Fodor's

THE AMALFI COAST, CAPRI, AND NAPLES

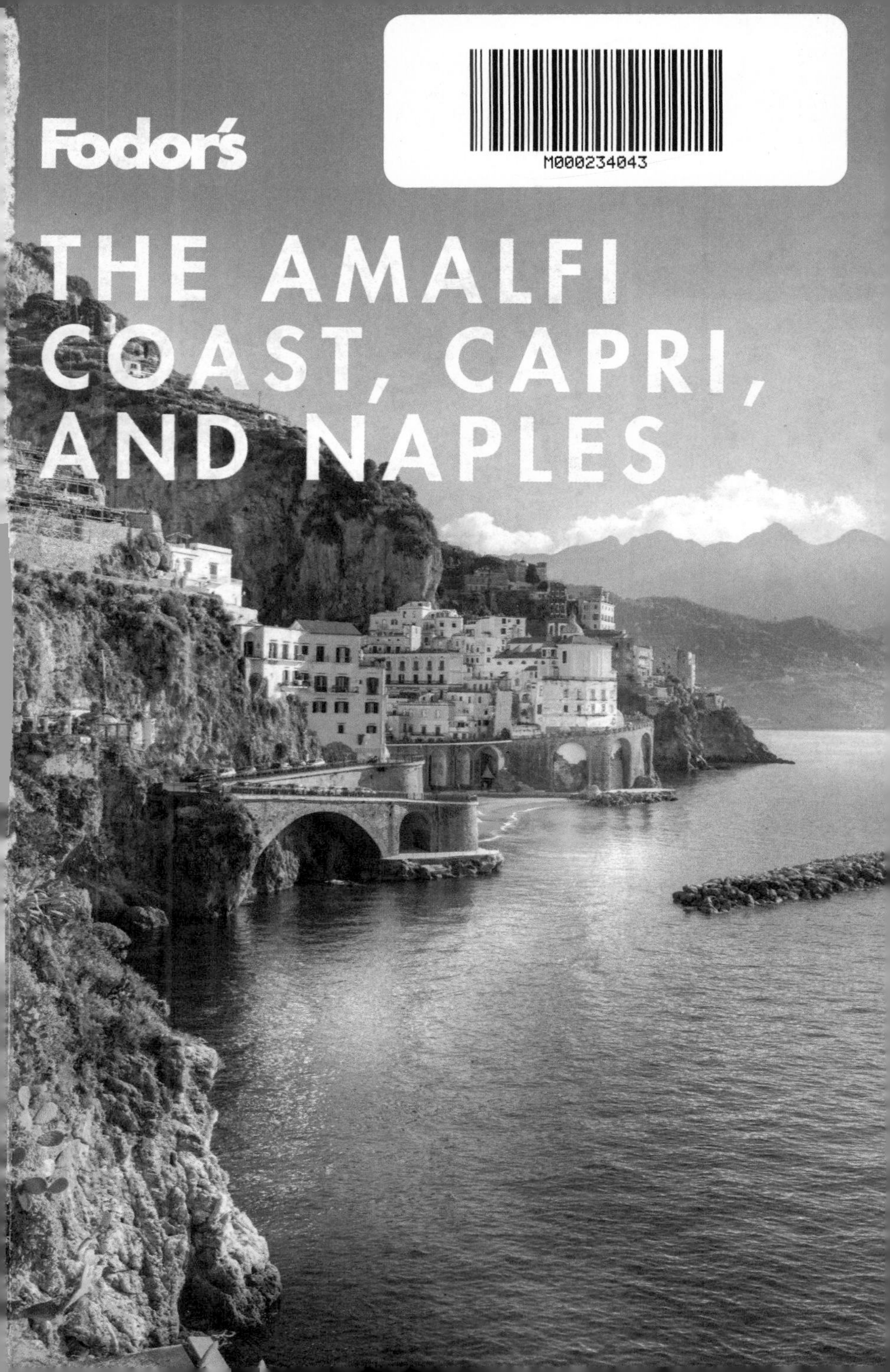

Welcome to the Amalfi Coast, Capri & Naples

Few regions of Italy claim as many iconic images as the corner of Campania that holds the Amalfi Coast, Naples, and the sun-splashed islands of Capri, Ischia, and Procida. If the colorful cliffside houses don't win your heart, the azure sea will. Driving the curving coastal road is exhilarating, so unwind with memorable Neapolitan fare, or go island hopping and explore grottoes and beaches. Cultural highlights are always nearby too, from the ruins of Pompeii and Herculaneum to the echoes of classical history in the vibrant streets of Naples and Sorrento.

TOP REASONS TO GO

★ **Food:** The home of great pizza, mozzarella, limoncello, and *spaghetti con le vongole.*

★ **Views:** The bluest bay in the world dazzles from Ravello's Belvedere of Infinity.

★ **Beaches:** Scenic, hidden coves line the Bay of Naples and make boat trips rewarding.

★ **Archaeology:** Pompeii and other evocative ruins transport you back to Roman times.

★ **Baroque Art:** Museums and churches shelter masterworks including three Caravaggios.

★ **Walking:** Slow exploration beckons—hiking Anacapri or strolling Naples' Spaccanapoli.

Contents

MAPS

Fodor's Features

Chapter 1

EXPERIENCE THE AMALFI COAST, CAPRI, AND NAPLES

20 ULTIMATE EXPERIENCES

The Amalfi Coast, Capri, and Naples offer terrific experiences that should be on every traveler's list. Here are Fodor's top picks for a memorable trip.

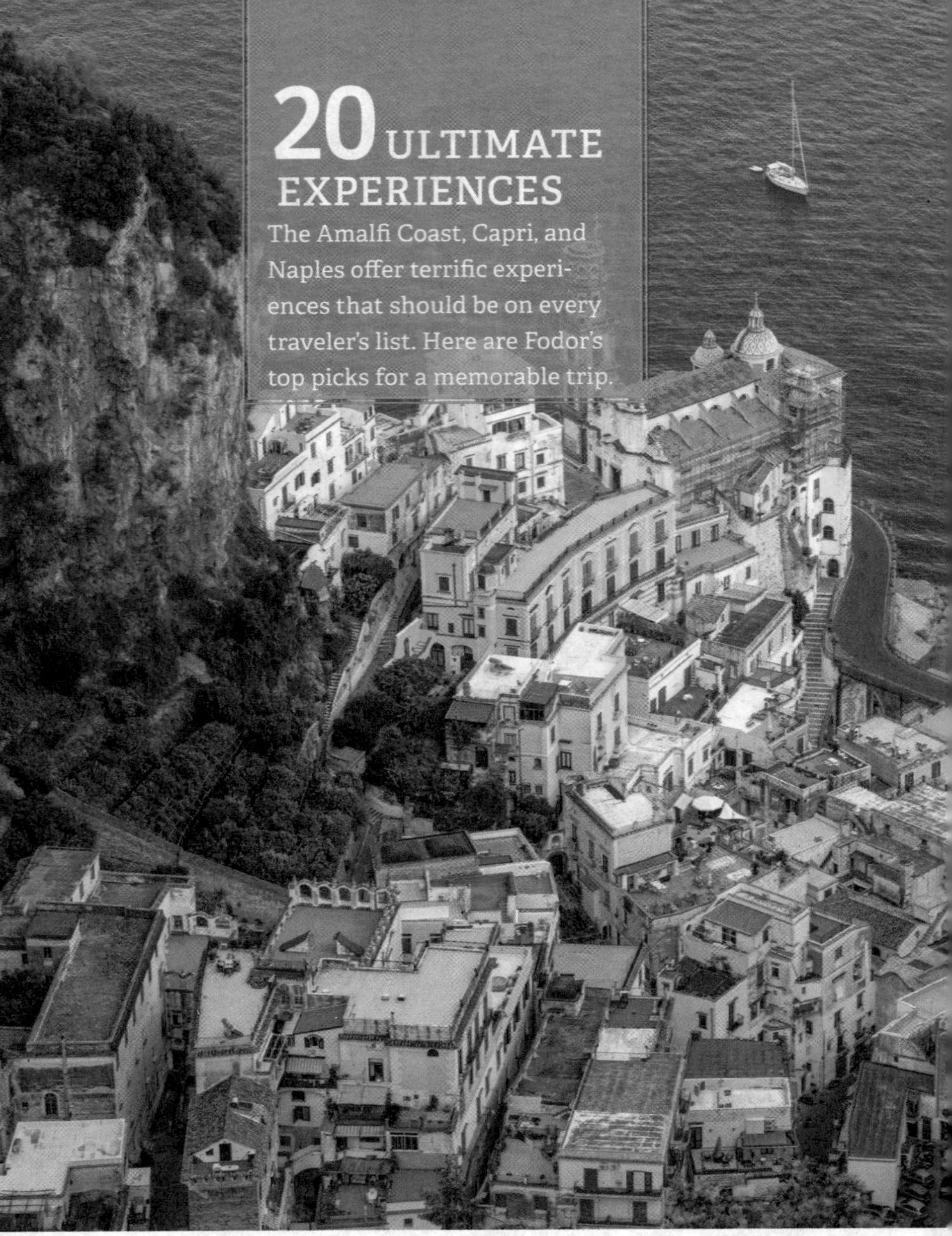

1 Be Charmed by Atrani

This tiny coastal hamlet is built in the dimple of a valley between two large cliffs, so the already diminutive medieval streets and arcaded lanes are even more quaint and romantic. There's also a charming little beach. *(Ch. 3)*

2 Discover Capri's Grottoes

You haven't fully experienced Capri until you've explored its rocky shoreline, a Swiss cheese of mysterious grottoes tucked into its myriad inlets and bays. *(Ch. 4)*

3 Marvel at Duomo di Sant'Andrea

The Duomo di Sant'Andrea is a mash-up of various styles (Baroque, Gothic, Byzantine, and Romanesque), but the Arab-Norman details are predominant. *(Ch. 3)*

4 Walk the Giro dell' Arco Naturale

The Giro dell' Arco Naturale is a stunning hike that takes you past some of Capri's most impressive natural wonders. *(Ch. 4)*

5 Sit and Contemplate at Certosa di San Giacomo

The palace complex of Certosa di San Giacomo has magnificent monastery gardens with exceptional views of the island. *(Ch. 4)*

6 Gaze Out From the Belvedere of Infinity

This sky-kissing terrace, set amid gorgeous gardens and overlooking the bluest bay in the world, is the high point of any trip to the Amalfi Coast. *(Ch. 3)*

7 Fall in Love with Ravello

Perched like an eagle's nest above the stunning coastline, Ravello has vertigo-inducing terraces, elegant gardens, and exudes an air of restrained glamour. *(Ch. 3)*

8 Chill Out at Le Sirenuse

In terms of pure bliss, an afternoon spent sitting by Le Sirenuse's lofty pool and soaking in the sun and scenery is time well spent. *(Ch. 3)*

9 Catch a Show at Teatro San Carlo

The Neoclassical Teatro San Carlo is one of the oldest opera houses in Europe and, next to La Scala in Milan, Italy's most famous. *(Ch. 7)*

10 Stay at Il San Pietro di Positano

The most opulent and storied hotel on the Amalfi Coast is a slice of heaven and an architectural wonder carved into the hillside just outside of Positano's historic center. *(Ch. 3)*

11 Visit the Museo Archeologico Nazionale

Many of the ancient mosaics, precious gold jewelry, and other artifacts from Herculaneum and Pompeii are preserved and expertly curated at this museum. *(Ch. 7)*

12 Explore Villa Jovis

The most impressive (and well-preserved) of Emperor Tiberius's 12 island residences, Villa Jovis is located on the island of Capri and has breathtaking views. *(Ch. 4)*

13 Take the Amalfi Drive

The road along the Amalfi Coast combines the thrills of a roller-coaster ride with spectacular rugged cliffs and seaside views. *(Ch. 3)*

14 Be Awed in Pompeii

The tragedy of Pompeii is our window into ancient Rome: most of Pompeii's regal homes, streets, amphitheaters (and sadly some people) were preserved for study. *(Ch. 6)*

15 Don't Miss Herculaneum

More compact and less crowded than the ruins of Pompeii, Herculaneum and most of its 5,000 inhabitants also perished during the eruption of Mt. Vesuvius. *(Ch. 6)*

16 Climb Mt. Vesuvius

The bay of Naples is dominated by the shadow of Mt. Vesuvius. Standing only 4,203 feet and rarely erupting, Mt. Vesuvius is not a threat these days. *(Ch. 6)*

17 Hike Il Sentiero degli Dei (Path of the Gods)

The Amalfi Coast's most popular and visually stunning hiking trail has spectacular views of Capri and the jagged peaks and colorful towns of the Amalfi Coast. *(Ch. 3)*

18 See Casa Rossa

Completed in 1899, Casa Rossa has a striking Pompeian red exterior and an eccentric 15th-century Aragonese tower. *(Ch. 4)*

19 Go Shopping Along Via Camarelle

Capri's Via Camarelle is a shopper's paradise, with high-end boutiques showcasing the wares of Italy's most celebrated designers. *(Ch. 4)*

20 Eat at Punta Tragara

Close to the city center, this Le Corbusier–designed hotel, with it's Michelin-starred rooftop restaurant, is lauded as one of the most beautiful on Capri. *(Ch. 4)*

WHAT'S WHERE

1 The Amalfi Coast. The hiking trail Il Sentiero degli Dei (the Path of the Gods) stretches above this spectacularly scenic corner of Campania, and the gods chose well. One of the most achingly beautiful places on Earth, the coast south of Sorrento is traversed by a road with seemingly hundred of turns, each with a view more stunning than the last. Here, sunbaked towns reveal their splendor around every bend: Positano, the world's most photographed fishing village; Amalfi, adorned with the coast's grandest cathedral; and sky-high Ravello, perched 1,500 feet over the famously blue Bay of Salerno.

2 Capri, Ischia, and Procida. History's hedonists have long luxuriated on Campania's islands. The most famous, rocky Capri, mixes natural beauty and *dolce vita* glamour. In summer, the day-trippers are legion, but even crowds don't spoil the charm. Twice the size of Capri, Ischia has Campania's most beautiful white-sand beaches and great spas and springs. Nearby Procida is a rugged island with multihue houses reflected in the bay.

3 Sorrento and the Sorrentine Peninsula. A Belle Époque treasure, with picturesque alleyways, palm-shaded cafés, and grande dame hotels, Sorrento has one of the world's most charming old towns, and a peninsula perfect for escaping the madding crowds.

4 The Bay of Naples. East of Naples lie Pompeii and Herculaneum, the most completely preserved cities of classical antiquity, along with Mt. Vesuvius, which buried them in ash and mud in AD 79. West of Naples is a fabled region, one where Nero and Hadrian had summer villas, Virgil composed his poetry, and the Apostle Paul landed to spread the gospel. Track their footsteps in ancient Baia and Cumae, where the oracle of Sybil bears testament to Italy's first Greek settlement.

5 Naples. Perhaps the most operatic city in the world, Naples can seduce you one moment and exasperate you the next. Unfolding like a pop-up history book, the city's canyon-like streets are packed with people, cafés, pizzerias, great museums, and an amazing number of Norman and Baroque churches.

Amalfi Coast, Capri, and Naples Today

The natural beauty and bounty of the Bay of Naples, and around 2,500 years of significant human settlement long ago made this part of the world a resort destination. Countless volcanic eruptions, earthquakes, plagues, invasions, and political problems have not dulled its luster. Today, mixing with its god-given shimmering shores, thermal waters, and wonderful food, contemporary life is vivid. From Posillipo to Positano, this area of Campania fascinates with its trappings of glamour and the complexity of a bitter-sweet Mezzogiorno lifestyle.

A PORTRAIT OF SOUTHERN ITALY

Southern Italy is slap-bang in the middle of the Mediterranean, so it's no wonder that it has experienced invasions and migrations for millennia, many of which have left their mark culturally, linguistically, and architecturally.

Southerners, despite the homogenizing influences of television and education, really *are* different from Italians farther north. Under an ostensibly sociable and more expressive exterior, they are more guarded when dealing with strangers, less at home with foreign languages, and more oriented toward the family than the community. The trappings of affluence, like cars and scooters, become essential status symbols here, which in part explains why Naples is congested and noisy.

A POLITICAL MIRE

Politics tends to be clientalistic in large swaths of the south. In this climate of mutual back-scratching and with unemployment rates twice the national average of 10%, the main preoccupation for many voters is *il posto fisso* (a steady job).

Votes are all too often cast for the politician who promises opportunities for career advancement—or lucrative contracts—preferably in the public sector. Over the years, this approach has insured inefficiencies, if not outright corruption.

The political landscape in Italy as a whole is less stable than in any other industrialized nation. The country has had a new government an average of about once a year since the end of World War II, and hopes are slim that the situation will change much in the near future.

This virtual turnstile outside the prime minister's office takes a toll on Italy in any number of ways: economic growth is slow in part because businesses are continually adapting to new sets of government policies, and polls show that rank-and-file Italians are increasingly cynical about their political institutions. As a result, they're much less likely to trust in or depend on the government than neighbors elsewhere in Europe do.

ECONOMIC UPS AND DOWNS

While the north has developed relatively rapidly in the past 50 years, the Italian entrepreneurial spirit in the south struggles to make good. Despite a pool of relatively cheap and willing labor, foreign investment across the entire south is merely one-tenth of that going to the northern region of Lombardy alone.

The discrepancy can be attributed in large part to the stifling presence of organized crime. Each major region has its own criminal association: in Naples, it's the Camorra. This system creates add-on costs at many levels, especially in retail.

It is not all bad news, though. Southern Italy has woken up to its major asset, its remarkable cultural and natural heritage. UNESCO lists 16 World Heritage sites in southern Italy alone, while the last decade has seen the creation of several national parks, marine parks, and regional nature preserves. Environmental and cultural associations have mushroomed as locals increasingly perceive the importance of preserving across the generations.

In general, the small average farm size in the south (5.8 hectares, less than 15 acres) has helped preserve a pleasing mosaic of habitats in the interior. Landscape and product diversity have been aided by the promotion of traditionally grown products by the European Union and its PDO (Protected Designation of Origin) project.

A GOURMET'S DELIGHT

The old joke says that three-quarters of the food and wine served in Italy is good … and the rest is amazing. In some sense, that's still true, and the "good" 75% has gotten even better.

Ingredients that in the past were available only to the wealthy can now be found even in the most remote parts of the country at reasonable prices. Dishes originally conceived to make the most of inferior cuts of meat or the least flavorful part of vegetables are now made with the best.

Italian restaurateurs seem determined to make the most of the country's reputation for good food. The same is true of Italian wine. Through investment and experimentation, Italy's winemakers are figuring out how to get the most from their vineyards. It's fair to say that Italy now produces more types of high-quality wine from more different grape varieties than any other country in the world.

THE BLACK MARKET

Nobody knows how big Italy's black-market economy is, though experts all agree it's massive. Estimates place it at anywhere from a fourth to a half of the official, legal economy. Put another way, if the highest estimates are correct, Italy's black-market economy is about as large as the entire economy of Mexico or India. If the black-market figures were added to Italy's official GDP, the country would leapfrog France, the United Kingdom, and China to become the world's fourth-largest economy.

The presence of the black market isn't obvious to the casual observer, but whenever a customer is not given a printed receipt in a store or restaurant, tobacco without a tax seal is bought from a street seller, or a product or service is exchanged for another product or service, that means the transaction goes unrecorded, unreported, and untaxed.

A COVID-CAMPANIA LEGACY

Like everywhere it seems, the COVID-19 pandemic has accelerated social and economic trends. In the region of Campania this is particularly true in the most sought-after corners of the Amalfi Coast and Capri. Restaurants and hotels in the more affordable categories have adapted in different ways. Some have refurbished, rebooted their brand and improved their facilities. Some have increased prices while others have dropped prices to attract dwindling visitor numbers. If you're thinking of splurging on one of Positano or Capri's chicest hotels expect to pay eye-watering amounts for just a night. In some cases prices have tripled. COVID it seems has made the rich and those that cater to their *Costiera Amalfitana*-lifestyle fantasizes even richer.

Classic Dishes from Naples and the Amalfi Coast

SFOGLIATELLE
Head to any bar for breakfast in Naples and you'll see people clasping one of these hornlike lobster tail pastries. This bar pastry classic is perfect for breakfast. The most popular kind is made of thin layers of pastry with a sweet custard filling.

VERA PIZZA NAPOLETANA
The flatbread meal that conquered the world started on the mean 17th-century streets of Napoli, eaten by the poor and given royal approval in 1889 by a certain Regina Margherita, the Queen Consort of Naples. For a true Neapolitan pizza, the purity of the ingredients are key.

RAGÙ DI CARNE ALLA GENOVESE
For the ultimate slow-cooked beef ragù this is the recipe, much loved in Naples, but relatively unknown outside Campania. Ask for the *bianco* (white) version from the 19th-century Cavalcanti cookbook—it has no tomatoes, but plenty of onions.

GRANITA DI LIMONE
In summer, you'll find vendors on street corners throughout the city and around the Bay of Naples selling the most refreshing crushed lemon ice.

SCIALATIELLI AI FRUTTI DI MARE
This classic summer seafood *primo* was invented on the Amalfi Coast in 1978, and is a mainstay on the Costiera especially. The shape of pasta is the key to retaining the sauce and scialatielli, a short, fatter version of fettuccine with a rectangular cross-section, does the job perfectly.

PARMIGIANA DI MELANZANE
Juices ooze and cheese melts in baked layers of fried eggplant, tomato, mozzarella—the best of Campanian sun-drenched produce—with the added salty kick of that noble Emilia-Romagna cheese Parmigiano Reggiano.

BABÀ
It may be Polish in origin, but Naples has taken the rum cake to new levels, developing suitably indulgent versions. There are many variations and shapes to try: *mignon*, *giganti*, or a *ciambella* being the most popular.

FRITTURA DI MARE
This dish not only encapsulates a Neapolitan spring or summer lunch but is also an integral part of the Christmas Eve feast. The fried seafood medley is made with the freshest seafood—commonly squid, prawns, red mullet, and anchovies—and best combined with a cold *birra* or Falanghina wine, gazing over the shoreline.

SPAGHETTI ALLE VONGOLE
Another simple Neapolitan pleasure and symbol of summer is also called *vermicelli alle vongole* and dates back to the end of the 1700s. It's all about the briny freshness of the carpet-shell clams (*vongole comuni* or *lupini sgusciati*). The classic white sauce (olive oil, garlic, white wine, chili, and parsley) can be whipped up in minutes.

Vera Pizza Napoletana

DELIZIA AL LIMONE
Most menus along the Amalfi Coast and some elsewhere in Campania have a *delizia al limone* on the *dolci* page. For its invention we don't go back that far; it was 1978 at a culinary event in Formia, up the coast toward Rome, when a Sorrentine pastry chef Carmine Marzuillo presented a soft sponge mound and whipped up some cream infused with Amalfi lemons.

SARTÙ DI RISO
This magnificent and rich Neapolitan classic reflects the city's cross-pollinating history. Sartù hails from the Spanish Aragonese court, which took the idea from the Arab world and brought it to Naples and Sicily. Today's recipe is a mound of rice flavored by a slow-cooked *ragù napoletano* and *polpettine* (small pork meatballs). A rich sauce may also contain eggplant, mushrooms, peas, sausage, boiled egg, and often provola or mozzarella cheese.

INSALATA CAPRESE
This simple salad named after the island and displaying the colors of the *bandiera tricolore italiana* (Italian flag) is all about the freshness and provenance of the ingredients; and nothing compares to slicing into the freshest, juiciest *mozzarella di bufala campana* and *pomodori freschi* with the sweet aroma and peppery-piquant combo of *basilico* and *olio di extra vergine*.

COLATURA DI ALICI
Anchovy drippings, anyone? Fermented anchovy sauce may sound gross, but this sauce has a kick that's been popular for millennia. Its origins lie in ancient Roman garum sauce, the staple flavoring to enliven any dish. Today, the place to sample it is Cetara on the Costiera Amalfitana, where it's made according to a centuries-old recipe.

ZUCCHINI ALLA SCAPECE
The fertile soil and benign climate in Naples helps produce wonderful vegetables, and this classic *contorno* of thin zucchini slices marinated in garlic, vinegar, and mint is a staple side dish on any *tavola napoletana*.

TORTA CAPRESE
Can cake be healthy? Well, the chocolate and almond torta Caprese—it was first made in Capri, apparently—is filled with life-giving and -affirming ingredients, and deserves to be deemed healthy, as it is gluten free and delicious.

Free Things to Do in Campania

MT. VESUVIUS
Mt. Vesuvius is not the towering threat that it was when it erupted in AD 79, so feel free to gaze into its smoking crater. A shuttle drops you at a point on the mountain where well-marked signs direct you up a 30-minute steep hike to the summit.

DUOMO (NAPLES)
Erected in the 1200s, Naples's main Duomo church is essentially a story of the city's tumultuous architectural history: ancient pagan columns share its interior with the 350-year-old richly decorated false wood ceiling, which in turn hides the original Gothic ceiling behind it.

IL SENTIERO DEGLI DEI (PATH OF THE GODS)
This is the Amalfi Coast's most popular and visually stunning hiking trail. The 4.8-mile trail runs between Agerola and Nocelle and, as the name implies, the views are breathtaking.

INCONTRI MUSICALI SORRENTINI
Sorrento's main cultural event features outstanding concerts and entertainment from the last week of August through the end of September. Though events happen throughout the city, many take place in the acoustically dramatic church of San Francesco's Moorish-style cloister.

LAGO D'AVERNO
Ancients believed Lago d'Averno was the doorway to the underworld. The lake's black water emits a pervasive sulfuric smell, ominous forested hills surround it, and Monte Nuovo looms over all.

MARINA DI FURORE
The best things in life are free, but not always easily accessible. The beach at Marina di Furore is a steep 944 steps down (and then back up). Hike down and enjoy one of the most private and pristine beaches in Italy. From here, there are lots of hiking options. The "Mad Bats' Path" is 3,000 steps of panoramic views that will keep you busy for a couple of hours.

GESÙ NUOVO (NAPLES)
Originally constructed as a palace, the 16th-century church of Gesù Nuovo is a striking contrast to the plain Romanesque facades of other nearby churches.

Spiaggia di Fornillo

The exterior is covered with pointy, faceted stones engraved underneath with Aramaic musical notes that together produce a 45-minute-long musical. The interior is resplendent with the Baroque sculptures of Naccherino and Finelli. The fine frescoes adorning its main nave were the work of Massimo Stanzione.

PIAZZA GARIBALDI (NAPLES)
Though still a little rough around the edges, Piazza Garibaldi has been completely revamped in recent years. The streets here are always lively and the city's largest Chinese population lives nearby, in case you're craving something other than Italian food.

RAVELLO FESTIVAL
What began in the 1950s as a quiet cultural gathering in the stunning mountain town of Ravello is today one of the most vibrant musical experiences that Italy has to offer. The annual festivities take place in the gardens of the ancient Villa Rufolo.

SPIAGGIA DI FORNILLO
As if there weren't enough outstanding qualities in the Amalfi Coast, Positano's Spiaggia di Fornillo is adored for its outstanding crystal clear waters. A favorite of Pablo Picasso, the beach's backdrops are the majestic pastel villas and buildings of Positano. Beachfront bars, restaurants, showers, toilets, and water-sports equipment rentals are all within walking distance.

HANG OUT IN A HARBOR
For a firsthand slice of southern Italian life and atmosphere, head to one of the coastline's beguiling harbors/marinas. Come at *alba* (dawn) to take golden-hour pics of the bobbling boats, seagulls, rusty anchors, and surrounding buildings. Down at pastel-hue Corricella on Procida, fishermen tend their nets and prepare to venture out to sea.

10 Best Churches in the Bay of Naples

SANTUARIO DEL SOCCORSO, ISCHIA
Sunset is often the magic hour to saunter along the Forio coastline and hang around this scenic whitewashed church on a promontory. Take a pew on the terrace to watch the 14th-century church blush as the burning embers of the day sink into the Mar Tirreno.

GESÙ NUOVO, NAPLES
Heralding the start of many a stroll through the Centro Storico is the sight of the austere diamond-pointed facade of the former Palazzo Sanseverino. Once inside, there's much to take the breath away, from the ornamental sumptuousness of the vault frescoes to the emotional intensity of the worshippers in its atmospheric corners and chapels.

DUOMO, NAPLES
Get a feel for the Neapolitans' fatalistic pagan-influenced relationship with the world, and its deadly hazards and deities, by spending some time in the colossal Duomo. Naples's cathedral is dedicated to the martyred early Christian San Gennaro, who was decapitated in 305. Three times a year, devotees focus on an old vial supposedly containing the blood of the saint and protectorate of Naples. An emotionally charged procession around the city leads into the Duomo, where the crowd implores the miracle of liquefaction: *liquefazione* symbolizes respite from the ever-looming disasters of famine, plague, revolt, earthquake, eruption, or defeat of the city's beloved soccer team, SSC Napoli. To glimpse the urn containing the saint's remains visit the chilling Cripta di San Gennaro.

PIO MONTE DELLA MISERICORDIA, NAPLES
Down the quiet end of dark, narrow, sticky, and slightly unnerving via dei Tribunali is this charitable body with an adjoining octagonal church. In 1601, seven wealthy men established an almshouse and Pio Monte della Misericordia charity for Naples's poor and destitute. Head through the arched loggia to the church bathed in natural light and gawk at one of Caravaggio's most powerful and brooding masterpieces, *The Seven Acts of Mercy* (1607) altarpiece.

SAN GIUSEPPE DEI RUFFI, NAPLES
Designed by Baroque master architect Lazzari, this 17th-century church in the Centro Storico is worth seeking out for its over-the-top splendor and unique *Messa* (Mass). Devotees and the curious rise early to witness the Sacramentine nuns in white and red habits process under the impressive cupola adorned with Francesco de Mura's dreamlike painting *Paradise* and the sweet sounds of the nuns singing early morning mass, reverberating around the cavernous space. Set the alarm early, as Mass begins daily at 8 am sharp.

SANTA CHIARA, NAPLES
One of the most photographed and much-loved expressions of life-affirming Neapolitan *gioia di vivere* (joy in life) can be enjoyed at this 14th-century church complex built by the Angevins. Take time out and stroll around the adjoining cloisters. The vibrant majolica-tiled

Santa Chiara

columns and seats depicting fruits of the fertile Campania soil and rural landscapes are perfect for quiet reflection after the hustle of Spaccanapoli.

SANTA MARIA ASSUNTA, POSITANO
The instantly recognizable dome and its cute cupola above can be seen all over the pastel-hue Positano, from the famous beach to the farthest *scalinatella* stairway high up on Path of the Gods. Inside, amid the 18th-century stucco work is the altar's Byzantine 13th-century painting on wood of Madonna with Child, known as the Black Virgin. The main draw though is deep in the crypts, where recently excavated remains of the original 13th-century church, funerary seating, and Roman villa frescoes are breathtaking.

DUOMO DI SANT'ANDREA, AMALFI
Originally conceived and erected in the 9th century, this prime piece of Arab-Norman extravagance was financed by Amalfi's once-mighty maritime trading republic that sailed east, so Byzantine influences abound. It's been changed and embellished many times since with a number of styles from Romanesque to Gothic, so there's much detail to get lost in here. Beyond the richly decorated facade and bronze doors, take time to linger in the Chiostro del Paradiso's lush palm-fringed gardens enclosed by interlaced Arabic arches.

DUOMO DI RAVELLO, RAVELLO
Up in lofty and lovely Ravello, leave the melee of coaches and day-trippers through a tunnel that leads to a more relaxed piazza. Eyes are drawn to the fresh, simple white-gleaming Romanesque cathedral with its 13th-century campanile. Beyond the rare and rather hefty bronze door (made in 1179 and apparently one of Italy's finest), the calming and sparse aesthetic continues inside this light-filled space. Within the cool stone walls, it's an intimate and refreshingly understated affair. Take time to examine the vibrantly decorated ambos with twisting columns sitting on lion pedestals.

SANTA MARIA A CETRELLA, CAPRI
Reaching this humbly rough-hewn church founded in the 14th century takes a bit of work, but it is well worth the pilgrimage. You'll be rewarded with a place made for some quiet reflection amid the flowery meadows (there's a hermitage here), and it's a fine spot to have a picnic, with lovely views down to the Faraglioni rocks.

Amazing Hikes on the Amalfi Coast

PATH OF THE GODS, AMALFI COAST, NAPLES
High up the limestone cliffs of the Amalfi Coast, centuries-old trails and mule tracks provide some of the most spectacular hiking in Europe. The classic Sentiero degli Dei route links the hilltop towns of Agerola to Nocelle, and is best tackled westward for the most awesome views.

LUNGOMARE DI NAPOLI, NAPLES
For the ultimate Neapolitan family *passeggiata*, head to this promenade, lined with restaurants and many an ornate statue and attraction en route. Its present form took shape after a cholera outbreak in 1884, when the nascent Italian state enacted Il Risanamento (urban renewal), sweeping away old fishing communities, and reclaiming land from the sea. Up until 2012, this sweep of coastline was spoiled by a roaring klaxon-cacophony of traffic, then Mayor Luigi de Magistris created the lungomare liberato (a waterfront freed of traffic).

VESUVIUS NATIONAL PARK, ERCOLANO, VESUVIUS
In addition to the short walk up to the crater rim of Vesuvius from the official car park, there are 11 trails within the Parco Nazionale di Vesuvio. Those after an epic trek should opt for Trail 4 through the Tirone Alto Forestry Nature Reserve established in 1974. On this seven-mile, six-hour hike, you can spot rare orchids and abundant wildlife including snakes, hares, foxes, lizards, and cuckoos. Between the trees there are views of the bay, up to the Gran Cono and toward the lava flows of 1944.

HERCULANEUM, ERCOLANO
Most people head straight to Pompeii to dig deeper into the history of the infamous AD 79 eruption, but this compact Roman resort is easier to get around and has riches aplenty. So far, only six *insulae* (blocks) have been excavated, but there's plenty to see within a manageable walking distance.

MONTE SOLARO, CAPRI
For the most tranquil and spellbinding hilltop atmosphere and views around the Gulfs of Naples and Salerno, this is the must-do Caprese excursion. To save the calf and thigh muscles take the serene chair-funicular ride from Anacapri up to the 589-meter terrace. Riding up in a single chairs, dangling over the small gardens and vegetable plots, is an ethereal experience. There's a café at the top and you can wander amid the macchia mediterranea scrub to gain different vantage points. Then you can either bound back down the path to Anacapri, take another dusty trail to the Cetrella church, or take the easy chairlift descent.

MONTE EPOMEO, ISCHIA
Ischia's 2,600-foot mountain is an extinct volcano with some otherworldly rock formations pitted with volcanic bubbles. The effort of taking the 45-minute walk from the charming piazza and church at Serrara, through Fontana and dusty woods, can be justly rewarded with a visit to

Valle dei Mulini

the terrace restaurant La Grotta del Fiore on the summit. The unusual 15th-century church and hermitage Chiesa di San Nicola is worth a look, too. On a clear day there are azure vistas over the Golfo di Napoli and to the distant smoking volcano of Stromboli.

PAESTUM

Visitors to mainland Italy's most important Greek ruins have the chance to walk in the footsteps of former resident Pythagoras and thousands of Grand Tourists. Amid the extensive grounds, enlivened in spring by butterflies fluttering around poppies and other wildflowers, there's ample space to escape the crowds; so after wandering between the Greek temples and Roman *macellum* (market), find a spot to sit and savor a picnic while contemplating the most captivating views.

SPACCANAPOLI, NAPLES

Spaccanapoli (literally split-Naples) and its parallel street Via dei Tribunali are the two east–west streets that cut through the ancient center of the Greek founded city of Neapolis. Along these *decumani* Neapolitan daily life is played out for all to see. Just go with the intoxicating flow—leave your valuables in a hotel safe and keep an open mind to fully explore. Although these long streets start up the hill of the Spanish Quarter most visitors begin by the Baroque obelisk Guglia dell'Immacolata.

CAPRI TOWN TO VILLA JOVIS, CAPRI

To reach Emperor Tiberius's infamous and colossal palace from which he ruled the Roman Empire AD 27–37 requires about an hour's hike from the Piazzetta, Capri Town. On the way you pass chic shops, along flower-fringed lanes and colonnaded gardens with many a *lucertola* (lizard) and *gatto* (cat) for company. For a dizzying view of a 1,000-foot drop with historic piquancy head to the Salto di Tiberio (Tiberius's Leap). Ancient scribes say that the emperor flung unwanted lovers, enemies, and even unlucky cooks into the sea below.

VALLE DEI MULINI, AMALFI

Also known as the Valle delle Ferriere, the Valley of the Mills is often explored from Amalfi, as a short excursion and welcome escape from the Amalfi crowds. For a more rewarding experience, there's a 4-mile path crisscrossing the Canneto River and passing through terraced lemon and olive groves. The ruins of stone mill buildings that once drove paper and lime production are welcome and picturesque spots to take a breather.

The 10 Creepiest Sights in Campania

CIMITERO DELLE FONTANELLE, NAPLES
In 1654 during the calamitous bubonic plague outbreak, some 250,000 bodies (over half the population of Naples) had to be deposited away from the living. Further plagues, wars, and volcanic disasters made it necessary to carve out this cathedral-like space to house the mounting bones.

CATACOMBE DI SAN GENNARO, NAPLES
Breathtaking Paleo-Christian art glows through the dank gloom of this creepy underground warren. Guided tours start outside the domed Chiesa di Madre di Buon Consiglio, exploring the captivating spaces first hewn from the volcanic tuff rock in the 2nd century.

TEMPLE OF ECHOES, BAIA (NAPLES)
Exploring the eerily empty Roman resort spa ruins of Baia can be a highly charged experience. This was once the lavish playground of pleasure-seeking emperors and scene of juicy plots and multiple murders, as documented by Roman biographer Suetonius.

CAPPELLA SANSEVERO, NAPLES
Down a side street off Spaccanapoli is this entrancing family chapel and brainchild of the mysterious and much-mythologized Prince Raimondo di Sangro (1710–71). His esoteric interests and tastes are on display here.

PLASTER CASTS, POMPEII
Among the most poignant echoes of the AD 79 eruption that buried Roman Pompeii are the chilling plaster casts of some its victims. After the first deluge of volcanic debris, many of the town's inhabitants stayed put, and were ultimately entombed.

CAVE OF THE SIBYL, CUMAE
To the west of Naples is Greek-founded Cumae. It's on the edge of the volcanic Fiery Fields, a steaming landscape of crater lakes, and inspiration for Virgil's Greco-Roman myths of the underworld. Amid these picturesque ruins is a curious 430-feet-long trapezoidal tunnel associated with magic deeds and ancient soothsayers. Here you can walk through the so-called Cave of the Sibyl, experiencing its otherworldly acoustics and chiaroscuro menace, imagining strange ancient ceremonies.

TOMB OF THE DIVER, MUSEO ARCHEOLOGICO NAZIONALE, PAESTUM
Within the austere Fascist-era museum are the frescoed panels of the Tomb of the Diver, buried within a funerary box in

Tomb of the Diver, Museo Archeologico Nazionale

about 475 BC and unearthed almost 2,500 years later, in 1968. Eyes are drawn to the arresting scene of a youth gracefully diving into water.

PALAZZO DELLE POSTE, NAPLES

Looming over Piazza Matteotti, this gargantuan Fascist-built post office seems more like an evil space station than a place to pick up some stamps. Its inhuman scale can leave you both cold and stupefied. Palazzo delle Poste is among a cluster of bombastic buildings that dicator Benito Mussolini built here in the 1930s. The curvilinear facade, simple forms, and imposing scale are examples of razionalista-funzionalista architecture.

OSPEDALE DELLE BAMBOLE, NAPLES

Ospedale delle Bambole (Doll's Hospital): just the name sounds like the title of a horror B-movie. Indeed, this very curious workshop/museum may have sweetness at its heart, but the disquieting, staring-eyed, limb-strewn visions that await may induce nightmares.

VILLA DEI PAPIRI AT MUSEO ARCHEOLOGICO NAZIONALE DI NAPOLI (MANN), NAPLES

Among the most spine-tingling sights in MANN (arguably the world's most impressive museum collection of Roman artifacts) is this set of lifelike bronze sculptures. Buried but preserved by the 80-feet-plus of volcanic debris that engulfed the lavish Villa dei Papiri at Herculaneum, they are some of the most soulful yet eerie Roman examples of an idealized human form, inspired by ancient Greek philosophy and aesthetics. Walking among these gracefully posed figures and peering into their piercing, concentrated expressions is uncanny—they seem poised to come to life at any moment.

The Best Places to Discover Volcanoes

Ischia

CRATER RIM OF VESUVIUS

Peering over the edge into the 650-foot-deep crater you can glimpse and even taste the acrid, sulfuric menace of Vesuvio's steamy fumaroles. Hearts may skip a beat after the odd, unnerving earth tremor. Up here the views of the bay and the surrounding area below—Pompeii, Herculaneum, Oplontis—hint at its immense eruptive might.

POMPEII'S PLASTER-CAST FIGURES

To get an idea of the merciless nature of Vesuvius, visit Pompeii to see the plaster-cast ghosts of some of its AD 79 victims. Archaeologist Giuseppe Fiorelli's casts freeze the positions of the incinerated Pompeians: a chilling reminder of how the earth's awesome natural power can take lives in an instant.

CAMPI FLEGREI

The Campi Flegrei, or Fiery Fields, is a complex caldera volcano that some scientists now deem to be Europe's largest supervolcano.

FUMAROLES AND THERMAL SPRINGS OF ISCHIA

The island of Ischia sits within the Campi Flegrei caldera, whose gargantuan

Pompeii's plaster-cast figures

magma chambers fuel the hydrothermal springs and fumaroles that soothe and heal thousands of spa-goers each day.

VILLA ROMANA
Although the Amalfi Coast is a limestone spur of the Apennines, without a fumarole or lava flow in sight, the communities some 13 miles from Vesuvius have been shaped by volcanology. By descending into the Villa Romana ruins by the beach at Positano, you are traveling through the volcanic debris spewed by the eruption of AD 79.

SOLFATARA CRATER
In this land scarred by constant tectonic activity, there is one steamy, fumarole-fizzing, and mud-bubbling 4,000-year-old crater that has become an emblem for volcanism in this part of the world. Solfatara was a bathing curiosity on the Grand Tour and has appeared in numerous movies and music videos, including Rossellini's *Journey to Italy* and Pink Floyd's *Live at Pompeii*.

BAIA
Down at the shoreline of Baia, the sea has swallowed part of the town, and at nearby Pozzuoli, marine mollusk bore-holes 20 feet up the Roman columns indicate that the sea was once much higher. These two towns attest to the shifting water levels—the rise and fall of the land surface caused by the constant emptying and filling of the magma chambers below.

HERCULANEUM
Walking down the sloping path into the Herculaneum archaeological site, you are struck by the enormity of the eruption that buried Pompeii. Scientists believe that Herculaneum was seared by a 900°F pyroclastic surge that roared down the mountain at 250 mph.

SAN SEBASTIANO
In 1944, liquid lava enveloped buildings and took off the church cupola, while walls of cooler lava crushed buildings. Today the curious can walk on those lava flows and enter modern buildings built in the 1950s and 1960s atop the lava and half-destroyed main street, Via Roma.

OSSERVATORIO VESUVIANO
Vesuvius remains the most closely monitored volcano on the planet; the research here started the science of volcanology.

Locations from Elena Ferrante's *My Brilliant Friend*

PIAZZA PLEBISCITO, NAPLES
In the novel the girls glimpse how the other half lives when they dress up and join Carmela, Pasquale, and Rino for a Metropolitana trip into the Centro Storico. It's Episode 5, "The Shoes," when this violent clash of Neapolitan districts and distant worlds shocks the viewer.

SPIAGGIA MARONTI, ISCHIA
Continuing Lenù's summer in Ischia, after an evening passeggiata with a gelato-slurping scene by Ischia Ponte, there's a moonlit walk on the dark volcanic sand of Maronti that culminates in a heart-to-heart chat between Lenù and Nino Sarratore.

IL RIONE, NAPLES
The gray and oppressive Rione quarter in the novel are based on a very Neapolitan kind of suburb and many believe that the Rione Luzzatti is Ferrante's inspiration. A film set based on the Rione was built for the acclaimed HBO series adaptation.

CHIAIA AND THE GALLERIA PRINCIPE, NAPLES
Continuing this evening *passeggiata* (stroll), the group walks along Via Toledo and around Chiaia, ending up in Piazza Amedeo. For the small screen, the action is transferred from Via Chiaia to the elegant, glass-canopied Victorian shopping mall Galleria Principe (it's less swanky in real life today and beside roaring traffic opposite the Museo Nazionale).

TRAGHETTO TO ISCHIA FROM MOLO SAN VINCENZO
By the end of Episode 5 there is a hint that the gloom and menace will lift (albeit momentarily) as Lenù walks with her mother along the old quayside of Molo San Vincenzo with its brick porticoes, backdropped by Vesuvio, Castel Nuovo, and Castel Sant'Elmo in the summer haze.

ISCHIA PORTO
In blue-tinted Episode 6, Lenù's bittersweet yet liberating Ischia adventure begins. Initial shots frame the outline of Monte Epomeo as the small ferry approaches Ischia. Disembarking at Ischia Ponte, she enters the quayside shouts and bustle of hotel hawkers, postcard peddlers, and *taralli* sellers with the Castello Aragonese in the distance On Via Luigi Mazzella, by the pastel fishermen's dwellings, Lenù boards a bright blue bus for Barano on the southern shores of the island.

Chiaia and the Galleria Principe

BARANO D'ISCHIA
At Nella Incardo's Barano villa, while first looking after an English family on holiday, Lenù begins to blossom. The scenes are filmed on a flower-filled Barano terrace backed by the lush hills of Ischia. The vibrancy and freedom of this new life outside the Rione is symbolized with lots of blue splashes: Lenù sports a 1950s blue swimsuit on the beach at Barano and, on entering the water, she recalls the sweet sensuality of swimming in the sea at Coroglio.

SEA GARDEN: BAGNO BATHING CLUB IN POSILLIPO
Lenù's coming-of-age tale continues when she takes a job babysitting the stationery shop owner's daughters, which takes her to the picturesque Posillipo bathing establishment, Sea Garden. This popular spot near Mergellina port in Naples was first opened in 1840 and is alleged to have been a favorite spot of Lord Nelson and his lover Lady Hamilton. Among the colorful umbrellas and beach huts, and the half-ruins of the17th-century Villa Donn'Anna, Lenù frolics in the sea, reads novels, and explores her sexuality with Antonio.

LUNGOMARE, NAPLES
In Episode 4, titled "Dissolving Margins," Lenù gets her first taste of life outside the Rione and glimpses of the splendor of the Neapolitan Riviera. After her father attempts to get Lenù a job at the Tribunale (courthouse), they walk to the waterfront at Via Nazario Sauro.

CORSO UMBERTO I
Toward the end of the novel and TV series, Lila and her pals head to a shop to try on wedding dresses on one of Napoli's main shopping streets. Corso Umberto I, nicknamed "Il Rettifilo" (The Straight Line) is a broad and long street that connects Piazza Garibaldi with Piazza Municipio.

What to Watch and Read

IL POSTINO (1994)

Filmed partly on Procida, Michael Radford's tender fictional story of a burgeoning friendship between a specially recruited island postman and the exiled Chilean poet Pablo Neruda is both heartbreaking and uplifting.

LA MANO DEL DIO (2021)

Academy Award–winning Neapolitan director Paolo Sorrentino's very personal coming-of-age drama is slow-burning and brimming with Napoletanità (Neapolitan-ess). It's 1984 and the city is gripped by an obsession, a dream... that the world's finest soccer player Diego Maradona is about to shun Europe's most glamorous teams and sign for SSC Napoli. Fabietto Schisa is caught up in the Maradona fever, while negotiating his way through teenage life and around his parents' tempestuous relationship. Then suddenly a tragedy, an act of god strikes the family. It rocks Fabietto's world and all those around him. Sorrentino's Fellini-esque movie is a life-affirming and poignant tale, and a vivid snapshot of 1980s Naples.

THE VESUVIUS CLUB (2004)

British comic actor, director, and writer Mark Gatiss's comic-book Edwardian secret agent Lucifer Box explores the fleshly and hair-raising underbelly of Naples in this fantasy romp of a spy-thriller. Investigating the mysterious death of Jocelyn Utterson Poop of the Diplomatic Service, the suave sleuth is drawn deeper and deeper into a shady, gaseous world of Masonic shenanigans, a smuggling racket, opium dens, Pompeian tunnels, and love trysts. Gatiss's preposterous and entertaining tale climaxes in a most-singular prison beneath Vesuvius where a bomb is set to ignite the magma chambers and destroy Italy.

THE VOLCANO LOVER BY SUSAN SONTAG (1992)

Sontag's novel, set largely in Naples, is based on the infamous late-1700s love triangle between Sir William Hamilton, the English Consul in the Neapolitan court; his voluptuous and intoxicating wife Emma (Lady Hamilton); and Lord Nelson of the English navy. The title derives from William Hamilton's passion for volcanology—he poured his passion into studying the activity of Vesuvius and Campi Flegrei, and amassing a fine art and antiquities collection during his time in Italy. With the backdrop of revolution and counter-revolution in Europe and Naples, the dashing eye-patched Lord Nelson and Emma become lovers, hole up together, and scandal ensues.

CAPRI-REVOLUTION (2018)

In director Mario Martone's film based on the life of German artist Karl Wilhelm Diefenbach, a commune of artists in 1914 find idyllic refuge on Capri as Europe about to be ravaged by war. The plot centers on the relationships between a Caprese peasant goat-herding girl, Lucia, the group of dissident northern Europeans led by Seybu, and an idealistic local doctor. It's very loosely based on the alternative dissident Russian community—including writer Maxim Gorky—who lived on Capri between 1907 and 1913. Some of the scenes are shot on Capri—on the rocky shore at Orrico and on the slopes of Monte Solaro—and elsewhere in Campania along the Cilento Coast.

ELENA FERRANTE'S NEAPOLITAN NOVELS (2012–15)

Worldwide critical acclaim and massive sales of the book series beginning with *My Brilliant Friend* have sparked massive interest in anarchic and complex Naples: its people, history, and the streets. Perhaps partly fueled by mystery surrounding the identity of the pseudonymous author of the Neapolitan Novels—it's been called Ferrante Fever—the Neapolitan Novels could be to post–World War II Naples what Dickens's novels are to Victorian London. Ferrante's novels bring the city to life as her vivid depictions—mixing the opulent, idyllic, and squalid—underlie the lifetime friendship of Elena and Lila, plus a cast of Neapolitan families and other characters farther north. Such is the worldwide clamor to get nearer to the vividly drawn characters and the city itself—increased by the excellent HBO small-screen adaptation—there's currently a boom in Ferrante-related tours and enthralled readers wandering around seeking locations in the tetralogy, clutching the books to their chest.

AVANTI! (1972)

In Billy Wilder's dark romantic movie comedy based on the 1968 Broadway play by Samuel A. Taylor, straight-laced Wendell Armbruster Jr. (Jack Lemmon) travels to Ischia to recover the body of his millionaire father. Digging for clues about the sudden death in an automobile accident, Wendell discovers that his Baltimore industrialist father had a British mistress with him in the flattened Fiat. A farce ensues involving a hotel valet, a maid, and the vineyard-owning Trotta family.

NAPLES '44: AN INTELLIGENCE OFFICER IN THE ITALIAN LABYRINTH BY NORMAN LEWIS (1978)

Naples *'44* is former British intelligence officer turned writer and novelist Norman Lewis's account of his experiences stationed in Naples at the end of World War II. In a diary format spanning September 1943 to October 1944, Lewis describes Naples as a city ravaged by war, famine, and then beset by a recent eruption of Vesuvius. It's considered one of the great wartime memoirs.

L'ORO DI NAPOLI (THE GOLD OF NAPLES) (1954)

This Vittorio de Sica–directed movie is a good place to start for those not familiar with a certain quartet of 20th-century Neapolitan stage and screen icons. Alongside director and actor De Sica is the Pozzuoli-born Sophia Loren; Rione Sanità native and comic genius Totò (born Antonio De Curtis); and a fellow embodiment of Neapolitan wit, guile, and expression, Eduardo de Filippo. With humor, tragedy, and humanity, the plot explores a variety of Neapolitan moods and *l'arte di arrangiarsi* (making-ends-meet) archetypes including a *pizzaiolo*, a gambler, a charlatan sage, and a clown.

PASSIONE (2010)

Italian-American actor John Turturro's love letter to Naples showcases Neapolitan music and dance, drawing on the influences from ancient Greeks, invading Saracens, and World War II American troops. His cross-genre musical collaborations are filmed as theatrical pieces amid Naples's scruffy backdrops, volcanoes, and Roman ruins. The film intersperses the musical dramas with interviews, impromptu piazza performances, and archival film footage.

POMPEII BY ROBERT HARRIS (2003)

Harris's book is probably the most gripping and well-researched novel written about the volcanic eruption of AD 79 and Roman life in the Bay of Naples. The story charts the life of a Roman engineer and the first pages set the scene in the rarely visited Piscina Mirabilis, a cathedral-like cistern fed by the Aqua Augusta aqueduct that supplied water to the nearby Roman fleet at Miseno. Here, Pliny the Younger observed the devastating and unexpected eruption.

Money-Saving Tips

EATING

Pizza rules the roost here, not just culturally, but also pricewise. The classic Margherita is likely to be the cheapest option on the menu, and even in costlier establishments will not break the bank (beware the cover charge in some restaurants, however). Many pizzerias also have an outside counter selling inexpensive fried delicacies, ideal for a quick snack. Keep an eye out for *tavole calde* (warm tables), which sell portions of pasta and secondi from behind a large counter—these are often take-away, and seating areas are generally very basic, but the food is good. Rustic trattorie are generally a better value than the classier joints, and their menus offer the same local ingredients, often prepared by the owner's mamma. Opt for the house wine—not only is it less expensive, it may well come from the family's own vineyard. You will probably be offered a complementary *limoncello* to round off your meal. For around €3, a *salumeria* will rustle up a sandwich for you—find a shady panoramic point for a picnic. In the evening if you'd like a break from a full meal visit a bar that does an *aperitivo* deal. Alongside your fancy drink you'll often be served a plate of cold cuts, cheeses, and other *stuzzichini* snacks, or be invited to fill a plate from a bounteous buffet.

LODGING

While five-star hotels will hit your wallet hard, there are many good value alternatives in the area. Bed-and-breakfasts and family-run hotels are good bets, and the owners' warmth and hospitality is a golden opportunity to integrate with the local culture; although some services may be basic, there is every chance they offer the same stunning views as the more upmarket establishments. Many hotels have half-board options, particularly in high season, and promote special offers on their websites. If you can avoid the peak summer season you will find that rates often drop by up to 30%. Consider also choosing a smaller town as a base, rather than the main urban areas. Near many of the big-name resorts like Positano, Sorrento, and Amalfi you'll find much more affordable lodgings. You may forgo the convenience of being in the center of the action, but you'll not only save money but often enjoy a more relaxing stay.

SHOPPING

The open-air markets are the place to head for money-conscious shoppers. There are a number of these in Naples, selling discount clothing, household items, and food. Bargains are harder to come by in resort areas, but stores drop prices by up to 70% in the summer sales—generally a three-week period in July. Outside that period you may have to dig deep for those one-of-a-kind pieces (e.g., Capri sandals, Positano beachwear), but think of the savings on the high street prices back home. Make sure to ask about tax-free shopping for foreign visitors.

TRAVEL

As European standards go, it is not expensive to travel around the region. Museum buffs will want to invest in the three-day Campania Arte Card (🌐 *www.campaniartecard.it*), which includes all transport, including the airport Alibus, as well as free entry to two sites and discounts to others, for €32. On the islands it is wiser to avoid the 24-hour ticket—you will probably not make enough trips to justify the cost. Bear in mind, too, that walking is often an option for shorter distances, and that those hundreds of steps on the Amalfi Coast are indeed easier to tackle going down than up!

Chapter 2

TRAVEL SMART

Updated by
Fergal Kavanagh

★ CAPITAL:
Rome

POPULATION:
60,327,235

LANGUAGE:
Italian

$ CURRENCY:
Euro

COUNTRY CODE:
39

EMERGENCIES:
112

DRIVING:
On the right

ELECTRICITY:
200v/50 cycles; plugs have two round prongs

TIME:
6 hours ahead of New York

WEB RESOURCES:
www.italia.it
www.amalfitouristoffice.it
www.positano.com
www.capritourism.com
www.ischia.it
www.visitnaples.eu

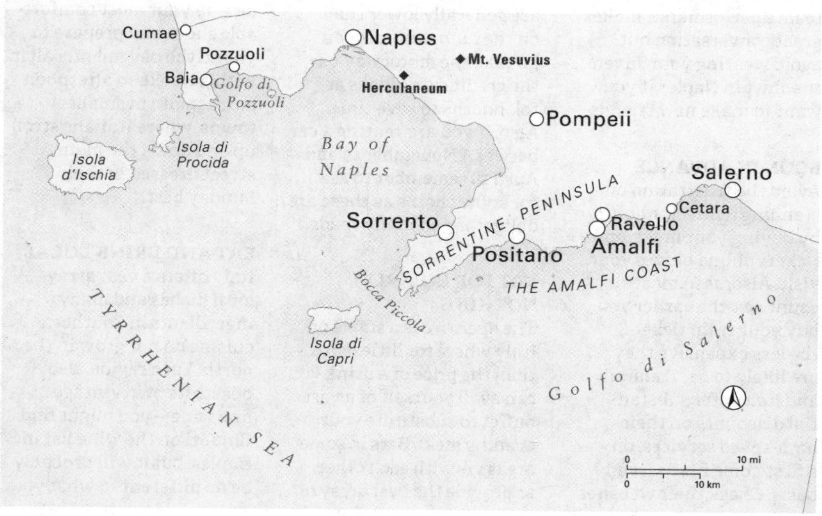

Know Before You Go

A TALE OF TWO COUNTRIES
Italy as we know it is just over 160 years old, united by Garibaldi in 1861, and traditions and customs die hard. Differences and rivalries between the wealthier north and the more relaxed south abound but you will need to spend time in both to live the full Italian experience.

DRINK YOUR FILL
Bottled water is available everywhere but often at an inflated price. Carry a refillable bottle and fill up for free at the strategically placed water fountains in cities. In restaurants bottled water (natural or *frizzante*) is the default but you can ask for tap water (*acqua del rubinetto*), although you may have to insist.

FOOTBALL CRAZY
Soccer—*calcio*—is taken very seriously in Italy with rivalries running deep. A little knowledge of a local team's performance makes great conversation but avoid wearing your Juventus shirt in Naples if you want to make new friends.

BOOK IN ADVANCE
Avoid the frustration of standing in line for hours by buying your museum tickets online before your visit. Also, as in most countries, the earlier you buy your train tickets, the less expensive they are likely to be. *Trenitalia* and *Italo* offer substantial discounts on their high-speed services, on a first-come first-served basis. Check their websites and prepare to be flexible with your travel times. Discounts are not offered on regional trains, nor is seat reservation possible, and tickets for these (unless bought online) must be stamped before boarding.

TAKE THE BACK ROADS
So you've rented a car? Why stick to the highways then? Much of Italy's beauty is off the beaten track, on winding mountain roads or coastal secondary roads, so take your time and wander a little. Not only will you save on tolls but gas prices are generally lower than on the *autostrade*. If you do take the motorway use the credit cards lanes at toll booths to save time. Also, if you are renting a car between November 15 and April 15 remember to ask for snow chains as these are obligatory on many roads.

EAT FOR (NEARLY) NOTHING
The *aperitivo* is a staple of Italy where for little more than the price of a drink you can avail yourself of a vast buffet to substitute your evening meal. Bars in some areas vie with each other to provide the best array of pasta dishes, *pizzette* and *panini*, so check out a few of them before taking your place at the table.

PLAN YOUR DAY
Mealtimes vary depending on where you are. Lunch in the north is from noon to 2 pm, while restaurants in the south will often serve until 3. You may have problems finding anywhere to eat in the north after 9 pm, the time most southerners are sitting down for dinner—restaurants here tend not to open until 7:30 pm. Also, shoppers beware, many stores are closed from 1 to 4:30 pm.

GET YOUR WALKING SHOES ON
The best, and often the only, way to see a city is on foot. In recent years many city and town centers have become pedestrianized and public transport works well (albeit generally better in the north). Hourly ticketed or private parking costs can add up, so when possible lace up your most comfortable shoes and prepare to pound the pavement. Fall in with a weekend afternoon *passeggiata* in smaller towns, where Italians stroll up and down the main street dressed in their Sunday best.

EAT AND DRINK LOCAL
Italy offers a vast array local dishes and many ingredients in Southern cuisine do not grow in the north. Each region also boasts its own vintage of fine wine—you might find Chianti on the wine list in Naples, but it will probably be no different to what you

drink at home. The local Campania wines, however, offer a far more authentic taste of the area.

WHAT YOU GET IN A BAR
Coffee culture is different here. Italians take their one-shot *espresso* standing at the counter at a bar—a place often also serving snacks as well as alcoholic drinks, usually closed in the evening. Pay the cashier for your drink, then place your receipt and, to emulate locals, a 10-cent tip on the counter, then place your order. If you choose to sit, there is usually a surcharge, whether there is table service or not. Also, if you order a *latte* you'll get a glass of milk.

NEVER PASS A RESTROOM
Public restrooms in train stations usually cost €1 and bars frown on the use of their services without making a purchase, so before you leave the hotel, restaurant, or museum, take advantage of the facilities.

DAY-TRIPPER
Lodging prices in tourist hot spots are at a premium during high season, but better deals can be found a little farther from the action. Consider booking outside town and taking a local train or bus to see the sights—you'll miss the evening atmosphere but can spend more on lunch. Avoid sleeping on local trains, however, as theft is common.

TAKE YOUR TIME
The Italian experience differs from region to region. It is unlikely you will be able to visit everywhere, so choose your destination and explore it at leisure. Quick in-and-out visits to cities will allow you to see the major sights but you'll miss out on each area's local atmosphere. High-speed trains whisk you from city to city, but the slower *regionali* get you there, too, at up to a quarter of the price.

BE ITALIAN
Food is one of Italy's defining features and locals continue to be horrified by the idea of pineapple on pizza—ketchup on tomato pasta is also a no-no. You do not need a knife to eat spaghetti (although a spoon to wind the pasta is allowed for beginners) and it is fine to pick your pizza up. Most restaurants have a cover charge, listed as bread on the menu, although waiters also appreciate a tip—this is standard (around 10%) in the south.

BEWARE OF SCAMS
Larger train stations often have porters insisting on carrying your bags, then charging a fee, so be firm. Also, as in all large cities, be careful where you store your wallet and valuables and avoid purchasing from street vendors.

ONE TICKET COVERS ALL
Many cities and towns sell a multiple day pass allowing access to different museums and sights—these offer great savings if you plan to visit a few attractions and some also offer deals on public transport.

LEARN THE LINGO
Most Italians have some command of English, although this not a fail-safe rule, particularly in the south. You can get by on hand gestures and pointing, but a *grazie* or *buongiorno* here and there will not go amiss. Avoid using *ciao* with people you do not know well.

THE PRICE IS RIGHT
Some stores and market stalls in tourist towns welcome haggling, so you might be able to knock a few euro off those handmade sandals in Capri.

DRESS LIKE A LOCAL
Italians are known for their style and would never visit a city wearing socks and sandals. Casual dress is fine, but if you don't want to stick out as a tourist, dress to impress. Also, when visiting churches, shoulders and legs should be covered.

CARRY CHANGE
Credit cards are accepted everywhere but for smaller purchases like a local bus ticket or a coffee in a bar, a few loose euro are far more welcome.

Getting Here and Around

Air

Most flights to Naples from North America and Australia make connections at Rome's Aeroporto Leonardo da Vinci (FCO) Fiumicino and Milan's Aeroporto Malpensa (MXP) Malpensa or another European airport. ITA Airways, Italy's national flag carrier, has the most nonstop flights to Rome and Milan, from which you can fly on to Naples. Flying time to Milan or Rome is approximately 8–8½ hours from New York, 10–11 hours from Chicago, 11½ hours from Dallas (via New York), and 11½ hours from Los Angeles. Flights from Rome to Naples are around 30 minutes and from Milan to Naples, about one hour. You can also take the FS airport train to Termini, Rome's main station, to connect with a train to Naples. It will take about 35 minutes to get from Fiumicino to Termini.

Just outside Naples, Aeroporto Capodichino (NAP) serves the Campania region. Completely renovated in 2009, it handles domestic and international flights, and is run by GESAC, part of BAA (British Airports Authority), the majority stakeholder.

FLIGHTS

As well as ITA Airways, other domestic and international carriers, such as British Airways, Aer Lingus, EasyJet, Ryanair, Volatea, Wizz Air and Transavia have direct connections between Naples and destinations in other European countries and may have slightly cheaper flights within Italy.

United Airlines connects New York's Newark Airport to Naples's Aeroporto Capodichino from May to mid October. ITA Airways offers nonstop flights to Italy from the United States as part of a transatlantic joint venture with Air France-KLM and Delta, with direct flights to Boston, Chicago, Miami, New York City, and seasonal flights to Los Angeles.

Boat

As one of the great harbors of the world, Naples offers a wide array of boat, ferry (*traghetti*), and hydrofoil (*aliscafo*) services between the city, the islands of the bay, the Sorrentine Peninsula, and other Mediterranean destinations. Hydrofoils leave from the main station of Molo Beverello—the port harbor of Naples opposite the Castel Nuovo (at the Municipio metro stop). Less frequent ferries leave from Calata Porta di Massa, a short distance to the east. Companies such as Caremar, SNAV, and Alilauro run services connecting Naples with Sorrento, Capri, Ischia, and Procida. The trip to Ischia and Procida is shorter and cheaper if you use the ferry that departs from Pozzuoli harbor (the nearest metro station is on the Cumana line at Pozzuoli). Next to the Molo Beverello is the Stazione Marittima (Molo Angioino), where larger ferries make trips to the Aeolian Islands, Sicily, and Sardinia.

Hydrofoil service is generally twice as fast as ferries and almost double the price. The service is considerably more frequent in summer. ⇨ *For specific information about boat, ferry, and hydrofoil travel between Naples and other destinations on the Bay of Naples and the Amalfi Coast, see the "Getting Here and Around" sections near the beginning of each regional chapter.* Car ferries operate to the islands of the Bay of Naples, but advance reservations are best.

FARES AND SCHEDULES

The website www.naplesbayferry.com lists ferry and hydrofoil schedules. As there are substantial seasonal variations, double-check departure times and days, especially when traveling farther afield on low-frequency services.

 Bus

Campania's bus network is extensive and in some areas buses can be more direct (and, therefore, faster) than local trains, so it's a good idea to compare bus and train schedules. Bus services outside cities are organized on a regional level, often by private companies, and the service is fairly reliable and uniform. ANM handles buses within Naples, while SITA services longer trips, including the Amalfi Coast. Itabus provides budget travel throughout Italy and FlixBus also has international routes. Most regional buses leave from the bus station behind Stazione Centrale, but be sure to check (SITA buses leave from Varco Immacolatella in the port area). All buses—as indeed all public transport—are no-smoking.

PAYING

Tickets are not sold onboard many local and regional buses so you must purchase them in advance (cash only) by machine (often no change given), at newsstands, at tobacconists, at metro stations, or at the bus station. Remember to time-stamp this ticket after you board as conductors sometimes do spot-checks. Keep in mind that many ticket sellers close for several hours at midday, so it's always wise to stock up on bus tickets when you have the chance.

 Car

Combine the cost of gasoline (prices on the islands can exceed €2 per liter, or $8.50 per gallon, at this writing), the ever-changeable dollar, the gridlock traffic in and around Naples, parking fees, and driving standards in southern Italy, and you get some good reasons for not traveling by car in Campania. There's an extensive network of *autostrade* (toll highways), complemented by equally well-maintained yet free *superstrade* (expressways). The ticket you're issued on entering an autostrada must be returned when you exit and pay the toll; on some shorter highways, like the *tangenziale* around Naples, the flat-rate toll (€1) is paid on exit; the Naples–Salerno toll (€2.10) is paid on entry. You can use your credit card at special lanes, identifiable by the blue sign. You simply slip the card into a designated slot at many autostrada locations, make paying tolls easier and faster.

If you want to hire a driver, this service can usually be arranged through hotels or travel agents. Agree on a flat daily rate beforehand, which will include the driver, car, and gasoline. In most cases you would be expected to pay extra for the driver's meals, as well as any parking fees incurred.

GASOLINE

Gas stations on autostrade are open 24 hours, otherwise they are generally open Monday–Saturday 7 am–7 pm with a break at lunchtime. Most stations also have self-service pumps (often cheaper than served), these are always available. Gas, so-called *benzina verde* ("green gasoline," or unleaded fuel), costs about

Getting Here and Around

€1.70–€1.85 per liter on the mainland. Confusingly, the Italian word *gasolio* means diesel fuel. It costs about €1.55 per liter (if you are renting a car, ask about the fuel type before you leave the agency).

PARKING

Parking space is at a premium in Naples and most towns, but especially in the *centri storici* (historic centers), which are filled with narrow streets and restricted circulation zones. It's often a good idea (if not the only option) to park your car in a designated (preferably attended) lot. When parking on the street, within the blue lines, pay at the nearby *parcometro,* a coin-only ticket machine. If driving to the more popular venues in Naples at night, you may be encouraged to park by a *parcheggiatore abusivo* (unlicensed parking attendant) who will expect a tip (about €1). Bear in mind that this will not stop your car from being clamped or towed away, and such practices are really just fueling the underground economy.

■ TIP→ **If you have baggage in the car, always park your car in an attended car park or garage.**

RENTALS

To rent a car in Italy, generally you must be at least 23 years old. Additional drivers must be identified in the contract and must qualify with the age limits. There may be an additional daily fee for more than one driver. Upon rental, all companies require credit cards as a warranty; to rent bigger cars (2,000 cc or more), you must often show two credit cards. Your driver's license may not be recognized outside your home country. An International Driver's Permit is a good idea. There are no special restrictions on senior-citizen drivers. Book car seats, required for children under age three, in advance (the cost is generally about €50 for the duration of the rental). Most rental cars have standard transmission; you must request an automatic and often pay a higher rate. Rates are usually lower if you book before you leave home.

RULES OF THE ROAD

Driving is on the right. Regulations are similar to those in the United States, except that a right turn is not permitted on a red light. Daytime use of headlights is obligatory on all roads outside urban areas, and seat belts must be worn at all times—despite high noncompliance rates in Campania. In most Italian towns the use of the horn is forbidden; a large sign, "Zona di Silenzio," indicates where. Elsewhere, according to the Italian Highway Code, horns can only be used in situations where there is "immediate and real danger." Some drivers interpret this as covering every sharp bend on the Amalfi Coast, although an alternative noise-free technique is to slow down and keep a foot hovering over the brake pedal. In winter you will be required to have snow chains. Speed limits are 130 kph (80 mph) on autostrade, 110 kph (70 mph) on superstrade, and 90 kph (55 mph) on state and provincial roads, unless otherwise marked. There are stiff sanctions for the use of handheld mobile phones while driving. Fines for driving after drinking are heavy, including the suspension of license and the additional possibility of six months' imprisonment.

The fastest trains in Italy are the state-run Freccia Rossa (red arrow) and the competing Nuovo Trasporto Viaggiatori (NTV) Italo. These operate between Rome and Naples (70 minutes), and also run the length of the peninsula, including Naples–Milan via Rome, Florence, and Bologna. The Intercity (IC) and *Interregionale* trains make more stops and are a little slower. *Regionale* and *locale* trains are the slowest; many serve commuters.

In Naples, all trains leave from the Stazione Centrale. Different trains—of varying speed and cost—connect Roma Termini and Napoli Centrale every hour (Alta Velocità and Italo: 1 hour 10 minutes, €48, second class; Intercity: about 2 hours 10 minutes, €27, second class. Substantial discounts are available when booking in advance).

There is a refreshment service on all long-distance trains, with mobile carts and a cafeteria or dining car. Tap water on trains is not drinkable. There's no smoking on any public transport in Italy. Potential confusion can arise in Pompeii, as the main-line station is a good 20-minute walk from the archaeological site. For the site, you need to take the Circumvesuviana network from Naples to Sorrento and get off at Pompei Scavi (35 minutes).

FARES AND SCHEDULES

To avoid long lines at station windows, you can buy tickets in advance online or at travel agencies displaying the Trenitalia or Italo emblem. The self-service machines in major stations will also save you time. Tickets can be purchased at the last minute; if you board without a ticket, you will have to pay a surcharge of €50 on application to train staff.

On trains without reservations, tickets must be date-stamped in the small yellow or green machines near the tracks before you board—if you forget, or didn't buy a ticket, you are liable to a hefty fine, over and above the fare to your destination. You can also buy train tickets for nearby destinations (within a 200-km [124-mile] range) at tobacconists.

USEFUL STATIONS

The Circumvesuviana rail line for points east stop on the lower level of Naples's Stazione Centrale. Destinations include Ercolano (Herculaneum), Pompei Scavi–Villa dei Misteri (Pompeii), and Sorrento. Note that there are two Circumvesuviana stations in the town of Pompeii, served by different lines. For the archaeological site, take the Sorrento line. There are also two railway lines that leave from the **Stazione Cumana** in Montesanto. Both head west, with one following the coast and stopping at Pozzuoli and Lucrino (near Baia), among other places. **Salerno's train station** is a stop on the Milan–Reggio Calabria line.

Essentials

Dining

Though pizza, mozzarella, and pasta with seafood are the flagship dishes in the Naples region, regional cuisine in Campania is both varied and distinctive. This is reflected by the choice of eateries, especially in Naples and Sorrento: meals range from on-the-hoof one-euro pizzas at kiosks, to earthy *osterie* serving *cucina povera* (land-based cuisine with a good dose of vegetables), and upscale restaurants where service, location, and *piatti* (dishes) should be worth the higher price tag. Italian restaurateurs have become sensitive to those with special dietary requirements, with vegetarian and gluten-free options widely available—be sure to ask, however, as bacon or kindred pork products may be used to flavor many land dishes but never appear as an item on the menu.

MEALS

A full-scale meal consists of a selection of *antipasti* followed by a *primo* (pasta or rice), then a *secondo* (meat or fish), rounded off with *frutta o dolci* (fruit or dessert).

The typical pizzeria fare in Naples includes *fritti* (deep-fried finger food), such as *crocchè* (fried mashed potatoes) and *arancini* (rice balls stuffed with mozzarella).

PAYING

Il conto—the restaurant check—includes tax and a cover charge per person, usually listed as *coperto* or *pane.* This should be a modest charge (around €2 per person), except at the most expensive restaurants. Although the vast majority of eateries now accept major credit cards, tips are still left in cash.

BARS

Bars are primarily places to get a coffee and a bite to eat, rather than drinking establishments. Many bars have a selection of panini warmed up on the griddle (*piastra*) and *tramezzini* (sandwiches made of untoasted white bread triangles). If you place your order at the counter, ask if you can sit down: some places charge for table service, others do not.

Unless otherwise noted, the restaurants listed in this guide are open daily for lunch and dinner.

WINES, BEER, AND SPIRITS

Refreshingly, there's a fairly low markup on bottled wines, and a liter of house wine rarely costs more than €8–€10. At the end of your meal you may well be offered some of the house liqueur, probably *limoncello* (a lemon-based liqueur with varying proportions of sugar) or *nocillo* (from green walnuts).

Italians have a relaxed attitude to alcohol consumption. In many homes, wine is a necessary accompaniment to any meal, like salt and olive oil. All bars and cafés are licensed to serve alcohol, and even takeaway pizzas can be enjoyed with a beer in a city park.

PRICES

Prices are per person for a main course at dinner, or if dinner is not served, at lunch.

Restaurant reviews have been shortened. For full information, visit Fodors.com.

What It Costs in Euros

$	$$	$$$	$$$$
AT DINNER			
under €15	€15–€24	€25–€35	over €35

Health and Safety

Although COVID-19 brought travel to a virtual standstill for most of 2020 and into 2021, vaccinations have made travel possible again. Remaining requirements and restrictions—including those for unvaccinated travelers—can, however, vary from one place (or even business) to the next. Check out the websites of the CDC and the U.S. Department of State, both of which have destination-specific, COVID-19 guidance. Also, in case travel is curtailed abruptly again, consider buying trip insurance. Just be sure to read the fine print: not all travel-insurance policies cover pandemic-related cancellations.

Naples, like any modern metropolis, has had certain problems with crime. Although great inroads have been made since the 1990s and the city today is as safe as many other big urban centers in Europe, you should continue to be vigilant, especially around the main rail station of Piazza Garibaldi where petty theft is common. In Italy, in general, violent crimes are rare.

■ TIP→ Distribute your cash, credit cards, IDs, and other valuables between a deep front pocket, an inside jacket or vest pocket, and a hidden money pouch. Don't reach for the money pouch once you're in public.

No matter where you are in Italy, dial 113 for all emergencies, or find somebody (your concierge, a passerby) who will call for you, as not all 113 operators speak English; the Italian word to use to draw people's attention in an emergency is *"Aiuto!"* (Help!, pronounced "ah-YOU-toh"). *"Pronto soccorso"* means "first aid" and when said to an operator will get you an *ambulanza* (ambulance).

The most common types of illnesses are caused by contaminated food and water. In Italy, tap water is safe to drink and eating out, even in tiny "hole-in-the-wall" places, is perfectly safe. As in every part of the world, avoid vegetables and fruits that you haven't washed or peeled yourself. If you have problems, mild cases of traveler's diarrhea may respond to Imodium (known generically as loperamide) or Pepto-Bismol. Be sure to drink plenty of fluids; if you can't keep fluids down, seek medical help immediately.

Immunizations

Make sure you are up-to-date on routine vaccines before every trip. These vaccines include measles-mumps-rubella (MMR) vaccine, diphtheria-tetanus-pertussis vaccine, varicella (chickenpox) vaccine, polio vaccine, and your yearly flu shot.

Lodging

Campania has a varied and abundant number of hotels, bed-and-breakfasts, *agriturismi* (farm stays), and rental properties. Throughout the cities and the countryside you can find very sophisticated, luxurious palaces and villas as well as rustic farmhouses and small hotels. Six-hundred-year-old *palazzi* and converted monasteries have been restored as luxurious hotels, while retaining the original atmosphere. At the other end of the spectrum, boutique hotels inhabit historic buildings using chic Italian design for the interiors. Increasingly, the famed Italian wineries are creating rooms and apartments for three-day to weeklong stays.

The lodgings we list are the cream of the crop in each price category. Properties are assigned price categories based on the range between their least- and most-expensive standard double room at high season (excluding holidays).

Essentials

Note that in peak-season months (usually June–September), some resort hotels require either half- or full-board arrangements, whereby your (increased) room tab includes one or two meals provided by the hotel restaurant. Note that the hotel prices in this book reflect basic room rates only.

RENTALS

AirBnB offers a wide range of properties throughout the region. Renting an apartment, a farmhouse, or a villa can be economical depending on the number of people in your group and your budget. Issues to keep in mind when renting an apartment in a city or town are the neighborhood (street noise and ambience), the availability of an elevator or number of stairs, the furnishings (including pots and pans and linens), and the cost of utilities. Inquiries about countryside properties should also include how isolated the property is.

PRICES

Prices are for a standard double room in high season.

Hotel reviews have been shortened. For full information, visit Fodors.com.

What It Costs in Euros			
$	$$	$$$	$$$$
FOR TWO PEOPLE			
under €125	€125–€200	€201–€300	over €300

Packing

In summer, stick with clothing that is as light as possible, although a sweater may be necessary for cool evenings, especially in the Lattari Mountains along the Amalfi Coast (even during the hot months). Sunglasses, a hat, and sunblock are essential, now more than ever due to global warming, which often sends the temperature soaring to 95°F or more in the middle of summer. But, contrary to myth, the sun does not shine all day, every day on Campania: brief summer thunderstorms are common in Naples, while typhoon-like storms occasionally arrive along the Amalfi Coast, so an umbrella will definitely come in handy. In winter bring a medium-weight coat and a raincoat; winters in Naples can be both humid *and* cold. Even in Naples, central heating may not be up to your standards, and interiors can be chilly and damp; take wools or flannel rather than sheer fabrics. Bring sturdy shoes for winter, and comfortable walking shoes in any season.

For sightseeing, pack a pair of binoculars; they will help you get a good look at Naples' wondrous painted ceilings and domes.

Passports

U.S. citizens need only a valid passport to enter Italy for stays of up to 90 days. Ensure that the passport is valid for six months after the date of arrival. Children are required to have their own passport.

■ TIP→ **Before your trip, make two copies of your passport's data page (one for someone at home and another for you to carry separately). Or scan the page and email it to someone at home and/or yourself.**

Tipping

If a 10%–15% service charge is added to your restaurant bill it's not necessary to leave an additional tip, although this charge does not actually go to the waiters, so a few euros will not go amiss. If service is not included, leave a cash tip of a couple of euros per person. At a hotel bar, tip €1 for a round or two of drinks; at a café, tip €0.10 per coffee.

Tip taxi drivers, particularly if the driver helps with luggage. On large group sight-seeing tours, tip guides about €5 per person for a half-day group tour, more if they are especially knowledgeable.

In hotels leave the chambermaid about €1 per day in a moderately priced hotel; tip a minimum of €1 for valet or room service. Double these amounts in an expensive hotel.

Tours

A knowledgeable guide can take you places that you might never discover on your own, and you may be pushed to see more than you would have otherwise. Whenever you book a guided tour, find out what's included and what isn't. Also keep in mind that the province of Naples has tour guides licensed by the government. Some are eminently qualified in relevant fields such as architecture and art history, but most, especially those that linger outside Pompeii have simply managed to pass the test (or purchase the license!). Tipping is appreciated, but not obligatory, for local guides.

U.S. Embassy/Consulate

The U.S. Embassy is in Rome and the U.S. Consulates General are in Florence, Milan, and Naples. If you are arrested or detained, ask police or prison officials to notify the U.S. Embassy or the nearest consulate immediately. All visitors, including U.S. citizens, are not allowed to bring laptops into the Embassy or Consulate General.

Visas

When staying for 90 days or less, U.S. citizens are not required to obtain a visa prior to traveling to Italy. Italian law requires you fill in a declaration of presence within eight days of your arrival, but the stamp on your passport at Airport Arrivals substitutes this. If you plan to travel or live in Italy or the European Union for longer than 90 days, you must acquire a valid visa from the Italian consulate serving your state *before you leave the United States.* Plan ahead because the process of obtaining a visa will take at least 30 days and the Italian government does not accept visa applications submitted by visa expediters.

When to Go

High Season: June through September is expensive and busy. In August, most Italians take their own summer holidays; cities are less crowded, but many shops and restaurants close. July and August can be uncomfortably hot.

Low Season: Winter offers the least appealing weather, though it's the best time for airfare and hotel deals and to escape the crowds. Many hotels close down for the winter months.

Value Season: By late September, temperate weather, saner airfares, and more cultural events can make for a happier trip. October is also great, but November is often rainy and (hence) quiet. From late April to early May, the masses have not yet arrived but cafés are already abuzz. March and early April can be changeable and wet.

Great Itineraries

Best of Naples, Capri, and the Amalfi Coast, 6 Days

Covering the principal sights of this fascinating region, this itinerary is ideal for energetic first-timers. Public transport is a well-oiled machine, and distances aren't too far. Driving is a disadvantage, as parking spots are exorbitantly priced and difficult to find.

DAY 1: NAPLES

Italy's most vibrant city can be a little rough around the edges, but Naples is a delight to discover, and most visitors end up falling in love with the city's alluring palazzi and spectacular pizza. Find a hotel in the atmospheric Centro Storico or near the Lungomare.

Logistics: 4 miles; airport bus to center (15 minutes).

DAY 2: NAPLES

Start the day at the **Museo Archaeologico Nazionale,** budgeting at least two hours for the collection of Greco-Roman treasures from all over Campania—this is an essential stop on the Pompeii trail. Next take Via Santa Maria di Costantinopoli and grab a coffee at one of the outdoor cafés in Piazza Bellini. From here, head down Via dei Tribunali for a pizza at one of the Centro Storico's many pizzerias. Continue along Tribunali, crossing Via Duomo, visiting the **Duomo** before continuing onto see Caravaggio's *The Seven Works of Mercy* at **Pio Monte della Misericordia.** Descend Via Duomo and turn right onto Spaccanapoli, the street that "splits Naples," cutting through the Centro Storico. It is, in fact, not just one street—Via San Biago Dei Librai becomes Via Benedetto Croce at Piazza San Domenico. Turn off here for a brief stop at the **Cappella Sansevero** with its remarkable Veiled Christ, a pinnacle of Masonic sculpture. Continue along Spaccanapoli to Piazza del Gesù and the churches of **Il Gesù Nuovo,** with its faceted stone facade, and **Santa Chiara**—stop here for a short rest in its magnificent majolica cloister. Heading downhill, turn left to follow Via Monteoliveto and Via Medina to the port and the **Castel Nuovo,** with its 15th-century triumphal entrance arch. Walk on past the **Teatro San Carlo,** Europe's oldest theater, just across from the Liberty style **Galleria Umberto I,** and on to the enormous **Palazzo Reale,** one-time residence of Charles of Bourbon. Cross the **Piazza del Plebiscito** with the **Basilico di San Francesco di Paola** and continue down to the seafront. Gaze at **Castel dell'Ovo**, Naples's oldest castle, then dine along the *lungomare.*

Logistics: This entire day is easily done on foot.

DAY 3: POMPEII AND SORRENTO

After breakfast, pack your luggage and head from Naples to **Pompeii,** one of the true archaeological gems of Europe. Allow a half day to get a feel for the place, then it's on to **Sorrento,** your first taste of the wonderful peninsula that marks the beginning of the fabled **Amalfi Coast.** Sorrento is touristy, but it may well be the Italian city of your imagination: cliffhanging, cobblestone-paved, and graced with a breathtaking variety of fishing ports and coastal views.

Logistics: 33 miles; car (1 hour) or train (1 hour) from Naples to Sorrento.

DAY 4: CAPRI

A short hydrofoil trip lands you at **Marina Grande,** the port of **Capri.** Take a boat to the oh-so-blue **Grotta Azzurra,** an hour's round trip, then join the queues for the funicular up to Capri town. Gaze at the jet set in **La Piazzetta,** then walk down Via Vittorio Emanele, past the Hotel Quisisana, itself a small village, and

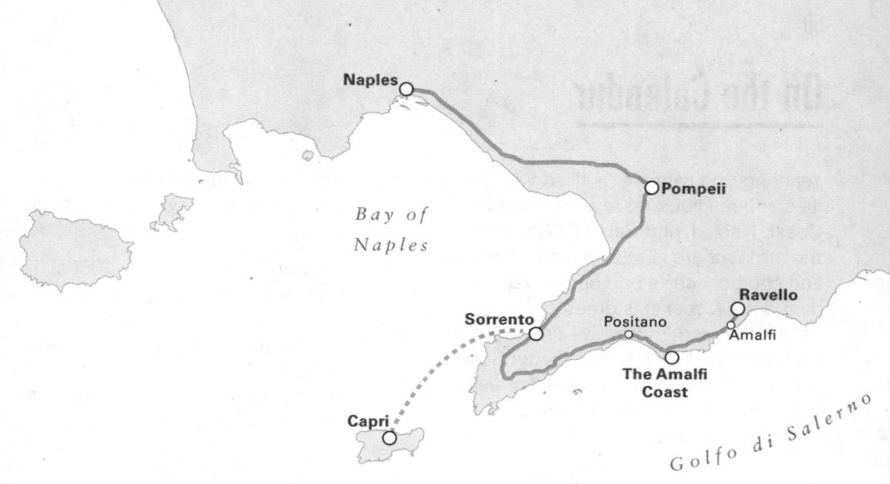

continue downhill to the **Certosa di San Giacomo,** a 14th-century Carthusian monastery. Wander around this magnificent structure, soaking in the island's history. Next, climb west for a few minutes to the **Giardini di Augusto,** with its stunning views of **I Faraglioni** and the winding Via Krupp. Return to the piazzetta and walk along Via Roma to the bus station, taking a 10-minute ride to **Anacapri.** Take the chairlift to **Monte Solaro** with its bay views, then down again to the charming **Villa San Michele,** former home of Swedish doctor and philanthropist Axel Munthe. Watch your time, however—there are not many direct buses from Anacapri to Marina Grande, so you will probably need to take a bus to Capri before returning to Marina Grande for your boat back to Sorrento.

Logistics: 9 miles; hydrofoil from Sorrento to Capri (25 minutes).

DAY 5: THE AMALFI COAST

Drivers, you are advised to leave your car behind today. After breakfast make your way to the train station where SITA buses make regular trips along the Amalfi Coast. The first stop, after an hour, is **Positano,** a must. It's one of the most visited towns in Italy for good reason: a vertical scene with white Moorish-style houses above blue-green seas make for a truly memorable setting. Walk 10 minutes down from the Sponda bus stop on the main road, wander around, sip a coffee, then head back up to the take the 40-minute bus ride to Amalfi. Stop for lunch, then visit the 9th-century cathedral **Duomo di Sant'Andrea.** A 35-minute climb uphill on a SITA bus takes you to the less-traveled town of **Ravello,** an aerie perched loftily above the coast. Don't miss the **Duomo** and its 12th-century bronze door, and the spectacular gardens of **Villa Rufolo** and **Villa Cimbrone** before settling in for dinner with a view.

Logistics: 24 miles; bus from Sorrento to Amalfi, Amalfi to Ravello (2 hours).

DAY 6: RAVELLO TO NAPLES

Amalfi is just a short ride down the hill, and from here you can retrace the route to Sorrento and on to Naples, or take a 75-minute ride on a SITA bus to Salerno. Regular trains make the 45-minute trip to Naples from here.

Logistics: 40 miles; bus from Ravello to Amalfi, Amalfi to Salerno, train from Salerno to Naples (2 hours 30 minutes).

On the Calendar

Yearlong, the calendar is filled with festivities and religious *feste* along the Amalfi Coast, Naples, and Capri. At Christmas, the atmosphere is festive, and orchestra and choir concerts pop up all over. Capodanno (New Year's) is greeted with a big celebration and impressive fireworks. In Catholic Italy, Good Friday, Easter Sunday, and Christmas are all excuses for lavish family occasions, with special foods and church ceremonies.

January/February

Carnival. Maiori, on the Amalfi Coast, holds a colorful 10-day celebration with parades and floats. ⊕ *www.grancarnevaledimaiori.it.*

March/April

Easter Processions. On Holy Thursday and Good Friday solemn hooded figures walk through various locations on the Sorrento peninsula, singing a Miserere chorus. ⊕ *www.processioni.com.*

May/June

Ischia Film Festival. The Ischia Film Festival takes over the Castello Aragonese for a week at the end of June, focusing—appropriately, given its unbeatable location—on films with stunning landscapes. ⊕ *www.ischiafilmfestival.it.*

Regata Storica delle Antiche Repubbliche Marinare (*Historical Regatta of the Ancient Maritime Republics*). In this historical pageant, four boats, each with eight oarsmen, represent the medieval maritime republics of Amalfi, Pisa, Genoa, and Venice. The prize is a scale-model gold-and-silver replica of an antique sailing ship. ⊕ *www.repubblichemarinare.org.*

Ravello Festival. Starting in the 1950s, Ravello became famous as the "City of Music," when concerts began to be performed in the spectacular gardens of the Villa Rufolo. The celebrated Ravello Festival runs June–October, and presents a variety of events from classical concerts as well as dance, opera, and jazz events. ⊕ *www.ravellofestival.com.*

July/August

Ischia Global Film & Music Festival. Since its inception in 2002, the Ischia Global Film & Music Festival has become an important festival, attracting top actors from around the world. ⊕ *www.ischiaglobal.com.*

Feast of Sant'Anna. There's a rich tradition in Ischian local festivals, with the Feast of Sant'Anna on July 26 holding pride of place with its skillful choreography and floating procession in the marina at Ischia Ponte below the Aragonese Castle. ⊕ *www.festadisantanna.it.*

Piano & Jazz Festival. This three-day event in late August sees the cream of Italian jazz musicians performing on the island of Ischia, at the Negumbo gardens and along Corso Rizzoli. ⊕ *www.pianoejazz.it.*

Festa dell'Assunta *(Feast of the Assumption).* Positano's star event of the year—and its main religious feast—is held on August 15, with a replica of the Byzantine icon of the Madonna with Child from Santa Maria Assunta carried from the church to the sea, commemorated by fireworks.

Sorrento Classica. This event features concerts and theatrical entertainments from the last week of August to the end of September, many held in the famous Moorish-style cloister of the church of San Francesco. 🌐 *www.societaconcerti-sorrento.it.*

September/October

Festa di San Gennaro. The liquefaction of the blood of Naples's patron saint is celebrated in the Duomo on September 19. In the unlikely event the miracle does not occur, disaster will fall upon the city.

Positano Premia La Danza Léonide Massine (*Positano Prize for the Art of Dancing*). The first week in September sees this celebration of dance that includes music concerts, and dance performances. 🌐 *www.positanopremialadanza.it.*

Torello Festa dell'Incendio. On the third Sunday of September, this time-stained medieval hamlet celebrates the Madonna Addolorata with an unforgettable fireworks display that has to be seen to be believed.

Sagra del Pesce (*Fish Festival*). The last Saturday in September brings this fabulous fish festival on Fornillo beach, with live music and plenty of seafood dishes to taste. 🌐 *www.festadelpesce.net.*

November/December

Festa di Sant' Andrea (*Feast of Saint Andrew*). Dedicated to Amalfi's patron saint and protector of seamen, this festival, which takes place on June 27 and November 30, is a religious celebration, with the summer festival commemorating the defeat of a 1544 pirate attack and the November festival honoring the death of St. Andrew.

Helpful Italian Phrases

BASICS

Yes/no	Sí/No	see/no
Please	Per favore	pear fa-**vo**-ray
Thank you	Grazie	**grah**-tsee-ay
You're welcome	Prego	**pray**-go
I'm sorry (apology)	Mi dispiace	mee dis-pee-**atch**-ay
Excuse me, sorry	Scusi	**skoo**-zee
Good morning/ afternoon	Buongiorno	bwohn-**jor**-no
Good evening	Buona sera	**bwoh**-na **say**-ra
Good-bye	Arrivederci	a-ree-vah-**dare**-chee
Mr. (Sir)	Signore	see-**nyo**-ray
Mrs. (Ma'am)	Signora	see-**nyo**-ra
Miss	Signorina	see-nyo-**ree**-na
Pleased to meet you	Piacere	pee-ah-**chair**-ray
How are you?	Come sta?	**ko**-may-**stah**
Hello (phone)	Pronto?	**proan**-to

NUMBERS

one-half	mezzo	**mets**-zoh
one	uno	**oo**-no
two	due	**doo**-ay
three	tre	Tray
four	quattro	**kwah**-tro
five	cinque	**cheen**-kway
six	sei	Say
seven	sette	**set**-ay
eight	otto	**oh**-to
nine	nove	**no**-vay
ten	dieci	dee-**eh**-chee
eleven	undici	**oon**-dee-chee
twelve	dodici	**doh**-dee-chee
thirteen	tredici	**trey**-dee-chee
fourteen	quattordici	kwah-**tor**-dee-chee
fifteen	quindici	**kwin**-dee-chee
sixteen	sedici	**say**-dee-chee
seventeen	dicissette	dee-chah-**set**-ay
eighteen	diciotto	dee-chee-**oh**-to
nineteen	diciannove	dee-chee-ahn-**no**-vay
twenty	venti	**vain**-tee
twenty-one	ventuno	**vent**-oo-no
thirty	trenta	**train**-ta
forty	quaranta	kwa-**rahn**-ta
fifty	cinquanta	cheen-**kwahn**-ta
sixty	sessanta	seh-**sahn**-ta
seventy	settanta	seh-**tahn**-ta
eighty	ottanta	o-**tahn**-ta
ninety	novanta	no-**vahn**-ta
one hundred	cento	**chen**-to
one thousand	mille	**mee**-lay
one million	un milione	oon **mill**-oo-nay

COLORS

black	Nero	**nair**-ro
blue	Blu	bloo
brown	Marrone	ma-**rohn**-nay
green	Verde	**ver**-day
orange	Arancione	ah-rahn-**cho**-nay
red	Rosso	**rose**-so
white	Bianco	bee-**ahn**-koh
yellow	Giallo	**jaw**-low

DAYS OF THE WEEK

Sunday	Domenica	do-**meh**-nee-ka
Monday	Lunedi	loo-ne-**dee**
Tuesday	Martedi	mar-te-**dee**
Wednesday	Mercoledi	**mer**-ko-le-**dee**
Thursday	Giovedi	jo-ve-**dee**
Friday	VenerdÌ	ve-ner-**dee**
Saturday	Sabato	**sa**-ba-toh

MONTHS

January	Gennaio	jen-**ay**-o
February	Febbraio	feb-**rah**-yo
March	Marzo	**mart**-so
April	Aprile	a-**pril**-ay
May	Maggio	**mahd**-joe
June	Giugno	**joon**-yo
July	Luglio	**lool**-yo
August	Agosto	a-**gus**-to
September	Settembre	se-**tem**-bre
October	Ottobre	o-**toh**-bre
November	Novembre	no-**vem**-bre
December	Dicembre	di-**chem**-bre

USEFUL WORDS AND PHRASES

Do you speak English?	Parla Inglese?	**par**-la een-**glay**-zay
I don't speak Italian	Non parlo italiano	non **par**-lo ee-tal-**yah**-no
I don't understand	Non capisco	non ka-**peess**-ko
I don't know	Non lo so	non lo **so**
I understand	Capisco	ka-**peess**-ko
I'm American	Sono Americano(a)	**so**-no a-may-ree-**kah**-no(a)
I'm British	Sono inglese	so-no een-**glay**-zay
What's your name?	Come si chiama?	**ko**-may see kee-**ah**-ma
My name is …	Mi chiamo…	mee kee-**ah**-mo
What time is it?	Che ore sono?	kay **o**-ray **so**-no
How?	Come?	**ko**-may
When?	Quando?	**kwan**-doe
Yesterday/today/ tomorrow	Ieri/oggi/domani	**yer**-ee/ **o**-jee/ do-**mah**-nee

This morning	Stamattina/Oggi	sta-ma-**tee**-na/ **o**-jee
Afternoon	Pomeriggio	po-mer-**ee**-jo
Tonight	Stasera	sta-**ser**-a
What?	Che cosa?	kay **ko**-za
What is it?	Che cos'è?	kay ko-**zey**
Why?	Perchè?	pear-**kay**
Who?	Chi?	**Kee**
Where is …	Dov'è…	doe-**veh**
the train station?	la stazione?	la sta-tsee-**oh**-nay
the subway?	la metropolitana?	la may-tro-po-lee-**tah**-na
the bus stop?	la fermata dell'autobus?	la fer-**mah**-ta del-ow-tor-**booss**
the airport	l'aeroporto	la-er-roh-**por**-toh
the post office?	l'ufficio postale	loo-**fee**-cho po-**stah**-lay
the bank?	la banca?	la **bahn**-ka
the hotel?	l'hotel...?	lo-**tel**
the museum?	Il museo	eel moo-**zay**-o
the hospital?	l'ospedale?	lo-spay-**dah**-lay
the elevator?	l'ascensore	la-shen-**so**-ray
the restrooms?	...il bagno	eel **bahn**-yo
Here/there	Qui/là	kwee/la
Left/right	A sinistra/a destra	a see-**neess**-tra/a **des**-tra
Is it near/far?	È vicino/lontano?	ay vee-**chee**-no/ lon-**tah**-no
I'd like …	Vorrei...	vo-**ray**
a room	una camera	**oo**-na **kah**-may-ra
the key	la chiave	la kee-**ah**-vay
a newspaper	un giornale	oon jore-**nah**-vay
a stamp	un francobollo	oon frahn-ko-**bo**-lo
I'd like to buy …	Vorrei comprare...	vo-**ray** kom-**prah**-ray
a city map	una mappa della città	**oo**-na **mah**-pa **day**-la chee-**tah**
a road map	una carta stradale	**oo**-na **car**-tah stra-**dahl**-lay
a magazine	una revista	**oo**-na ray-**vees**-tah
envelopes	buste	**boos**-tay
writing paper	carta de lettera	**car**-tah dah **leyt**-ter-rah
a postcard	una cartolina	**oo**-na car-tog-**leen**-ah
a ticket	un biglietto	oon bee-**yet**-toh
How much is it?	Quanto costa?	**kwahn**-toe **coast**-a
It's expensive/ cheap	È caro/ economico	ay **car**-o/ ay-ko-**no**-mee-ko
A little/a lot	Poco/tanto	**po**-ko/**tahn**-to
More/less	Più/meno	pee-**oo**/**may**-no

Enough/too (much)	Abbastanza/ troppo	a-bas-**tahn**-sa/tro-po
I am sick	Sto male	sto **mah**-lay
Call a doctor	Chiama un dottore	kee-**ah**-mah-oondoe-**toe**-ray
Help!	Aiuto!	a-**yoo**-to
Stop!	Alt!	ahlt

DINING OUT

A bottle of …	Una bottiglia di...	**oo**-na bo-**tee**-lee-ah dee
A cup of …	Una tazza di...	**oo**-na **tah**-tsa dee
A glass of …	Un bicchiere di...	oon bee-key-**air**-ay dee
Beer	La birra	la **beer**-rah
Bill/check	Il conto	eel **cone**-toe
Bread	Il pane	eel **pah**-nay
Breakfast	La prima colazione	la **pree**-ma ko-la-**tsee**-oh-nay
Butter	Il Burro	eel **boor**-roh
Cocktail/aperitif	L'aperitivo	la-pay-ree-**tee**-vo
Dinner	La cena	la **chen**-a
Fixed-price menu	Menù a prezzo fisso	may-**noo** a **pret**-so **fee**-so
Fork	La forchetta	la for-**ket**-a
I am vegetarian	Sono vegetariano(a)	**so**-no vay-jay-ta-ree-**ah**-no/a
I cannot eat …	Non posso mangiare	non **pose**-so mahn-gee-**are**-ay
I'd like to order	Vorrei ordinare	vo-**ray** or-dee-**nah**-ray
Is service included?	Il servizio è incluso?	eel ser-**vee**-tzee-o ay een-**kloo**-zo
I'm hungry/ thirsty	Ho fame/sede	oh **fah**-meh/**sehd**-ed
It's good/bad	È buono/cattivo	ay **bwo**-bo/ka-**tee**-vo
It's hot/cold	È caldo/freddo	ay **kahl**-doe/**fred**-o
Knife	Il coltello	eel kol-**tel**-o
Lunch	Il pranzo	eel **prahnt**-so
Menu	Il menu	eel may-**noo**
Napkin	Il tovagliolo	eel toe-va-lee-**oh**-lo
Pepper	Il pepe	eel **pep**-peh
Plate	Il piatto	eel pee-**aht**-toe
Please give me …	Mi dia...	mee **dee**-a
Salt	Il sale	eel **sah**-lay
Spoon	Il cucchiaio	eel koo-kee-ah-yo
Tea	tè	tay
Water	acqua	**awk**-wah
Wine	vino	**vee**-noh

Contacts

AIRPORT INFORMATION Aeroporto Capodichino. (*NAP*). ✉ *5 km (3 miles) north of Naples* ☎ *081/7896259* 🌐 *www.aeroportodinapoli.it.* **Aeroporto di Milano Malpensa.** (*MXP*). ✉ *45 km (28 miles) north of Milan* ☎ *02/232323* 🌐 *www.milanomalpensa-airport.com.* **Aeroporto di Roma Fiumicino.** (*FCO, aka Leonardo da Vinci*). ✉ *35 km (20 miles) southwest of Rome* ☎ *06/65951* 🌐 *www.adr.it.*

AIRLINE CONTACTS ITA Airways. ✉ *Via Venti Settembre 97, Rome* ☎ *06/85960020 Rome office, 877/7931717 toll-free from U.S., 800/936090 toll-free from Italy* 🌐 *www.itaspa.com.*

CARRIERS Caremar. ☎ *081/18966690* 🌐 *www.caremar.it.* **Navigazione Libera del Golfo.** (*NLG*). ☎ *081/8071812 Sorrento office, 081/5520763 Naples Port office* 🌐 *www.navlib.it.* **SNAV.** ☎ *081/4285555* 🌐 *www.snav.it.* **Tirrenia.** ☎ *0299/76028132* 🌐 *www.tirrenia.it.*

BUS INFORMATION ANM. ✉ *Via G. Marino 1, Naples* ☎ *800/639525* 🌐 *www.anm.it.* **FlixBus.** ☎ *30/300137300 head office, Germany* 🌐 *www.flixbus.com.* **Itabus.** ☎ *06/88938232* 🌐 *www.itabus.it.* **SITA.** ✉ *Varco Immacolatella, inside Molo Beverello port, Naples* ☎ *089/3866701* 🌐 *www.sitasudtrasporti.it.*

Car

LOCAL CAR AND DRIVER DriviNaples. ☎ *329/4214496* 🌐 *www.drivinaples.com.* **Your Driver In Italy.** ☎ *328/9486675* 🌐 *www.yourdriverinitaly.com.*

MAJOR AGENCIES Sicily By Car. ☎ *091/6390111, 800/334440 toll-free in Italy* 🌐 *www.autoeuropa.it.*

EMERGENCY SERVICES ACI Emergency Service. ☎ *803116* 🌐 *www.aci.it.*

INFORMATION Circumvesuviana. ☎ *800/211388* 🌐 *www.eavsrl.it.* **Stazione Cumana.** ✉ *Piazzetta Montesanto, near Montesanto Metro station* ☎ *800/211388 toll-free* 🌐 *www.eavsrl.it.* **Trenitalia and Italo.** ✉ *Piazza Garibaldi,* ☎ *892021 Trenitalia, in Italy: fee, 06/68475475 Trenitalia, from abroad, 892020 Italo, in Italy: fee, 06/89371892 Italo, from abroad* 🌐 *www.trenitalia.com, www.italotreno.it.*

INFORMATION AND PASSES Eurail. 🌐 *www.eurail.com.* **Rail Europe.** 🌐 *www.raileurope.com.*

Chapter 3

THE AMALFI COAST

Updated by
Nick Bruno

Sights	Restaurants	Hotels	Shopping	Nightlife
★★★★★	★★★★☆	★★★☆☆	★★☆☆☆	★☆☆☆☆

WELCOME TO THE AMALFI COAST

TOP REASONS TO GO

★ **Positano, a world made of stairs:** Built like a steep amphitheater leading into the sea, Positano's pastel buildings and *scalinatelle* stairways always charm.

★ **Amalfi, captivating history and charm:** Offering a dazzling layer cake of civilizations—Norman, Saracen, and Arab-Sicilian—this medieval town is so picturesque, it's easy to see why it's the namesake of the entire coastline.

★ **Furore, art in the hills:** This "town that doesn't exist," with no discernible center, is perched between the sea and sky and decorated with murals by local and international artists.

★ **Villa Cimbrone, Ravello:** No one should miss the spellbinding gardens of this villa and its Belvedere of Infinity, set like an eagle's nest 1,500 feet above the sea.

★ **Grecian glory:** Paestum has three sublime temples sitting side by side—some of the best preserved of ancient architectural monuments anywhere.

1 Positano. The ultimate pastel-brushed, tumbling-to-the-seaside village moves between sophisticated-luxe, beachcomber-casual, and selfie-reverential posing. Sheltered by Monte Comune (which keeps things warmer in the winter), Positano's three districts—the Sponda Lower Town, the central Mulini area, and the Chiesa Nuovo Upper Town—are connected by endless staircases offering views well worth the blistered feet.

2 Praiano. This charming clifftop resort with spectacular sea views is a hidden gem along the Amalfi Coast.

3 Marina di Praia. Praiano's picturesque harbor with pebbly beach sits within a fissure between rocky cliffs.

4 Furore. Beloved of hikers, this sprawling hamlet combines artsy retreat, terraced vineyards, and a fiord-trapped beach with a tempestuous past.

5 Conca dei Marini. Put on the map by 1960s jet-setters, this tiny but exceedingly picturesque harbor hideaway rubs shoulders with the luminous Emerald Grotto.

6 Amalfi. Nestled between the green Valle dei Mulini and the blue Gulf of Salerno, this buzzy resort is threaded with beguiling, rambling passages, testimony to its Norman and Arab-Sicilian past. The glory of the city's days as a medieval maritime republic is most evident in its fantastic cathedral. The

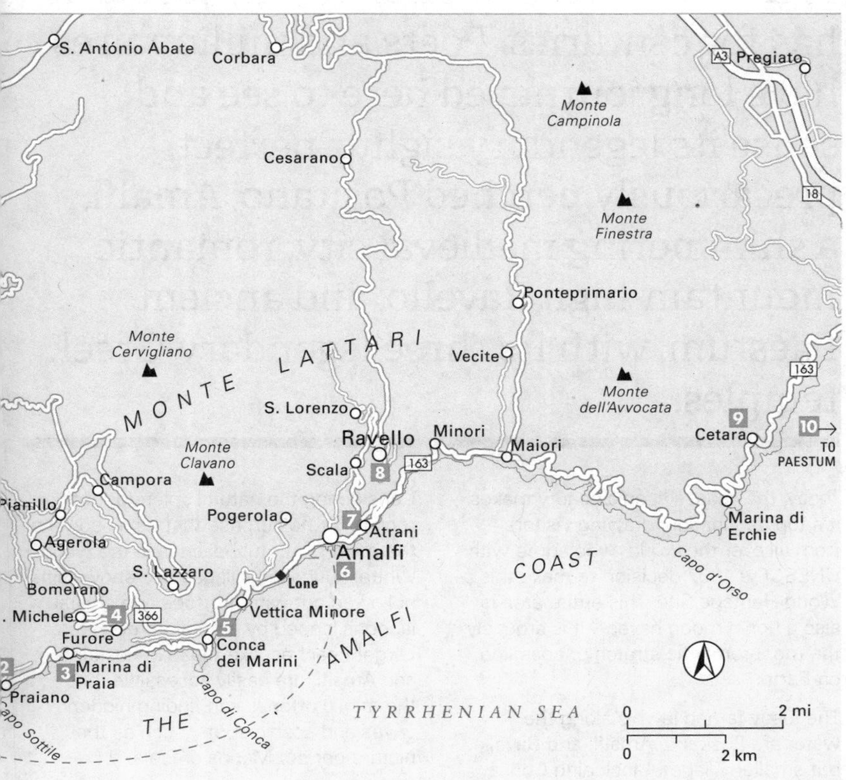

transportation hub of the coast, Amalfi's waterfront Piazza Flavio Gioia serves as the terminus for SITA's major bus routes.

7 **Atrani.** This tiny medieval town just outside of Amalfi offers a quiet and scenic break from its livelier neighbor.

8 **Ravello.** Just beyond the Valley of the Dragon lies Ravello, perched "closer to the sky than the sea" atop Monte Cereto and set over the breathtaking Bay of Salerno. Famed for its beautiful gardens (one of which inspired Wagner), its ethereal bluer-than-blue vistas, and its incredible mountain setting, Ravello is one of Italy's most beautiful towns.

9 **Cetara.** Off the Amalfi Drive's main drag is the costiera's earthiest charmer, with its fishermen's beach and famed anchovy-rich seafood restaurants.

10 **Paestum.** With its Greek temples and Roman ruins in flowery meadows, this vision of a lost city makes a rousing finale to any Grand Tour.

One of the most gorgeous places on Earth, this corner of the Campania region captivates visitors today just as it has for centuries. Poets and millionaires have long journeyed here to see and sense its legendary sights: perfect, precariously perched Positano; Amalfi, a shimmering medieval city; romantic mountain-high Ravello; and ancient Paestum, with its three legendary Greek temples.

Today, the coast's scenic beauty makes it a top destination, drawing visitors from all over the world, who agree with UNESCO's 1997 decision to make this a World Heritage Site. This entire area is also a honeymoon haven—it is arguably the most romantic stretch of coastline on Earth.

The justly famed jewels along the water are Positano, Amalfi, and Ravello, but smaller villages—including Conca dei Marini, Furore, Atrani, Scala, and Cetara—offer their own charms. The top towns along the Amalfi Drive may fill up in high season with tour buses, but in the countryside not much seems to have changed since the Middle Ages: mountains are still terraced and farmed for citrus, olives, and wine, and the sea is dotted with fishermen's boats. Vertiginously high villages, dominated by the spires of *chiese* (churches), are crammed with houses spilling down hillsides to the bay and navigated by flights of steps called *scalinatelle* often leading to outlooks that take your breath away.

Considering the natural splendor of this region, it's no surprise that it has some of the most beautiful beaches in the world. White, sunbaked villages rise above cliffs hollowed out with grottoes and crystal lagoons lapped by emerald green water. Larger beaches, like those in Positano and Amalfi, are easily accessible, but the magic often lies in finding hidden coves and scenic spots, such as the picture-perfect Marina di Praia.

Semitough daily realities lurk behind the scenic splendor of the Costiera Amalfitana, most notably the extremes of driving the twisty roads, the endless steps, and virtually nonexistent parking. So what? For a precious little time, you are in a land of unmarred beauty.

MAJOR REGIONS

Emerging from the Sorrentine peninsula's northern coast, the Amalfi Drive wriggles its way 8 km (5 miles) south to La Costiera Amalfitana proper, starting with the pastel-hue beach-chic **Positano,** the jet-set famous **Conca dei Marina** harbor, and the nearby cliffside resorts and secluded cove hamlets of **Marina di Praia** and **Furore.** In **Amalfi,** day-tripper throngs ooh and aah over the hodgepodge flamboyance of the *duomo* (cathedral), the medieval passages, and the verdant Valle dei Mulini views—between rounds of souvenir shopping, beach lounging, and eating, of course. Just around the coastal promontory, cute Atrani (Italy's smallest municipality), is where Amalfi's doges were crowned and found tranquil respite. Farther west and just beyond the Valley of the Dragon lies serene **Ravello,** with its gorgeous gardens and grand terrace vistas. Along the Amalfi Drive past modern Minori and Maiori, there's an earthy charm to **Cetara,** with its fishermen's beach and famed anchovy-rich seafood restaurants. Leapfrog over chaotic Salerno, and head toward the Cilento Coast, where you'll find the fertile Sele Plain and **Paestum,** famed for the finest temples of ancient Magna-Graecia on the Italian mainland. A fitting contemporary finale to the Grand Tour of the 17th to 19th centuries is a culinary pilgrimage to Tenuta Vannulo farm, where you'll encounter wallowing buffalo and the finest mozzarella on the planet.

Planning

When to Go

The coast is at its best in April, May, and early June. The weather is generally pleasant, and hotels and restaurants have just reopened for the season. By May the seawater is warm enough, by American standards, for swimming, but you can often have the beach to yourself, as Italians shy away at least until June. Temperatures can be torrid in summer, and the coast is swarming with visitors—during August all of Italy flocks to the shores. The early fall months are more relaxing, with gentle, warm weather; swimming temperatures often last through October. Many restaurants and hotels close down for the winter.

Planning your Time

The Amalfi Coast is laid out in the easiest possible way for touring—beginning to the west in Positano, proceeding east along the coastline for 19 km (12 miles) to Amalfi. From here it's less than 7 km (4½ miles) farther east to Ravello, the coast's other absolute must. If an overview of these three fabled spots is all you seek, three days will suffice. To experience a few more of the area's splendors, you'll need a minimum of five days. If staying in one place is a priority, and you will not be exploring much, pick a base—the obvious candidates are Positano, Amalfi, and Ravello—but it's best to arrange to stay overnight in at least two of these destinations.

Getting Here and Around

BOAT

Positano and Amalfi can be reached by ferry service. To get to smaller towns, make arrangements with private boat companies or independent fishermen recommended by the tourist office or your hotel. Ferries operated by Travelmar and Gescab serve Positano, Amalfi, Salerno, Sorrento, Capri, and other locations within the region. Tickets can be purchased at booths on piers and docks. Ferry service generally only runs from late spring through the beginning of November.

CONTACTS Gescab. ☎ *081/4285555* 🌐 *www.gescab.it.* **Travelmar.** ☎ *089/872950* 🌐 *www.travelmar.it.*

BUS

Most travelers tour the Amalfi Drive by bus. SITA Sud (Sicurezza Trasporti Autolinee South) buses make the trip many times daily 6 am–10 pm (less often on

Amalfi Coast History

Legends abound about the first settlements on the Amalfi Coast. The Greeks were early colonizers at Paestum to the south, and Romans fled their own sacked empire in the 4th century to settle the steep coastal ridge now called the Lattari Mountains because of the milk, or *latte*, produced there. Roman ruins of grand villas in Minori, Positano, and other locations along the coast indicate the area has been prized for its beautiful setting since ancient times. Despite frequent incursions by covetous Lombards, Saracens, and other hopefuls, the medieval Maritime Republic of Amalfi, with its ruling dogi, maintained its domination of the seas and coast until the Normans began their conquest of southern Italy in the 11th century.

By 1300, Naples, the capital of the Angevin Kingdom, had become the dominant ruler of the region and remained so until Italy unified in the mid-19th century. After the creation of the Amalfi Coast road in the mid-19th century, tourism blossomed, first with Grand Tour travelers and then with artists and writers who spread the word about this nearly forgotten coastline. Today, travelers from around the world come to admire the Costiera Amalfitana, with its unforgettable turquoise-to-sapphire sea and timeless villages.

Sunday, bank holidays, and major festival days). The bus from Sorrento to Amalfi stops at Positano (at Chiesa Nuova and Sponda), Praiano, and Conca dei Marini along the way. SITA bus drivers will stop anywhere on the main route as long as you state your destination when boarding. Tickets cost from €1.30 for a *corso semplice* (one-stop journey) to €12 for a 24-hour Costierasita pass. Tickets must be purchased in advance and inserted in the time-stamp machine when you enter the bus; vendors can be found in cafés, bars, and newsstands. For more about bus travel along the coast, see the feature "The Amalfi Drive" in this chapter.

CONTACTS SITA Sud. ☎ *342/6256442* 🌐 *www.sitasudtrasporti.it.*

CAR

Running between the Sorrentine peninsula and Salerno, Strada Statale 163 (State Highway 163, or the Amalfi Drive) can be reached from Naples via the A3 Autostrada to Castellammare di Stabia, then linked to Sorrento via Statale 145. When driving round-trip, many choose to go only in one direction on the seaside road, going the other way via the inland highway threading the mountains. If you drive, be prepared to pay exorbitant parking fees, and consider yourself lucky when you find a parking space. If you are feeling flush or are traveling with a group and can share costs, consider hiring a driver for airport transfers and minitours of the coast.

CONTACTS Benvenuto limos. ✉ *Via G. Marconi 150, Positano* ☎ *089/8424226 office, 310/4245640 U.S. number* 🌐 *www.benvenutolimos.com.* **Sorrento Silver Star.** ✉ *Corso Italia 288/a, Sorrento* ☎ *081/8771224 office hours, 339/3888143 Massimo Annunziata's cell phone* 🌐 *www.sorrentosilverstar.com.*

TRAIN

The towns of the Amalfi Coast aren't directly accessible by train, but you can take one to Sorrento or Salerno and then board a SITA Sud bus. The Circumvesuviana railway and seasonal (mid March–October) and faster Campania Express run along the curve of the Bay of Naples from Naples to Sorrento. The Milan–Reggio Calabria state-railway train stops in Salerno, whose station here is a good place to pick up buses serving the Amalfi Coast.

CONTACT Circumvesuviana. ☎ *800/211388* 🌐 *www.eavsrl.it.*

Restaurants

No surprise here: dining on the Amalfi Coast revolves largely around seafood. Dishes are prepared using the short, rolled handmade *scialatielli* or large *paccheri* pasta and adorned with local *vongole* (clams) or *cozze* (mussels) and other shellfish. Octopus, squid, and the fresh fish of the season are always on the menu for the second course. Cetara has been famous for its *alici* (anchovies) since Roman times, and even produces *alici* bread. Eateries range from beachside trattorias to beacons of fine dining with stupendous views.

Prices in the reviews are the average cost of a main course at dinner or, if dinner isn't served, at lunch. Restaurant reviews have been shortened. For full information, visit Fodors.com.

What it Costs in Euros

$	$$	$$$	$$$$
RESTAURANTS			
under €15	€15–€24	€25–€35	over €35

Hotels

Most lodgings in this part of Campania have been owned by the same families for generations, and whether the owner is plain mamma-and-papà or an heir to a ducal line, personality is evident. Along with local management may come quirks, even in the fanciest establishments, but the 21st century has wrought change, and with it, numerous 19th-century cliffside villas and palazzi, with their big gardens and grand staircases, huge baths and tile floors, have been transformed into luxury hotels. Happily, you don't need to be a millionaire to enjoy comfy lodgings along the Amalfi Coast: there are many less expensive options.

When booking, note that a few hotels may require a minimum stay for the peak periods of July and August and around holidays. If you're traveling by car and reserving rooms in advance, ask about parking fees, which can be as high as €25 per day.

Prices in the reviews are the lowest cost of a standard double room in high season. Hotel reviews have been shortened. For full information, visit Fodors.com.

What it Costs in Euros

$	$$	$$$	$$$$
HOTELS			
under €125	€125–€200	€201–€300	over €300

Tours

City Sightseeing

BUS TOURS | These bright red sightseeing buses are an excellent way to explore the Amalfi Coast while avoiding some of the crowds on the regular SITA buses: their mainstay tour is from Sorrento to Amalfi with a stop in Positano. ✉ *Sorrento* ☎ *081/18257088* 🌐 *www.city-sightseeing.it/it/costiera-amalfitana/* 🎫 *From €15.*

Vesuvius vs. Pompeii

GUIDED TOURS | With experienced local guides, this small company offers half-day and full-day tours of Naples, Pompeii, Vesuvius, Capri, Sorrento, and other destinations in Campania. ✉ *Sorrento* ☎ *333/6409000* 🌐 *www.vesuviusvspompeii.com.*

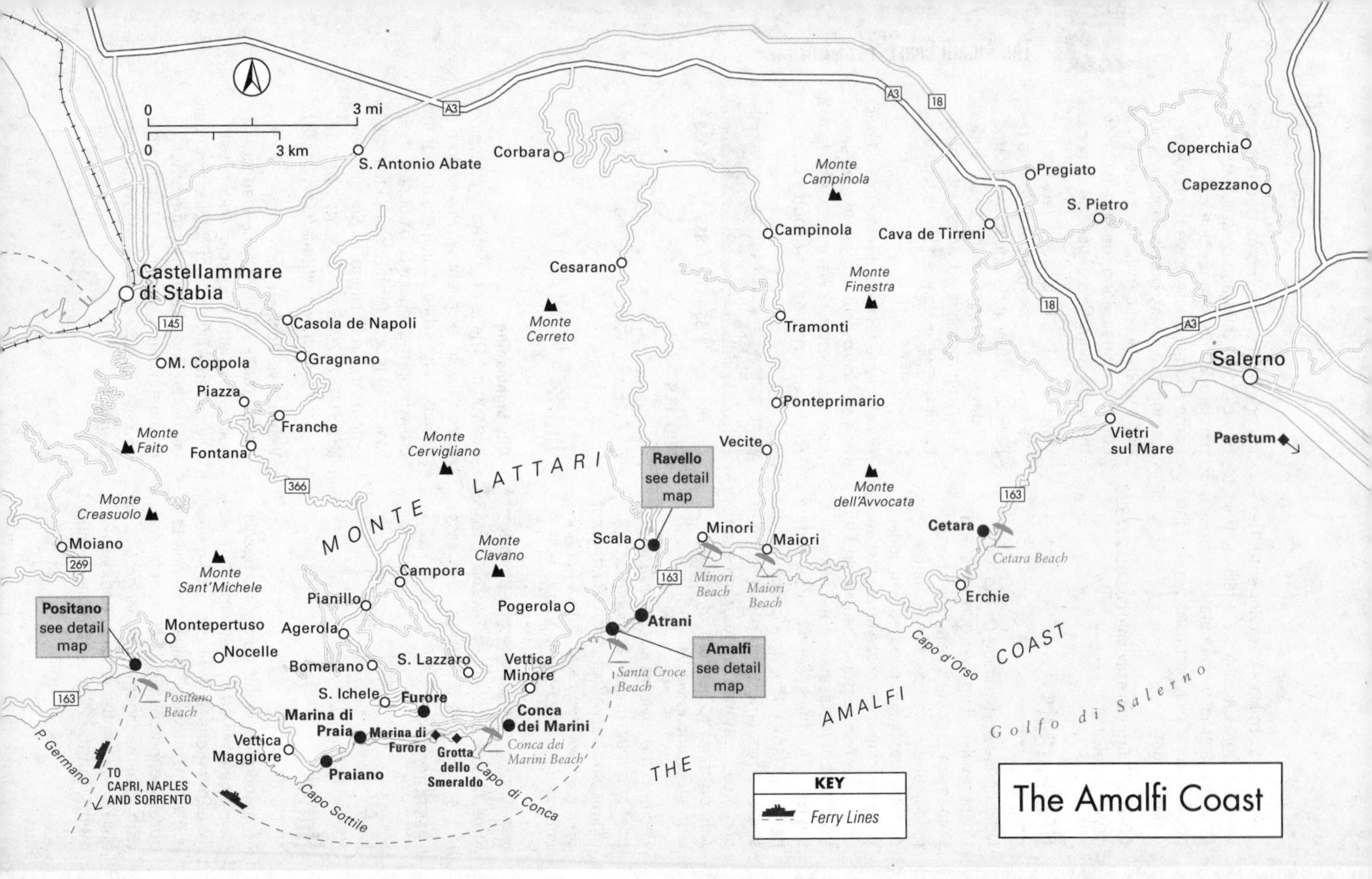

The Amalfi Coast
KEY
Ferry Lines
0
3 mi
0
3 km
Castellammare di Stabia
S. Antonio Abate
Corbara
Coperchia
Pregiato
Capezzano
S. Pietro
Monte Campinola
Campinola
Cava de Tirreni
Cesarano
Monte Finestra
Casola de Napoli
Monte Cerreto
Tramonti
Salerno
M. Coppola
Gragnano
Piazza
Franche
Ponteprimario
Monte Faito
Fontana
Monte Cervigliano
Vecite
Vietri sul Mare
Paestum
MONTE LATTARI
Ravello see detail map
Monte dell'Avvocata
Monte Creasuolo
Moiano
Monte Sant'Michele
Monte Clavano
Campora
Scala
Minori
Maiori
Cetara
Cetara Beach
Minori Beach
Maiori Beach
Erchie
Pianillo
Pogerola
Positano see detail map
Montepertuso
Agerola
Atrani
Amalfi see detail map
Nocelle
Bomerano
S. Lazzaro
Vettica Minore
Santa Croce Beach
Capo d'Orso
COAST
S. Ichele
Furore
Positano Beach
Marina di Praia
Marina di Furore
Grotta dello Smeraldo
Conca dei Marini
Conca dei Marini Beach
AMALFI
Golfo di Salerno
Vettica Maggiore
Praiano
P. Germano
TO CAPRI, NAPLES AND SORRENTO
Capo Sottile
Capo di Conca
THE
A3
18
145
366
269
163

Positano's History

A name now known worldwide, its origins could be a corruption of the Greek "Poseidon," or derived from a man named Posides, who owned villas here during the time of Claudius; or even from Roman freedmen, called the Posdii. The most popular theory is that the name "Positano" comes from Pestano (or Pesitano), a 9th-century town by a Benedictine abbey near Montepertuso, built by refugees of Paestum to the south, whose homes had been ransacked by the Saracens.

Pisa sacked the area in 1268, but after an elaborate defensive system of watchtowers was put in place, Positano once again prospered, briefly rivaling Amalfi. As a fiefdom of Neapolitan families until the end of the 17th century, Positano produced silk and, later, canvas goods, but decline began again in the late 18th century. With the coming of the steamship in the mid-19th century, some three-fourths of the town's 8,000 citizens emigrated to America—mostly to New York—and it eventually regressed into a backwater fishing village. That is, until artists and intellectuals, and then travelers, rediscovered its prodigious charms in the 20th century. Picasso, Stravinsky, Diaghilev, Olivier, Steinbeck, Klee—even Lenin—were just a few of this town's talented fans. Lemons, grapes, olives, fish, resort gear, and, of course, tourism keep it going, but despite its shimmery sophistication and overwrought popularity, Positano's chief export remains its most precious commodity: beauty.

Positano

56 km (35 miles) southeast of Naples, 16 km (10 miles) east of Sorrento.

When John Steinbeck visited Positano in 1953, he wrote that it was difficult to consider tourism an industry because "there are not enough [tourists]." Alas, there are more than enough now, and the town's vertical landscape with pastel-hue houses, drapes of bright pink bougainvillea, and sapphire-blue sea make it easy to understand why.

The most photographed fishing village in the world, this fabled locale is home to some 4,000 *positanesi,* who are joined daily by hordes arriving from Capri, Sorrento, and Amalfi. The town clings to the Monti Lattari with arcaded, cubist buildings, set in tiers up the mountainside, in shades of rose, peach, purple, and ivory.

GETTING HERE AND AROUND

SITA buses serve Positano from Amalfi from Sorrento. Purchase tickets prior to boarding at a *tabaccheria* (tobacconists) or *edicola* (newsstand). Buses pass through town every 40 minutes or so in both directions, departing Amalfi or Sorrento 6:30 am–7 pm. The bus has two main stops in Positano: Transita, or Upper Town—near the large church of Santa Maria delle Grazie, or Chiesa Nuova—and Sponda, closer to the Lower Town, to the east of the main beach. Summer ferries serve Positano from Amalfi, Sorrento, Capri, and Salerno. The ferry and hydrofoil ticket office in Positano is beside the Spiaggia Grande; ferries to Amalfi, Sorrento, and Capri are available at the dock under Via Positanesi d'America, near the public beach in the center of town. By car, take the Statale 163 (Amalfitana) from outside Sorrento or Salerno.

Local Mobility Amalfi Coast buses regularly ply even the smallest roads and

Beautiful Positano may be the most photographed fishing village in the world.

make more stops than SITA buses. The local sky-blue vehicles frequently ply the one-and-only one-way Via Pasitea, hairpinning from Transita to Piazza dei Mulini then up to the mountains and back, making a loop through the town every half hour. Two other lines link Positano with Praiano and Nocelle. Warning: bus services are unreliable. The taxi stand is at the top of Via dei Mulini.

If their hotels don't provide parking, most car travelers leave their wheels either in one of the few free parking spaces on the upper Sorrento–Amalfi main road or in one of the scarce and pricey garages a few minutes' walk from the beach. The best bet for day-trippers is to get to Positano early enough so that space is still available. (Even those arriving by SITA bus should get a morning start, as traffic on the Amalfi Drive becomes heavy by noon.)

A word of advice: wear comfortable walking shoes and be sure your back and legs are strong enough to negotiate those picturesque, but daunting and ladderlike *scalinatelle*. In the center of town, where no buses can go, you're on your own from Piazza dei Mulini: to begin your explorations, make a left turn onto the boutique-flanked Via dei Mulini and head down to the Palazzo Murat, Santa Maria Assunta church, and the beach—one of the most charming walks of the coast.

VISITOR INFORMATION

CONTACTS Ufficio di Turismo - Comune di Positano. ✉ *Via Regina Giovanna 13,* ☎ *334/9118563.*

Sights

Palazzo Murat

NOTABLE BUILDING | Past a bevy of resort boutiques, head to Via dei Mulini to view the prettiest garden in Positano: the 18th-century courtyard of the Palazzo Murat, named for Joachim Murat, who sensibly chose the palazzo as his summer residence. This was where Murat, designated by his brother-in-law Napoléon as King of Naples in 1808, came to forget the demands of power and lead a simpler life. He built this grand abode (now a hotel) near the church of Santa Maria Assunta, just steps from the main beach. ✉ *Via dei Mulini 23, Positano* ☎ *089/875177* 🌐 *www.palazzomurat.it.*

Santa Maria Assunta

CHURCH | The Chiesa Madre, or parish church of Santa Maria Assunta, lies just south of the Palazzo Murat, its green-and-yellow majolica dome topped by a perky cupola visible from just about anywhere in town. Built on the site of the former Benedictine abbey of Saint Vito, the 13th-century Romanesque structure was almost completely rebuilt in 1700. The last piece of the ancient mosaic floor can be seen under glass behind the altar. Note the carved wooden Christ, a masterpiece of devotional religious art, with its bathetic face and bloodied knees, on view before the altar. At the altar is a Byzantine 13th-century painting on wood of Madonna with Child, known popularly as the Black Virgin. A replica is carried to the beach every August 15 to celebrate the Feast of the Assumption. Legend claims that the painting was once stolen by Saracen pirates, who, fleeing in a raging storm, heard a voice from on high saying, "*Posa, posa*" (Put it down, put it down). When they placed the image on the beach near the church, the storm calmed, as did the Saracens. Embedded over the doorway of the church's bell tower, set across the tiny piazza, is a medieval bas-relief of fishes, a fox, and a pistrice (the mythical half-dragon, half-dog sea monster). This is one of the few relics of the medieval abbey of Saint Vito. The Oratorio houses historic statues from the Sacristy; renovations to the Crypt have unearthed part of an extensive Roman Villa buried by the AD 79 eruption (see Villa Romana). ✉ *Piazza Flavio Gioia, Positano* ☎ *089/875480* 🌐 *www.chiesapositano.it.*

★ Via Positanesi d'America

PROMENADE | **FAMILY** | Just before the ferry ticket booths to the right of Spiaggia Grande, a tiny road that is the loveliest seaside walkway on the entire coast rises up and borders the cliffs leading to Fornillo Beach. The road is named for the town's large number of 19th-century emigrants to the United States—Positano virtually survived during World War II thanks to the money and packages their descendants sent back home. Halfway up the path lies the Torre Trasìta (Trasìta Tower), the most distinctive of Positano's three coastline defense towers. Now a residence occasionally available for summer rental, the tower was used to spot pirate raids. As you continue along the Via Positanesi d'America, you'll pass a tiny inlet and an emerald cove before Fornillo Beach comes into view. ✉ *Via Positanesi d'America, Positano.*

★ Villa Romana

HISTORIC SIGHT | Painstaking excavations begun in 2003 below the oratory of Santa Maria Assunta are now open to the public and showcase tantalizing traces of Positano's vast Roman settlement buried by the AD 79 eruption. Through volcanic debris some 30 feet below the piazzetta is a cool subterranean world with different captivating chambers and crypts. The new entrance by the campanile leads to the most recently discovered Roman villa excavations, which sit below the Cripta Superiore with its spine-tingling funereal seating, reserved for Positano's most upstanding 18th-century citizens (i.e., the wealthy wanting to book a pew in heaven), members of the Confraternita del Monte dei Morti. Among the Roman artifacts are vibrant frescoes, ornate stucco reliefs, intricate bronzes and ceramics, and the mother of all stone mortars. Another entrance nearby leads to the Cripta Inferiore, with two naves, marble columns and later additions. ✉ *Piazza Flavio Gioia 7, Positano* ☎ *331/2085821* 🌐 *marpositano.it* 🎫 *€15.*

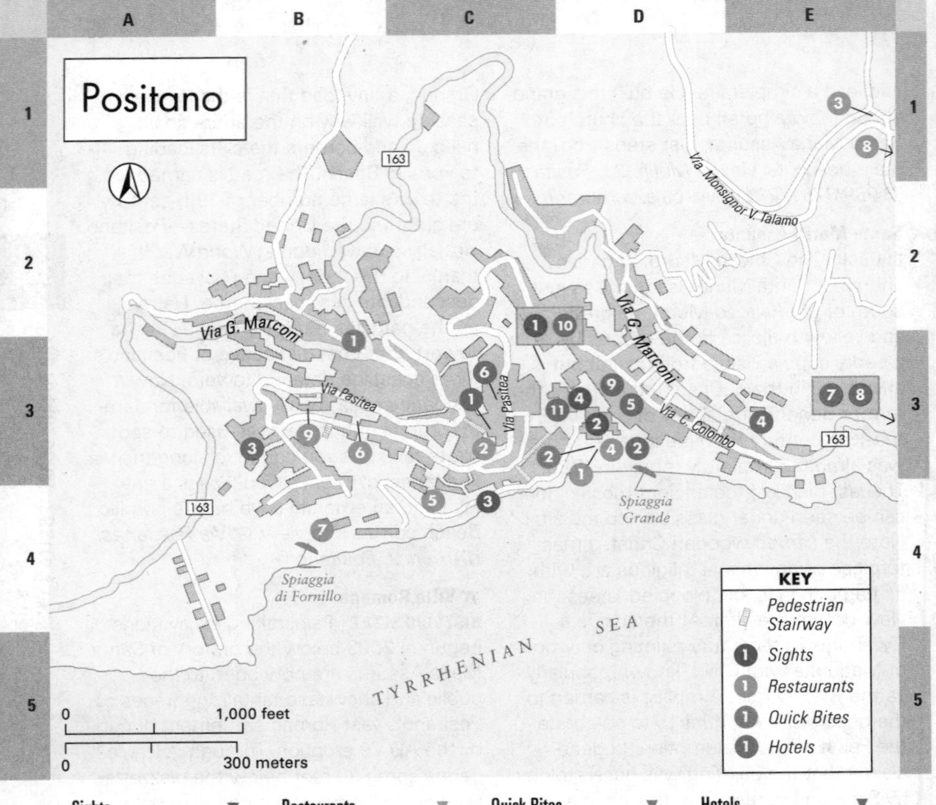

Sights

1 Palazzo Murat........... **D3**
2 Santa Maria Assunta... **D3**
3 Via Positanesi d'America................. **C4**
4 Villa Romana **D3**

Restaurants

1 Chez Black............... **D3**
2 Da Vincenzo............... **C3**
3 Il Ritrovo **E1**
4 La Cambusa **D3**
5 Lo Guarracino............ **C4**
6 Next2........................ **B3**
7 Pupetto..................... **B4**
8 Santa Croce **E1**
9 Saraceno D'Oro......... **B3**

Quick Bites

1 Bar Internazionale...... **B3**
2 Paradise Lounge Bar .. **D3**

Hotels

1 Casa Albertina **C3**
2 Hotel Buca di Bacco... **D3**
3 Hotel Conca d'Oro...... **B3**
4 Hotel Eden Roc **E3**
5 Hotel L'Ancora **D3**
6 Hotel Poseidon........... **C3**
7 Il San Pietro di Positano................. **E3**
8 La Fenice **E3**
9 Le Sirenuse............... **D3**
10 Palazzo Murat........... **C3**
11 Villa Flavio Gioia **D3**

Above It All: Montepertuso and Nocelle

Thousands of travelers head to Positano every summer for some escapist entertainment, but how do *you* escape *them*? The answer lies way up in the Lattari Mountains, where two adorable villages perch on rocky spurs 1,700 feet above Positano's coastline. It's hard to believe two such different settlements share the same air space as their jet-set neighbor while managing, for the most part, to escape the glare of discovery.

Take Positano's local bus 3 km (2 miles) to the village of **Montepertuso** (Pierced Mountain). This sky-high village is where Emperor Frederick II of Sicily bred and trained hawks; some feathery descendants—mainly kestrels and peregrine falcons—still nest on seemingly precarious ledges around the area.

The dramatic hole in the arched rock (*arco naturale*) below Monte Sant'Angelo a Tre Pizzi is one of only three in the world that both the sun's and the moon's rays can penetrate (April to July); the other two are in India. Try to see it in the morning, when the sun shines through.

Legend says the hole was created when the devil challenged the Madonna to a contest: whoever pierced the rock would own the village. In 10 attempts, the devil could only scratch the limestone, but when the Madonna touched the rock, it crumbled, the sky appeared, and she walked right through, sinking the devil into the hole. On July 2, a holy performance, games, and fireworks commemorate the Virgin's success.

The Positano bus continues from Montepertuso to just above the "lost" mountainside village of **Nocelle,** but many skip the ride and choose to hike instead. Along a well-paved road, then a curving, tree-shaded pathway, you skirt bottomless crevasses, hike under towering cliffs, and climb stairways that are relatively easy going. Finally, Nocelle appears and, in two minutes, the hamlet fully reveals itself: a stone alley, a scattering of houses and stairways, a pint-size piazza, a church.

Oh, yes, and a "panaromantic" view—the kind that resets your inner clock. Sheep bleat, children giggle, birds call melodiously, and the rustling wind congratulates you on being far from the madding crowd.

Beaches

The Marina is the main boating area, with taupe, semi-sandy Spiaggia Grande the largest and widest beach of the six or so in the area. Fishermen—once the dominant workforce—now function as a cooperative group, supplying local kitchens; they can be seen cleaning their colorful, flipped-over boats and mending their torn nets throughout the day, seemingly oblivious to the surrounding throngs. To the west of town is the less-crowded Spiaggia del Fornillo, which you can get to by walking the gorgeous Via Positanesi d'America (leading from Spiaggia Grande). Fornillo is worth the walk, as it is quieter and hemmed in by impressive cliffs. To the east of Positano is a string of small, pretty beaches, separated by coves—La Porta, Arienzo, San Pietro, and Laurito—most of which are accessible only by boat. At all beaches you will need to pay to rent sun beds and umbrellas, and they can cost plenty—up to €25 per person.

Spiaggia di Fornillo

BEACH | FAMILY | Positano regularly receives a Bandiera Blu (Blue Flag) in recognition of its water quality, safety, and services offered. The Spiaggia Grande (large beach) has the glorious, rainbow-hue backdrop of the town, but for a more informal atmosphere and lush vegetation, follow the Via Positanesi d'America to the Fornillo beach. Almost 300 meters long and now managed by Hotel Pupetto, the beach was a favorite of Pablo Picasso because of its position between the medieval Trasita and Clavel towers. **Amenities:** food and drink; lifeguards; showers; toilets; kayak; water sports. **Best for:** snorkeling, swimming. ✉ *Via Fornillo, Positano* 🌐 *www.hotelpupetto.it/en/hotel-beach-positano.*

Spiaggia Grande

BEACH | FAMILY | The walkway from the Piazza Flavio Gioia leads down to Spiaggia Grande, Positano's main beach, bordered by an esplanade and some of the town's busiest restaurants. Surrounded by the spectacular amphitheater of houses and villas that leapfrog up the hillsides of Monte Comune and Monte Sant'Angelo, this remains one of the most picturesque beaches in the world. **Amenities:** food and drink; lifeguards; showers; toilets; water sports. **Best for:** swimming; people-watching; photography. ✉ *Spiaggia Grande, Positano.*

Restaurants

Chez Black

$$$ | SOUTHERN ITALIAN | Although it caters to day-tripping coachloads, this nautically themed restaurant, whose waiters wear sailor uniforms, is a local institution that's hard to beat for its sceney location right on the Spiaggia Grande. The people-watching is good (Denzel Washington is reportedly a regular), and the friendly staff is happy to guide you through specialties such as *zuppa di pesce* (fish soup) and *spaghetti con ricci di mare* (spaghetti with sea urchins). **Known for:** buzzy atmosphere and late-evening tourist party vibe; not necessarily the best value given the quality of the food; house gin, lemon, and crème de menthe aperitivo, the grotta dello smeraldo. [$] *Average main: €25* ✉ *Via del Brigantino 19, Positano* ☎ *089/875036* 🌐 *www.chezblack.it* ⏲ *Closed Nov.–Feb.*

Da Vincenzo

$$ | SOUTHERN ITALIAN | Established in 1958, this family-run place pairs generations of tradition and genuine love of hospitality with ever-evolving innovation, reflected in the exceptional takes on classic Neapolitan dishes and the stylish, up-to-date yet rustic decor. Expect a truly warm welcome and a menu with both *mare* (sea) and robust *terra* (land) mainstays such as grilled octopus, shoulder of lamb, and eggplant Parmesan. **Known for:** busy outside terrace with views; sumptuous dolci, including cheesecake; charming hosts, from the owner to the young waitstaff. [$] *Average main: €24* ✉ *Via Pasitea 172/178, Positano* ☎ *089/875128* 🌐 *www.davincenzo.it* ⏲ *Closed Tues. lunch and Nov.–Mar.*

Il Ritrovo

$$ | SOUTHERN ITALIAN | FAMILY | In the tiny town square of Montepertuso, 1,500 feet up the mountainside from Positano (call for the free shuttle service to and from), the Ritrovo has been noted for its cucina for more than 20 years. The menu showcases food from both the sea and the hills: try the *scialatielli ai frutti di mare* accompanied by well-grilled vegetables; the house specialty *zuppa saracena,* a paella-like affair brimming with assorted seafood; and the lemon tiramisu, perhaps paired with one of 80 different kinds of a homemade liqueur, including carob and chamomile options. **Known for:** amiable padrone Salvatò, who also runs a cooking school; trademark zuppa saracena (seafood soup); airy, tranquil

Eating Well on the Amalfi Coast

Locals say they have "one foot in the fishing boat, one in the vineyard"—and a fortunate stance it is, as you can count on eating simple, fresh, seasonal food, and lots of it, with *tutti i sapori della campagna verace* (all the true flavors of the countryside). From the gulfs come *pesce alla griglia* (grilled fish), calamari, *aragosta* (lobster), and *gamberone* (shrimp). Wood oven–baked thin-crust pizzas start with the classic Margherita (tomato sauce, basil, and cheese) and Marinara (with tomato, garlic, and oregano) and go from there to infinity.

La Cucina Costiera seems more sensuous amid all this beauty. Sundried tomatoes and chili peppers hang in bright red cascades on balconies and shopfronts. Ingredients grown in terraced plots include plump olives pressed into oil or eaten whole, tiny spring *carciofi* (artichokes), and sweet figs. *Sponzini*, or *pomodori del pendolo*, the tomatoes carried from Egypt long ago by fishermen, grow in the mountains and muddy fields of Furore and Conca dei Marini. Eggplant, asparagus, and mushrooms thrive in the mountainous areas of Ravello, Scala, and Tramonti. Soft *fior di latte* (cow's-milk cheeses) are from the high hill pastures of Agerola, while the world's best buffalo mozzarella comes from Paestum.

Pasta is often served with seafood, but regional dishes include *crespelle al formaggio*—layers of crepes with béchamel sauce—and fettuccine-like *scialatielli*, often a house specialty, served with varied sauces. Clams and pasta baked in a paper bag—*al cartoccio*—is popular in Amalfi. In Positano, try traditional squid with potatoes, stuffed peppers, and slow-simmering ragù (tomato sauce with meat, garlic, and parsley). Around Cetara, anchovies are still transformed into the famed sauce called *garum*, handed down from the Romans. A lighter version is *colatura di alici*, an anchovy sauce developed by Cistercian monks near Amalfi, served on spaghetti as a traditional Christmas Eve treat. South of Salerno, you can visit working farms, and make friends with the buffalo, before sampling the best mozzarella known to mankind. Artichokes are also a specialty of the Paestum area. For the sweet tooth, don't miss the unusually good chocolate-covered eggplant or a moist cake made with lemons grown along the coastline and sometimes soaked with a bit of limoncello, a traditional lemon liqueur.

Wine here is light, drinkable, and inexpensive, and often consumed mere months after crushing; don't be surprised if it's the color of beer, and served from a jug (*sfuso*, "loose wine"). Practically all of it comes from Campania, often from the town or village in which it's poured, perhaps even from the restaurant's own centuries-old vines. Little of it transports well. Furore, Gragnano, and Ravello produce good bottled wines, both *rosso* (red) and *bianco* (white) with Furore's Cuomo perhaps the finest white wine.

Although a few restaurants are world-renowned, most are family affairs, with papà out front, the kids serving, and mamma, aunts, and even old *nonna* in the kitchen. Smile a bit, compliment the cuisine, and you're apt to meet them all.

mountainside location. $ *Average main: €23* ✉ *Via Montepertuso 77, Montepertuso* ☎ *089/812005* 🌐 *www.ilritrovo.com* ⏲ *Closed mid-Jan.–mid-Feb.*

La Cambusa

$$$ | **SOUTHERN ITALIAN** | Two bronze lions flanking the steps hint at a refined restaurant experience. Indeed, in its light-filled dining room or on its intimate terrace, La Cambusa serves lighter, more elegant seafood dishes (linguine with mussels and fish with potatoes and tomato sauce are favorites) than its "pack-em-in" Spiaggia Grande neighbors. **Known for:** showcases the freshest seafood; people-watching central; prime spot looking over Spiaggia Grande. $ *Average main: €28* ✉ *Piazza Amerigo Vespucci 4, Positano* ☎ *089/875432* 🌐 *www.lacambusapositano.com* ⏲ *Closed Nov.–Mar.*

Lo Guarracino

$$ | **SOUTHERN ITALIAN** | This partly arbor-covered restaurant is a romantic place to enjoy *scialatielli di mare* (seafood pasta) above the waves, with a terrace vista that takes in the cliffs, the sea, the Li Galli islands, Spiaggia del Fornillo, and Torre Clavel. **Known for:** romantic Robinson Crusoe–esque terrace; family-made liquori digestivi including a wild-herb number (agrumi); seafood and wood-fired pizza. $ *Average main: €24* ✉ *Via Positanesi d'America 12, Positano* ☎ *089/875794* 🌐 *www.loguarracinopositano.it* ⏲ *Closed Jan.–Mar.*

Next2

$$$ | **SOUTHERN ITALIAN** | Wrought-iron gates open from scenic Via Pasitea into Next2's *bianco e nero*–chic courtyard, replete with a cocktail bar and a whiff of edgy, youthful swagger. You can watch the talented *squadra* at work in the open kitchen crafting elegant, subtly flavored creations such as the *Caprese* starter, the seared tuna *secondo*, and—for those with bigger, bolder appetities—the *frittura di mare* (fried seafood medley). **Known for:** cocktails with novel, fresh infusions; delectable dessert pairings such as pear and walnut ice cream; exquisite-looking small-portioned dishes. $ *Average main: €28* ✉ *Via Pasitea 242, Positano* ☎ *089/8123516* 🌐 *next2.it* ⏲ *No lunch.*

Pupetto

$$ | **SOUTHERN ITALIAN** | **FAMILY** | A long spacious terrace overlooking the sea is the main feature of this simple yet superb-value spot—part of the family-friendly Hotel Pupetto, most of whose guest rooms have lovely water views, too. Feast on fresh grilled seafood and tasty pizza under lemon trees along Spiaggio di Fornillo and almost within octopus-tentacle grasp of your lounge chair. **Known for:** tranquil evening dining with a seaside stroll; eggplant parmigiana, salads, and grilled veggie options; buzzy flip-flop beachside lunching. $ *Average main: €18* ✉ *Hotel Pupetto, Via Fornillo 37, Positano* ☎ *089/875087* 🌐 *www.hotelpupetto.it* ⏲ *Closed Nov.–mid-Apr.*

Santa Croce

$$ | **SOUTHERN ITALIAN** | About 1,400 feet above sea level on the Path of the Gods, this low-key place in the dreamy hamlet of Nocelle delivers fortifying, superb-value plates to hikers and adventurous day-trippers. Try to get a window seat so that you can gaze over Positano, Li Galli islands, and the Fariglioni of Capri while sampling fresh pastas, seafood, and grilled meats; homemade desserts; or, on Saturday evening, exquisite pizza made in an olivewood-fired oven. **Known for:** relaxed, rustic vibe; fresh produce grown on the doorstep; lofty perch with divine views. $ *Average main: €17*

Continued on page 77

THE AMALFI DRIVE

The vertical village of Positano

If travelers do nothing else along this coast, they have to experience the Amalfi Drive, a cliff-hugging stretch of road that tests their faith in civil engineering. One of the most beautiful coastal drives in the world, this "route of 1,001 bends" offers breathtaking views.

It is an experience like no other. The road seems miraculously interwoven with the coastline, clinging to the cliffs, tunneling through mountains, and seamlessly blending with the towns it connects. Without the road the only way to explore this dramatic coastal setting is by boat or hiking the zigzagging mule paths that were once the only means of transportation—many of which are still used to connect remote villages. While the vertiginous drive may be frightening at first, keep your eyes open for views of bays of turquoise-to-sapphire water, timeless cliff-top villages, and pinnacles of rock. Pack your camera and stop along the route at the many overlooks to savor the views as blue sky and sea blend into one magical panorama with the rugged coastline as the backdrop.

POSITANO TO CONCA DEI MARINI

Positano

POSITANO The most beautiful vertical village in the world suffered from its confined space, so when it grew, it grew up the mountainside.

VETTICA MAGGIORE More priceless than any landscape painting in the National Gallery is the panorama you get from Vettica's seaside piazza and its San Gennaro church.

MARINA DI PRAIA Wedged between two soaring cliffs is this adorable harbor, crammed with dollhouse–issue chapel, restaurant, and beach.

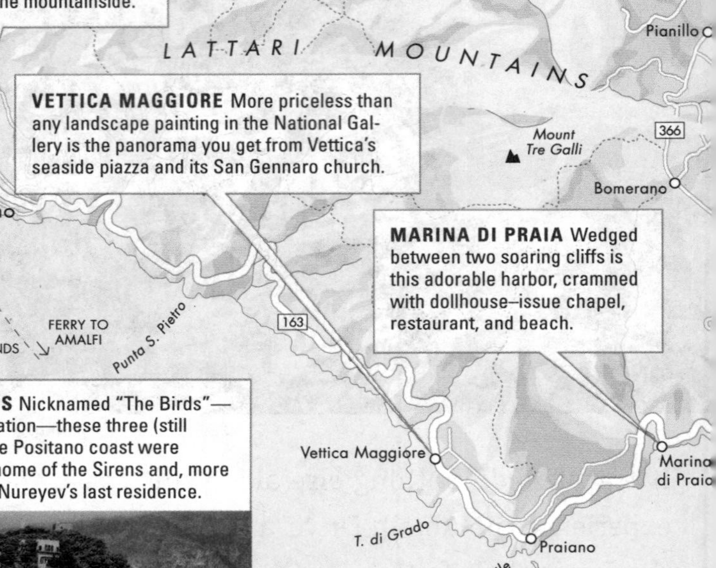

LI GALLI ISLANDS Nicknamed "The Birds"—owing to their formation—these three (still private) islets off the Positano coast were famed as Homer's home of the Sirens and, more recently, as Rudolf Nureyev's last residence.

A GUIDE TO THE DRIVE

Statale (Highway) 163—the Amalfi Drive,—was hewn from the lip of the Lattari Mountains and completed in 1852, varying from 50 feet to 400 feet above the bay. You can thank Ferdinand, the Bourbon king of the Two Sicilies, for commissioning it, and Luigi Giordano for designing this seemingly improbable engineering feat. A thousand or so gorgeous vistas appear along these almost 40 km (25 miles), stretching from just outside Sorrento stretching from just outside Sorrento to Vietri sul Mare. John Steinbeck once joked that the Amalfi Drive "is carefully designed to be a little narrower than two cars side by side" so the going can be a little tense: the slender two lanes hovering over the sheer drops sometimes seem impossible to maneuver by auto, let alone by buses and trucks.

Many travelers arrive from Sorrento, just to the north, connecting to the

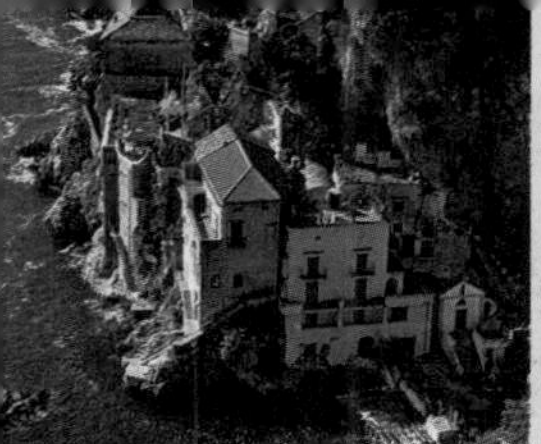

Conca dei Marini Beach

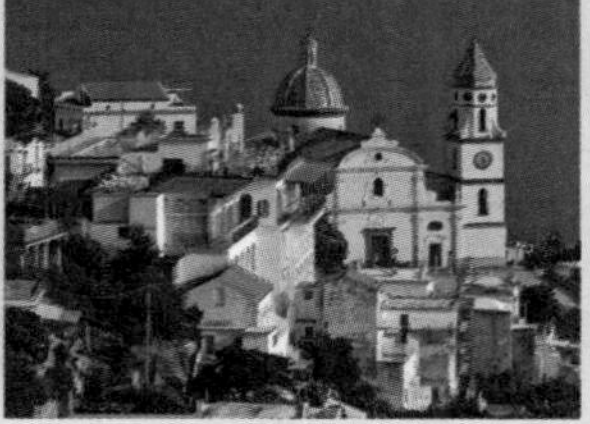

Vettica Maggiore

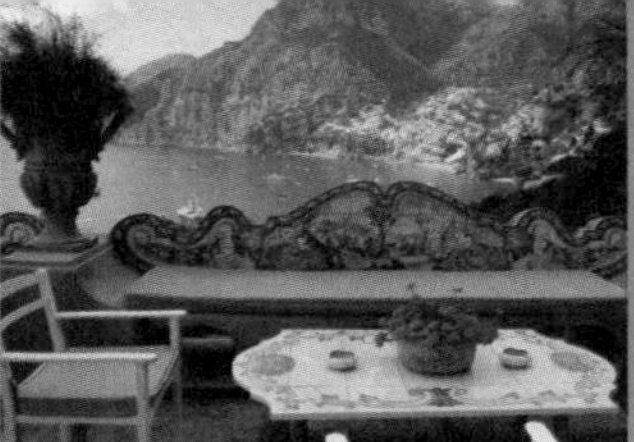

Il San Pietro di Positano

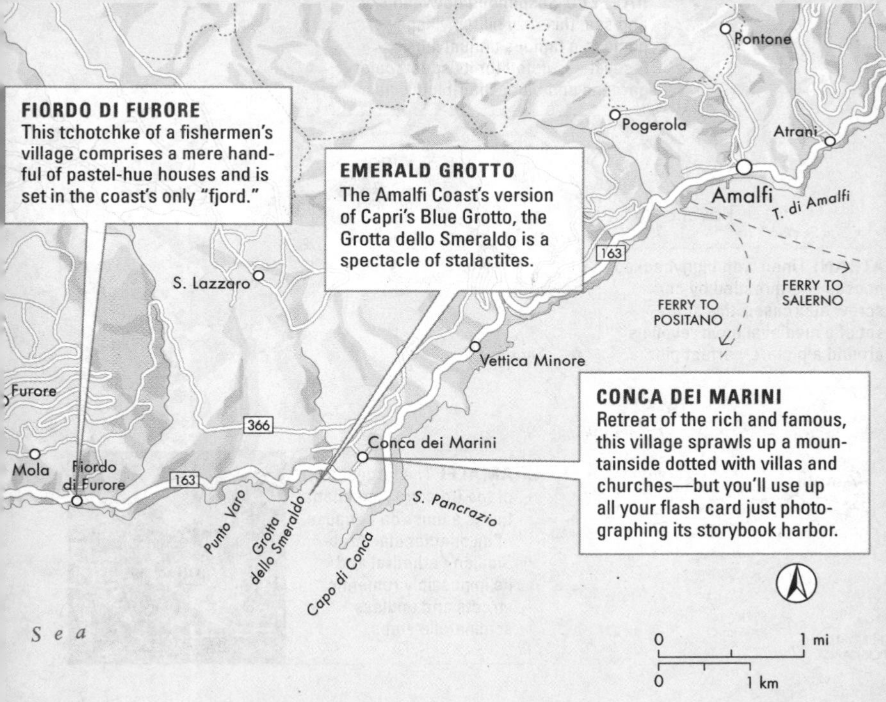
FIORDO DI FURORE
This tchotchke of a fishermen's village comprises a mere handful of pastel-hue houses and is set in the coast's only "fjord."
EMERALD GROTTO
The Amalfi Coast's version of Capri's Blue Grotto, the Grotta dello Smeraldo is a spectacle of stalactites.
CONCA DEI MARINI
Retreat of the rich and famous, this village sprawls up a mountainside dotted with villas and churches—but you'll use up all your flash card just photographing its storybook harbor.
Pontone
Pogerola
Atrani
Amalfi
T. di Amalfi
163
FERRY TO SALERNO
FERRY TO POSITANO
S. Lazzaro
Vettica Minore
Furore
366
Conca dei Marini
Mola
Fiordo di Furore
163
S. Pancrazio
Punto Varo
Grotta dello Smeraldo
Capo di Conca
Sea
0
1 mi
0
1 km

coast through Sant'Agata sui Due Golfi on the Statale 145—the Strada del Nastro Azzurro (Blue Ribbon Road), whose nickname aptly describes its width, and the color at your alternating right and left. The white-knuckle part, or, as some call it, the Via Smeraldo (Emerald Road), begins as the road connects back to Statale 163, threading through coastal ridges at Colli di S. Pietro, and continuing to wend its way around the Vallone di Positano. From ravine to ravine, Positano then begins to beckon out your window, appearing and disappearing. Just east of Positano, at Punta San Pietro, Statale 163 again winds sharply around valleys, deep ravines, and precipices, affording more stunning ridge views. Past Praiano, the Furore gorge is crossed by viaduct. From here on to Amalfi, the ridges soften just a bit.

A DIRECT ROUTE

If you think a road is just for getting from here to there, the Amalfi Drive is not for you. So if you want to leapfrog over all the thrills, opt for the high mountain pass called the Valico di Chiunzi, easily reached via the A3 Naples–Salerno Autostrada from the exit at Angri.

AMALFI TO CETARA

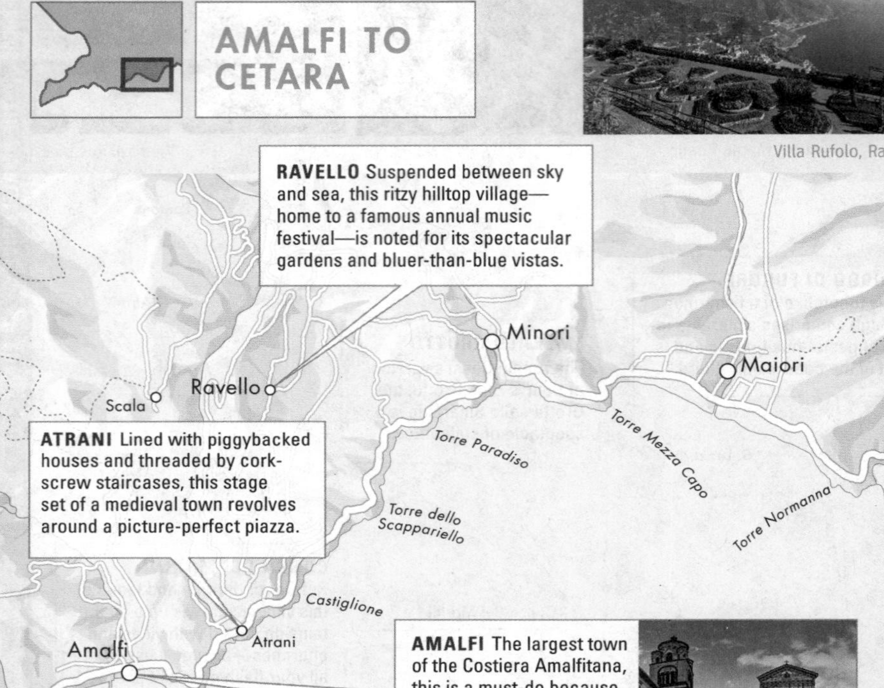

Villa Rufolo, Ravello

DOING THE DRIVE BY CAR

With countless twists and turns, the Amalfi Drive succeeds in making every driver into a Gran Turismo pro. In fact, at times you may feel you've entered the Amalfi Indy: the natives joke that the English complete the "course" in two hours, the Italians in a half hour. The drive is studded with stops built off the roadside for you to pull into safely and experience what your passengers are oohing and ahhing about. The round reflecting mirrors set along major curves in the road intend to show if others are coming around a bend, but honk before narrow curves to let oncoming traffic know about you, and listen for honks from oncoming curves. Buses and trucks will sometimes require you to back up; if there's a standoff, take it in stride, as it goes on all the time. At various points on the drive, stewards will stop larger vehicles so that cars can pass. Note that the road inevitably is closed some days due to landslides, especially in winter and early spring.

Villa Cimbrone, Ravello

Atrani

Cetara

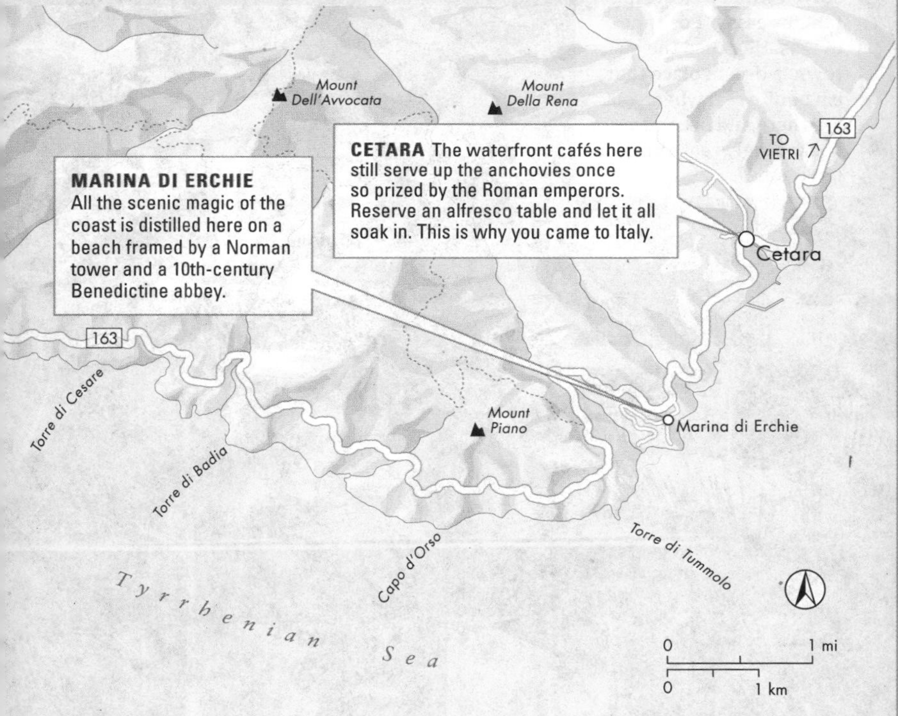

MARINA DI ERCHIE
All the scenic magic of the coast is distilled here on a beach framed by a Norman tower and a 10th-century Benedictine abbey.

CETARA The waterfront cafés here still serve up the anchovies once so prized by the Roman emperors. Reserve an alfresco table and let it all soak in. This is why you came to Italy.

Mount Dell'Avvocata

Mount Della Rena

TO VIETRI

163

Cetara

163

Torre di Cesare

Torre di Badia

Mount Piano

Marina di Erchie

Torre di Tummolo

Capo d'Orso

Tyrrhenian Sea

0 1 mi

0 1 km

DOING THE DRIVE BY BUS

There's one main reason why you should forget the car and opt for taking one of the convenient and inexpensive SITA buses that travel the route usually once an hour (www.sitasudtrasporti.it): the view is much better. Thanks to the mighty elevation of bus seats, you can see over the highway's low stone barrier. The best views can be yours if you sit on the sea side of the bus (on your right as you board the bus if you're starting in Sorrento, on your left if you begin in Amalfi). The trip between Sorrento and Amalfi generally takes between 90 and 120 minutes. Buses make regular stops at all the main destinations: happily, the driver will stop anywhere on the main route as long as you inform him of your destination, be it hotel or fork in the road, when boarding.. Note that buses fill up in the summer months, and the locals aren't usually orderly when it comes to making a line. There are storage areas below the bus for luggage.

Did You Know?

The hotel Sirenuse is where John Steinbeck stayed while writing his famous essay "Positano" in 1953. He called the town "a dream place that isn't quite real when you are there and becomes beckoningly real after you have gone."

✉ *Via Nocelle 19, Nocelle* ☎ *089/811260* ⊙ *Closed weekdays mid-Nov.–mid-Mar.*

★ Saraceno D'Oro

$$ | SOUTHERN ITALIAN | Although open for lunch, this reliable restaurant—tellingly popular with the *Positanesi*—truly comes into its own in the evening. Living up to its name, the ambience is distinctly Moorish without being kitschy; wood-fired pizza and hearty *costiera* seafood dishes dominate the menu. **Known for:** one of the best scialatielli di scoglio (classic seafood pastas) around; delizia di limone dessert; friendly staff guides you through the menu and the history. $ *Average main: €19* ✉ *Via Pasitea 254, Positano* ☎ *089/812050* 🌐 *www.saracenodoro.it* ⊙ *Closed Nov.–Dec. 26 and Jan. and Feb.*

Coffee and Quick Bites

Bar Internazionale

$ | CAFÉ | More than just a place to wait for the bus—it's at the main SITA Chiesa Nuova bus stop—Bar Internazionale is a meeting place for locals and visitors alike, a happy spot where you can read newspapers from several countries while nursing a creamy cappuccino. Many visitors only experience Positano in a tourism bubble, so this is good spot to mingle with working *positanesi*. **Known for:** good coffee; local hangout; nice vibe. $ *Average main: €4* ✉ *Via G. Marconi 306, Positano* ☎ *089/875434.*

Paradise Lounge Bar

$ | SANDWICHES | FAMILY | With an outdoor terrace overlooking the Spiaggia Grande, this is an ideal stop for a coffee, a sandwich, or an ice cream. By night, MTV music pumps from the stereo and the clamor of sporting events blares from the four large-screen TVs, as movers, groovers, and soccer fans from around the globe sip cocktails after a hard day on the beach. **Known for:** pastries, pizza, and panini; warm counter service; fab gelato artigianale. $ *Average main: €5* ✉ *Via del Saracino 32, Positano* ☎ *089/811915* ⊙ *Closed Mon.*

Hotels

Casa Albertina

$$$ | HOTEL | Clinging to a cliff, this little house is beloved for its homey restaurant; its owners, the Cinque family; and its Italianate charm, complete with rooms that have high ceilings, tile floors, bright fabrics, and sea and coastline views. **Pros:** sunny room balconies or terraces; quieter setting away from crowds; nearby access to Fornillo beach. **Cons:** 300 steps down to (and back up from) the main beach; dated decor; slightly removed from the action. $ *Rooms from: €265* ✉ *Via della Tavolozza 3, Positano* ☎ *089/875143* 🌐 *www.casalbertina.it* ⊙ *Closed Nov. and Dec.* 🛏 *20 rooms* 🍽 *Free Breakfast.*

★ Hotel Buca di Bacco

$$$$ | HOTEL | Above the Spiaggia Grande, a fisherman's tavern later converted into a guesthouse—where some of the airy guest rooms have sea views and others overlook the majolica dome of Santa Maria Assunta—has long held center stage, as evidenced by the photos of glitterati guests (Steinbeck, Hemingway, Jackie Kennedy) that line the walls. **Pros:** right on the beach; uninterrupted sea views from many rooms; a whirlpool tub with a view. **Cons:** no pool; street noise in lower-level rooms; tricky to reach if not arriving by boat. $ *Rooms from: €325* ✉ *Via Rampa Teglia 4, Positano* ☎ *089/857699* 🌐 *www.bucadibacco.it* ⊙ *Closed Nov.–Mar.* 🛏 *46 rooms* 🍽 *Free Breakfast.*

Hotel Conca d'Oro

$$$ | HOTEL | True to the word "gold" in its name, this bright, burnished, wedding-cake of a hotel shines brightly from its hillside perch amid a citrus-filled garden and terraces; guest rooms have chintz fabrics, antique furnishings, boldly patterned floor tiles, ceiling fans, and balconies that overlook the sea. **Pros:** removed from the bustle of the town; handy for Fornillo beach stairs;

fab terrace with pool and whirlpool tub. **Cons:** unusual electronic room locks; lots of steep steps; somewhat distant from the action. *Rooms from: €300 Via Boscariello 16, Positano 089/875111 www.hotel-concadoro.com Closed Jan. and Feb. 37 rooms Free Breakfast.*

Hotel Eden Roc

$$$ | **HOTEL** | The closest hotel to the Sponda bus stop, this luxury property (perfect for either couples or families) has spectacular views and service and spacious, pastel-hue guest rooms—all with terraces overlooking the town and some with whirlpool tubs. **Pros:** large rooms; good on-site amenities (gym, steam bath, wellness center, rooftop pool); magical views. **Cons:** some rooms are dated; a bit of a climb from the town center; on the main road (take care as you exit the hotel). *Rooms from: €290 Via G. Marconi 110, Positano 089/875844 www.edenroc.it Closed mid-Nov.–Feb. 25 rooms Free Breakfast.*

Hotel L'Ancora

$$$$ | **HOTEL** | Set back a little from the main road and a short walk up from the main beach, this hotel has commanding views and bright guest rooms decorated with local artwork and boldly patterned mosaic tile. **Pros:** bright and sunny; not far from the Sponda bus stop; all rooms have balconies or terraces and sea views. **Cons:** some rooms lack views; no on-site pool; a slight climb from the main drag. *Rooms from: €500 Via Cristoforo Colombo 36, Positano 089/875318 www.hotelancorapositano.com Closed Nov.–Mar. 18 rooms Free Breakfast.*

Hotel Poseidon

$$$$ | **HOTEL** | The Poseidon is more than just another hotel with an amazing view and a terrace, thanks, in no small part, to the on-site Beauty Center L'Onda with its gym, Turkish bath, and massage and other treatments. **Pros:** gorgeous panoramic terraces; cozy bar area with fireplace; great customer service and help with excursions. **Cons:** poor soundproofing so can be noisy; some rooms are on the small side; a steep climb from the town center. *Rooms from: €850 Viale Pasitea 148, Positano 089/811111 www.hotelposeidonpositano.it Closed Nov.–mid-Apr. 48 rooms Free Breakfast.*

★ Il San Pietro di Positano

$$$$ | **HOTEL** | Favored by the glitterati, the San Pietro is several leagues above town (a shuttle bus whisks you back and forth), far from the crowds and paparazzi but camera-ready nevertheless, with seven levels of gardened terraces and a stunning interior that mixes the modern (the hotel was built in the early 1970s) with the magnificent (great antiques, elegant Vietri tilework). **Pros:** picture-perfect views from the terrace; mixing with the Modigliani-sleek jet-setters; super-ambitious and stylish restaurant menu. **Cons:** not all rooms served by the elevator; service can be stand-offish; too far away from Positano to take a stroll. *Rooms from: €2010 Via Laurito 2, Positano 089/812080 www.ilsanpietro.it Closed Nov.–Mar. 57 rooms Free Breakfast.*

La Fenice

$$$ | **HOTEL** | This tiny, unpretentious hotel on the outskirts of Positano beckons with bougainvillea-laden views, castaway cottages, and a turquoise seawater pool—all perched over a private beach where a boat can whisk you away to Capri. **Pros:** small private beach with kayaks; secluded pool; family owned. **Cons:** lots of steps; roadside rooms are small and noisy; a 10-minute walk to town. *Rooms from: €230 Via G. Marconi 4, Positano 089/875513 www.lafenicepositano.com Sometimes closed Dec.–Feb. 14 rooms Free Breakfast.*

★ Le Sirenuse

$$$$ | **HOTEL** | As legendary as its namesake sirens, this 18th-century palazzo has long set the standard for luxury in Italian hotels: it opened in 1951 with just 12 rooms (John Steinbeck stayed here while writing "Positano" for *Harper's Bazaar* in 1953) and now sprawls over eight floors, where extravagantly stylish guest rooms are accented with antiques and fine linens. **Pros:** unrivaled views, including from poolside terrace; gorgeous artworks around every corner; many rooms have whirlpool tubs. **Cons:** can be noisy; lower-priced rooms are small; a bit of a climb from the town center. *$ Rooms from: €2128 ✉ Via Cristoforo Colombo 30, Positano ☎ 089/875066 🌐 www.sirenuse.it ⏲ Closed Nov.–Mar. 58 rooms 🍴 Free Breakfast.*

Palazzo Murat

$$$$ | **HOTEL** | A central-yet-secreted location, an infinity pool below the cupola of Santa Maria Assunta, and a magical bougainvillea-draped patio garden are among the things that make the Murat an extraordinary place to stay. **Pros:** once a regal residence; shops and passeggiata on the doorstep; stunning garden and surroundings. **Cons:** not all balconies secluded; constant stream of curious day-trippers; only five rooms have seaside views. *$ Rooms from: €650 ✉ Via dei Mulini 23, Positano ☎ 089/875177 🌐 www.palazzomurat.it ⏲ Closed Nov.–Mar. 31 rooms 🍴 Free Breakfast.*

Villa Flavio Gioia

$$$ | **HOTEL** | If you're eager to settle in for a while, this charming villa, a private home for centuries, has a prime location overlooking Piazza Flavio Gioia (the Spiaggia Grande is but a hop, skip, and flip-flop away) and bright mini-apartments, each with a cooking area and a terrace or large balcony. **Pros:** convenient location; ideal for longer stays; helpful staff can help with excursions. **Cons:** no pool; some rooms have no views; one-week minimum stay for certain periods of the year. *$ Rooms from: €300 ✉ Piazza Flavio Gioia 2, Positano ☎ 089/875222 🌐 www.villaflaviogioia.it ⏲ Closed Nov.–Mar. 13 rooms 🍴 No Meals.*

Nightlife

La Zagara

COCKTAIL LOUNGES | Come evening, things heat up at this bar and pasticceria where a local pianist tickles the ivories and summer sees DJ jams on the leafy terrace. *✉ Via dei Mulini 8, Positano ☎ 089/875964 🌐 www.lazagara.com ⏲ Closed Nov.–Mar.*

L'Alternativa

GATHERING PLACES | The Tiffany-blue hut by the ferry ticket office at the far end of Spiaggia Grande is a refreshingly no-frills spot for a granita or snack by day or late night cocktail or bottle of Peroni beer. Expect a friendly and unpretentious crowd where local fishermen mix with young visitors who congregate in and around the harbor seats into the evening. *✉ Molo Spiaggia Grande, Positano ⏲ Closed Jan.–Mar.*

Music on the Rocks

DANCE CLUBS | The owners of the restaurants Chez Black and Le Terrazze run this popular bar/club (est.1972), which occasionally hosts live music. Set in a seaside cave off Spiaggia Grande, it's a grinning, cheese-fest of pop tunes, dayglo lighting, and loungey nooks frequented by a lot of twentysomething visitors, a few middle-age locals, and the occasional celebrity (think Lenny Kravitz, Kate Moss, and Denzel Washington). Special events aside, entrance is free. *✉ Via Grotte dell'Incanto 56, Positano ☎ 089/875874 🌐 www.musicontherocks.it ⏲ Closed Nov.–Mar.*

Set on its own clifftop promontory, the Grand Terrace of the San Pietro hotel is lined with beautiful majolica-tiled benches (inspired by those of the cloisters of Naples's Santa Chiara church).

Shopping

Although the traditional gaudily colored and lace-trimmed Positano-style clothes have started to look frou-frou and dated, some contemporary designers are putting a 21st-century spin on the fashion. Goods still range from haute to kitsch, often-tight tops and casual skirts in vibrant hues, with prices generally higher than in other coastal towns. The fabric industry here began long ago with silk, canvas, and hand embroidery, then made headlines in 1959 when Positano introduced Italy to the bikini. The most concentrated shopping area, and the least difficult to maneuver, is the mazelike area near the cathedral by the beach, where the crowded pedestrian pathway literally runs through boutiques. Lining steep alleyways covered with bougainvillea, small shops display items such as local foodstuffs, wood, lace, pottery, wines and limoncello, and ceramics; you'll even find artisans who can hand-stitch a pair of stylish sandals while you wait.

Antica Sartoria

MIXED CLOTHING | Come here for colorful local fashions at reasonable prices; there's also a location closer to the beach, on Via del Brigantino. ✉ *Piazza dei Mulini 1/3, Positano* ☎ *089/812200* 🌐 *www.anticasartoriapositano.it.*

Ceramica Casola

CERAMICS | The colorful ceramics at this gorgeous factory showroom along the Amalfi Coast road east of Positano include vases, plates, decorative tiles, wall hangings, and outdoor sculptures. The shop also has a small boutique in hilltop Scala, along the coast. ✉ *Via Laurito 49, Positano* ☎ *089/811382* 🌐 *www.ceramicacasola.com* ⏲ *Closed Sun. Nov.–Mar.*

★ **Da Vincenzo Shop**

HOUSEWARES | Sister shop of the nearby restaurant, this place is well worth visiting for its selection of vibrant house wares—stripey mugs, majolica ceramics, aprons, dishcloths—and stylish utensils including solid-wood chopping boards. ✉ *Via Pasitea 200, Positano* ☎ *089/875128* 🌐 *www.davincenzo.it.*

★ Delicatessen Positano
FOOD | Here, you can grab a light lunch or pick up some picnic supplies before or after shopping for limoncello, vino, and biscotti. ✉ *Via dei Mulini 5, 13, 15, Positano* ☎ *089/875489.*

Marilù
WOMEN'S CLOTHING | It's worth popping in for their super-Positanese floaty dresses and other cotton and linen attire—their second and original shop is at Via del Saracino 16, near the Spiaggia Grande beach. ✉ *Via dei Mulini 17, Positano* ☎ *089/811709* 🌐 *www.marilumoda.com.*

Sapori e Profumi di Positano
FOOD | Here you can find anything it's conceivably possible to make that smells and tastes of the venerable *limone*—be sure to ask if the product you want really contains the bulbous *sfusato amalfitano.* ✉ *Via dei Mulini 6, Positano* ☎ *089/812055* 🌐 *www.saporidipositano.com* ⏲ *Closed Jan. and Feb.*

Square Gallery
ART GALLERIES | This gallery, along with its branch in Capri, exhibits contemporary art by Italian and international artists. ✉ *Via dei Mulini 16, Positano* ☎ *089/875257* 🌐 *www.liquidartsystem.com.*

Activities

BOAT EXCURSIONS

From Spiaggia Grande you can board a scheduled day boat or hire a private one for as long as you'd like, to visit Capri, the Emerald Grotto in Conca dei Marini, or coves and inlets with small beaches. A favorite boating destination nearby are the rocky Li Galli islets (6 km [4 miles] southwest), seen from any point in Positano, whose name derives from their importance in Greek mythology—resembling pecking birds, the islands were said to be the home of the sirens, part human, part feathered. Originally the site of an ancient Roman anchorage, the islands have always held an allure, tempting purchasers in search of an exclusive paradise: Russian choreographer Leonide Massine in 1925, and, in 1988, dancer Rudolf Nureyev, who discovered the islands in 1984 when he came to accept the Positano Prize for the Art of Dancing, given each year in honor of Massine. The islands now belong to a Sorrento hotelier, who also purchased the renowned Villa Treville (🌐 *www.villatreville.com*), formerly owned by the famed film and opera director Franco Zeffirelli. This is a pricey destination, though: the suite named for Zeffirelli runs €8,000 per night in high season, and even a "budget" room costs €3,000. Boating past the islands is the closest most visitors can get to experiencing the natural beauty and history of the Li Galli.

Cassiopea
BOATING | Boating excursions to Capri, the Li Galli islands, and along the Amalfi Coast can be organized through Cassiopea, which rents motorboats and Zodiacs by the hour. Their sunset cruise with prosecco is a magical way to end a day in Positano. Look out for the orange stand on Spiaggia Grande. ✉ *Spiaggia Grande, Positano* ☎ *338/8474700 cell phone Roberto, 339/1115538 cell phone Maddy* 🌐 *www.cassiopea-positano.com.*

L'Uomo e il Mare
BOATING | This small company conducts boating excursions along the Amalfi Coast and to Capri. Rides cost from €100 per person, including lunch onboard, less if you skip the meal. ✉ *Spiaggia Grande pier, Positano* ☎ *089/811613, 339/6646646 cell phone Andrea* 🌐 *www.gennaroesalvatore.it.*

Praiano

5 km (3 miles) southeast of Positano, 1 km (½ mile) northwest of Marina di Praia.

Praiano has less wealth and sophistication than its more famous neighbors and more olive and lemon trees than tourists. From afar, it looks as alluring as a landscape painting. Up close, apart from the town piazza and the nativity scenes in an enclave on the eastern edge of town, it can easily feel like just a village-along-a-road. However, meandering off the main road to explore the quiet spots and scenic views reveals a peaceful oasis that captivates many travelers.

The town's name comes from *Plagianum,* as the people who first inhabited the site were called. Back in the 13th century, King Charles I of Anjou founded a university here, the doges of Amalfi established a summer residence, and, for a while, Praiano was renowned for its silk industry. But the decline of Amalfi's 12th-century maritime republic hit hard; the charming parish church of San Luca, at the top of the village, is a reminder of those headier times. A medieval lookout tower on the rocks still keeps guard over the coast, and hidden coves are for boating, bathing, and sunning off the rocks. The views are splendid, especially at sunset looking toward Positano, and you can clearly see as far as the Faraglioni rocks in Capri from here.

What really makes Praiano worth a stop is the vast bayside piazza, in the Vettica Maggiore area of the village; it almost seems to levitate over the water. This is a fine place to stretch your legs and view distant Positano, the coast, and the sea. Paved with an intricate, colorful pattern in majolica, the piazza is a fitting setting for the Chiesa di San Gennaro, rebuilt in the 16th century, with its notably ornate facade and a gleaming majolica-tile dome. Paintings from the 16th and 17th centuries include *Martyrdom of St. Bartholomew,* by Giovanni Bernardo Lama, decorating the side chapel. You'll find a pretty but hard-to-reach cliffside beach if you follow the "Spiaggia" signs from the church; it's at the end of an olive grove, hidden at the bottom of the hillside, next to a tiny anchorage.

GETTING HERE AND AROUND

By car, take the Statale 163 (Amalfitana) from outside Sorrento or Salerno. There is SITA bus service from Sorrento, Positano, and Amalfi.

VISITOR INFORMATION

CONTACTS Ufficio Informazioni Turistiche di Praiano. (*Praiano Tourist Office*) ✉ *Via Gennaro Capriglione 116b, Praiano* ☎ *089/874557* 🌐 *www.praiano.org.*

Restaurants

Cala Gavitella

$$$ | **SOUTHERN ITALIAN** | Reaching this beach club might take some effort—by boat or steep steps—but the seaside views, warm welcome, and simple but incredibly fresh seafood dishes are just rewards. By day, it's an enchanting spot for lunch or quick bites between dips; on summer evenings, there's often live music. **Known for:** secluded, all-day sunbathing and swimming; friendly and gregarious staff; locally caught seafood including totano (meaty mollusco). [$] *Average main: €26* ✉ *Via Gavitella 1, Praiano* ☎ *350/5821514* 🌐 *www.lagavitella.it.*

Hotels

Grand Hotel Tritone

$$$$ | **HOTEL** | From afar on the Amalfi Drive, this looks like a shimmering white palazzo, and although its interior isn't decorated palatially, it nevertheless offers unfussy, light-filled charm—not to mention flagstone terraces and gardens set amid rock pinnacles that take full advantage of the dizzying location. **Pros:** flagstone terraces; gorgeous private

beach; retreat-like tranquillity. **Cons:** a walk along the busy road to get to Praiano; some might find the whole package a tad dated; early '60s standard-issue guest rooms. *$ Rooms from: €387 ✉ Via Campo 5, Praiano ☎ 089/874333 🌐 www.hoteltritonepraiano.com ⏲ Closed mid-Oct.–Mar. 59 rooms 🍽 Free Breakfast.*

Hotel Open Gate

$$ | **HOTEL** | With much the same views as the multimillion-dollar villas nearby, this small family-run Praiano pad is a great-value option. **Pros:** coastal views at a fraction of the price of other properties; simple rooms; wonderful terrace. **Cons:** can be noisy; beds are not the plushest; on the Amalfi Drive. *$ Rooms from: €160 ✉ Via Roma 38, Praiano ☎ 089/874148 🌐 www.hotelopengate.it ⏲ Closed Nov.–Mar. 12 rooms 🍽 Free Breakfast.*

Marina di Praia

3½ km (2 miles) southeast of Positano, 2 km (1 mile) west of Vallone di Furore.

Just east of Praiano, the scenic hamlet of Marina di Praia is nestled by the sea at the bottom of a dramatic chasm. This is the only anchorage along this rocky stretch surrounding Praiano where you can hire a boat and dock it, and enjoy a comfortable day at the beach. With its long-lost fishing village atmosphere, scenic setting, and beautiful beach for swimming, it's a great spot to take a break while driving along the Amalfi Coast. Don't miss its year-round nativity scene, nestled within cliffs above a small beach. It also has some excellent seafood restaurants, a hotel, and a tiny church. The legendary disco, L'Africana, is tucked away on a pretty, winding path along the sea.

GETTING HERE AND AROUND

By car, take the Statale 163 (Amalfitana) from outside Sorrento or Salerno. Take the SITA bus from Sorrento–Positano–Amalfi, or the local bus from Praiano. The town itself is easily walkable.

Restaurants

Alfonso a Mare

$$$ | **SOUTHERN ITALIAN** | A landmark restaurant and hotel nestled in the Marina di Praia cove, Alfonso a Mare occupies a rustic flagstone structure that once was a dry haul for boats. Noteworthy menu options include the antipasti, the freshly caught fish, and the seafood pastas. **Known for:** fresh seafood; gorgeous beach location; dining on the sea deck. *$ Average main: €26 ✉ Via Marina di Praia 6, Furore ☎ 089/874091 🌐 www.alfonsoamare.it ⏲ Closed mid-Nov.–Feb.*

Hotels

Hotel Onda Verde

$$$$ | **HOTEL** | On a rock jutting dramatically above the tiny cove of Marina dei Praia and overlooking a Saracen tower and coastal ridges, this popular, picturesque hotel has gorgeous flower-fringed terraces and public rooms with panoramic glass walls and marble flooring; it's also near the legendary L'Africana disco, so after a night of partying, you can climb into bed without having to drive. **Pros:** comfortable, stylish rooms; various massages and treatments; parking included in rates. **Cons:** not great for mingling as you might never leave the hotel; poolside service lacking; a bit of a walk to get here. *$ Rooms from: €310 ✉ Via Terramare 3, Praiano ☎ 089/874143 🌐 www.ondaverde.it ⏲ Closed Nov.–mid-Mar. 25 rooms 🍽 Free Breakfast.*

Did You Know?

The tiny Marina di Furore sits some 3,000 steps below its town. The harbor was once the site of a paper mill, but today is one of the Amalfi Coast's most impressive swimming spots.

Nightlife

L'Africana

DANCE CLUBS | Off a mile-long footpath from the Marina del Praia—or accessed via an elevator from Statale 163—L'Africana is a golden-oldie classic from the 1960s. With an open-to-the-sea atmosphere, a cave for a dance floor, and wildish shows with partial nudity, you can party the night away here, as Jackie Kennedy once did. The nightclub runs boats from Positano on Saturday—transfer can also be arranged from other points along the coast. Just ring them to get picked up. ✉ *Via Terramare 2, Praiano* ☎ *089/874858, 351/8112728 cell phone* 🌐 *www.africanafamousclub.com.*

Furore

18 km (12 miles) northeast of Positano, 14 km (9 miles) northeast of Praiano.

Furore stretches for 8 km (5 miles) along the panoramic winding road climbing the Monti Lattari hills toward Agerola. Its nickname as the *paese che non c'è,* the "town that doesn't exist," comes from the absence of any real focal point, or piazza, in the town. Yet, endearingly, it has billed itself as the *paese dipinto,* the "painted town," as the walls are the "canvas" for an array of murals by local and international artists, who have mostly represented the traditions and culture of their town. This open-air "gallery" was first initiated in 1980 with just three murals, and is regularly added to, with a different scene appearing around every bend. Other than artists, the most important residents of Furore are the local vintners. Townsfolk are said to live with one foot in a boat and one in a vineyard, and terraced vineyards cling to Furore's hillsides. Many vines uniquely grow horizontally from the stone walls, maximizing the use of the land here.

GETTING HERE AND AROUND

By car, take the Castellammare exit from the A3 motorway and follow the signs to Gragnano and Agerola, or take the Statale 163 (Amalfi Drive), and climb the hill 2 km (1 mile) west of Amalfi. There's a SITA bus service from Sorrento, and Positano. As for the Vallone di Furore, by car, take the Statale 163 (Amalfitana) from outside Sorrento or Salerno. There's SITA bus service from Positano and Amalfi. Walking around the town is not the ideal option, as it stretches 8 km (5 miles). The murals are on the sides of walls and houses along the winding main road.

Sights

Cantine di Marisa Cuomo
(*Marisa Cuomo Cellars*)

WINERY | The most famous of Furore's vineyards is the Gran Furor Divina Costiera estate, where top-quality "extreme" wines (so-called because of the grape-growing conditions) have been produced since 1942. Now named for owner Andrea Ferraioli's wife, the winery has won countless awards all over the world. Among the most lauded vintages is the Bianco Fiorduva, a white wine made from grapes that are allowed to over-ripen a bit. Daughter Dorotea organizes tastings, and the cellar, hewn from the hillside Dolomitic limestone rock, can be visited; call for details and reservations (required). Andrea is also a talented photographer, so don't miss the opportunity to see his stunning shots of the surrounding region. If you visit, ask to view the part of the stone wall (not far from the cellar) where you can see a magnificent 100-year-old horizontal vine. ✉ *Via Giambattista Lama 16/18, Furore* ☎ *089/830348* 🌐 *www.marisacuomo.com* 🕒 *No tours Sun Nov.–Mar.*

★ **Marina di Furore**

VIEWPOINT | From the lofty top of Furore, 944 steps (count 'em!) lead down to Marina di Furore, nearly hidden away in a fjord. Set on the coast, this enchanting hamlet—perhaps 10 houses?—beckons to most travelers as their SITA buses pass over it on a towering viaduct that each summer is the site of the Mediterranean Cup High-Diving Championship. The locale's name derives from the "furor" of stormy water that once rushed down the Torrente Schiato here, now a mere trickle. Adorning the gorge is a fishermen's village scene fit for a Neapolitan *presepe* (with some houses renovated for Anna Magnani during the filming of Roberto Rossellini's *L'Amore* in 1948); these buildings and the adjoining paper mill were abandoned when the tiny harbor closed. Today, the sleepy hamlet only comes to life during the summer months when the colorful houses are complemented by sunbathers who follow the narrow pathway down to the secluded beach. From the beach, the Sentiero della Volpe Pescatrice ("fox-fish's path") and the Sentiero dei Pipistrelli Impazziti ("mad bats' path") climb up some 3,000 steps and were built to portage goods from the harbor to the town of Furore. The hard walk up takes a couple of hours, as you climb from sea to sky. To see any of this by car, you have to pay to park in the rest area some 450 yards away on the Amalfi side of the gorge, just before the gas station. Unless you're in pretty good shape, it's better to boat to the beach and just rubberneck. ✉ *Via Trasita, Fiordo di Furore, Furore.*

Restaurants

Bacco

$$ | **SOUTHERN ITALIAN** | Opened in 1930, this longtime favorite named for the Greek god of wine is, appropriately, run by the Cuomo wine family. The terrace has one of the coast's of the best views, and the menu features simple but delicious mountain and sea fare, including *ferrazzuoli alla Nannarella* (named after actress Anna Magnani, a past patron, and featuring fresh pasta with tomatoes, tuna, swordfish, and pine nuts) and *vermicelli cu o' pesce fujuto,* a dish with no fish despite its moniker (the flavor of the local tomatoes provides the *piscine parfumo).* **Known for:** excellent Furore wine and tasting events; gluten-free options; former patron Anna Magnani's dish ferrazzuoli alla Nannare. $ *Average main: €22* ✉ *Via Giambattista Lama 9, Furore* ☎ *089/830360* 🌐 *www.baccofurore.it* ⏲ *Closed Tues. and Jan.–Mar.*

Conca dei Marini

2 km (1 mile) east of Vallone di Furore, 4 km (2½ miles) southwest of Amalfi.

A longtime favorite of the off-duty rich and famous, Conca dei Marini (the name means "seafarers' basin") hides many of its charms, as any sublime hideaway should. On the most dramatic promontory of the coast, the town was originally a province of ancient Rome called Cossa and later became an important naval base of the Amalfi Republic. Much later, it became a retreat for high-profile types, including Jacqueline Kennedy, automaker Gianni Agnelli of Fiat, and film producer Carlo Ponti, who erected a white villa here by the sea (for his first wife, not Sophia Loren). You can see why: the green of terraced gardens competes with (and loses to) the blue sea, while the town's distinctive houses flanking the ridges have thick, white walls, with cupolas, balconies, and external staircases, testimony to former Arabic, Moorish, and Greek settlements. Below, on Capo di Conca, a promontory once used as a cemetery, a 16th-century coastal tower dramatically overlooks the sea. On a curve in the road sits the village's most noteworthy attraction, the Emerald Grotto. While it all might seem overly tourist-focused at first glance, pause long enough in Conca dei Marini and you'll quickly discover the intense beauty that is its most lasting attraction.

The coast's leading hideaway for off-duty celebrities, Conca dei Marini is landmarked by its 16th-century watchtower.

GETTING HERE AND AROUND

By car, take the Statale 163 (Amalfitana) from outside Sorrento or Salerno. There's SITA bus service from Positano and Amalfi. The town is easily walkable, but be prepared to climb a lot of steps!

Sights

Grotta dello Smeraldo (*Emerald Grotto*)
NATURE SIGHT | FAMILY | The tacky road sign, squadron of tour buses, Dean Martino–style boatmen, and freeform serenading (Andrea is the king of the grotto crooners) scream tourist trap, but there is, nevertheless, a compelling, eerie *bellezza* in the rock formations and luminous waters here. The karstic cave was originally part of the shore, but the lowest end sank into the sea. Intense greenish light filters into the water from an arch below sea level and is reflected off the cavern walls. You visit the Grotta dello Smeraldo, which is filled with huge stalactites and stalagmites, on a large rowboat. Don't let the boatman's constant spiel detract from the experience—just tune out and enjoy the sparkles, shapes, and brilliant colors. The light at the grotto is best from noon to 3 pm. You can take an elevator from the coast road down to the grotto, or in the summer you can drive to Amalfi and arrive by boat (€10, excluding the grotto's €6 admission fee). Companies in Positano, Amalfi, and elsewhere along the coast provide passage to the grotto, but consider one of the longer boat trips that explore Punta Campanella, Li Galli, and the more secluded spots along the coast. ✉ *Via Smeraldo, west of Capo di Conca, Conca dei Marini* ☎ *089/831535* 🎫 *€6* 🕒 *Closed in adverse weather conditions.*

San Pancrazio
CHURCH | For Conca in excelsis, head up the hill on Via Don Amodio, opposite the Hotel Belvedere, to Conca dei Marini's northern reaches. Your reward after a short climb up the hillside roads and steep scalinatelle is the stunningly sited neo-Byzantine church of San Pancrazio, set in a palm-tree garden. Opposite this church, in the direction of Positano, is a

road leading to Punta Vreca, a sky-high lookout over the coast. Climbing farther up the scalinatella San Pancrazio will take you to the tiny town piazza. ✉ *Via Don Gaetano Amodio, Conca dei Marini.*

Sant'Antonio di Padova

CHURCH | Spectacularly cantilevered hundreds of feet over the coastline on a stone parapet, this elegant Neoclassical white church is also known as Chiesa Principale di San Giovanni Battista. It's only open for Sunday-morning services, but if for a quick peek at other times you might ask locals if someone (*il custode*: caretaker) has a key to open the church. Just ask, *"Dov'è la persona che ci potrebbe far visitare la chiesa?"* For those who want to see churches in coastal villages, this may be the only way to gain entry. ✉ *Via Sant'Antonio, Conca dei Marini.*

Santa Maria della Neve

VIEWPOINT | A must-do in Conca dei Marini is the jaunt down the staircase to the left of the Hotel Belvedere that delivers you to the town's dollhouse-size harbor, Santa Maria della Neve, and darling little chapel of the same name. You'll pass by some gorgeous houses on your way to one of the most idyllic sights along the entire coast. The view of the harbor from the Amalfi Drive high atop the hill is a prime photo op. ✉ *Marina di Conca, Conca dei Marini.*

Beaches

Conca dei Marini Beach

BEACH | With its wonderful patches of emerald set in a blue-glass lagoon, Conca dei Marini's harbor is one of the most enchanting visions on the coast. Descend (and later ascend!) the steps past the Borgo Marinaro houses (a colony for off-duty celebrities) and down to the harbor, set with cafés and a little chapel dedicated to Santa Maria della Neve that seems to bless the picture-perfect beach. **Amenities:** food and drink; lifeguards; showers; toilets. **Best for:** snorkeling, swimming. ✉ *Marina di Conca, Conca dei Marini.*

Lido Capo di Conca

BEACH | Landmarked by its giant Saracen Tower, the Capo di Conca protects bathers from the western winds. Here at this privately run beach with a bar and restaurant, it is the water that compels: infinite shades of aquamarine, lapis, and emerald shimmering in sunshine, glowing silver in moonlight, and becoming transparent in the rocky coves. **Amenities:** food and drink; lifeguards; pool; showers; toilets. **Best for:** diving; snorkeling; swimming. ✉ *Via Capo di Conca, Conca dei Marini* ☎ *089/831512* 🌐 *www.capodiconca.it.*

Hotels

Hotel Belvedere

$$$ | **HOTEL** | Set in a grande-dame villa—featuring salons top-heavy with overstuffed sofas, a ravishing seawater-pool area, and a rocky beach—the tranquil Belvedere is equidistant from Conca dei Marini's lagoon and Saracen tower and can arrange shuttle service for trips to Amalfi. **Pros:** local-flavor restaurant; a home away from home; large bright rooms with terrace views. **Cons:** no elevator to the beach; away from the action; busy Amalfi Drive entrance (be careful as you exit the doorway). $ *Rooms from: €285* ✉ *Via Smeraldo 19, Conca dei Marini* ☎ *089/831282* 🌐 *www.belvederehotel.it* ⏲ *Closed mid-Oct.–mid-Apr.* *36 rooms* 🍽 *Free Breakfast.*

★ **Monastero Santa Rosa Hotel & Spa**

$$$$ | **HOTEL** | One of Italy's most exclusive retreats—in a 17th-century monastery on dramatic coastal cliffs—this boutique hotel has just 20 rooms, all with vaulted ceilings, Italian antiques, modern amenities, sumptuous bathrooms, and dazzling

Amalfi's History

Amalfi's origin is cloudy. One legend says that a general of Constantine's army named Amalfo settled here in 320; another tale has it that Roman noblemen from the village of Melphi (in Latin, "a Melphi"), fleeing after the fall of the empire, were first in these parts, shipwrecked in the 4th century on their way to Constantinople. Myth becomes fact by the 6th century, when Amalfi is inscribed in the archives as a Byzantine diocese. Its geographic position was good defense, and the distance from Constantinople made its increasing autonomy possible. Continuously hammered by the Lombards and others, in 839 it rose against and finally sacked nearby Salerno, to which its inhabitants had been deported. In the 10th century, Amalfi constructed many churches and monasteries and was ruled by judges, later called *dogi*—self-appointed dukes who amassed vast wealth and power.

From the 9th century until 1101, Amalfi remained linked to Byzantium but also was increasingly independent and prosperous, perhaps the major trading port in southern Italy. Its influence loomed large, thanks to its creation of the Tavole Amalfitane, a code of maritime laws taken up by most medieval kingdoms. Amalfi created its own gold and silver coins—or *tari*, engraved with the cross of Amalfi—and ruled a vast territory. With trade extending as far as Alexandria and Constantinople, it became Italy's first maritime republic, ahead of Pisa, Venice, and Genoa; the population swelled to about 100,000. As William of Apulia wrote in the 11th century, "No other city is richer in silver, cloth, and gold."

But the days of wine and doges were about to end. In the 11th century Robert Guisgard of Normandy first aided, then sacked the town, and the Normans from Sicily returned, after a short Amalfitan revolt, in the 12th century. Then, when the Republic of Pisa twice conquered it, Amalfi fell into decline, hastened by a storm in 1343, then by an indirect blow from Christopher Columbus's discoveries, which opened the world beyond to competing trade routes. By the 18th century, the town had sunk into gloom, looking to its lemons and handmade paper for survival. After the state road was built by Ferdinand, the Bourbon king of Naples, in the 19th century, Amalfi evolved into a tourist destination, drawing Grand Tour–era travelers like Richard Wagner, Henry Wadsworth Longfellow, and Henrik Ibsen, all of whom helped spread Amalfi's fame.

views framed by Mediterranean gardens. **Pros:** excellent service; gorgeous gardens and infinity pool; meticulously restored property with spa. **Cons:** a bit remote; some rooms could be more spacious; out of reach for many budgets. [$] *Rooms from: €902* ✉ *Via Roma 2, Conca dei Marini* ☎ *089/8321199* 🌐 *www.monasterosantarosa.com* 🕓 *Closed Nov.–mid-Apr.* *20 rooms* 🍽 *Free Breakfast.*

Amalfi

18 km (11 miles) southeast of Positano, 32 km (20 miles) west of Salerno.

At first glance, it's hard to imagine that this resort destination was one of the world's great naval powers, and a sturdy rival of Genoa and Pisa for control of

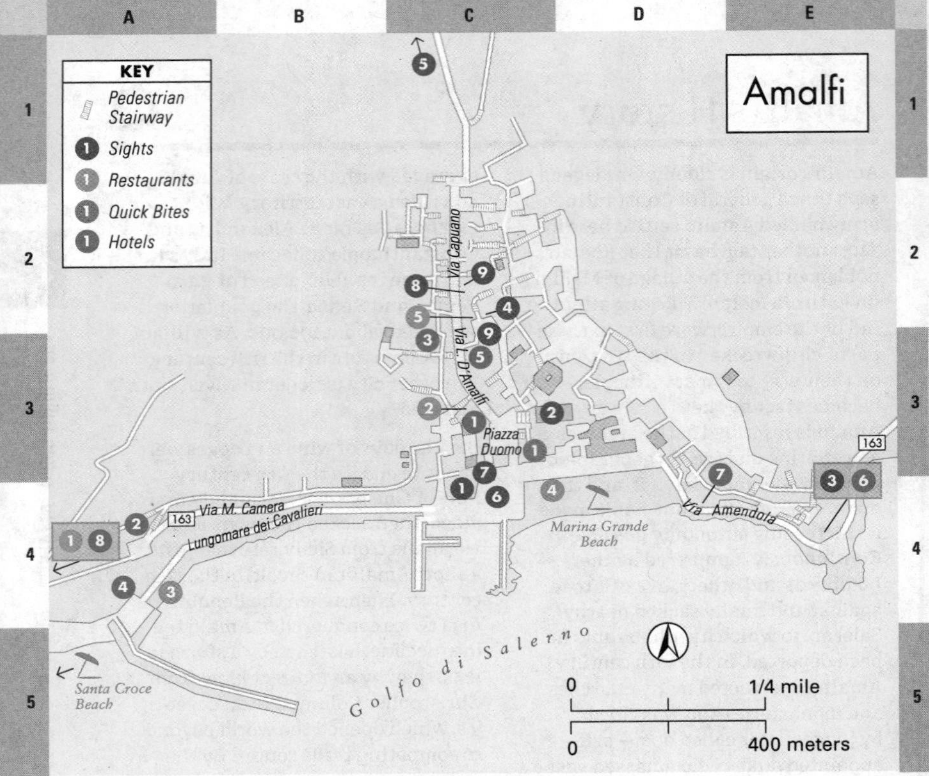

Sights

1 Arsenale della Repubblica C4
2 Duomo di Sant'Andrea C3
3 Hotel Luna Convento E4
4 Maria Santissima Addolorata C2
5 Museo della Carta C1
6 Piazza Flavio Gioia C4
7 Porta della Marina C3
8 Santa Maria Maggiore C2
9 Supportico Rua C2

Restaurants

1 Da Ciccio: Cielo Mare Terra A4
2 Da Gemma C3
3 Lo Smeraldino A4
4 Stella Maris C4
5 Taverna Buonvicino C2

Quick Bites

1 Pasticceria Andrea Pansa C3

Hotels

1 Albergo Sant'Andrea C3
2 Grand Hotel Convento di Amalfi A4
3 Hotel Amalfi C3
4 Hotel Aurora A4
5 Hotel Floridiana C3
6 Hotel Luna Convento E4
7 Hotel Marina Riviera ... D4
8 Hotel Santa Caterina ... A4

the Mediterranean in the 11th and 12th centuries. Once the seat of the Amalfi Maritime Republic, the town is set in a verdant valley of the Lattari Mountains, with cream-color and pastel-hue buildings tightly packing a gorge on the Bay of Salerno. The harbor, which once launched the greatest fleet in Italy, now bobs with ferries and blue-and-white fishing boats. The main street, lined with shops and *pasticcerie,* has replaced a raging mountain torrent, and terraced hills flaunt the green and gold of lemon groves. Bearing testimony to its great trade with Tunis, Tripoli, and Algiers, Amalfi remains honeycombed with Arab-Sicilian cloisters and covered passages. In a way Amalfi has become great again, showing off its medieval glory days with sea pageants, convents-turned-hotels, ancient paper mills, covered streets, and its glimmering cathedral.

GETTING HERE AND AROUND

By car, take the Statale 163 (Amalfitana) from outside Sorrento or Salerno, or take the Angri exit on the A3 motorway and cross the mountainous Valico di Chiunzi. Take the SITA bus from Sorrento–Salerno, or summer ferries from Sorrento or Salerno. The special express SITA bus from Naples departs Monday–Saturday at 9 am, 2:30 pm, and 5:30 pm from the port (Varco Immacolalatella); catching this bus makes for an easy and scenic ride back to the city, allowing you to bypass a transfer from the bus to the Circumvesuviana railway in Sorrento. Note, however, the Amalfi–Naples bus leaves at 6:20 am!

In Amalfi you can purchase tickets prior to boarding at any tobacco shop displaying a SITA sticker; all SITA buses leave Amalfi from Piazza Flavio Gioia. One way to tour Amalfi and the surrounding area is aboard an open-top City Sightseeing bus.

Amalfi's compact tourist center is split between the bustling *lungomare* (waterfront), with its public and private transportation hubs, and the piazza in front of the Duomo. Parking is a big problem, as the tiny lot on the seafront (€3 per hour) fills up fast. There is a huge car park carved into the mountainside 400 yards east of the town. Still, traveling here via ferry and bus or staying in a hotel with a parking garage are good ideas. Amalfi is a small town and is best visited on foot. Once you explore the main sights near the waterfront, take off and explore the medieval center, then escape to the outskirts and the terraced hills of the Valle dei Mulini, site of Amalfi's ancient paper mills.

VISITOR INFORMATION

CONTACTS Azienda Autonoma di Cura, Soggiorno e Turismo. (*Amalfi Tourist Office*) ✉ *Corso Reppubliche Marinare 27, Amalfi* ☎ *089/871107* 🌐 *www.amalfitouristoffice.it.*

Sights

★ **Arsenale della Repubblica** (*Arsenal of the Republic*)

HISTORIC SIGHT | From the middle of the 11th century, Amalfi's center of shipbuilding, customs houses, and warehouses was the Arsenale, today the only (partially) preserved medieval shipyard in southern Italy. Ships and galleys up to 80-feet long, equipped with up to 120 oars, were built at this largest arsenal of any medieval maritime republic. Two large Gothic halls here now host the Museo della Bussola e del Ducato Marinaro di Amalfi (Museum of the Compass and Maritime Duchy of Amalfi) with exhibitions and artifacts from Amalfi's medieval period, including paintings, ancient coins, banners, and jeweled costumes. The highlight is the original 66-chapter draft of the code of the Tavole Amalfitane, the sea laws and customs of the ancient republic, used throughout the Italian Mediterranean from the 13th to the 16th century. The Tavole established everything from prices for boat hires to procedures to be followed in case of a shipwreck. Long one of the treasures of the Imperial Library of Vienna, the draft

Did You Know?

Arab-Norman design can be seen throughout Amalfi, including in the Duomo di Sant' Andrea, where the style predominates in a mix of Gothic, Romanesque, Byzantine, and Baroque influences.

was returned to Amalfi after more than 500 years. Ten of the arsenal's original 22 stone piers remain; the others were destroyed by storms and changes in the sea level on this ever-active coast. ✉ *South of Piazza dei Dogi, at Via Camera, by waterfront, Largo Cesareo Console 3, Amalfi* ☎ *089/8736204* 🌐 *arsenalediamalfi.it* 🎫 *€4* ⏲ *Closed Mon. and Tues.*

★ **Duomo di Sant'Andrea**

CHURCH | Complicated, grand, delicate, and dominating, the 9th-century Amalfi cathedral has been remodeled over the years with Romanesque, Byzantine, Gothic, and Baroque elements, but retains a predominantly Arab-Norman style. Built around 1266 as a burial ground for Amalfi's elite, the cloister, the first stop on a tour of the cathedral, is one of southern Italy's architectural treasures. Its flower-and-palm-filled quadrangle has a series of exceptionally delicate intertwining arches on slender double columns. The chapel at the back of the cloister leads into the 9th-century basilica, now a museum housing sarcophagi, sculpture, Neapolitan goldsmiths' artwork, and other treasures from the cathedral complex. Steps from the **basilica** lead down into the **Cripta di Sant'Andrea** (Crypt of Saint Andrew). The cathedral above was built in the 13th century to house the saint's bones, which came from Constantinople. Following the one-way traffic up to the cathedral, you can admire the elaborate polychrome marbles and painted, coffered ceilings from its 18th-century restoration. ✉ *Piazza Duomo, Amalfi* ☎ *089/871324* 🌐 *museodiocesanoamalfi.it* 🎫 *€4* ⏲ *Generally closed early Jan. and Feb. except for daily services.*

Hotel Luna Convento

NOTABLE BUILDING | The legendary St. Francis of Assisi founded this 13th-century former monastery that retains its original cloister, famous for its distinctive Arab-Sicilian arcaded columns and crypt with frescoes. Two centuries ago the property was transformed into the Amalfi Coast's earliest hotel. The many noteworthy guests include Henrik Ibsen, who wrote much of his play *A Doll's House* here. The hotel also owns the landmark Torre Saracena (Saracen Tower), now home to a bar and nightspot, which sits across the highway and stands guard over Amalfi's seaside promontory. ✉ *Via Pantaleone Comite 19, Amalfi* ☎ *089/871002* 🌐 *lunahotel.it.*

Maria Santissima Addolorata (*Our Lady of Sorrows*)

CHURCH | This church is adjacent to the confraternity founded in 1765 to organize Amalfi's Good Friday celebrations, a short stroll up the Salita Brancia behind the Duomo. The entrance gate bears a late-Gothic bas-relief of the Crucifixion, once belonging to nobility from the nearby village of Scala and identified by its coat of arms at the foot of the cross. The interior is Neoclassical, with a coffered ceiling and a harmonious scale; note the 16th-century marble Madonna and Child in the sacristy. Opening times for this church are erratic, but Mass is held on Saturday afternoon. ✉ *Largo Santa Maria Maggiore, Amalfi.*

★ **Museo della Carta** (*Paper Museum*)

HISTORY MUSEUM | FAMILY | Uphill from town, the Valle dei Mulini (Valley of the Mills) was for centuries Amalfi's center for papermaking, an ancient trade learned from the Arabs, who learned it from the Chinese. Beginning in the 12th century, former flour mills were converted to produce paper made from cotton and linen. The paper industry was a success, and by 1811 more than a dozen mills here, with more along the coast, were humming. Natural waterpower ensured that the handmade paper was cost-effective. Yet, by the late 1800s the industry had moved to Naples and other more geographically accessible areas. Flooding in 1954 closed most of the mills for good, and many have been converted into private housing. The Museo della Carta

The piazza outside Amalfi's Duomo is a lively gathering place.

(Museum of Paper) opened in 1971 in a 15th-century mill. Paper samples, tools of the trade, old machinery, and the audio-visual presentation are all enlightening. You can also participate in a paper-making laboratory. ✉ *Via delle Cartiere 23, Amalfi* ☎ *089/8304561* 🌐 *www.museodellacarta.it* 🎫 *€5, includes guided tour; €7 with paper-making experience* 🕑 *Closed Feb. and Mon. Nov.–Jan.*

Piazza Flavio Gioia

PUBLIC ART | A statue, set in an ironically disorienting traffic roundabout in front of the harbor, honors the *Amalfitano* credited with inventing the maritime compass in the Middle Ages. Many say it was the Chinese who invented the compass, passing the idea along to the Arabs, who traded with Amalfi; Gioia may have adapted it for sea use (for the record, some historians believe there was no such person as Gioia). ✉ *On waterfront, Piazza Flavio Gioia, Amalfi.*

Porta della Marina

PUBLIC ART | This gateway "door" to the harbor bears a huge ceramic panel, created by Renato Rossi in the 1950s, commemorating the trade routes of the republic during the Middle Ages. In one example, ships loaded with Italian timber sold the wood for gold in North Africa, then used the gold to buy gems, spices, and silks in Asia to trade back in Italy. Walk 200 feet along Corso delle Repubbliche Marinare, past the tourist office, to see the ceramic panel created by Diodoro Cossa in the 1960s. The scenes illustrate local historical highlights, among them Roman refugees establishing themselves in nearby Scala in the 4th century, the founding of Amalfi by these same Romans, Amalfi's commercial and diplomatic role in the Mediterranean, the arrival of St. Andrew's body, and the invention of the maritime compass. ✉ *Across from Piazza Flavio Gioia, next to arsenal, Amalfi.*

Experiencing the Amalfi Coast: Boating

People take to boats here with the ease that others use around buses and subways. Ferries and hydrofoils run on regular schedules during high season. The waters are calm and beckoning, and boating for pleasure frees you from the tension of coastal driving, giving a different perspective on the coast, so try to arrange to spend at least one day on the water. Bright red-and-blue fishing boats are for hire by the day or for a few hours at the major harbors of Sorrento, Positano, and Amalfi, and by almost any beach wherever you see fishermen.

Boats can take you around the Sorrento area, to the Emerald Grotto, to Capri and offshore islets, to major towns, and otherwise inaccessible cove beaches. They will drop you off and pick you up, or stay with you, depending on your budget. Look for established sites on major beaches and come a day or so ahead to reserve and bargain, especially if you're with a group.

Pricing starts at around €150 per day, more or less, depending on the market, the season, and your talent at haggling. If in doubt, ask for recommendations about local boatmen at your hotel or at the town tourist board. And don't expect fishermen to speak much English; you'll have to learn to speak with your hands, as many Italians do.

Santa Maria Maggiore

CHURCH | As inscribed on a capital at the entrance, one Duke Mansone I had this church constructed in 986. Though the layout is Byzantine, a 16th-century overhaul inverted the entrance and high altar, and the decoration is now mostly Baroque. The campanile dates from the 12th century, and there's a noteworthy 18th-century crèche. Church hours are erratic; check with the Duomo for when Mass is scheduled. ✉ *Near Maria Santissima Addolorata, Largo Santa Maria Maggiore, Amalfi.*

Supportico Rua

HISTORIC DISTRICT | A tunnel-like passageway also known as Via dei Mercanti, the evocative Supportico Rua was the main thoroughfare of medieval Amalfi, when the main road was a raging torrent. Still the town's most fascinating "street," it is especially wonderful when the light from alleys and windows plays on its white walls. Stretching almost the length of the main street, it ends at a medieval-era *contrada,* or neighborhood, with a fountain known as Capo di Ciuccio (donkey's head), where mules would refresh themselves after the climb down from the hills. ✉ *Adjacent to Via Pietro Capuano, Amalfi.*

Beaches

Marina Grande Beach

BEACH | **FAMILY** | Amalfi's main beach stretches along the front of town and is popular with both locals and visitors. During the summer months, the beach is covered with rows of brightly colored sun beds and umbrellas, each color indicating a different swimming establishment generally associated with the restaurant overlooking the beach. The water is clear, especially in the mornings, and the swimming is good. Both ends of the beach have free areas, which are popular with locals and families. The beach has large pebbles, so if you're planning a leisurely day then renting a sun bed is recommended. **Amenities**: food and drink;

Amalfi's Luscious Lemons

Lemons as big as oranges and oranges as big as grapefruits are cultivated on the seemingly endless net-covered pergolas of the Amalfi Coast. From linguine with lemon at trattorias to lemon soufflés at fancy restaurants, the yellow citrus is everywhere. All parts are used, as can be seen from the delicious habit of baking raisins, figs, or pieces of cheese wrapped in lemon leaves, bound up with thin red thread.

Not only are lemons a main component of meals and drinks, but they are also used as a remedy for everything from flu to bunions. But the most renowned end product is that local *digestivo* known as limoncello, which captures in a bottle the color, fragrance, and taste of those tart-sweet lemons. Drink it cold in a tiny, frosty glass or after a shot of hot espresso—a golden memory quenched with each sip.

lifeguards; showers; toilets. **Best for**: swimming. ✉ *Corso delle Repubbliche Marinare, Amalfi.*

Santa Croce Beach

BEACH | Named for the ruins of a chapel found in the beach's grotto, the rocky beach of Santa Croce is located below the village of Vettica Minore, west of Amalfi, but is reachable only by boat from Amalfi. Paradise for swimmers, the water is crystal clear and the surrounding coast is studded with emerald grottoes—stronger swimmers can admire a natural arch in the rock, about 150 meters west (locals say that kissing your *bella* while swimming underneath ensures everlasting love). With a delightful restaurant and sun-bed rental available, this is a relaxing beach experience. **Amenities:** food and drink; lifeguards; showers; toilets. **Best for:** snorkeling; swimming. ✉ *Amalfi.*

Restaurants

★ Da Ciccio: Cielo Mare Terra

$$ | **SOUTHERN ITALIAN** | Featuring, as its name suggests, stunning views of sky, sea, and land and run by the fourth generation of the *famiglia* Cavaliere (sommelier Giuseppe, front-of-house manager Antonio, and chef Marco), this restaurant just outside of town serves exquisite dishes made with fresh local produce—often from its own *orto* garden and the sea below. Many diners opt for the aromatic theater *al tavolo* of the signature *spaghetti al cartoccio dal 1965* (spaghetti with clams, olives, capers, tomatoes, and oregano), which the ever-smiling Antonio removes from baking paper, mixes, and serves. **Known for:** aperitivo on the panoramic terrace; free shuttle service from Amalfi and around; warm family-run place with home-grown produce. $ *Average main: €24* ✉ *Via Giovanni Augustariccio 21, Amalfi* ☎ *089/831265, 0345/3538935 for shuttle service* 🌐 *www.ristorante-daciccio.com* 🕒 *Closed Tues. No lunch Mon.–Thurs.*

Da Gemma

$$$ | **SOUTHERN ITALIAN** | Diners in the know have sung the praises of this understated landmark since 1872. Imaginative sauces turn plates of risotto and paccheri pasta into one-off culinary experiences; tile floors, white tablecloths, and a terrace set above the main street create a soothing ambience. **Known for:** signature feast fish soup to end all fish soups; novel risotto and pasta dishes; freshest sea and mountain produce. $ *Average main: €27* ✉ *Via Fra Gerardo Sasso 9, Amalfi* ☎ *089/871345* 🌐 *www.trattoriadagemma.com.*

Lo Smeraldino

$$ | **SEAFOOD** | **FAMILY** | Open since 1949, this airy, popular restaurant on Amalfi's almost-emerald waterfront dishes out reasonably priced seafood and *cucina tipica Amalfitana* (Amalfi Coast cuisine) such as lemon and zucchine tagliatelle *alla Nerano* and excellent grilled fish. You can see the boats bringing in the day's catch, and at night pizza is served on the terrace amid the twinkling lights of hills, sea, and sky. **Known for:** super waterside location; very popular with families in the summer; classic Campania pasta dishes. *Average main: €21 Piazzale dei Protontini 1, Amalfi 089/871070 www.ristorantelosmeraldino.it Closed Wed. Sept.–June, and Jan. and Feb.*

Stella Maris

$$ | **SOUTHERN ITALIAN** | **FAMILY** | With its white awnings and prime location on the beach (where you can rent sun beds), Stella Maris is likely the first restaurant you'll encounter on arriving in Amalfi. Dine or enjoy an aperitivo on the terrace, in front of the glass walls or on the beach—all the while gazing at the fishing boats bobbing in the bay or the sun worshipers tanning on the shore. **Known for:** classic seafood frittata; fab desserts including delizia di limone; sun lounger dining service. *Average main: €19 Via della Regione 2, Amalfi 089/872463 www.stella-maris.it Closed Dec.–Feb.*

Taverna Buonvicino

$$ | **SOUTHERN ITALIAN** | In the heart of medieval Amalfi, with alfresco seating in the *piazzetta* outside the churches of Santa Maria Maggiore and the Maria Santissima Addolorata, this place has a magical atmosphere. The menu features simple seasonal dishes like grilled squid, octopus, and buffalo steak—all lovingly crafted using grandma's recipes. **Known for:** paranza seafood medley; seasonal dishes and catch of the day; twinkly, tranquil courtyard. *Average main: €22 Largo Santa Maria Maggiore 1–3, Amalfi 089/8736385 www.facebook.com/TavernaBuonVicino Closed Jan. and Feb.*

Coffee and Quick Bites

★ Pasticceria Andrea Pansa

$ | **NEOPOLITAN** | Amalfi's famed historic pasticceria (est.1830) is a must-visit for a breakfast capuccino and sflogliatella or lip-smacking limoncello with delizia al limone dessert. For the full indulgence grab a table outside but remember it's a lot cheaper and atmospheric consuming *al banco* (at the bar) watching the patrons and smartly attired *baristi*. **Known for:** delicious chocolates, biscotti, and candied fruits; cakes galore including torta Caprese, pastiera, and colomba; tables on the piazza. *Average main: €6 Piazza Duomo 40, Amalfi 089/871065 www.pasticceriapansa.it.*

Hotels

Albergo Sant'Andrea

$$ | **HOTEL** | Just across from the magnificent steps leading to Amalfi's cathedral, this tiny, family-run *pensione* has a cute "Room with a View" lobby that's as big as a Victorian closet and guest rooms (most overlooking the Duomo) that range from cozy to vast. **Pros:** great location on the main square; friendly, reliable budget option; divine Duomo views. **Cons:** on the piazza, so expect noise; simple, dated decor; steep flight of steps to entrance. *Rooms from: €150 Via Duca Mansone I, Amalfi 089/871145 www.albergosantandrea.it Closed Feb. and Mar. 8 rooms Free Breakfast.*

★ Grand Hotel Convento di Amalfi

$$$$ | **HOTEL** | This fabled medieval monastery was lauded by such guests as Longfellow and Wagner, and though recently modernized, it still retains some of its historic charm, including Victorian lecterns, Savonarola chairs, and a celebrated Arab-Sicilian cloister; once stark monk cells are now comfy contemporary

guest room cocoons, some with wicker settees and beds. **Pros:** a slice of paradise; sublime terrace and garden walkways; impeccable service. **Cons:** limited dining options; a 10-minute walk to town; traditionalists will miss some of its old-world charm. *Rooms from: €1071 Via Annunziatella 46, Amalfi 089/8736711 www.ghconventodiamalfi.com Closed Jan.–mid-Mar. 53 rooms Free Breakfast.*

Hotel Amalfi

$$ | HOTEL | Up a tiny side street not far from the Piazza Duomo, the unassuming Hotel Amalfi offers decent value in the heart of Amalfi; though rooms are standard and somewhat characterless, expect a friendly welcome and a roof terrace where you can breakfast in the warm morning sun. **Pros:** great central location; leafy lemon-scented garden; best rooms have balcony views, one has a whirlpool tub. **Cons:** no access without negotiating steps; basic breakfast; rooms are not very exciting. *Rooms from: €160 Via dei Pastai 3, Amalfi 089/872440 www.hamalfi.it 40 rooms Free Breakfast.*

Hotel Aurora

$$$ | HOTEL | This well-run little hotel is a good deal for those who prefer absorbing rays on the beach to hiking the highlands; ask for a room with a sea view and private terrace. **Pros:** away from the madding crowds; ideal for a beach-based trip; verdant breakfast terrace. **Cons:** smaller rooms are a bit cramped; car access is a problem; a bit of a walk to town. *Rooms from: €209 Piazzale dei Protontini 7, between Scalo d'Oriente and Lungomare dei Cavalieri, Amalfi 089/871209 www.aurora-hotel.it Closed Nov.–Mar. 29 rooms Free Breakfast.*

Hotel Floridiana

$$ | HOTEL | The one-time residence of Pisani (in the 12th century) has simple and comfortable rooms with historical touches—look for the frescoed ceiling in the former ballroom, now the dining room. **Pros:** rooftop whirlpool tub; in the heart of the ancient marine town; interesting excursions can be arranged. **Cons:** unreliable air-conditioning; the mezzanine rooms not for everybody; the rooms face inward, no sea view. *Rooms from: €170 Via Brancia 1, Amalfi 089/8736373 www.hotelfloridiana.it Closed Nov.–Mar. 13 rooms Free Breakfast.*

Hotel Luna Convento

$$$$ | HOTEL | Founded as a convent in 1222, allegedly by St. Francis of Assisi himself, the hotel has coved ceilings, graceful arches, marble columns, Flemish artwork, religious artifacts, antique furnishings, and mosaic flooring—all of which blend seamlessly with modern comforts. **Pros:** dripping with history; 270-degree view; secluded bathing area. **Cons:** due for a refurb; roadside rooms noisy; seawater pool is across a busy road from the hotel. *Rooms from: €360 Via P. Comite 33, Amalfi 089/871002 www.lunahotel.it Closed Jan.–mid-Mar. 43 rooms Free Breakfast.*

Hotel Marina Riviera

$$$$ | HOTEL | This hotel graces a coastal promontory, once the site of fisherman's cottages, in Amalfi town itself, so many of the rooms and the breakfast terrace have dreamy views. **Pros:** to-die-for views; wonderful pool; special breakfast balcony views. **Cons:** fronts busy road; high price for the location; entrance difficult to find. *Rooms from: €396 Via Pantaleone Comite 19, Amalfi 089/871104 www.marinariviera.it Closed Nov.–Mar. 34 rooms Free Breakfast.*

Hotel Santa Caterina

$$$$ | HOTEL | Owned by the Gargano family for generations, this quietly elegant, supremely comfortable hotel has long been one of the treasures of the coast; indeed, it once served as a romantic escape for Elizabeth Taylor and Richard

Burton. **Pros:** gorgeous terrace gardens with secluded suites; wonderful view of the town; fab sea-level pool area where you might see staff catching octopus. **Cons:** exorbitantly priced food and drink; formal and rather overattentive service; away from the main town. *Rooms from: €1122* ✉ *Strada Amalfitana 9, Amalfi* ☎ *089/871012* 🌐 *www.hotelsantacaterina.it* *Closed Nov.–mid-Mar.* *66 rooms* *Free Breakfast.*

Nightlife

Amalfi doesn't have many clubs for music or dancing. However, flyers and posters often go up announcing concerts and theatricals during the peak summer months.

Marina Grande Lounge Bar
COCKTAIL LOUNGES | Part of the Marina Grande restaurant and beach club, this bar is a great spot to toast the waves with a cocktail, *aperitivo,* or glass of wine. ✉ *Viale della Regione 4, Amalfi* ☎ *089/871129* 🌐 *www.ristorantemarinagrande.com.*

Shopping

Leading off from Piazza Duomo is the main street of Amalfi, Via Lorenzo d'Amalfi, which is lined with some of the loveliest shops on the coast. While it can be crowded during the day, be sure to take a stroll along here in the evening.

Bazar Florio
LEATHER GOODS | Leather goods are popular items in small shops along the main streets; one good option is Bazar Florio, whose fair and friendly owner's stock includes handbags, wallets, and backpacks. ✉ *Via Pietro Capuano 5/7, Amalfi* ☎ *089/871980* 🌐 *www.amalfibazar.com.*

★ **Cioccolato Andrea Pansa**
CHOCOLATE | Affiliated with the Pasticceria Andrea Pansa bakery and coffee shop just across Piazza Duomo, this tiny chocolate shop packs a sweet punch. All of the confections are handmade in its Piazza Municipio workshop. Try the candied lemon rinds dipped in chocolate, an Amalfi specialty. (Remember: you pay double to eat in.) ✉ *Via Lorenzo d'Amalfi 1, Amalfi* ☎ *089/873282* 🌐 *www.andreapansa.it.*

Edicolé - Mondadori Point
BOOKS | This shop near the tourist office makes a great stop if you're pining for English-language newspapers or need a poolside paperback or a book on Amalfi's history. ✉ *Corso Delle Repubbliche Marinare 17, Amalfi* ☎ *089/871180.*

★ **La Scuderia del Duca**
STATIONERY | A publisher of fine handmade paper, prints, and books, La Scuderia sells beautiful art tomes as well as lovely postcards, hand-crafted leather journals, stationery, desk accessories, and objets d'art. ✉ *Via Cardinale Marino del Giudice, Amalfi* ☎ *089/872976* 🌐 *www.carta-amalfi.it.*

Milleunaceramica
CERAMICS | For a colorful selection of ceramics—many with Arabic influences—by artists in Vietri sul Mare and along the Amalfi Coast, check out this shop on Amalfi's main street. ✉ *Via Pietro Capuano 36, Amalfi* ☎ *089/872670* 🌐 *www.milleunaceramica.com.*

Mostacciuolo
JEWELRY & WATCHES | A well-known and respected family of coral craftsmen has run this shop since 1930. ✉ *Piazza Duomo 22, Amalfi* ☎ *089/871552* 🌐 *coralandcameo.com.*

Atrani

1 km (½ mile) east of Amalfi, 5 km (3 miles) southwest of Ravello.

In some respects this stage-set of a medieval town is a secret treasure: set in a narrow valley between two cliffs, this is the smallest municipality in southern Italy and is refreshingly quiet compared

The heart of the pretty town of Atrani looks for all the world just like an opera set.

to its much more popular neighbor Amalfi. Especially when viewed from the sea, the town looks like an amphitheater ready for a royal pageant. Its closely packed, dollhouse-scale backstreets are filled with pastel-and-white houses and shops, fragrant gardens, arcaded lanes, and spiraling *scalinatelle.* But the hamlet's stellar attractions are its medieval and Baroque churches, which dominate the skyline, as well as its charming beach.

Atrani is often overlooked by tourists, who drive right by it over the riverbed of the Torrente Dragone. It looks little changed from the days when it was closely linked to the Amalfitan republic, the residential choice of its aristocracy. In 1578 it gained its independence from Amalfi, with which it maintains a friendly rivalry.

Pretty Piazza Umberto I, entirely enclosed by four-story houses, is the setting for the basics of Italian life for Atrani's less than 1,000 residents: general store, coffee shop, bar, tabacchi, restaurants, and barber. An arcade to one side offers a glimpse of the beach, fishing boats, and the sea beyond. Often used as a filming location due to its historic character, find a place at a table in the piazza, sit back, and enjoy the authentically old-fashioned setting.

GETTING HERE AND AROUND

Atrani is a 10-minute walk from the eastern outskirts of Amalfi—take the seaside stairs off the drive, just after the tunnel. By car, take the Statale 163 (Amalfitana) from outside Sorrento or Salerno. There's SITA bus service from Amalfi and Salerno. The town itself is highly walkable; Piazza Umberto I is the town center.

Sights

San Salvatore de Birecto

CHURCH | In the Middle Ages, the 10th-century church of San Salvatore de Bireto played an important role in the crowning of new doges for the Republic of Amalfi. The name Birecto likely comes from the Semitic word *biru,* meaning a small stream of water, referring to the fact that the church is built on an arch right over a stream—today a narrow road leading through Atrani. The church was remodeled in the 1800s but has received a careful restoration to reveal some aspects of its medieval past, including Arab-influenced Gothic designs, ancient ceramic tile work, and religious artifacts like a curious 12th-century marble plaque showing two peacocks. The paneled bronze doors cast in the 11th century came from Constantinople, as did the doors in the Amalfi Duomo, both testimonies to the cultural and commercial exchange between the Republic of Amalfi and the Orient. ✉ *Piazza Umberto I, Atrani.*

Santa Maria Maddalena (*Church of Saint Mary Magdalene*)
CHURCH | With its scenic setting on the edge of Atrani with the Amalfi Coast road curving around its base, the Santa Maria Maddalena church certainly has the most eye-catching setting of any building along the coastline. Sixteenth-century paintings attributed to Amalfi Coast artists adorn this church that was built in 1274 and given a Baroque facade in 1852. Majolica tiles cover the dome, and the bell tower has an octagonal belfry similar to the campanile of the Carmine church in Naples. Among the treasures here are the altar, with its richly colored marbles, and the aforementioned paintings, *St. Magdalene between St. Sebastian and St. Andrew* by Giovannangelo D'Amato of Maiori, and *The Incredulity of St. Thomas* by Andrea da Salerno. However, the view from the charming piazza in front of the church is alone worth the climb. ✉ *Via Protopisani, Atrani.*

A' Paranza
$$ | SOUTHERN ITALIAN | Atrani's most reliable option (since 1986), where each day's fare depends entirely on the seafood catch, is an intimate place on the main walkway at the back of the piazza. White coved ceilings and immaculate linens are offset by a colorful naive-art mural of fishermen mending *paranze* (trawler nets). **Known for:** freshest catch of the day; refined yet relaxed; chef's seafood tasting menu. $ *Average main: €22* ✉ *Via Dragone 1/2, Atrani* ☎ *089/871840* 🌐 *www.ristoranteparanza.com* ⏲ *Closed Tues. Sept.–June, and Jan.*

Le Arcate
$$ | SOUTHERN ITALIAN | Under the old fishermen's arches of Atrani you can choose from an extensive menu that features great-value seafood scialatielli, paccheri, and other *primi* as well as 20-odd wood-fired pizza options. Get a table on the large beach-view terrace to lean over and see where your meal came from. **Known for:** bountiful prix-fixe options; beach views and warm hospitality; catch of the day cooked grilled or all'acqua pazza. $ *Average main: €21* ✉ *Largo Buonocore, under arcades of roadway leading down to Atrani's beach, Atrani* ☎ *089/871367* ⏲ *Closed Mon. mid-Sept.–mid-June, and mid-Jan.–mid-Feb.*

Palazzo Ferraioli
$$ | HOTEL | Occupying a 19th-century villa up the steps from Atrani's harbor, this hotel has unrivaled beach vistas and a pop-art design-theme, evident in both the modern lobby and in the colorful, individually designed guest rooms, each one dedicated to a movie actress. **Pros:** spa center; the finest villa in town; solarium views. **Cons:** slightly removed from the action; quirky movie star-pad decor not for all; all those steps. $ *Rooms from: €197* ✉ *Via Campo 16, Atrani* ☎ *089/872652* 🌐 *www.palazzoferraioli.it* ⏲ *Closed mid-Oct.–mid-Apr.* *25 rooms* *Free Breakfast.*

Villa San Michele
$$$ | HOTEL | Built into the rocky shoreline just outside Atrani, this small, friendly, family-run hotel has the feel of a private villa hideaway, one with peaceful, lemon- and flower-scented terraces that tumble down the cliffs and access to the Mar Tirreno waves. **Pros:** fresh simply furnished rooms with balconies; on-site restaurant with terrace views; next to the SITA bus stop. **Cons:** a few rooms only have Juliet balconies; tricky walking the SS163 coastal road especially at night; a lot of steps to tackle. *Rooms from: €210* ✉ *Via Carusiello 2, Atrani* ☎ *089/872237* 🌐 *www.hotel-villasanmichele.it* ⏲ *Closed Nov.–Mar.* *12 rooms* 🍽 *Free Breakfast.*

Ravello

6½ km (4 miles) northeast of Amalfi, 29 km (18 miles) west of Salerno.

Positano may focus on pleasure, and Amalfi on history, but cool, serene Ravello revels in refinement. Thrust over the Bay of Salerno on a mountain promontory, below forests of chestnut and ash, above terraced lemon groves and vineyards, Ravello early on beckoned the affluent with its island-in-the-sky views and secluded defensive positioning. Gardens out of the *Arabian Nights,* pastel *palazzi,* tucked-away piazzas with medieval fountains, architecture ranging from Romano-Byzantine to Norman-Saracen, and those sweeping blue-water, blue-sky vistas have inspired a panoply of large personalities, including Wagner and Boccaccio, princes and popes, aesthetes and hedonists, and a stream of famous authors from Virginia Woolf to Tennessee Williams. Today, many visitors flock here to discover this paradisical place, some to enjoy the town's celebrated music festival, others just to stroll through the hillside streets to gape at the bluer-than-blue panoramas of sea and sky.

At the Villa Rufolo, the noted Ravello Festival is held in its shaded gardens. Here, Wagnerian concerts are often held to pay homage to the great composer, who was inspired by these gardens to compose scenes of *Parsifal.* With the exception of the Villa Rufolo, concerts and the occasional event at the Auditorium Oscar Niemeyer, the hush lingers. Empty, narrow streets morph into whitewashed staircases rising into a haze of azure, which could be from the sea, the sky, or a union of both. About the only places that don't seem to be in slow motion are Piazza Duomo, in front of the cathedral, during the evening passeggiata, or cafés at *pranzo* (luncheon) or *cena* (dinner). The town likes to celebrate religious festivals throughout the year—perhaps the most beautiful is the blossom-strewn celebration of Corpus Domini (usually the end of May or beginning of June), when Piazza del Duomo is ornamented with sidewalk pictures created with flower petals.

GETTING HERE AND AROUND

By car, take the hill road climbing just east of Atrani, or take the Angri exit on the A3 motorway and cross the mountainous Valico di Chiunzi. SITA and City Sightseeing buses make the run up and down the mountain between Ravello and Piazza Flavio Gioia in Amalfi, where you can catch the main Amalfi Drive bus to Sorrento. In Ravello, you can purchase tickets prior to boarding at Bar Calce (Via Boccaccio 11). There are about two buses every hour. Open-top City Sightseeing buses make a dozen or so trips daily from Amalfi (and connect with the more modern beach towns of Minori and Maiori). Piazza del Duomo is the town's central point, with (as you face the Duomo) Via Roma to the left (north), Via San Giovanni del Toro straight ahead (east) up the steps of Via Wagner, and Via dei Rufolo to the right (south). Although cars must park in the municipal lot, most arriving buses deposit their passengers near the hillside tunnel that leads to Piazza del Duomo.

The Perils of the Ravello Bus

Once known as "*la città più tranquilla, solitaria e silenziosa del mondo,*" the mountaintop town of Ravello has been discovered by hordes of tourists, meaning it's not quite so tranquil as it used to be. Nowhere is that more evident than on the bus ride into town. There are one or two buses an hour (depending on the time of day and they stop running early some days) up to Ravello from Amalfi, and each is often crammed to seemingly twice its capacity.

Once the crowds have packed in, the fun really begins, as the bus weaves its way up the mountain. There are so many switchbacks you'll think the bus is going to deposit you back in Amalfi. The road is so narrow in places that it can only alternatively accommodate one-way traffic—of course, the payoff for this trying bus ride is heavenly Ravello. Be sure to get a bus schedule, get to the bus stop early, and don't expect orderly lines.

VISITOR INFORMATION

CONTACTS Azienda Autonoma Soggiorno e Turismo. ✉ *Piazza Fontana Moresca, 10,* ☎ *089/857096.*

Sights

Auditorium Oscar Niemeyer

ARTS CENTER | Crowning Via della Repubblica and the hillside, which overlooks the spectacular Bay of Salerno, Auditorium Niemeyer is a startling piece of modernist architecture. Designed with a dramatically curved, all-white roof by the Brazilian architect Oscar Niemeyer (designer of Brasília), it was conceived as an alternative indoor venue for concerts, including those of the famed summer Ravello Festival, and is now also used as a cinema. The subject of much controversy since its first conception back in 2000, it raised the wrath of some locals who denounced such an ambitious modernist building in medieval Ravello. They need not have worried. The result, inaugurated in 2010, is a design masterpiece—a huge, overhanging canopied roof suspended over a 400-seat concert area, with a giant eye-shape window allowing spectators to contemplate the extraordinary bay vista during performances. ✉ *Via della Repubblica 12, Ravello.*

★ Duomo

CHURCH | Ravello's first bishop, Orso Papiciò, founded this cathedral, dedicated to San Pantaleone, in 1086. Rebuilt in the 12th and 17th centuries, it retains traces of medieval frescoes in the transept, an original mullioned window, a marble portal, and a three-story 13th-century bell tower playfully interwoven with mullioned windows and arches. The 12th-century bronze door has 54 embossed panels depicting Christ's life, and saints, prophets, plants, and animals, all narrating biblical lore. Ancient columns divide the nave's three aisles, and treasures include sarcophagi from Roman times and paintings by the southern Renaissance artist Andrea da Salerno. Most impressive are the two medieval pulpits: the earlier one is inset with a mosaic scene of Jonah and the whale, while the more famous one opposite boasts exquisite mosaic work and six twisting columns sitting on lion pedestals. In the crypt is the **Museo del Duomo**, which displays 13th-century treasures from the reign of Frederick II of Sicily. ✉ *Piazza del Duomo, Ravello* ☎ *089/858311* 🎫 *€3.*

Ravello's History

The town itself was founded in the 9th century, under Amalfi's rule. Residents prosperous from cotton tussled with the superpower republic and elected their own doge in the 11th century; *Amalfitani* dubbed them *ribelli* (rebels). In the 12th century, with the aid of the Norman King Roger, Ravello even succeeded in resisting Pisa's army for a couple of years, though the powerful Pisans returned to wreak destruction along the coast. Even so, Ravello's skilled seafaring trade with merchants and Moors from Sicily and points east led to a burgeoning wealth, which peaked in the 13th century, when there were 13 churches, four cloisters, and dozens of sumptuous villas. Neapolitan princes built palaces and life was privileged.

Ravello's bright light eventually diminished, first through Pisa's maritime rise in the 14th century, then through rivalry between its warring families in the 15th century. When the plague cast its shadow in the 17th century, the population plummeted from upward of 30,000 to perhaps a couple of thousand souls, where it remains today. When Ravello was incorporated into the diocese of Amalfi in 1804, a kind of stillness settled in. Despite the decline of its power and populace, Ravello's cultural heritage and special loveliness continued to blossom. Gardens flowered and music flowed in the ruined villas, and artists, sophisticates, and their lovers filled the crumbling palazzi. Grieg, Wagner, D.H. Lawrence, Chanel, Garbo and her companion, conductor Leopold Stokowski, and then, slowly, tourists, followed in their footsteps.

Giardini del Vescovo (*Monsignore*)
GARDEN | A one-time bishop's residence that dates from at least the 12th century, the Villa Episcopio (formerly Villa di Sangro) today hosts concerts and exhibitions and has an open-air theater in its splendid gardens—the same gardens where André Gide found inspiration for his novel *The Immoralist,* where Italy's King Vittorio Emanuele III abdicated in favor of his son in 1944, and where Jackie Kennedy enjoyed breaks from her obligations as First Lady during a much publicized 1962 visit. Wheelchair access is via a new ramp on via San Giovanni del Toro. ✉ *Via Richard Wagner/Via dei Episcopio, Ravello* 🎫 *Free.*

Mamma Agata
SCHOOL | If you fancy learning how to make some of the things you've been eating, Mamma Agata, who has cooked for Elizabeth Taylor, Federico Fellini, Jackie Kennedy, and Marcello Mastroianni, will take you into her kitchen—with the almost obligatory stunning view—and walk you through the preparation of the area's pasta dishes and sweets. A morning session is followed by lunch—that you will have seen made. ✉ *Piazza San Cosma 9, Ravello* ☎ *089/857845* 🌐 *www.mammaagata.com* 🎫 *Cooking class and lunch cost €250* ⏲ *Closed weekends, and Nov.–mid-Mar.*

Monastero di Santa Chiara (*Monastery of St. Clare*)
RELIGIOUS BUILDING | Along the path to the Villa Cimbrone lies this 13th-century monastery. The majolica flooring is one of its special elements, along with the matronaeum, or women's gallery, the only one left on the Amalfi Coast. Although the monastery is only open to the public for the early-morning Sunday service and special events (such as the Festa di Santa

The view from Villa Cimbrone's Belvedere of Infinity may be the finest on the coast.

Chiara on August 11), the wheel used to deliver food (and at one time unwanted children) to the nuns is just inside the entrance and can be seen anytime. ✉ *Via Santa Chiara 9, Ravello* ✥ *Near entrance of Villa Cimbrone* 🌐 *www.sorelleclarisseravello.it.*

★ **Museo del Corallo** (*Coral Museum*)
ART MUSEUM | To the left of the Duomo, the entrance to this private museum is through the tempting shop CAMO, and both are the creation of master-craftsman-in-residence Giorgio Filocamo. The museum celebrates the venerable tradition of Italian workmanship in coral, harvested in bygone centuries from the gulfs of Salerno and Naples and crafted into jewelry, cameos, and figurines. The fascinating collection, not confined solely to coral work, includes a painting of Sisto IV from the 14th century. Look also in particular for a carved Christ from the 17th century, for which the J. Paul Getty Museum offered $525,000 in 1987 (the offer was refused), and a tobacco box covered in cameos, one of only two in the world. There is also a statue of the Madonna dating to 1532. Giorgio has crafted coral for Pope John Paul II, the Clintons, and Princess Caroline, as well as numerous Hollywood stars. ✉ *Piazza Duomo 9, Ravello* ☎ *089/857461* 🌐 *www.museodelcorallo.com* 🎫 *Free.*

Piazza Fontana Moresca
PLAZA/SQUARE | Below the Hotel Parsifal in the center of a traffic circle stand two stone lions on a fanciful 1,000-year-old fountain that still spews water into a ciborium basin taken from the Duomo. Unfortunately, the lions are reproductions; the originals were stolen years ago. Just beyond the fountain along Via Lacco there's a viewpoint taking in the coastline and down the valley to the town of Maiori. ✉ *Viale Gioacchino d'Anna, near Via Lacco, Ravello.*

San Giovanni del Toro
CHURCH | Across the tiny piazza from the Hotel Caruso is the noted 11th-century church of San Giovanni del Toro. Its evocative interior has three high apses and a crypt with 14th-century frescoes of

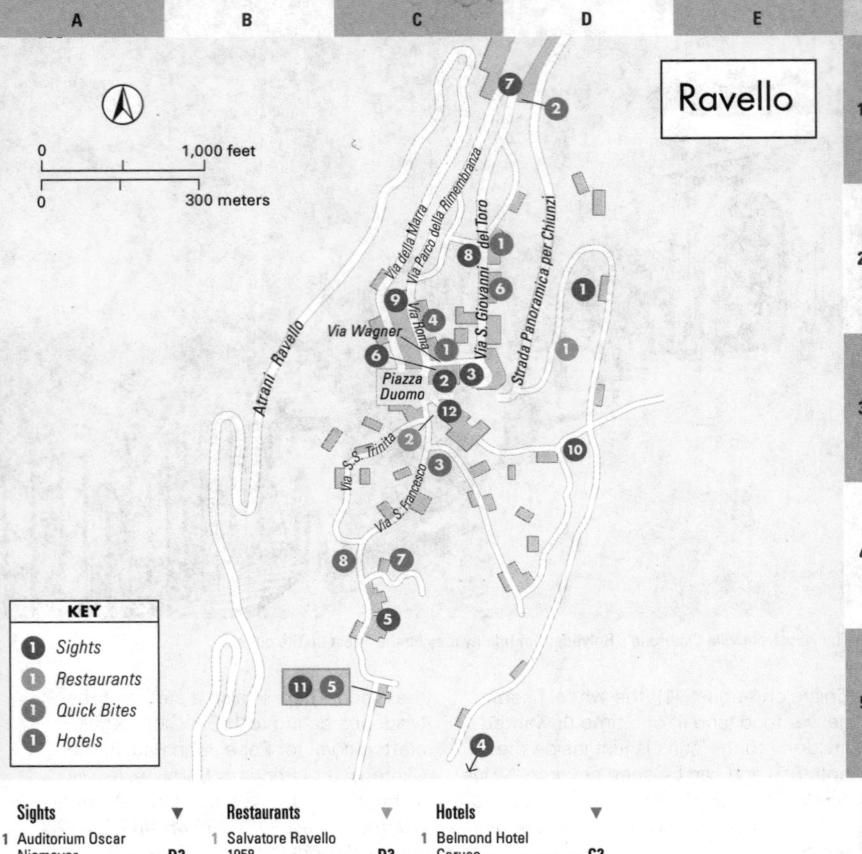

Sights

1 Auditorium Oscar Niemeyer **D2**
2 Duomo **C3**
3 Giardini del Vescovo **C3**
4 Mamma Agata **C5**
5 Monastero di Santa Chiara **C4**
6 Museo del Corallo **C3**
7 Piazza Fontana Moresca **D1**
8 San Giovanni del Toro ... **C2**
9 Santa Maria a Gradillo..................... **C2**
10 Santissima Annunziata **D3**
11 Villa Cimbrone............ **C5**
12 Villa Rufolo................ **C3**

Restaurants

1 Salvatore Ravello 1958...................... **D3**
2 Vittoria **C3**

Quick Bites

1 Giardini Caffè Calce **C3**

Hotels

1 Belmond Hotel Caruso **C2**
2 Hotel Parsifal............ **D1**
3 Hotel Rufolo **C3**
4 Hotel Toro.................. **C2**
5 Hotel Villa Cimbrone **C5**
6 Palazzo Avino **C2**
7 Villa Amore **C4**
8 Villa Maria Hotel......... **C4**

Christ and the apostles. A 12th-century *ambo* (pulpit) by Alfano da Termoli startles the eye with its blue Persian majolica and four columns topped with elaborate capitals. The chapel of the Coppola family in the left aisle has an exceptional 14th-century relief of St. Catherine of Alexandria. The small church's three porticos adorned with lunettes show an Arabian influence, and the tripartite back facade is exquisite. Restoration work on the church commenced in 2003, with no sign of being completed. The church has some erratic summer opening hours; inquire about them at the Duomo or Azienda Autonoma Soggiorno e Turismo. ✉ *Piazza San Giovanni del Toro, Ravello.*

Santa Maria a Gradillo

CHURCH | A 13th-century church with a graceful dome, Santa Maria a Gradillo was where the town noblemen gathered to discuss civic issues; its atrium collapsed in the 18th century. The small Sicilian-Saracenic bell tower has two light mullion windows. Ask about the church's most current opening hours at Duomo or Azienda Autonoma Soggiorno e Turismo. ✉ *Via Gradillo, Ravello.*

Santissima Annunziata

RELIGIOUS BUILDING | With its oft-photographed bell towers and scenic location below Villa Rufolo, the deconsecrated church of Santissima Annunziata is one of Ravello's most recognizable features, dating from the 13th century, when it was constructed for the wealthy Fusco family. The adjoining oratory was the 15th-century seat of the flagellating Confraternity of Battent. The church is generally closed to the public except for special events, such as performances by the Ravello Concert Society (check the website for upcoming recitals). For an up-close look at the exterior, exit the Villa Rufolo and take a sharp right to reach the Via dell'Annunziata stair path, which plummets you down the hillside right past the church and to the scenic Via della Repubblica. ✉ *Via dell' Annunziata, Ravello* ✣ *Located down approximately 90 steps from entrance of Villa Rufolo* 🌐 *www.ravelloarts.org.*

★ Villa Cimbrone

GARDEN | To the south of Ravello's main square, a somewhat hilly 15-minute walk along Via San Francesco brings you to Ravello's showstopper, the Villa Cimbrone, whose dazzling gardens perch 1,500 feet above the sea. This medieval-style fantasy was created in 1905 by England's Lord Grimthorpe and made world famous in the 1930s when Greta Garbo found sanctuary from the press here. The Gothic *castello-palazzo* sits amid idyllic gardens that are divided by the grand Avenue of Immensity pathway, leading in turn to the literal high point of any trip to the Amalfi Coast—the **Belvedere of Infinity**. This grand stone parapet, adorned with stone busts, overlooks the entire Bay of Salerno and frames a panorama the late writer Gore Vidal, a longtime Ravello resident, described as the most beautiful in the world. The villa itself is now a five-star hotel. ✉ *Via Santa Chiara 26, Ravello* ☎ *089/857459* 🌐 *www.villacimbrone.it* 🎫 *€7.*

★ Villa Rufolo

GARDEN | Directly off Ravello's main piazza is the Villa Rufolo, home to some of the most spectacular gardens in Italy, framing a stunning vista of the Bay of Salerno, often called the "bluest view in the world." If one believes the master storyteller Boccaccio, the villa was built in the 13th century by Landolfo Rufolo, whose immense fortune stemmed from trade with the Moors and the Saracens. Norman and Arab architecture mingle in a welter of color-filled gardens so lush the composer Richard Wagner used them as inspiration for Klingsor's Garden, the home of the Flower Maidens, in his opera *Parsifal*. Beyond the Arab-Sicilian cloister and the Norman tower lie the two terrace gardens. The lower one, the "Wagner Terrace," is often the site of Ravello Festival concerts. Highlights of the house are its Moorish cloister—an

Arabic-Sicilian delight with interlacing lancet arcs and polychromatic palmette decoration—and the 14th-century Torre Maggiore, or Klingsor's Tower. ✉ *Piazza del Duomo, Ravello* ☎ *089/857621* 🌐 *www.villarufolo.it* 🎫 *€7, extra charge for concerts.*

Restaurants

Salvatore Ravello 1958
$$ | SOUTHERN ITALIAN | Adjacent to the Hotel Graal and sharing the same glorious view of the Bay of Salerno, this restaurant has a large terrace and a contemporary-styled dining area beside an open kitchen. Seasonal Campanian produce is transformed into some of the most exquisite plates in town, and the friendly staff knows their *fagioli.* **Known for:** artistic presentation; daily specials might include seasonal rabbit, lamb, tuna; unusual, tasty bread options. $ *Average main: €24* ✉ *Via della Repubblica 2, Ravello* ☎ *089/857227* ⏲ *Closed Mon. in winter.*

Vittoria
$$ | PIZZA | FAMILY | Just south of the Duomo, this airy, unfussy place with coved stone ceilings is a good bet for an informal bite. The *pizza al forno di legna* with fresh toppings is the star attraction: locals praise it, and even Gore Vidal allegedly approved. **Known for:** Campanian classics, including seafood frittura and eggplant parmigiana; very popular with locals and tourists; extensive menu. $ *Average main: €20* ✉ *Via dei Rufolo 3, Ravello* ☎ *089/857947* 🌐 *www.ristorantepizzeriavittoria.it.*

Coffee and Quick Bites

Giardini Caffè Calce
$ | SOUTHERN ITALIAN | Right on Piazza Duomo, this café is a popular pit-stop for coffee, *sfogliatelle* pastries, and ice cream, as well as simple pasta dishes, salads, and *pizze.* With an alfresco area and three guest rooms, this is a favorite of locals and visitors alike. **Known for:** tranquil garden and covered area; haven from the piazza throng; good for a leisurely snack. $ *Average main: €10* ✉ *Via Wagner 3, Ravello* ☎ *329/9756500 mobile.*

Hotels

Belmond Hotel Caruso
$$$$ | HOTEL | In a grand palazzo on the highest point of Ravello, with some buildings dating from the 16th century and with a Bay of Salerno panorama that's incomparable and timeless, this member of the exclusive Belmond hotel brand has been a slice of hospitality paradise since the 19th century; today, it shimmers with modern luxuries amid its frescoes, Norman arches, and beautifully terraced garden. **Pros:** infinity pool; spacious suites with terraces; complimentary boat and shuttle services. **Cons:** service can be inconsistent; overrated restaurant; out of most visitors' price range. $ *Rooms from: €2375* ✉ *Piazza San Giovanni del Toro 2, Ravello* ☎ *089/858801* 🌐 *www.hotelcaruso.com* ⏲ *Closed Nov.–mid-Apr.* 🛏 *50 rooms* 🍴 *Free Breakfast.*

Hotel Parsifal
$$ | HOTEL | In 1288, this diminutive property overlooking the coastline housed an order of Augustinian friars; today the intact cloister hosts travelers intent on enjoying themselves under the coved ceilings of the former *eremitani scalzi* (shaved hermit) cells. **Pros:** staying in a former Ravello convent; open year-round; charming manager and his family dote on Americans. **Cons:** minimum three-night stay in some periods; tiny rooms; some may not like the '70's vibe. $ *Rooms from: €190* ✉ *Viale Gioacchino d'Anna 5, Ravello* ☎ *089/857144* 🌐 *www.hotelparsifal.com* 🛏 *17 rooms* 🍴 *Free Breakfast.*

Hotel Rufolo
$$$ | HOTEL | FAMILY | The quarters might be snug and simply furnished, but many have balconies with gorgeous sea and

sky vistas framed by the palm trees of the Villa Rufolo, just below the hotel. **Pros:** parking included in room rates; beautiful views over Villa Rufolo; great pool and spa services. **Cons:** dated decor; overpriced: paying for the location; car park clutters the entrance. *Rooms from: €275 Via San Francesco 1, Ravello 089/857133 www.hotelrufolo.it Closed Jan.–Mar. 34 rooms Free Breakfast.*

Hotel Toro

$$ | **HOTEL** | Two minutes from the Duomo, this relaxing, good-value, little place with a garden, antiques, and a history that includes stays by some illustrious artistic guests (e.g., the composer Edvard Grieg and the artist M.S. Escher) has been family-run for three generations. **Pros:** a small piece of Ravello's artistic history; very central; friendly, helpful staff. **Cons:** space rather cramped; may lack finesse for some; long flight of steps to climb. *Rooms from: €150 Via Roma 16, Ravello 089/857211 www.hoteltoro.it Closed Nov.–mid-Apr. 10 rooms Free Breakfast.*

★ **Hotel Villa Cimbrone**

$$$$ | **HOTEL** | Suspended over the azure sea and set amid legendary rose-filled gardens, this Gothic-style castle was once home to Lord Grimthorpe and a hideaway for Greta Garbo; since the 1990s, it's been an exclusive if pricey visitors haven, with guest rooms ranging from palatial to cozy. **Pros:** gorgeous pool and views; top-rated restaurant; surrounded by beautiful gardens. **Cons:** special place comes at a price; daily arrival of respectful day-trippers; a longish hike from town center (porters can help with luggage). *Rooms from: €750 Via Santa Chiara 26, Ravello 089/857459 www.villacimbrone.com Closed Nov.–mid-Apr. 19 rooms Free Breakfast.*

Palazzo Avino

$$$$ | **HOTEL** | Once home to the aristocratic Sasso family, this 12th-century palazzo—replete with a marble lobby (the former chapel), rooftop hot tubs, and a waterfall—once hosted a *Parsifal*-absorbed Wagner and was a 1950s hideaway for Ingrid Bergman and director Roberto Rossellini. **Pros:** beach Club House 15-minute drive away; stunning pool and terraces; a serene retreat dripping in history. **Cons:** some rooms tiny; overrated restaurant and overpriced food; out of most travelers' price range. *Rooms from: €1194 Via San Giovanni del Toro 28, Ravello 089/818181 www.palazzoavino.com Closed Nov.–Mar. 43 rooms Free Breakfast.*

Villa Amore

$$$ | **HOTEL** | A 10-minute walk from the Piazza Duomo, this secluded hotel with a garden is family-run and shares the same exhilarating view of the Bay of Salerno as Ravello's most expensive hotels. **Pros:** wonderful views; good value restaurant; inexpensive alternative to its illustrious neighbors. **Cons:** long flight of steps to reach entrance; some rooms are very cramped and without views; away from the main drag. *Rooms from: €210 Via dei Fusco 5, Ravello 089/857135 www.villaamore.it Closed Nov.–Mar. 12 rooms Free Breakfast.*

Villa Maria Hotel

$$$ | **HOTEL** | Hued in glowing terracotta, adorned with gorgeous flowers, and fronted by a vast garden terrace, the Villa Maria offers more sunny warmth than Ravello's more formal hotels—not to mention a delightfully friendly staff (thanks to the hands-on management of the Palumbo family) and a convenient restaurant. **Pros:** friendly staff; gorgeous restaurant terrace; spacious rooms. **Cons:** pool is at the adjacent hotel; tricky access via steps; most rooms face the valley, not the coast. *Rooms from: €250 Via Santa Chiara 2, Ravello 089/857255 www.villamaria.it Closed Nov.–mid-Mar. 23 rooms Free Breakfast.*

Did You Know?

Ravello's Villa Cimbrone, with some of the most heralded gardens along the Amalfi Coast, was where Greta Garbo chose to hide from the press in 1937.

Performing Arts

Unless there's an event at the Auditorium Oscar Niemeyer, there's little nightlife activity other than the concerts offered by the Ravello Concert Society and the Ravello Festival. A few cafés and bars are scattered about, but the general peacefulness extends to evening hours. Hotels and restaurants may offer live music and can advise you about the few nightclubs, but around these parts the sound is soft and classical—or silence.

★ Ravello Concert Society
CONCERTS | The society runs a yearlong program at the Annunziata concert venue, the Ravello Art Centre (formerly the Grand Caruso Wine Cellars), and elsewhere, including places in the neighboring town of Scala. Most concerts are held at 8:30 pm, with occasional performances starting at 6:30 pm. ✉ *Ravello* ☎ *089/8424082* 🌐 *www.ravelloarts.org.*

Shopping

★ Ceramiche d'Arte Carmela
CERAMICS | The store ships its Vietri-made and other hand-painted ceramics all over the world. Bargaining might result in a discount of 10% or even more if you have a talent for it. There are also opportunities for gaining hands-on experience at the showroom and workshop, a three-minute walk away in a courtyard at Via Roma 20. ✉ *Via dei Rufolo 16, Ravello* ☎ *089/857303* 🌐 *www.ceramichedarte-carmela.com.*

Gruppo Petit Prince
ART GALLERIES | Between March and October, this shop sells colorful stationery, prints, and artworks amid the Gothic cloisters of the Complesso Monumentale San Francesco. There's also an attractive branch in Piazza Duomo at the corner of Via Roma. ✉ *Via San Francesco 9, Ravello* ☎ *089/858033* 🌐 *www.gruppopetitprince.it.*

★ Ravello Gusti & Delizie
FOOD | This *oleoteca* is *the* place to taste and shop for the costiera's finest extra virgin olive oil as well as quality *oro verde* from other regions. You'll also find delicacies from all over Italy, including intriguing lemon products—candies, candles, soaps, and even lemon honey. ✉ *Via Roma 28/30, Ravello* ☎ *089/857802.*

Cetara

3 km (2 miles) northeast of Erchie, 4 km (2½ miles) southwest of Vietri.

Tourists tend to take a pass on the village of Cetara. A quiet fishing village below orange groves on Monte Falerzo, it was held in subjugation to greater powers, like most of these coastal sites, throughout much of its history. From its days as a Saracen stronghold in the 9th century, it became the final holding of Amalfi at the eastern edge of the republic, which all through the 11th and 12th centuries tithed part of Cetara's fishing catch, *ius piscariae*—the town's claim to fame. It is rumored that the village's Latin name comes from this big catch—*cetaria* (tuna net), though Cetara is more renowned these days for its anchovies. Thousands of years ago, salted and strained, they became a spicy liquid called *garum*, a delicacy to the rich of ancient Rome. Garum, as well as the lighter *colatura di alici*, can be purchased at local grocery stores or at Cetarii, on the beachfront.

GETTING HERE AND AROUND

By car, take the Statale 163 (Amalfitana) from outside Sorrento or Salerno, or take the Angri exit on the A3 motorway and cross the mountainous Valico di Chiunzi. The SITA bus line runs here from Amalfi and Salerno. The town's only road leads to the beach.

Paestum is the site of remarkably well-preserved Greek temples, including the Tempio di Cerere.

Sights

Back in the days of the Caesars, this little town was known for its outstanding seafood and its special garum recipe, which is a funky fish sauce similar to what's used in Asian cuisine today. Gourmands still flock here to eat like emperors, while others head here because the waterfront is so delightfully laid-back and "real." Other than the charmingly scenic waterfront, there are no sights of note, other than the church of San Pietro, near the harbor.

Chiesa Parrocchiale di San Pietro Apostolo
CHURCH | Dedicated to Cetara's patron saint, the church of San Pietro Apostolo has its origins in 988, its vibrant majolica-tiled cupola soaring over Neoclassical exteriors visible all around Cetara. Set in the Borgo Marinaro fishing quarter and suitably dedicated to the protector of fisherman, the church's bronze doors (inaugurated in 2005) by Battisto Marello (1948-) depict the saint with keys to the Kingdom of Heaven beside brother Sant'Andrea holding fishing nets and writhing fish. See if you can spot Christ overseeing all in the background. Popping into focus among the late Baroque interiors of marble-work, statuary and painting is a wonderful, recent stained glass window addition (1993). Center stage again are the fraternal apostles amid a Saint Peter's Basilica in Rome, Cetara skyline, sheep, and busy fishing folk. ✉ *Piazza S. Pietro, Cetara* ☎ *089/2595060* 🎫 *Free.*

Beaches

Cetara
BEACH | A medieval Norman tower provides a spectacular landmark for this beach on Cetara's picturesque marina. With blue-and-white boats lying on the sand, anchovy-fishing boats in the harbor, and children playing in the adjacent park, the beach is a hive of activity—stretch out your towel and enjoy the buzz. The water here is clean, and the lido has a cool bar and sun beds for rent. The sun shines here until late afternoon, so if you stay long enough that hunger strikes, try the fried anchovies in the Cuopperia on

the marina. Served in paper cones, *cuoppi* are the local fast food. **Amenities:** food and drink; lifeguards; showers; toilets. **Best for:** snorkeling; swimming. ✉ *Via Marina, Cetara.*

Restaurants

Acqua Pazza

$$ | SEAFOOD | Locals along this part of the coast rave about this tiny restaurant a short stroll up from the harbor. The environment is modest—a spare interior with a few tables—but the seafood served is remarkably fresh. **Known for:** catch of the day cooked all'acqua pazza; seasonal seafood menu; linguine alla colatura di alici. *Average main: €23 ✉ Via Garibaldi 38, Cetara ☎ 089/261606 🌐 www.acquapazza.it ⏲ Closed Mon. mid-Oct.–mid-Apr.*

Al Convento

$$ | SOUTHERN ITALIAN | FAMILY | Occupying part of a former convent, this restaurant opened in the 1960s receives glowing reviews for its varied and tasty preparations involving anchovies. For the adventurous there are dishes such as spaghetti *con colatura* (with a modern version of garum); less adventurous types can try one of the excellent pizzas made in a wood-fired oven. **Known for:** adventurous misto di colatura dish; veggie, Fiorentina steak and pizza options; low-key yet ethereal ambience. *Average main: €20 ✉ Piazza San Francesco 16, Cetara ☎ 089/261039 🌐 www.alconvento.net ⏲ Closed Wed. Oct.–Apr.*

Hotels

Cetus

$$$ | HOTEL | Cetara's leading hotel is set in a white stucco building that seems to have emerged right out of the rock in the cliffs above the beach; an on-site restaurant has a breathtaking terrace and excellent seafood. **Pros:** epic vistas floating above the sea; private beach away from the crowds; spacious airy rooms all with sea views. **Cons:** not ideal for walking; steep descent to beach; 350 yards from town along Amalfi Drive. *Rooms from: €260 ✉ Corso Umberto I 1, Cetara ☎ 089/261388 🌐 www.hotelcetus.com 37 rooms Free Breakfast.*

Shopping

★ Cetarii

FOOD | At this shop opened in 1995, you can buy a bottle of *colatura di alici* (achovy sauce) and various types of tuna *sott'olio* amid a cornucopia of quality products sourced locally and from father reaches of the Mezzogiorno. ✉ *Via Largo Marina 48/50, Cetara ☎ 089/261863 🌐 www.cetarii.it.*

Paestum

56 km (27 miles) southeast of Cetara, 44 km (25 miles) southeast of Salerno, 99 km (62 miles) southeast of Naples.

For history buffs, a visit to Campania is not complete without seeing the ancient ruins of Paestum. A visit to the ruins to stroll past the incredibly well-preserved temples and see the top-notch collection at the Museo Nazionale is a great day trip from the Amalfi Coast or Naples.

The archaeological ruins can be reached via train as the Paestum train station (Stazione di Paestum) is located about 800 yards from the ruins. Access can be gained through the perfectly preserved archway **Porta Sirena,** or—if driving—through the northern gate of **Porta Aurea.**

GETTING HERE AND AROUND

By car, take the A3 motorway south from Salerno, take the Battipaglia exit to SS18. Exit at Capaccio Scala. Take a CSTP or SCAT bus hourly from Salerno or the State railway from Salerno or Naples.

VISITOR INFORMATION

CONTACTS Azienda Autonoma Soggiorno e Turismo di Paestum. (*Paestum Tourist Office*) ✉ *Via Magna Grecia 887,* ☎ *0828/811016* 🌐 *www.infopaestum.it.*

Sights

★ Greek Temples

RUINS | One of Italy's most majestic sights lies on the edge of a flat coastal plain: the remarkably preserved Greek temples of Paestum. This is the site of the ancient city of Poseidonia, founded by Greek colonists probably in the 6th century BC. When the Romans took it over in 273 BC, they Latinized the name to Paestum and changed the layout of the settlement, adding an amphitheater and a forum. Much of the archaeological material found on the site is displayed in the Museo Nazionale, and several rooms are devoted to the unique tomb paintings—rare examples of Greek and pre-Roman pictorial art—discovered in the area.

At the northern end of the site opposite the ticket barrier is the Tempio di Cerere (Temple of Ceres). Built in about 500 BC, it is thought to have been originally dedicated to the goddess Athena. Follow the road south past the Foro Romano (Roman Forum) to the Tempio di Nettuno (Temple of Poseidon), a showstopping Doric edifice with 36 fluted columns and an entablature (the area above the capitals) that rivals those of the finest temples in Greece. Beyond is the so-called Basilica. It dates from the early 6th century BC. The name is an 18th-century misnomer, though, since it was, in fact, a temple to Hera, the wife of Zeus. Try to see the temples in the early morning or late afternoon when the stone takes on a golden hue. ✉ *Via Magna Grecia, Paestum* ☎ *0828/811023 ticket office* 🌐 *www.museopaestum.beniculturali.it* 🎫 *Site and museum: Mar.-Nov. €12, Dec.-Feb. €6.*

★ Tenuta Vannulo—Buffalo Farm and Shop

FARM/RANCH | **FAMILY** | Foodies, families, and the curious flock to this novel farm attraction that celebrates humane animal husbandry, organic mozzarella di bufala, and other wonderful products. A tour of the ranch run by the Palmieri family—headed by the serene octogenerian Antonio—brings you nose to glistening snout with probably the most pampered buffalo in the world. Some 600 of them wallow in pools, get a mechanical massage, and flap their ears to classical music. The shop/restaurant is the place to taste and take away cheese, ice cream, yogurt, chocolate, and leather products. ✉ *Contrada Vannulo, Via Galileo Galilei 101, Capaccio, Paestum* ☎ *0828/727894* 🌐 *www.vannulo.it* 🎫 *€5 guided tours; book in advance.*

Hotels

Azienda Agrituristica Seliano

$$ | **B&B/INN** | At this working farm about 3 km (2 miles) from Paestum's Greek temples, befriend the resident dogs so they will accompany you on country walks or bike rides, and opt for half-board to enjoy home-produced mozzarella and rich buffalo stew; you'll dine at a table with other guests before withdrawing to your charming wood-beamed guest room in one of the 19th-century baronial buildings. **Pros:** a great taste of a working farm; cooking classes; a banquet every evening. **Cons:** rustic, dated decor; not for non–dog fans; confusing to find. 💲 *Rooms from: €140* ✉ *Via Seliano, Paestum* ☎ *0828/723634* 🌐 *www.agriturismoseliano.it* ⏲ *Closed Nov.–Mar.* 🛏 *14 rooms* 🍽 *Free Breakfast.*

Chapter 4

CAPRI, ISCHIA, AND PROCIDA

Updated by
Fergal Kavanagh

Sights ★★★★★ | Restaurants ★★★★★ | Hotels ★★★★★ | Shopping ★★★★☆ | Nightlife ★★★☆☆

WELCOME TO CAPRI, ISCHIA, AND PROCIDA

TOP REASONS TO GO

★ **The living room of the world:** Pose oh-so-casually with the beautiful people sipping Campari on La Piazzetta, the central crossroads of Capri Town, a stage-set square that always seems ready for a gala performance.

★ **Spa-laden Ischia:** Ischia has gorgeous spas famed for their seaweed soaks and fango mud cures.

★ **Marina di Corricella, Procida:** Tiny Procida has numerous harbors, but none will have you reaching for your camera as quickly as this rainbow-hued, horizontal version of Positano.

★ **Anacapri's Heights:** Be sure to be nice to the bus driver when you take the precipitously steep road up to Capri's blufftop village—you're nearly a thousand feet above the Bay of Naples here.

★ **Island bounty:** Feast on Capri's ravioli, salad, and chocolate cake, Ischia's wild rabbit, Procida's sweet lemon *lingua di bue* (cow's tongue)—and of course seafood aplenty.

1 Capri. Capri is a balmy destination that has been the darling of tourism for 2,500 years. Although its hotels and restaurants rank among the priciest around, its incomparable views and natural wonders are free, as are all of the drop-dead gorgeous walking trails. Sadly for your wallet, though, a visit of just a few days might not be enough.

2 Ischia. More than twice the size of Capri, lesser-known Ischia has paradisial white-sand beaches, thermal hot-spring spas, and fewer day-trippers. Its medieval castle on its own island is one of the loveliest locations on the planet. Neapolitans vacation here (for up to two months!), so Ischia is an authentic Italian experience.

3 Procida. Although it's a short trip, 3 km (2 miles) from the mainland, this little volcanic outcropping remained a secret to many until it was declared the 2022 Italian Capital of Culture. Sun, cliffs, and sea combine to create the distinctive atmosphere so memorably immortalized in the film *Il Postino*.

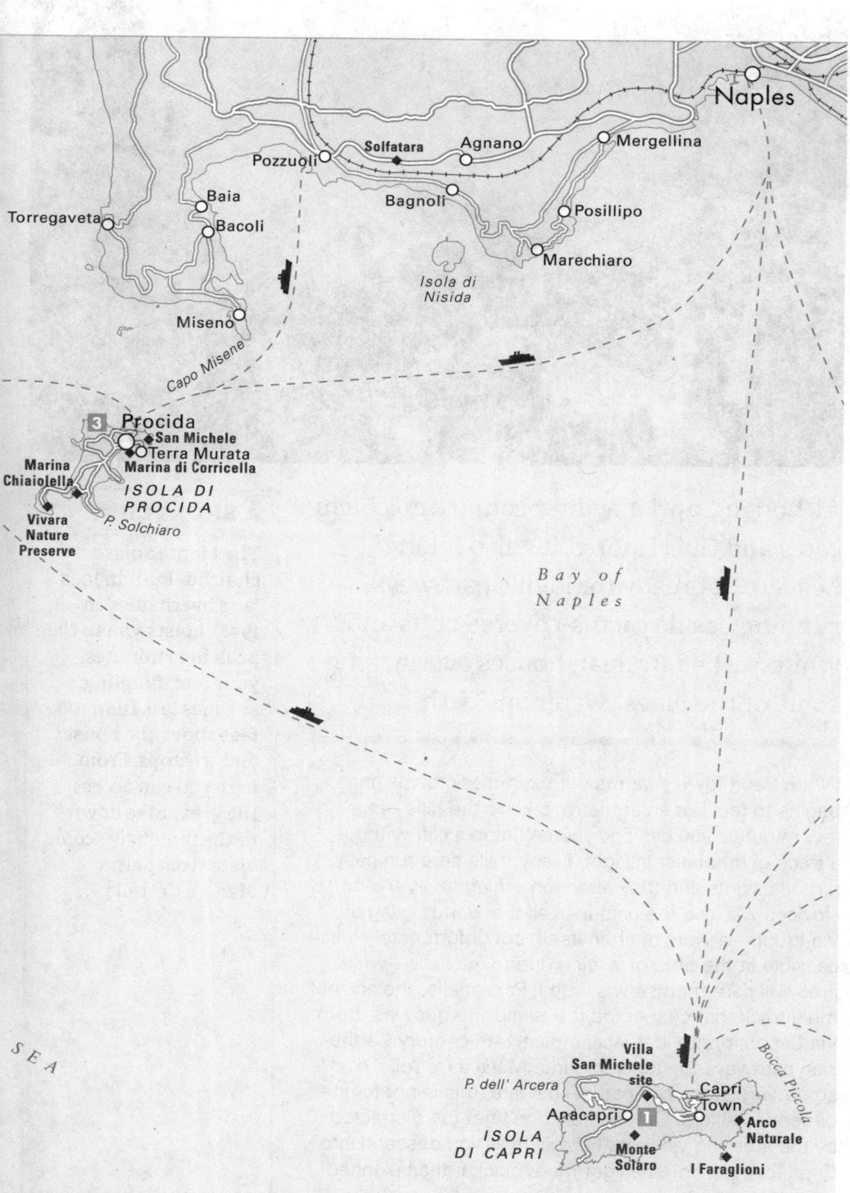
Naples
Mergellina
Agnano
Solfatara
Pozzuoli
Bagnoli
Baia
Torregaveta
Bacoli
Posillipo
Marechiaro
Isola di Nisida
Miseno
Capo Misene
Procida
San Michele
Terra Murata
Marina di Corricella
Marina Chiaiolella
ISOLA DI PROCIDA
Vivara Nature Preserve
P. Solchiaro
Bay of Naples
SEA
Villa San Michele site
P. dell' Arcera
Capri Town
Bocca Piccola
Anacapri
Arco Naturale
ISOLA DI CAPRI
Monte Solaro
I Faraglioni

CAPRI IS FOR WALKERS

Atop Monte Solaro leading to lovely views

Although Capri may first conjure up chichi cafés and Gucci stores, it's also hiking heaven. Get ready for idyllic pathways running beside cactus-covered cliffs and whitewashed Arabian houses overlooking some of the bluest water on Earth.

When Capri Town swarms with summer crowds and begins to feel like an ant farm, take to the hills—in a few minutes, you can find yourself atop a cliff without a trace of humanity in sight. Many trails here run past famous sights and they offer something for everyone. Novices will love the unique-in-all-the-world zigzag of Via Krupp—a work of art in itself, but unfortunately inaccessible at the time of writing due to rockfalls—while pros will dare themselves with Il Passetiello, the ancient mule track that connected the island's two towns, from Via Capodimonte in Anacapri past 14th-century Carthusian pathways to stunning Santa Maria a Cetrella, plus some *very* steep cliff paths—beware, this is not for inexperienced hikers. On this trail, don't get too distracted by the amazing view of I Faraglioni as you descend into Capri Town, or you may get there quicker than planned!

A SHORTCUT

The Monte Solaro chairlift, built in 1952 (and overhauled in 1998), hoists you to the peak in 13 minutes, your feet dangling, at times less than 100 feet above the houses and treetops. From here you can access the great hike down to the famously scenic vista from Santa Maria a Cetrella.

IL SENTIERO DEI FORTINI

One of the most beautiful coastal walks in the world, this "Path of the Forts" stretches along the western side of the island for 5.2 km (3.2 miles). Jaw-dropping views are accented by four Saracen fortresses (used mainly during the Napoleonic wars). Starting from the Grotta Azzura (Blue Grotto), you soon meet the first fort, Fortino di Orrico, set just 30 meters (100 feet) above the water. The path continues through rich Mediterranean maquis to Fortino di Mesola, with great views around this strategically placed fort. The path then rises past Fortino del Pino to the tiny Fortino del Tombosiello and then ends at the famous Faro lighthouse. Along the path, ceramic panels—inscribed with reflective haikus—describe your surroundings, the final touch to this unmissable open-air ecomuseum. This walk is not difficult, but lasts up to five hours, with no watering spots along the way, so bring lots of water!

BELVEDERE MIGLIARA TO PUNTA CARENA

The 40-minute walk along the paved Via Migliara from Anacapri to the Belvedere Migliara—with one of the most beautiful views on the island—and the Philosophy Park may be some folks' idea of a hike, but the blisters are truly worth it when you head on down the mountainside via the tiny path for 20 minutes to the Torre della Guardia, a Saracen tower once belonging to Axel Munthe. Stone steps take you down to Punta Carena, with its shell-shape rocky bay: perfect for a well-deserved swim!

Via Krupp

The Lighthouse at Punta Carena from the Belvedere di Migliara

SCALA FENICIA

Workout fans will have no hesitation in climbing up (of course!) the 921 steps of the—probably—Greek (Phoenician)-built steps, once the main "road" from Capri to Anacapri. From Marina Grande follow the street (not the funicular) to Capri Town for five minutes until you see the signpost on your right. A paved residential path then takes you to the base of the stairway, with the next stop (apart from some time to catch your breath!) just under Villa San Michele, 290 meters (950 feet) above the sea. Take a break shortly before the top, just before passing under the main car road, to admire the 17th-century chapel of Sant'Antonio da Padova, dedicated to the patron saint of Anacapri.

GIRO DELL'ARCO NATURALE

Where else can you see the Arco Naturale, the Grotta di Matermaia, Villa Malaparte, and I Faraglioni in under two hours? This is a truly spectacular walk.

The islands off Naples are so different from each other that you wonder how they can possibly be in the same bay—indeed, some would say that Capri, Ischia, and Procida are not true water mates, as they lie just beyond the bay's outer fringes. More tellingly, their contrasts go beyond mere geology and vegetation. They all occupy different niches in the traveler's mind.

Capri panders to the whims of the international jet set. Ischia serves the needs of a predominantly German and Italian clientele. Procida—the closest to the mainland—is more dependent on the weekend and summer influx of Neapolitans. But together, the islands of Capri, Ischia, and Procida—chosen by the Greeks, the supreme connoisseurs and aesthetes of antiquity, as their first base in Italy—combine a broad and delightful gamut of experiences.

Islandophiles, of course, have always had a special love for Capri (the first syllable is accented—"*Ca*-pri"). Italy's most glamorous seaside getaway, this craggy, whale-shape island has an epic beauty: cliffs that are the very embodiment of time, bougainvillea-shaded pathways overlooking the sea, trees seemingly hewn out of rock. Capri has always been a stage shared with the Beautiful People, often an eclectic potpourri of duchesses who have left their dukes at home, fading French film actresses, pretenders to obscure thrones, waspish couturiers, and sleek supermodels.

Today Capri continues to attract thousands of visitors. On summer days the port and *piazzetta* are often crammed, so if you can visit in spring or fall, do so. Yet even the crowds are not enough to destroy Capri's charm. The town itself is a Moorish stage of sparkling white houses, tiny squares, and narrow medieval alleyways hung with flowers, while its hillsides are spectacular settings for luxurious seaside villas. The mood is modish but somehow unspoiled. Retreat when the day-trippers take over by offering yourself to the sun at your hotel pool or exploring the hidden corners of the island. Even in the height of summer, you can enjoy a degree of privacy on one of the many paved paths that have been mapped out through species-rich Mediterranean maquis, winding around the island hundreds of feet above the sea.

Recent years have seen a diversification of the experiences offered on the three islands. Once entirely dependent on its thermal springs, Ischia is now the archaeological front-runner in the bay, thanks to its noted museum in Lacco Ameno. Procida, as Italy's Capital of Culture in

2022, has opened up to tourism, with some newer, smaller hotels remaining open throughout the year. All the islands are well served by road networks, with buses plying the main roads and a funicular on Capri reaching the main town from the Marina Grande, as well as a chairlift ascending to the top of Monte Solaro (1,932 feet) from Anacapri.

MAJOR REGIONS

Fantastic grottoes, soaring conical peaks, caverns great and small, plus villas of the emperors and thousands of legends brush **Capri** with an air of whispered mystery. Capri's two main hubs are **Capri Town** (on the saddle between Monte Tiberio and Monte Solaro) and **Anacapri,** higher up (902 feet). On arriving at the main harbor, **Marina Grande,** everyone heads for the famous funicular, which ascends (and descends) several times an hour. Once you're taken up to Anacapri by bus, you can reach even greater island heights via the spectacular chairlift that ascends to the top of Monte Solaro (1,932 feet) from Anacapri's town center.

Ischia is renowned for it's gardens and inviting natural hot baths. Most of the island's maritime traffic is channeled into **Ischia Porto,** with some arrivals at **Casamicciola** and **Forio,** burgeoning resorts and busy spa centers. The Castello Aragonese in **Ischia Ponte,** which is a vast medieval complex, is one of the island's main historic sights; **Lacco Ameno,** with its immense archaeological heritage and more upscale ambience, is a good base for exploring the north of the island; **Forio** is famous for the grand gardens of La Mortella and the Poseiden thermal baths; and **Sant'Angelo** is a magical fishing village at the La Roja promontory.

Procida is Europe's most densely populated island—just over 10,000 people. Though there are some lovely oasis, like **Marina Corricella** and **Isola di Vivara,** which seem to have been bypassed by modern civilization. Picturesquely scenic, with breath taking views from 11th-century **Terra Murata** and **Abbazia di San Michele,** it's no surprise that Procida has strong artistic traditions and is Italy's Capital of Culture in 2022.

Planning

When to Go

April, May, and early June is a good time to visit the islands; the weather is usually good, and hotels and restaurants have just reopened for the season. It gets terribly hot in summer, and visitors crowd the limited space available, particularly in August. Things quiet down in the early fall, and the weather is generally pleasant.

Planning Your Time

Each of the three islands has its own individual charm—the chic resort of Capri, the volcanic spas of Ischia, and the rustic Procida. If you are unable to overnight, it is worth getting to Capri as early in the morning as possible to see the main sites before the human tsunami hits the island. Take a round-the-island boat trip and gaze at the natural beauty of the Fariglioni and the Blue Grotto, two of the unmissable sights on this fabled isle.

If archaeology and history are at the top of your list of priorities, choosing between Ischia and Capri can be difficult. Ischia has the added bonus of its natural thermal baths, with its waters healing ailments since Roman times—if you want the gamut of natural saunas and access to a dreamy beach, head to Poseidon in Forio or landscaped Negombo in Lacco Ameno.

Moving around Capri to the main sites is generally easier—and can be done in a day if pushed—while Ischia calls for more chilling out at your destination. If time is limited, Procida and its magical waterfront, as immortalized in the Oscar-winning film *Il Postino,* can be tacked on to your stay as a day trip from Ischia or from the mainland.

Getting Here and Around

BOAT

Lying equidistant from Naples (about 25 km [16 miles]), Ischia and Capri stand like guards at the main entrance to the Bay of Naples, with Ischia to the west and Capri to the south, while Procida is like a small stepping-stone halfway between Ischia and Capo Miseno (Cape Misenum), on the mainland. The islands can be reached easily from various points in and near Naples, and the port of Pozzuoli is the closest to Ischia and Procida. Nevertheless, most people head first to Capri using hydrofoils from the main port terminal in Naples—the Molo Beverello. Ferries are far less frequent, and leave from the nearby Calata Porta di Massa. There are also boat connections between the islands.

■ TIP→ For details, see the "Getting Here and Around" sections for each island in this chapter.

You should buy a single ticket rather than a round-trip, which would tie you to the same line on your return journey. Day-trippers need to remember that the high-season crowds on the last ferries leaving the islands make this crossing riotously reminiscent of packed subways and buses back home; in addition, rough bay waters can also delay (and even cancel) these boat rides.

BUS

Once on the islands you can do without a car, as the bus service is good—the trip from Capri to Anacapri is breathtaking both for its views and the sheer drops just inches away. Tickets should be bought before boarding, and then stamped on the bus.

TAXI AND SCOOTER

For those with (much) deeper pockets, microtaxis are readily available to whiz you to your destination. Renting a scooter on Ischia gives you the freedom to explore at will, as well as giving you that real Italian experience. Much of Capri is pedestrianized, but a scooter will make it easier to get to the more far flung sites in Anacapri.

Restaurants

The islands' restaurants offer top-quality food, from Mamma's home cooking to Michelin-star dining experiences. Capri's eateries unsurprisingly cater to more sophisticated palettes, with innovative seafood creations, while less expensive, yet authentic spots are ubiquitous in Ischia and Procida. Ischia is renowned for its wild rabbit dishes.

Prices in the reviews are the average cost of a main course at dinner or, if dinner isn't served, at lunch. Restaurant reviews have been shortened. For full information, visit Fodors.com.

What it Costs in Euros

	$	$$	$$$	$$$$
RESTAURANTS				
	under €15	€15–€24	€25–€35	over €35

Hotels

On Capri, hotels fill up quickly, so book well in advance to be assured of getting first-pick accommodations. Although island prices are generally higher than those on the mainland, it's worth paying the difference for an overnight stay. Once the day-trippers have left center stage and headed down to the Marina Grande for the ferry home, the streets regain some of their charm and tranquillity.

Although Ischia can be sampled piecemeal on day excursions from Naples, given the size of the island, you'd be well advised to arrange a stopover. Ischia is known for its natural hot-water spas, and many hotels have a wellness or beauty center, meaning you may be tempted not to venture any farther than the lobby for the duration of your stay. Hotels in Procida tend to be family-run and more down-to-earth. Note that booking is essential for the summer months, when half board may be required. Most hotels close from November to Easter, when the season is at its lowest.

Prices in the reviews are the lowest cost of a standard double room in high season. Hotel reviews have been shortened. For full information, visit Fodors.com.

What it Costs in Euros

	$	$$	$$$	$$$$
HOTELS	under €125	€125–€200	€201–€300	over €300

Tours

Vesuvius vs. Pompeii
GUIDED TOURS | There is a selection of tour operators in the area; one reputable company is Vesuvius vs. Pompeii, who offer guided walking tours and organize transfers. ✉ *Capri* ☎ *333/6409000 mobile* 🌐 *www.vesuviusvspompeii.com.*

Capri

Fantastic grottoes, soaring conical peaks, caverns great and small, plus villas of the emperors and thousands of legends brush Capri with an air of whispered mystery. Emperor Augustus was the first to tout the island's pleasures by nicknaming it Apragopolis (City of Sweet Idleness) and Capri has drawn escapists of every ilk since. Ancient Greek and Roman goddesses were moved aside by the likes of Jacqueline Onassis, Elizabeth Taylor, and Brigitte Bardot, who made the island into a paparazzo's paradise in the 1960s. Today, new generations of glitterati continue to answer the island's call.

Life on Capri gravitates around the two centers of Capri Town (on the saddle between Monte Tiberio and Monte Solaro) and Anacapri, higher up (902 feet). The main road connecting Capri Town with the upper town of Anacapri is well plied by buses. On arriving at the main harbor, the Marina Grande, everyone heads for the famous funicular, which ascends (and descends) several times an hour. Once you're lofted up to Anacapri by bus, you can reach the island heights by taking the spectacular chairlift that ascends to the top of Monte Solaro (1,932 feet) from Anacapri's town center. Within Capri Town and Anacapri foot power is the preferred mode of transportation, as much for convenience as for the sheer delight of walking along these gorgeous street and roads.

GETTING HERE AND AROUND

Capri is well connected with the mainland in all seasons, though there are more sailings April–October. Hydrofoils, Seacats, and similar vessels leave from Molo Beverello (below Piazza Municipio) in Naples, while far less frequent car ferries leave from Calata Porta di Massa, 1,000 yards to the east. There's also service to and from Sorrento's Marina Piccola. Much of Capri is pedestrianized, and a car is a great hindrance, not a help.

Several ferry and hydrofoil companies ply the waters of the Bay of Naples, making frequent trips to Capri. Schedules change from season to season; the tourist office's website (🌐 *www.capritourism.com*) gives updated departure times. However, you can't return to Naples after the last sailing (11 pm in high season, often 8 pm or even earlier in low season). There's little to be gained—sometimes nothing—from buying a round-trip ticket, which will just tie you down to the return schedule of one line. Book in advance in spring and summer for a Sunday return to the mainland.

Many of Capri's sights are reasonably accessible by either boat or bus, although some require walking for up to an hour. The bus service is relatively cheap (€2) and frequent, while taxis are likely to cost 10–20 times as much as public transport. Don't buy a *biglietto giornaliero* (day pass) for the bus unless you're thinking of covering almost every corner of the island—it costs €7, so you would need to make four separate trips to make it pay, and it doesn't include the funicular nor the routes to the Grotta Azzurra and Faro. The tour bus company Staiano offers an alternative, less crowded service in more modern vehicles, for the same price, leaving from 200 yards east of the funicular station at Marina Grande.

FERRIES AND HYDROFOILS

In summer, Alilauro has a service from Sorrento (€20.70, travel time 25 minutes). Its offshoot Alicost offers weekday jet-foil service from the Amalfi Coast, with a round-trip from Amalfi costing €29.50 (travel time 65 minutes). Caremar has up to seven ferry departures per day from Calata Porta di Massa (€14.80 slow, €20.30 fast; travel time of 1 hour 20 minutes). Four ferries leave daily from Sorrento (€16.90, travel time 25 minutes).

Gescab is the umbrella body for transportation to the islands. Navigazione Libera Del Golfo has up to five hydrofoil departures per day from Molo Beverello (€24, travel time 40 minutes), and up to four per day from Sorrento (€20.70, 25 minutes). SNAV offers a hydrofoil almost every hour from Molo Beverello (€22.70, travel time 40 minutes).

CONTACTS Alilauro. ✉ *Capri* ☎ *081/4972222 Alilauro, 089/871483 Alicosta* 🌐 *www.alilauro.it, www.alicost.it.* **Caremar.** ✉ *Capri* ☎ *081/18966690* 🌐 *www.caremar.it.* **Gescab.** ✉ *Capri* ☎ *081/7041911* 🌐 *www.gescab.it.* **Navigazione Libera Del Golfo.** ✉ *Capri* ☎ *081/5520763* 🌐 *www.navlib.it.* **SNAV.** ✉ *Capri* ☎ *081/4285555* 🌐 *www.snav.it.*

SCOOTERS

CONTACTS Oasi Motor. ✉ *Via Cristoforo Colombo 47, Marina Grande* ☎ *334/3532975* 🌐 *www.oasimotorcapri.it.* **Rent a Scooter.** ✉ *Via Roma 70, Capri* ☎ *081/8375863* 🌐 *caprirentscooter.com.*

TOURS

BOAT TOURS

Many outfitters provide boat tours of the island—you can also hire your own speedboat or *gommone* (dinghy). If time is short, catch a tour on a larger, quicker, and sometimes more fun-packed boat—some operators offer guided tours, with a lively combination of anecdotes (and folk songs!) to accompany you throughout; proffer a gratuity of a euro or two if you are happy with the trip.

Note: Tour passengers often have to purchase separate tickets (€14) to use the rowboats that tour the Blue Grotto. Check when signing up for your giro cruise.

Capri Boats

BOAT TOURS | Those wanting to experience the "Capri moon" over the Faraglioni, nighttime fishing expeditions, and an array of gozzo tours should contact this outfitter. They rent boats at €190 for two hours. ✉ *Via Cristoforo Colombo 27, Marina Grande* ☎ *338/6080158* 🌐 *www.capriboats.com.*

Capri Relax Boats

BOAT TOURS | One of the best and most stylish of the outfitters, Capri Relax has a really comprehensive range of tours. The island tour will take you into caves that larger boats can't reach, and their flexibility allows you to decide the itinerary. ✉ *Via Cristoforo Colombo 34, Marina Grande* ☎ *331/6084109* 🌐 *www.caprirelaxboats.com.*

Capri Sea Service
BOAT TOURS | A panoply of options are offered, from gozzo tours to prebooked diving trips. ✉ *Via Cristoforo Colombo 64, Marina Grande* ☎ *081/8378781* 🌐 *www.capriseaservice.com.*

Capri Whales
BOAT TOURS | These tours are virtually living island history, as owner Gennarino Alberino claims his family has been here for more than 700 years—he was one of the divers who unearthed the ancient marble statues found in the Blue Grotto. Each of his boats is furnished with freshwater showers, bathrooms and iceboxes. Gennarino and his family's knowledge of the island is encyclopedic, and few others can match it. You can rent your own boat from €100. ✉ *Via Cristoforo Colombo 17, Marina Grande* ☎ *081/8375833* 🌐 *www.capriwhales.it.*

Laser Capri
BOAT TOURS | For those who want to make a tour on a larger, sturdier sightseeing boat, Laser has a fleet of larger ships that can take up to 100 people. Tickets cost €18 for a full-island tour (add €14 for the row boat to the Blue Grotto). Their ticket booth is 200 yards east of the funicular station. ✉ *Via Cristoforo Colombo 69, Marina Grande* ☎ *081/8375208* 🌐 *www.lasercapri.com.*

Leomar
BOAT TOURS | Based on the beach at Marina Grande next to the bus stop, Leomar offers full-day speedboat rentals for €140–€170 per hour, six people maximum. They also offer canoe and pedalboat rentals. ✉ *Spiaggia Marina Grande, Capri* ☎ *081/8377181.*

Motoscafisti Capri
BOAT TOURS | With offices right on the dock at Marina Grande, this cooperative of gozzo boat owners offers two set tours that leave on the hour. Admission is €20–€21 (both €18 online) depending on choice of tour; maximum number is 30 people per boat. Both the "Blue" and "Yellow" tours include the Blue Grotto. ✉ *Molo 0, Marina Grande* ☎ *081/8377714* 🌐 *www.motoscafisticapri.com.*

BUS TOURS

Staiano
GUIDED TOURS | In addition to providing a sleek alternative to Capri's local bus service, this family-run business has been offering island tours for over 60 years. ✉ *Via Don Giobbe Ruocco 36, Capri* ☎ *081/8374401* 🌐 *www.staianotourcapri.com.*

VISITOR INFORMATION

CONTACTS Azienda Autonoma di Cura, Soggiorno e Turismo. ✉ *Piazza Umberto I,* ☎ *081/8370686* 🌐 *www.capritourism.com.*

Marina Grande

Besides being the main harbor gateway to Capri and the main disembarkation point for the mainland, Marina Grande is usually the starting point for round-island tours and trips to the Grotta Azzurra. The marina has faded in the glare of neon since the days when it was Sophia Loren's home in the 1960 film *It Started in Naples.* Originally a conglomeration of fishermen's houses built on ancient Roman foundations, it's now an extended hodgepodge of various architectural styles, with buildings that almost exclusively service the tourist industry. Warehouses and storerooms in which fishermen once kept their boats and tackle are now shops, restaurants, and bars, most either tacky or overpriced. To the west, however, lie three sights worth exploring: the historic 17th-century church of San Costanzo, the ruins of the Palazzo a Mare (the former palace of emperor Augustus), and the chic **Baths of Tiberius beach.**

GETTING HERE AND AROUND

Ferries and hydrofoils bring you here from Naples and Sorrento.

Capri's Roman History

Of all the peoples who have left their mark on the island during its millennia of history, the Romans with their sybaritic wealth had the greatest effect in forming the island's psyche. Capri became the center of power in the Roman Empire when Tiberius scattered 12 villas around the island and decided to spend the rest of his life here, refusing to return to Rome even when, 10 years on, he was near death. With reports that he became a dirty old man only interested in orgies, he used Capri as a base to run the ancient Roman Empire. All Tiberius's hard work and happy play—he also indulged in his secret passion for astronomy here—were overlooked by ancient scandalmongers, prime among them Suetonius, who wrote: "In Capri they still show the place at the cliff top where Tiberius used to watch his victims being thrown into the sea after prolonged and exquisite tortures. A party of mariners were stationed below, and when the bodies came hurtling down, they whacked at them with oars and boat-hooks, to make sure they were completely dead." Thankfully, present-day Capri is less fraught with danger for travelers, or even to dignitaries from afar. The main risks now are overexposure to the Mediterranean sun, overindulgence in pleasures of the palate, and a very sore wallet.

CONTACTS Oasi Motor. ✉ *Via Cristoforo Colombo 47, Marina Grande* ☎ *334/3532975* 🌐 *www.oasimotorcapri.it.*

Beaches

Bagni di Tiberio
BEACH | The free beach at Marina Grande, under the J.K. Place hotel, is usually crowded, so social go-getters prefer the historic Bagni di Tiberio beach to the east. Here you can swim around the ruins of Tiberius's Palazzo a Mare and dine at the family-run beach club. Entrance, including boat from Marina Grande, is €14, a sun bed is €12, and an umbrella is €7. **Amenities:** food and drink; lifeguards; showers; toilets. **Best for:** snorkeling; swimming. ✉ *Via Palazzo a Mare 41, Marina Grande* ☎ *081/8370703* 🌐 *www.bagnitiberio.com.*

Restaurants

Da Paolino (*Lemon Trees*)
$$$ | **SOUTHERN ITALIAN** | A grove of 130 lemon trees provides the unique setting for this popular restaurant near Marina Grande and down a winding road in a residential area, toward the Bagni di Tiberio. The ubiquitous citrus perfumes the air as you tuck into a *bomba*—a fried pizza stuffed with mozzarella cheese, ham, and tomato—or one of the many lemon-based desserts. **Known for:** fresh local cooking; citrus-based deserts; its lemon-grove setting. $ *Average main: €25* ✉ *Via Palazzo a Mare 11, Marina Grande* ☎ *081/8376102* 🌐 *www.paolino-capri.com* ⏲ *Closed Nov.–mid-Apr.*

Hotels

★ **J. K. Place**
$$$$ | **HOTEL** | Occupying an 1876 villa above Marina Grande harbor, southern Italy's most glamorous hotel makes other Capri accommodations seem dull. **Pros:** exquisite pool; free shuttle to town;

pleasant walk to the magical Tiberio beach. **Cons:** pool visible from main road; only for high rollers; expensive. *Rooms from: €1182 Via Provinciale Marina Grande 225, Capri 081/8384001 www.jkcapri.com Closed mid-Oct.–mid-Apr. 22 rooms Free Breakfast.*

Villa Marina

$$$ | HOTEL | Although it's one of the island's newest properties, a setting above Marina Grande amid lush terraced gardens evokes a time when the island was an artists' paradise; most of the sumptuous, modern guest rooms look out over the bay, and each one is individually decorated and named for a Capri luminary. **Pros:** those views; gorgeous gardens; friendly, helpful staff. **Cons:** small pool; impersonal rooms; a 10-minute uphill climb to Capri Town. *Rooms from: €280 Via Prov. Marina Grande 191, Capri 081/8376630 www.villamarinacapri.com Closed Nov.–Easter 22 rooms Free Breakfast.*

Capri Town and Nearby

This fantasy of white-on-white Capriote architecture, flower-filled window boxes, and stylish boutiques rests on a saddle between rugged limestone cliffs to the east and west, where huge herds of *capre* (goats) once roamed, hence the name of the island. Beyond Capri Town lies some of the island's most spectacular sights, including I Faraglioni and the Villa Jovis. As you disembark at the marina quay, note that unlike the other islands in the Bay of Naples, Capri is not of volcanic origin but was formed by marine deposits laid more than 100 million years ago and then uplifted during plate tectonic activity in the Pleistocene era (as recently as 1–2 million years ago); Monte Tiberio, to the south of the Marina Grande, and Monte Solaro, to the west, powerfully attest to these upheavals.

GETTING HERE AND AROUND

From the main harbor, Marina Grande, follow the crowds to the main ticket office for the famous funicular, located near where the pier juts out into the harbor. Look for the rounded arcadelike entrance set in the wall of stores and houses. The funicular heads up from the Marina Grande to the main attraction, Capri Town, the island's hub, which lies above in the saddle of the island. Across the way from the funicular office are ticket offices for many boat lines, near the small police station, plus for tickets to take buses up the hill to Capri Town and Anacapri. Staiano also provides a bus service from the port.

Conveniently located at the traffic hub of the island, Rent a Scooter offers scooters from €25 for two hours (add €5 in August). They also rent boats at €130 for two hours.

CONTACTS Rent a Scooter. *Via Roma 70, Capri 081/8375863 caprirentscooter.com.*

Sights

Arco Naturale (*Natural Arch*)

NATURE SIGHT | One of Capri's most famous natural wonders, this geologic arch framing Punto Massullo is all that remains of a large limestone cave that has suffered the erosive effects of wind and rain over the millennia. Once a cave that was likely hollowed out by wave action, it broke apart when lifted up to its present position, hundreds of feet above sea level, in relatively recent geological times (about 1–2 million years ago). *Via Arco Naturale, at end of Via Matermania, Capri.*

Certosa di San Giacomo

HISTORIC SIGHT | An eerie atmosphere hangs around neglected corners of this once-grand, palatial complex between the Castiglione and Tuoro hills, which was for centuries a Carthusian monastery dedicated to St. James. It was founded between 1371 and 1374, when

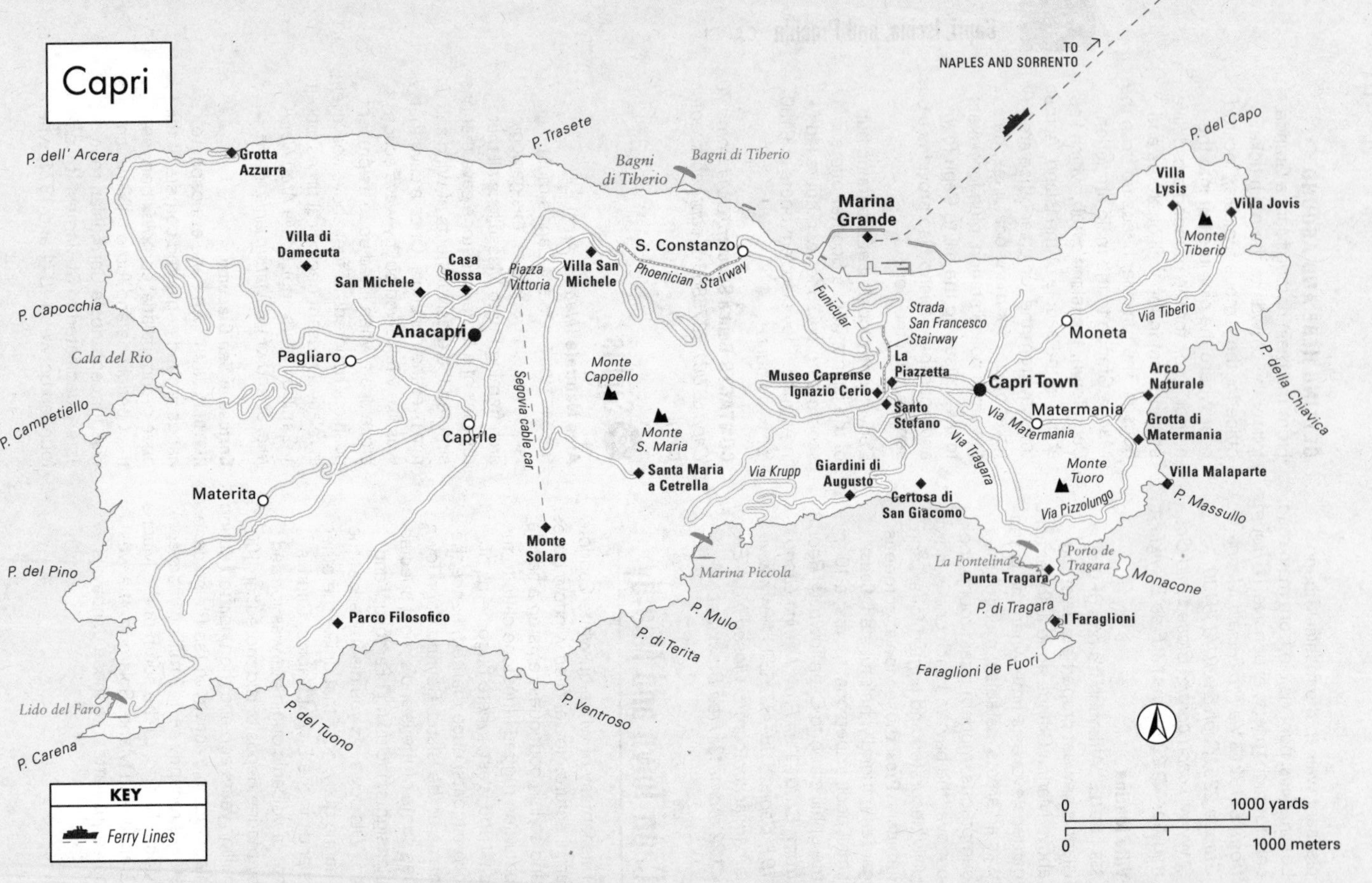
Capri
TO NAPLES AND SORRENTO
P. dell' Arcera
Grotta Azzurra
P. Trasete
Bagni di Tiberio
Bagni di Tiberio
Marina Grande
P. del Capo
Villa Lysis
Villa Jovis
Monte Tiberio
Villa di Damecuta
Casa Rossa
Piazza Vittoria
Villa San Michele
S. Constanzo
Phoenician Stairway
San Michele
P. Capocchia
Funicular
Strada San Francesco Stairway
Via Tiberio
Moneta
P. della Chiavica
Anacapri
Cala del Rio
Pagliaro
Monte Cappello
La Piazzetta
Museo Caprense Ignazio Cerio
Capri Town
Arco Naturale
Matermania
Santo Stefano
Via Matermania
Grotta di Matermania
P. Campetiello
Caprile
Monte S. Maria
Segovia cable car
Via Tragara
Giardini di Augusto
Monte Tuoro
Villa Malaparte
Santa Maria a Cetrella
Via Krupp
Certosa di San Giacomo
Via Pizzolungo
P. Massullo
Materita
Monte Solaro
Marina Piccola
La Fontelina
Porto de Tragara
Punta Tragara
Monacone
P. del Pino
P. Mulo
P. di Tragara
I Faraglioni
Parco Filosofico
P. di Terita
Faraglioni de Fuori
Lido del Faro
P. Ventroso
P. del Tuono
P. Carena
KEY
Ferry Lines
0
1000 yards
0
1000 meters

Classic Capri: A Good Walk

Capri Town

This walk will take three- to five hours. You'd be well advised to avoid the hot midday hours in summer. Pick up a map of Capri and start at Piazza Umberto I, better known locally as **La Piazzetta.** You can take the funicular up from the harbor area of **Marina Grande**, or opt for the 15-minute climb on a former mule track starting from the small square on the quayside called Largo Fontana.

Admire the majolica decoration of the clock tower dial and inspect the 17th-century church of **Santo Stefano,** then forge your way across to Via Le Botteghe; if you're thinking about a picnic lunch, you can stock up at a supermarket here. Take the small Via Madonna delle Grazie behind the fruit stall to see the **Chiesa di Sant'Anna,** with its restored 14th-century frescoes. The farther away you get from La Piazzetta, the quieter this pedestrianized road becomes. Via Le Botteghe becomes Via Fuorlovado and then Via Croce, developing gradually into an avenue fringed by flowering vines and trees.

The East Coast

After about 10 minutes, at the Caffé Manari, the road to the Arco Naturale branches off to the right. Follow the signs for Arco Naturale along Via Matermania for about 15 minutes until the path forks (Arco Naturale to the left, Grotta di Matermania to the right). Art and archaeology buffs will instead want to continue straight on at the bar and up Monte Tiberio.

A turnoff along the way takes you to the **Villa Lysis,** one of Capri's most legendary private homes (look for the signpost off Via Tiberio). Return to Via Tiberio and continue—the hike may take 45 minutes up the hill—to reach **Villa Jovis.**

Unrivaled views

Peer at the **Arco Naturale,** but remember the path is a cul-de-sac, so you will have to retrace your steps. Then, take the hundreds of steps—and we mean hundreds—down to the **Grotta di Matermania**, an impressive natural cave where ancient Romans worshipped the goddess Cybele every dawn.

The path then levels out for one of the most beautiful seaside walks in the world—the Via Pizzolungo. This path continues south high above the shoreline, affording fine views of Punta Massullo where **Villa Malaparte** perches over the sea. Farther on is a panoramic point from which you can gaze at **I Faraglioni.** As you continue west, look first for the Villa Solitaria, built in the early 1900s by famed Capriote architect Edwin Cerio, then look for the towering rock pinnacle Pizzo Lungo (High Point), which the ancients thought was the petrified form of Polyphemus, the giant blinded by Odysseus's men.

Back to the town

At the end of the Giro dell'Arco Naturale (Natural Arch Circuit) is the **Punta Tragara**, another panoramic point, which marks your arrival back in Capri Town. From here take Via Tragara, until it joins with Via Camerelle. Look for a left turn down Via Cerio to the **Certosa di San Giacomo**, a former monastery. Retrace your steps until you get to Via Serena, a mere five-minute walk from the Piazzetta.

Villa Jovis was the home of Emperor Tiberius during the final years of his rule over ancient Rome.

Queen Giovanna I of Naples gave Count Giacomo Arcucci, her secretary, the land and the means to create it. The count himself then became devoutly religious and retired here until his death. After the monastery was sacked by the pirates Dragut and Barbarossa in the 16th century, it was thoroughly restored and rebuilt—thanks in part to heavy taxes exacted from the populace. The Quarto del Priore hosts occasional art exhibitions from international artists, but the showstopper here is the Museo Diefenbach, with restored large canvases by influential German painter K.W. Diefenbach, who visited Capri in 1899 and stayed until his death in 1913. ✉ *Via Certosa, Capri* ☎ *081/8376218* 🎫 *€6, with audio guide* ⏲ *Closed Mon.*

★ Giardini di Augusto

(*Gardens of Augustus*)

GARDEN | From the terraces of this beautiful public garden, you can see the village of Marina Piccola below—restaurants, cabanas, and swimming platforms huddle among the shoals—and admire the steep, winding Via Krupp, actually a staircase cut into the rock. Friedrich Krupp, the German arms manufacturer, loved Capri and became one of the island's most generous benefactors. Sadly, the path down to Marina Piccola is closed indefinitely due to the danger of rockfalls. ✉ *Via Matteotti, beyond monastery of San Giacomo, Capri* 🎫 *€1.*

Grotta di Matermania

NATURE SIGHT | Set in the bowels of Monte Tuoro, this legend-haunted cave was dedicated to Cybele, the Magna Mater, or Great Mother of the gods—hence the somewhat corrupted name of the cave. A goddess with definite eastern origins, Cybele did not form part of the Greek or Roman pantheon: worship of her was introduced to Italy in 204 BC at the command of the Sibylline oracle, supposedly for the purpose of driving Hannibal out of Italy. At dawn the cave is touched by the rays of the sun, leading scholars to believe it may also have been a shrine where the Mithraic mysteries were celebrated. Hypnotic rituals, ritual sacrifice

The Islands through the Ages

In terms of settlements, conquests, and dominion, the history of the islands echoes that of Campania's mainland. For eastern Mediterranean traders in the second and first millennia BC, Capri and Ischia were both close enough to the mainland to provide easy access to trade routes and impervious enough to afford natural protection against invaders.

Ischia, or Pithekoussai, as it used to be called—a word probably derived from the Greek term for a large earthenware jar (*pithos*) rather than the less plausible word, *pithekos*, meaning monkey—is renowned in classical circles as the first colony founded by the Greeks on Italian soil, as early as the 8th century BC.

Capri, probably colonized in the 7th century BC, a century or so later than Ischia, is amply described in the early years of the Roman Empire by authors such as Suetonius and Tacitus, as this was the island where Tiberius spent the last 10 years of his life.

After the breakup of the Roman Empire, the islands, like many other parts of the Mediterranean, suffered a succession of incursions. Saracens, Normans, and Turks all laid siege to the islands at some stage, between periods of relative stability under the Swabians, the Angevins, the Aragonese, and the Spanish.

After a short interregnum under the French at the beginning of the 19th century, a period of relative peace and prosperity ensued. Over the next century, from the opening of its first hotel in 1822, Capri saw an influx of visitors which reads like a "who's who" of literature and politics, especially in the first decades of the 20th century. Ischia and Procida established themselves as holiday resorts much later, with development taking place from the 1950s onward.

of bulls, and other orgiastic practices made this cave a place of myth, so it's not surprising that later authors reported (erroneously) that Emperor Tiberius used it for orgies. Nevertheless, the cave was adapted by the Romans into a luxurious nymphaeum (small shrine), but little remains of the original structure, which would have been covered by tesserae, polychrome stucco, and marine shells. If you want to see the few ancient remains, you have to step inside the now-unprepossessing cavern. ✉ *Giro del'Arco Naturale, Capri.*

★ I Faraglioni

NATURE SIGHT | Few landscapes set more artists dreaming than that of the famous Faraglioni—three enigmatic, pale-ocher limestone colossi that loom out of the sea just off the Punta Tragara on the southern coast of Capri. Soaring almost 350 feet above the water, the Faraglioni have become for most Italians a beloved symbol of Capri and have been poetically compared to Gothic cathedrals or modern skyscrapers. The first rock is called Faraglione di Terra, since it's attached to the land; at its base is the famous restaurant and bathing lido Da Luigi, where a beach mattress may accompany the luncheon menu. The second is called Faraglione di Mezzo, or Stella, and little boats can often be seen going through its picturesque tunnel, which was caused by sea erosion. The rock farthest out to sea is Faraglione di Scopolo and is inhabited by a wall lizard species with a striking blue belly, considered a local variant by biologists although legend has it that they were originally brought as pets

Did You Know?

I Faraglioni, Capri's landmark rock formation, rises to a height of 350 feet. Plus, the rock farthest from shore, known as the Faraglione di Scopolo, is home to a blue-tinted lizard found nowhere else.

from Greece to delight ancient Roman courtiers. ✉ *End of Via Tragara, Capri.*

La Piazzetta

PLAZA/SQUARE | The English writer and Capriophile Norman Douglas called this square, officially known as Piazza Umberto I, "the small theater of the world." The rendezvous point for international crowds, this *"salone"* became famous as the late-night place to spot heavenly bodies—of the Hollywood variety, that is: Frank Sinatra, Rita Hayworth, Julie Christie, Julia Roberts, and Mariah Carey are just a few of the celebs who have made La Piazzetta the place where the rich and famous come to watch other rich and famous folk. These days, if the high flyers bother to make an appearance, they're likely to show up at 8 in the evening for an aperitivo and some peppery *tarallucchi* bread sticks, with a possible return visit for a late-night limoncello.

In any event, the square is never less than picturesque and has been a natural crossroads and meeting point since Roman times. The religious complex of Santo Stefano was built around the square in the 17th century, but the clock tower and Municipio, or town hall (once the archbishop's palace) are the only remnants of its cathedral. Capri's version of Big Ben—the charming bell tower, or Torre dell'Orologio—is perched over the ancient gateway. ✉ *At intersection of vias Botteghe, Longano, and Vittorio Emanuele, Capri.*

Museo Caprense Ignazio Cerio

HISTORY MUSEUM | Former mayor of Capri Town, designer of the island's most ravishing turn-of-the-20th-century villas, author of delightfully arcane books, and even paleontologist par excellence, Edwin Cerio was Capri's leading genius and eccentric. His most notorious work was a Capri guidebook that all but urged tourists to stay away. His most beautiful work was the Villa Solitaria—once home to famed novelist Compton Mackenzie and set over the sea on the Via Pizzo Lungo path. He also set up this small but interesting museum, which conserves finds from the island. Room 1 displays Pleistocene fossils of pygmy elephant, rhino, and hippopotamus, which all grazed here 200,000–300,000 years ago, when the climate and terrain were very different. Although much of the island's important archaeological finds have been shipped off to Naples, Room 4 displays a scantily labeled collection of vases, mosaics, and stuccowork from the Greek and Roman periods. The terrace gives unrivalled views of the piazzetta and the bay, and was where Clark Gable took breakfast in Vittorio De Sica's 1960 film *It Started In Naples.* ✉ *Piazzetta Cerio 5, Capri* ☎ *081/8376681, 081/8370858* 🌐 *www.centrocaprense.org* 🎫 *€3* 🕒 *Closed Sun.*

Punta Tragara

VIEWPOINT | The "three sons of Capri" can be best seen from the famous lookout point at Punta Tragara at the end of gorgeous Via Tragara. At this point, a path—marked by a plaque honoring the poet Pablo Neruda, who loved this particular walk—leads down hundreds of steps to the water and the feet of I Faraglioni, and perhaps to a delightful lunch at one of the two lidos at the rock base: Da Luigi, a household name in the Bay of Naples, or La Fontelina, an exclusive sun-drenched retreat nearby. After lunch, habitués then hire a little boat to ferry them back to nearby Marina Piccola and the bus back to town. Near the start of the Neruda path turn left to find the most gorgeous seaside walk in Capri—the Via Pizzolungo. Another place to drink in the view of I Faraglioni, which is most romantic at sunset, is the Punta Del Cannone, a hilltop belvedere reached beyond the Certosa di San Giacomo and the Giardini di Augusto. ✉ *End of Via Tragara, Capri.*

Santo Stefano

CHURCH | Towering over La Piazzetta, with a dome that is more sculpted than constructed and with *cupolettas* that seem molded from frozen zabaglione, Capri's mother church is a prime example of *l'architettura baroccheggiante*—the term historians use to describe Capri's fanciful form of Baroque architecture. Often using vaulting and molded buttresses (because there was little wood to be found on such a scrubby island to support the ceilings), Capri's architects became sculptors when they adapted Moorish and Grecian styles into their own "homemade" architecture. Sometimes known unglamorously as the ex-cathedral, the church was built in 1685 by Marziale Desiderio of Amalfi on the site of a Benedictine convent (founded in the 6th century), whose sole relic is the clock tower campanile across the Piazzetta. As in so many churches in southern Italy, there has been a good deal of recycling of ancient building materials: the flooring of the high altar was laid with polychrome marble from Villa Jovis, while the marble in the Cappella del Sacramento was removed from the Roman villa of Tragara. Inside the sacristy are some of the church treasures, including an 18th-century large silver bust of San Costanzo, the patron saint of Capri, whose holy day is celebrated every May 14. ✉ *Piazza Umberto I, Capri* ☎ *081/8370072* 🌐 *www.fondazionesancostanzo.it.*

★ Villa Jovis

RUINS | In Roman times, Capri was the site of 12 spacious villas, but Villa Jovis is both the best preserved and the largest, occupying nearly 23,000 square feet. Named in honor of the ancient Roman god Jupiter, or Jove, the villa of the emperor Tiberius is riveted to the towering Rocca di Capri like an eagle's nest overlooking the strait separating Capri from Punta Campanella, the tip of the Sorrentine Peninsula. A powerful reminder of the importance of the island in Roman times, the site is even more compelling because of the accounts of the latter years of Tiberius's reign between AD 27 and 37, written by authors and near-contemporaries Suetonius and Tacitus. The Salto di Tiberio (Tiberius's Leap) is where ancient gossips believed Tiberius had enemies (among them his discarded lovers and even unfortunate cooks) hurled over the precipice into the sea some 1,000 feet below. From La Piazzetta allow 45 minutes each way for the walk to this site. ✉ *Via A. Maiuri, Capri* ☎ *081/8374549* 🎟 *€6, with audioguide* ⏲ *Closed Jan. and Feb. and Tues. Oct.–Mar.*

★ Villa Lysis

HISTORIC HOME | Opened to the public in 2003, this legendary villa was originally known as the Villa Fersen, after Baron Jacques d'Adelsward-Fersen, the builder. Fleeing to the island from a scandal involving Parisian schoolboys, the French aristocrat had this white stucco pile designed by Edouard Chimot in 1903 in shimmering Belle Époque style, replete with gilded-mosaic columns and floors looted from the island's ancient Roman sites. Past the impressive columned entrance, inscribed in stone with "Amori et Dolori Sacrum" (A Shrine to Love and Sorrow), the baron would retire to write poems and paint pictures in his Stile Liberty ("Liberty Style," or Art Nouveau) salons. Sadly all the furnishings are gone, but you can still gasp at the ballroom open to the sea and the large smoking room in the basement, where, in a tiled pool, Fersen committed suicide by ingesting a lethal mix of opium and Champagne in 1923. Outside are magical terraces with views to rival the adjacent Villa Jovis. ✉ *Via Lo Capo, Via Lo Capo 33, Capri* ☎ *081/8386111 for Capri municipal office* 🎟 *€2* ⏲ *Closed Wed. and Nov.–Feb.*

Villa Malaparte

HISTORIC HOME | Nicknamed the Casa Come Me (House Like Myself) and perched out on the rocky Punta Massullo, this villa is considered by some historians to be a great monument of 20th-century architecture. Built low to

Did You Know?

After being off limits for 32 years, winding Via Krupp was reopened in 2008, complete with a plaque unveiled by Italian president Giorgio Napolitano proclaiming the road a symbol of liberty and an homage to beauty. It is now closed again, with no sign of reopening.

Active Capri

Unsurprisingly, these islands are a haven for fans of water sports. Apart from the ample opportunities for swimming in crystal-clear water (but if it's sandy beaches you want, avoid Capri), both Ischia and Procida have long-established scuba-diving centers. Windsurfers should head to Ischia, while Procida is the ideal place to rent a yacht for short or long trips. Boat and canoe rental is available on all three islands. You might prefer, however, to just avail yourself of the thermal baths for which Ischia is renowned.

With their high peaks, both Capri and Ischia offer spectacular trekking opportunities. Ischia's Monte Epomeo, at 2,582 feet, is somewhat more challenging than the 1,932 feet of Monte Solaro in Capri, especially as on the latter you can choose to use the chairlift for one leg (if not both) of the trip.

The path from Capri Town to I Faraglioni is one of the most beautiful seaside walks in the world, although a strong competitor is the five-hour trek past four Napoleonic towers on the island's west coast.

be part of the ageless landscape, the red-hue villa was designed in Rationalist style by the Roman architect Adalberto Libera in the late 1930s for its owner Curzio Malaparte (author of the novel *La Pelle,* which recounts various World War II experiences in Naples). Unfortunately, the aesthetic concerns of the villa are inextricably entailed with political ones: Curzio Malaparte was a full-blown Fascist, and the only reason why this house was allowed to be built along this otherwise unsullied stretch of coast was by special fiat from none other than Mussolini. Malaparte was unhappy with the design and made a number of alterations during the construction phase, including the famous trapezoidal staircase that seems to grow out of the roof. The villa is private, but if you want to see it up close, it was featured as a suitably striking backdrop for Brigitte Bardot in Jean-Luc Godard's underrated film *Contempt* (1963). ✉ *Giro dell'Arco Naturale, Capri.*

Beaches

La Fontelina

BEACH | Rather than visiting public beaches, many sun worshippers opt to enjoy the island's fabled *stabilimenti balneari* (private bathing lidos), some of which offer real relaxation and unbelievable views. One of the most famous is La Fontelina, open April–October. At the foot of the Faraglioni rocks, the lido has a magical setting. There's no beach here, so the lido isn't suitable for children, and booking in advance is essential. You can get to La Fontelina by using a rocky path that begins at the end of Via Tragara; others prefer to take a ferry (€6) from the more accessible Marina Piccola during the afternoon. The excellent but pricey restaurant is only open for lunch. **Amenities:** food and drink; lifeguards; showers; toilets. **Best for:** snorkeling; swimming. ✉ *Località Faraglioni, Via Faraglioni 2, Capri* ☎ *081/8370845* 🌐 *www.fontelina-capri.com* 🎫 *€36, includes locker and sun chair; €18 beach umbrella.*

Marina Piccola

BEACH | Although Capri is not noted for fine beaches, Marina Piccola is generally considered to have the best beach on the island. It's certainly the most historic: Homer believed this to be the legendary spot where the Sirens nearly snared Odysseus. Expect to pay about €16 per person for the use of showers, lockers, and a sun chair/sun bed. It's definitely worth investing in snorkeling gear, as the sea is rich in marine life, and visibility is often excellent. **Amenities:** food and drink; lifeguards; showers; toilets. **Best for:** snorkeling; swimming. ✉ *Capri.*

Restaurants

Al Caprì

$$ | **SOUTHERN ITALIAN** | This sleek restaurant with an unrivaled bay view is on busy street just steps from the Piazzetta. Passersby often gather to study the menu and drop in for a quick bite, though dishes such as *scialatielli con aragosta* (homemade pasta with lobster) or *paccheri al coccio* (pasta with shellfish) deserve hours to savor. **Known for:** a celebrity favorite; efficient friendly service; stunning views. $ *Average main: €20* ✉ *Via Roma 38, Capri* ☎ *081/8377108* 🌐 *www.ristorantealcapri.it.*

Al Grottino

$$ | **SOUTHERN ITALIAN** | In a 14th-century building close to the Piazzetta, this small, friendly, family-run restaurant has arched ceilings, autographed photos of famous patrons, and lots of atmosphere. Specialties include scialatielli *ai fiori di zucchine e gamberetti* (with zucchini flowers and shrimp) and *cocotte* (housemade pasta with mussels, clams, and shrimps), but the owner delights in taking his guests through the menu of regional dishes. **Known for:** gluten-free options; Caprese specialties with the freshest ingredients; good value for Capri. $ *Average main: €20* ✉ *Via Longano 27, Capri* ☎ *081/8370584* 🌐 *www.ristorantealgrottino.net* ⏲ *Closed Nov.–late Mar.*

Aurora

$$$ | **SOUTHERN ITALIAN** | Often frequented by celebrities, whose photographs adorn the walls inside and out, the island's oldest restaurant offers courtesy and *simpatia* (irrespective of your star status), a sleekly minimalist interior, and tables outside along a chic thoroughfare. The cognoscenti start by sharing a pizza *all'Acqua*—thin-crust, with mozzarella and a sprinkling of *peperoncino* (chili)—but the *gnocchetti al pesto con fagiolini croccanti e pinoli* (dumplings with pesto, beans, and pine nuts) and house-made sweets are good, too. **Known for:** incredible wine cellar and choice; Papà Gennaro's unusually light pizza all'Acqua; historic jet-set hangout. $ *Average main: €28* ✉ *Via Fuorlovado 18/22, Capri* ☎ *081/8370181* 🌐 *auroracapri.com* ⏲ *Closed Nov.–Easter.*

Il Geranio

$$ | **SOUTHERN ITALIAN** | Take the steps up to the right just before the Giardini di Augusto to find this romantic spot, where outdoor seating is staggered on the layered terraces, commanding a fine view of the Fariglioni. The menu combines the best of local and international cooking, specializing in both meat and seafood dishes. **Known for:** wide choice of dishes; vast wine list; stunning views. $ *Average main: €18* ✉ *Via Matteotti 8, Capri* ☎ *081/8370616* 🌐 *www.geraniocapri.com* ⏲ *Closed mid-Oct.–mid-Apr.*

La Canzone del Mare

$$$ | **SOUTHERN ITALIAN** | Although it's not primarily a restaurant, a luncheon dominated by fresh seafood and vegetables in the covered pavilion of this legendary bathing lido of the Marina Piccola is Capri at its most picture-perfect. With two seawater pools, a rocky beach, and I Faraglioni in the distance, it was the erstwhile haunt of Gracie Fields, Emilio Pucci, Noël Coward, and any number of 1950s and '60s glitterati. **Known for:** famous dolce vita–era haunt, now very crowded; sunset wine and peaches served with stuzzichini (appetizers); open terrace overlooking Marina Piccola. [$] *Average main: €35* ✉ *Via Marina Piccola 93, Capri* ☎ *081/8370104* 🌐 *www.lacanzonedelmare.com* ⏲ *No dinner. Closed Oct.–mid-Apr.*

★ La Capannina

$$$ | SOUTHERN ITALIAN | Near the busy piazzetta and long one of Capri's most celebrity-haunted restaurants, La Capannina has a discreet flower-decked veranda that's ideal for dining by candlelight. Specialties change daily depending on the season, but the menu always includes ravioli capresi, linguine *con lo scorfano* (with scorpion fish), and an exquisite "Pezzogna" (sea bream cooked whole and topped with a layer of potatoes). **Known for:** seafood dishes; wine bar next door; walls strewn with photos of celebrity clientele. [$] *Average main: €26* ✉ *Via Le Botteghe 12b, Capri* ☎ *081/8370732* 🌐 *www.capanninacapri.com* ⏲ *Closed Nov.–mid-Mar.*

La Fontelina

$$$ | SOUTHERN ITALIAN | Given its position right on the water's edge, seafood is almost de rigueur here, but also expect fabulous fresh vegetable creations like *polpette di melanzane* (eggplant fritters), and then dip into the vegetable buffet. La Fontelina also functions as a lido, with steps and ladders into fathoms-deep blue water, and this location—accessible on foot from Punta Tragara or by boat from Marina Piccola (10 minutes; €25 up to four passengers)—makes it a good place to spend a delightfully comatose day. **Known for:** chef Mario's daily seafood specials; shuttle boat from Marina Piccola; lunch stop for beach-club bathers. [$] *Average main: €28* ✉ *Via Faraglioni 2, Capri* ☎ *081/8370845* 🌐 *www.fontelina-capri.com* ⏲ *No dinner. Closed mid-Oct.–Easter.*

Le Camerelle

$$$ | SOUTHERN ITALIAN | When you've had enough of the florid Caprese decor, head to this restaurant, where the interior design is Parisian but the ambience evokes New York's trendy Meatpacking District. You can't go wrong with the fresh fish or spaghetti *alla Nerano* (with zucchini, basil, and Parmigiano cheese), and the wine list is a hefty 23 pages. **Known for:** vast and worldly wine list; people-watching; sleek atmosphere. [$] *Average main: €30* ✉ *Via Camerelle 81/83, Capri* ☎ *081/8378677* 🌐 *www.facebook.com/lecamerelle* ⏲ *Closed mid-Oct.–Mar.*

Le Grottelle

$$$ | SOUTHERN ITALIAN | This extremely informal trattoria enjoys a distinctive setting up against limestone rocks not far from the Arco Naturale, with the kitchen in a cave at the back. Whether you stumble over it (and are lucky enough to get a table) or intentionally head for it after an island hike, Le Grottelle will prove memorable, thanks to the ambience, the views of Li Galli islands, and a menu that includes ravioli and local rabbit but is best known for seafood dishes such as linguine *con gamberetti e rucola* (with shrimp and arugula). **Known for:** cool grotto interiors; seafood dishes; breathtaking cliff-clinging location. [$] *Average main: €25* ✉ *Via Arco Naturale 13, Capri* ☎ *081/8375719* ⏲ *Closed Nov.–mid-Mar.*

Pulalli

$$ | ITALIAN | Under the shadow of the Piazzetta's clock tower, this is a pleasant spot to dine above the bustle of the square. Simple local dishes such as ravioli capresi and linguine al limone are accompanied by one of over 150 labels on the wine list; tapas-style snacks are served for those who want a predinner aperitivo. **Known for:** wine list; friendly owner; prime location. [$] *Average main:*

Continued on page 144

CAPRI BY BOAT

To savor Capri to the fullest you must sail its blue waters as well as wander through its squares and gardens. Happily, the famous "giro" cruises around the island allow you to enjoy the perfect sailing safari.

Sooner or later, the beautiful coastline of Capri will lure you to its shores, where you'll be in good company: ancient heroes, emperors, Hollywood divas, and legions of mere mortals have been answering the same siren call from time immemorial. Fact is, you haven't fully experienced Capri until you've explored its rocky shoreline, a veritable Swiss cheese of mysterious grottoes tucked into its myriad inlets and bays. As you'll learn, the Blue Grotto may be world famous, but there's also a Green Grotto, a Yellow Grotto, a Pink, and a White. And unless you possess fins, the only way to penetrate many of these secret recesses is to book yourself on one of the island's giro (tour) cruises—they have been an iconic Caprese experience since the 19th century. Offered by a flotilla of companies ranging from bare-bones to high luxe, these roundabout tours—many last only two hours but you can also sign on for daylong cruises—give you the chance to travel the island's "highway," marvel at sights immortalized in 1,001 travel posters, and, for one magical afternoon, take possession of one of the horseshoe-shape inlets where movie stars are as much at home as dolphins.

above, Capri's iconic Faraglioni rock formation

A "GIRO" TOUR AROUND CAPRI

An aquatic version of the famous Italian *passeggiata* (stroll), the Capri giro cruise is offered on two main types of boat. The classic craft is a *gozzo*—once the traditional fishing boat of the Bay of Naples, it now varies in comfort from luxe (shower, lunch, aperitif) to basic (BYO *panino*). Or opt for a *gommone*, a speedboat: this gives you a chance to create your own itinerary—but watch out for gas prices. Coastal highlights are outlined below, but you can always opt to follow your instincts, take an inviting side lagoon, and while the day away in one of the innumerable small inlets.

Grotta Bianca

STARTING YOUR ROUNDS

Capri's gateway harbor, the **Marina Grande**, is where most giro cruises start. Time, budget, weather, and confidence will determine your choice of tour—long or short, cheap or ritzy, guided or independent—but the more extensive ones should cover the following sites. East of the marina lies the **Grotta del Bove Marino** (Sea Lion's Cave). Listen for the distinctly mammalian howl, amplified naturally by the cave walls: local fishermen may tell you the creature is still in residence, but what you're hearing is the wail of the wind and sea. You soon reach **Punta Capo**, marked by its welcoming statue of the Madonna del Soccorso. Here, atop the **Rocca di Capri**—Capri's own Gibraltar—catch a glimpse of the **Villa Lysis**, a 19th-century Xanadu that clings like a wasps' nest to the cliff and, perched atop the looming peak, the ruins of Emperor Tiberius's fabled **Villa Jovis**.

Villa Jovis

SEA FOR YOURSELF

Rounding Capri's eastern coast you arrive at the **Grotta dei Polpi**, originally named for its abundance of octopus and cuttlefish; recently fished dry, it is now called the Coral Cave. Past a gorge, you'll arrive at **Grotta Meravigliosa**—the "cave of marvels," as its innumerable stalagmites and stalactites prove (look, as most people do, for one that is said to resemble the Madonna). You'll need a sweater and even a scarf in here—it's glacial even in peak summer.

Farther along is the **Grotta Bianca** (White Grotto),

Marina Grande

whose opal waters—their color is due to the mix of seawater and deep-spring water—shimmer against a spectacularly jagged white backdrop; past the entrance a large crevice has produced a natural swimming pool, known as the Piscina di Venere (Pool of Venus). Entering the **Cala di Matermania**, spot the distant square-shaped sea rock known as Il Monacone, once home to a hermit-monk who kept a net hanging off its side (woe betide any fisherman who did not throw in some fish!). Astride the promontory of **Punta Massullo** is that modernist red-hued **Villa Malaparte**.

Past the ancient Roman port of **Tragara** lies the famed **Faraglioni**, the earthen powerhouse of three massive rocks rising from the sea that remain the scenic masterpiece of Capri. The "Faraglione di Terra" is linked to land and nestles two famous lido restaurants, Da Luigi and La Fontelina. The next rock monolith out is the "Faraglione di Mezzo" (Middle)—this one has the tunnel that is so much fun to sail through—while the farthest one out is the Scopolo, or "Faraglione di Fuori" (External). If you have an expert guide ask him to take you into the little blue grotto—a small cave illuminated by an underwater window of aquamarine light—tucked behind the Faraglioni.

Faraglioni

Villa Malaparte

Cala di Matermania

WATER COLORS

Farther on sits the **Grotta Albergo Marinari**. Despite its name, there is no hotel here; the cave was used by sailors as shelter from sudden sea storms. Next lies the **Grotta Oscura**, whose deceptively narrow entrance opens up to reveal the largest cave on the island, its two large oval caverns a showplace of stunning light reflections. Drifting up the southern coast of Capri, the zigzagging drama of **Via Krupp** threads its way over the hillside to chic **Marina Piccola**. It was here on the Scoglie delle Sirene (Siren's Rock), immortalized in Canto XII of the *Odyssey*, that mermaids tried to lure Odysseus, the world's first tourist, onto its hazardous shoals.

Faro

Just after **Punta Ventroso** look for the Cala di San Costanzo, where a "face" in the rock presumably resembles St. Costanzo, the patron saint of Capri. A few hundred meters farther on is the **Grotta Verde** (Green Grotto), whose waters resemble an enormous deep-sea daiquiri, and which in turn is followed by the **Grotta Rossa**, whose red hue is caused by algae buildup. A little way beyond is the

Marina Piccola

Grotta dei Santi (Saints' Cave), whose rocky outcrop resembles human figures at prayer. Take some time to enjoy the truly stunning waters of **Cala Marmolata**, which you'll sail through before coming to the lighthouse, or **Faro**. Sail the length of the west coast to the cape landmarked by the Torre Damecuta. From the Gradola shore you will find your spectaculafinale, the **Grotta Azzurra** (Blue Grotto).

MAKING THE MOST OF THE GROTTA AZZURA

Today, many travelers visit Capri's fabled Grotta Azzurra (Blue Grotta) using tour boats departing either from Capri's Marina Grande or from the small embarkation point below Anacapri (reached by bus from Anacapri Town). This approach can prove frustrating: you have to board one boat to get to the grotto, then transfer to a smaller one to pass through the 3-foot-high cave opening, and then are allowed—due to the midday traffic jam of boats—disappointingly little time once inside the cave. Instead, in late afternoon—not midday—take the bus from Anacapri's Piazza Vittoria to the Strada della Grotta Azzurra. Interested in protecting the early-afternoon hours for their traditional siesta, many native Capresi insist that the optimum time to see the unearthly blue is between 10 AM and 1 PM. However, more objective observers advise that the best time is around 4 PM or 5 PM, when the raking light of the sun is most brilliant. At this hour, many—though not all—of the boatmen have departed along with the tour buses, so you may have the Blue Grotto pretty much to yourself.

€26 from Marina Grande, €12.50 by rowboat from Grotta Azzurra

9–1 hr before sunset, closed if sea is even minimally rough

Grotta Azzurra

€18 ✉ Piazza Umberto I, 4, Anacapri ☎ 081/8374108 🌐 www.facebook.com/pulallicapri ⏲ Closed Tues. and Dec.–Mar.

Hotels

★ Capri Tiberio Palace

$$$$ | HOTEL | Offering guests comfort, style, luxury, and sigh-inducing views since the 19th century, this hotel is a short walk from the piazzetta—near the action, but not quite in the thick of it. **Pros:** friendly staff; traditional and kosher restaurant; pure luxury. **Cons:** tiny gym; the pool is too close to the restaurant; no port-to-door guest shuttle. *$ Rooms from: €599 ✉ Via Croce 11–15, Capri ☎ 081/9787111 🌐 www.capritiberiopalace.com ⏲ Closed Nov.–mid-Apr. 54 rooms 🍽 Free Breakfast.*

Il Gatto Bianco

$$$ | HOTEL | The spot where Jacqueline Kennedy famously sought refuge from the paparazzi is still a wonderful place to experience a quintessentially Capresi atmosphere, particularly in the public spaces, featuring a blue-on-white bar area, majolica-lined stairs, and antique-y accents. **Pros:** central location; wonderful atmosphere; a one-time jet-set favorite. **Cons:** no sea view; terrace is fully enclosed; perhaps too close to the action. *$ Rooms from: €201 ✉ Via Vittorio Emanuele 32, Capri ☎ 081/8370203 🌐 www.gattobianco-capri.com ⏲ Closed Nov.–mid-Mar. 40 rooms 🍽 Free Breakfast.*

La Minerva

$$$$ | HOTEL | A onetime private home, this friendly and welcoming hotel has become a Capri favorite, where most of the bright, airy rooms have panoramic terraces—shaded in bougainvillea and overlooking the Faraglioni and Villa Malaparte. **Pros:** the views; the garden; family-run. **Cons:** down a sidestreet with steps; pricey; a 10-minute climb to the Piazzetta. *$ Rooms from: €650 ✉ Via Occhio Marino 8, Capri ☎ 081/8377067 🌐 www.laminervacapri.com ⏲ Closed Nov.–Mar. 18 rooms 🍽 Free Breakfast.*

La Palma

$$$ | HOTEL | Capri's oldest hotel (1822) doesn't rest on its laurels: it's attentively run and glamorous, from the gleaming lobby to the courtyard lined with coves and columns featuring archetypal Caprese "zabaglione" stucco to the plush rooms with fresco-like art and dolce vita accents. **Pros:** the most central of Capri's luxury hotels; real island glamour; magical courtyard. **Cons:** rather far from the sea; the terrace can get crowded; perhaps too central. *$ Rooms from: €300 ✉ Via V. Emanuele 39, Capri ☎ 081/8370133 🌐 www.lapalma-capri.com ⏲ Closed Nov.–Easter 70 rooms 🍽 Free Breakfast.*

La Scalinatella

$$$$ | HOTEL | If you're bronzed, beautiful, or both, this is your kind of hotel—a white Moorish mansion that evokes Hollywood-style Capri, complete with hillside terraces (indeed, the name means "little stairway"), winding paths, bougainvillea arbors, and an *Architectural Digest* opulence. **Pros:** all rooms have a sea view; his-and-her bathrooms; heated pool. **Cons:** main pool visible from main road; a lot of steps; a bit removed from the center. *$ Rooms from: €530 ✉ Via Tragara 10, Capri ☎ 081/8370633 🌐 www.scalinatella.com ⏲ Closed Nov.–Mar. 31 rooms 🍽 Free Breakfast.*

La Tosca

$$ | HOTEL | Up a tiny side street above the Certosa, this simple, quiet hotel offers unassuming vibes, terrace views, and reasonable rates. **Pros:** simple, unadorned charm; quiet spot near Capri Town; pleasant, helpful owner. **Cons:** rooms might seem to lack panache; books up early; not all rooms have good views. *$ Rooms from: €165 ✉ Via Birago 5, Capri ☎ 081/8370989 🌐 www.latoscahotel.com ⏲ Closed Nov.–Feb. 11 rooms 🍽 Free Breakfast.*

★ Punta Tragara

$$$$ | HOTEL | Designed by Le Corbusier, this former private villa was the site of a secret wartime meeting between Churchill and Eisenhower; today, it's one of Capri's most beautiful hotels, with a breathtaking location on Punta Tragara; public areas adorned with baronial fireplaces, gilded antiques, and travertine marble; and guest rooms that are simultaneously sumptuous and cozy-casual. **Pros:** decadent and luxurious; two gorgeous pools; wonderful views of the famed Faraglioni rocks. **Cons:** small gym; some find the style dated (others find it a plus); a 15-minute walk from the center. *$ Rooms from: €950 ✉ Via Tragara 57, Capri ☎ 081/8370844 ⊕ www.hoteltragara.com ⏲ Closed mid-Oct.–mid-Apr. 44 rooms 🍽 Free Breakfast.*

Quisisana

$$$$ | HOTEL | Some say Capri has three villages: Capri Town, Anacapri, and this landmark hotel, which looms large in island mythology, attracts utterly devoted guests, and has an enormous lobby and theater-cum-convention center that are 1930s jewels designed by noted modernist Gio Ponti. **Pros:** luxe atmosphere on a large scale; top spa facilities; stumbling distance from La Piazzetta. **Cons:** not quite as ritzy as in bygone days; convention-size and far from cozy; minimum three- or five-night stay some periods. *$ Rooms from: €490 ✉ Via Camerelle 2, Capri ☎ 081/8370788 ⊕ www.quisisana.com ⏲ Closed Nov.–mid-Mar. 147 rooms 🍽 Free Breakfast.*

Villa Krupp

$$ | B&B/INN | Occupying a beautiful house overlooking the idyllic Gardens of Augustus, this hostelry (once the home of Maxim Gorky, whose guests included Lenin) has comfy beds in plain but spacious rooms, some of which have south-facing terraces and awesome views. **Pros:** a historical home; much-needed porter service; stunning views. **Cons:** breakfast doesn't match the views; simple rooms; a lot of steps to negotiate. *$ Rooms from: €170 ✉ Viale Matteotti 12, Capri ☎ 081/8370362 ⊕ www.villakrupp.com ⏲ Closed mid-Oct.–mid-Apr. 12 rooms 🍽 Free Breakfast.*

Villa Sarah

$$$ | HOTEL | This yellow, two-story, Mediterranean-style hostelry—complete with Capri's signature round windows and a setting amid lovely gardens in a pleasant residential district—has lots of Caprese spirit and simple but homey and brightly accented rooms that will make you feel like a guest in a private villa. **Pros:** gorgeous pool; unfussy decor; lush gardens. **Cons:** small pool; many rooms tiny; a long and steep climb from the Piazzetta. *$ Rooms from: €250 ✉ Via Tiberio 3/a, Capri ☎ 081/8377817 ⊕ www.villasarah.it ⏲ Closed Nov.–Mar. 20 rooms 🍽 Free Breakfast.*

As would be expected, Capri offers a fair spread of evening entertainment, especially on weekends and during the busier months of July and August, when many upper-crust mainland Italians occupy their island vacation homes. For music that's fairly gentle on the ears, try one of the traditional *taverne,* which are peculiar to Capri Town. There are also several dance clubs and piano bars from which to choose, but the nightlife is more laid-back than Naples or even Ischia. On summer nights the place to be seen showing off your tan and sipping your extra-dry martini is the Piazzetta. Capri Town has the island's most popular late-night spots, often found in cellars.

Anema e Core

LIVE MUSIC | Anema e Core means "soul and heart" in Caprese dialect. This popular place is tucked down a quiet sidestreet, a two-minute walk from the Piazzetta. Admission (€50) includes an eclectic range of lightish live music after 11 pm and a drink from the bar. No food is served, so come well sated. There's

Did You Know?

The Torre Dell'Orologio in Capri Town's famed Piazetta has been a central meeting place since Roman times. It's a great place to people-watch.

no dancing here officially, though some patrons—including celebrities—occasionally take to the tables. The spot is closed Monday and is usually open 9 pm–3 am; reservations are essential on weekends. ✉ *Via Sella Orta 1, Capri* ☎ *325/4742508* 🌐 *www.anemaecore.com.*

Capri Rooftop

COCKTAIL LOUNGES | On top of the Hotel Luna, with breathtaking views over the Faliglioni, this bar is open all day, and is the perfect place for a breather between visits to the Certosa San Giacomo and the Giardini di Augustus. After dark, it becomes the most beautiful nightspot in Capri. ✉ *Hotel Luna, Via Matteotti 7, Capri* ☎ *081/8378147* 🌐 *www.caprirooftop.com.*

La Capannina Wine Bar - Grapperia

WINE BARS | Antique prints line the walls of this tasteful bar just across the alley from the Capannina restaurant. By day it is an informal eatery. ✉ *Vico San Tommaso 1, Capri* ☎ *081/8370732* 🌐 *www.capanninacapri.com.*

Performing Arts

Culturally speaking, Capri has a fairly long hibernation, awakening briefly for the New Year celebrations. Recitals and other low-key cultural events are held in October and January in the Centro Caprense Ignazio Cerio, though June–September the island comes alive with various events, including an outdoor concert season. In general, for information about cultural events and art exhibitions, ask at the local tourist information office or scan the posters in shop windows.

The Certosa di San Giacomo is the cultural heart of the island, hosting events throughout the year. Concerts are held in the two attractive cloisters from June through September. July sees the Certosa International Arts Festival, hosting film screenings, recitals, and readings while the New Year's Eve festivities are eclipsed by the film festival Capri Hollywood (🌐 *www.capri-world.com*).

Capri also caters to the literati, with Le Conversazioni (🌐 *www.leconversazioni.it*), presenting well-known authors reading from their works in Piazzetta di Tragara. Held at the beginning of July, previous editions have featured David Byrne, Patti Smith, Martin Amis, and Ethan Coen.

Shopping

Although Capri is unlikely to be a bargain-hunter's paradise, shopping here is an experience in its own right. Frustratingly though, goods are often displayed without price tags, which means you have to shop Italian-style: decide whether you like an article first and then inquire about its price, rather than vice versa.

Bottega Capri

SHOES | Sandals are a Capri specialty. With a family business stretching back to 1917, owner Vincenzo Faiella is justifiably proud of his made-to-measure footwear. Expect to pay €70–€110 for a carefully handcrafted pair. ✉ *Via Le Botteghe 21, Capri* ☎ *081/8377425.*

Capri Watch

JEWELRY & WATCHES | For more than 20 years these watchmakers have produced the distinctive, jeweled Capri Watch—the full range is available here. ✉ *Via Camerelle 21, Capri* ☎ *081/8377148* 🌐 *www.capricapri.com.*

Carthusia

PERFUME | If you're looking for something that's easily portable to take back from Capri, then eau de toilette, potpourri, or perfumed soap might be just the thing. Carthusia has been making perfumes since 1948, but—as they will proudly tell you—the tradition of perfumery on the island stretches back hundreds of years to the days of Queen Giovanna of Anjou. You can see the perfumes being made through a window at the factory, close to the Certosa di San Giacomo. ✉ *Factory, Via Matteotti 2d, Capri* ☎ *081/8370368* 🌐 *www.carthusia.com.*

Chantecler

JEWELRY & WATCHES | Some tax-free "bargains" might be possible from Capri institution Chantecler, where you can find miniature replicas of the San Michele's Bell of Good Fortune. ✉ *Via Vittorio Emanuele 51, Capri* ☎ *081/8370544* 🌐 *www.chantecler.it.*

Da Costanzo

SHOES | Da Costanzo has been the "king" of Caprese sandalmakers since Jackie O, Sophia Loren, and Grace Kelly all purchased pairs here in the good old days. ✉ *Via Roma 49, Capri* ☎ *081/8378077.*

La Campanina

JEWELRY & WATCHES | Named after San Michele's bell, Capri's good luck symbol, La Campanina has crafted distinctive local brooches since 1950. Owner Lina was responsible for the replica of the bell that was presented to President Roosevelt at Christmas in 1944 (this is now on display at the Museum of the Franklin D. Roosevelt Library in New York). The shop is also Capri's official Rolex dealer. ✉ *Via Vittorio Emanuele 18/20, Capri* ☎ *081/8370643* 🌐 *www. lacampaninacapri.com.*

La Capannina Più

SOUVENIRS | With a selection of more than 1,000 wines (including kosher varieties) as well as marmalades and local Capri "stone" sweets (chocolate-covered almonds), this is an ideal place for connoisseurs to purchase gifts or souvenirs, especially given that the shop ships all over the world, as well as providing a service for yachts. ✉ *Via Le Botteghe 79, Capri* ☎ *081/8378899* 🌐 *www.capanninacapri.com.*

La Conchiglia

BOOKS | La Conchiglia offers the largest selection of books on Capri and publishes many sumptuous tomes through its own imprint. There's also a branch in Anacapri. ✉ *Via Le Botteghe 12, Capri* ☎ *081/8376577* 🌐 *www.edizionilaconchiglia.it.*

La Parisienne

MIXED CLOTHING | Capri's main shopping streets—the Via Vittorio Emanuele and Via Camerelle, down the road from the island's main square, La Piazzetta—are crammed with world-famous names (Gucci, Prada, Dolce & Gabbana, Ferragamo, Hermès). But if you're overwhelmed by the choice and are looking for something stylish but distinctively Capri—in an astonishing range of colors—check out the bright hand-block prints on clothes, bags, and shoes by Neapolitan Livio De Simone at La Parisienne. This is also a good place to purchase copies of the original Capri pants. ✉ *Piazza Umberto I 7, Capri* ☎ *081/8370283* 🌐 *www.laparisiennecapri.it.*

Liquid Art System

ART GALLERIES | In the heart of Capri Town, this gallery is a favorite for collectors and enthusiasts of contemporary art, with paintings by local and international artists availabe to buy. They also have a branch in Anacapri and are responsible for the installations that dot the island in summer months. ✉ *Via V. Emanuele 56, Capri* ☎ *081/8378828* 🌐 *www.liquidartsystem.com.*

Russo Capri

MIXED CLOTHING | The boutiques of Roberto Russo are favored by fashion folk. Russo Capri has one of the island's largest selections of casual chic clothes. ✉ *Via F. Serena 8–10, Capri* ☎ *081/8388200 office, 081/8388265 store* 🌐 *www.russocapri.com.*

Activities

Although there are several tennis courts on the island, most have restricted access, so people looking to burn excess energy tend to do so at sea level or below. For naturalists, bird-watching is particularly good in spring and autumn as Capri lies on a migration pathway, and botany lovers will be thrilled by the island's various nature trails, especially April–June.

Capri Gym A.D.
HEALTH CLUB | For a simple workout, the Capri Fitness A.D., down the steps at the Ristorante Villa Jovis, allows one-off visits. ✉ *Via Roma 36, Capri* ☎ *331/7612571* 🎫 *€15.*

Anacapri and Nearby

One of the most breathtaking bus rides anywhere follows the tortuous road from Capri Town 3 km (2 miles) up a dramatic escarpment to Anacapri. At 902 feet over the bay, Anacapri is the island's only other town and leading settlement on the island's peaks, poetically referred to as the Monte Sirene (Siren Heights). Crowds are thickest around the square, which is the starting point of the chairlift to the top of Monte Solaro and a short walk from Villa San Michele, the main magnet up here for tour groups. Allow plenty of time when traveling to or from Anacapri, as space on the local buses is usually at a premium. Alternatively, the athletically inclined can hike from close to Marina Grande up to Anacapri by taking the 921 steps of the Scala Fenicia (the Phoenician Stairway, more likely to have been built by the Greeks than the Phoenicians) to Villa San Michele. Needless to say, most people will want to tackle the Scala Fenica going down, not up. As a fitting finale to a visit to Anacapri, take the convenient bus down the hill to the water's edge and the fabled Grotta Azzurra.

GETTING HERE AND AROUND

There's regular bus service to Anacapri from Marina Grande or Capri Town (Piazzetta d'Ungheria).

Sights

★ **Casa Rossa** (*Red House*)
HISTORIC HOME | Capri is famous for its villas built by artists, millionaires, and poets who became willing prisoners of Capri during the Gilded Age. Elihu Vedder, Charles Coleman, Lord Algernon, and the Wolcott-Perry sisters were some of the people who constructed lavish Aesthetic Movement houses. Built by the American colonel J.C. MacKowen, this particular villa, near the center of Anacapri, was erected between 1876 and 1899. With walls hued in distinctive Pompeian red, the villa incorporates a noted 15th-century Aragonese tower. A historian and archaeologist, MacKowen wrote a guide to Capri and brought to light marble fragments and statues inside the Blue Grotto, thus revealing and validating its importance as a nymphaeum in Roman times; the statues are displayed here. Local legend says that Anacapri's menfolk locked their women in Casa Rossa when they went to work in Naples, but the villa now houses a permanent exhibition called "The Painted Island," featuring 32 canvases from masters such as Brancaccio and Carelli, depicting images of Capri in the 19th and 20th centuries. A collection of oils by 20th-century Milan landscape artist Carlo Perindani was added in 2015. Don't miss the views from the highest roof terrace in central Anacapri, taking in Monte Solaro and Ischia. ✉ *Via G. Orlandi 78, Anacapri* ☎ *081/8382193* 🎫 *€4, €1 for ticket holders of chairlift or Villa San Michele.*

Grotta Azzurra
CAVE | Only when the Grotta Azzurra was "discovered" in 1826, by the Polish poet August Kopisch and Swiss artist Ernest Fries, did Capri become a tourist destination. The watery cave's blue beauty became a symbol of the return to nature and revolt from reason that marked the Romantic era, and it soon became a required stop on the Grand Tour. In reality, the grotto had long been a local landmark. During the Roman era—as testified by the extensive remains, primarily below sea level, and several large statues now at the Certosa di San Giacomo—it had been the elegant, mosaic-decorated nymphaeum of the adjoining villa of Gradola. Historians can't quite agree if it was simply a lovely little pavilion where rich

patricians would cool themselves or truly a religious site where sacred mysteries were practiced. The water's extraordinary sapphire color is caused by a hidden opening in the rock that refracts the light. At highest illumination the very air inside seems tinted blue. Locals say the afternoon light is best from April to June, and the morning in July and August.

The Blue Grotto can be reached from Marina Grande or from the small embarkation point below Anacapri on the northwest side of the island, accessible by bus from Anacapri. If you're pressed for time, however, skip this sometimes frustrating and disappointing excursion. You board one boat to get to the grotto, then transfer to a smaller boat that takes you inside. If there's a backup of boats waiting to get in, you'll be given precious little time to enjoy the gorgeous color of the water and its silvery reflections. ✉ *Capri* 🎫 *From €15 from Marina Grande via various companies, then €14 by rowboat with Coop. Battellieri* 🕑 *Closed if the sea is even minimally rough.*

★ Monte Solaro

VIEWPOINT | An impressive limestone formation and the highest point on Capri (1,932 feet), Monte Solaro affords gasp-inducing views toward the bays of both Naples and Salerno. A serene 13-minute chairlift ride will take you right to the top (refreshments available at the bar), where you can launch out on a number of scenic trails on the western side of the island. Picnickers should note that even in summer it can get windy at this height, and there are few trees to provide shade or refuge. ✉ *Piazza Vittoria, Anacapri* ☎ *081/8371428* 🌐 *www.capriseggiovia.it* 🎫 *€9 one-way, €12 return* 🕑 *Closed chairlift in adverse weather.*

Parco Filosofico (*Philosophical Park*)

GARDEN | Frustrated by Capri's ongoing commercial overdevelopment, Swedish professor Gunnar Adler-Karlsson acquired the land around the Belvedere di Migliara with the intention of maintaining an ecologically pure area. Covering 11,000 square meters (36,000 square feet), paths lead through rich Mediterranean maquis with more than 60 ceramic panels lining the way with quotes from great thinkers from Aristotle to Einstein. Allegedly the first of its kind in the world, just feet away from one of the most gorgeous views in the world, this park is devoted to peace and reflection. A complete guide, called "Meditation Upon Western Wisdom," is available from the adjacent Da Gelsomino restaurant. ✉ *Via Migliara, Anacapri* 🌐 *www.philosophicalpark.org* 🎫 *Free.*

San Michele

CHURCH | In the heart of Anacapri, the octagonal Baroque church of San Michele, finished in 1719, is best known for its exquisite majolica pavement designed by Solimena and executed by the *mastro-riggiolaro* (master tiler) Chiaiese from Abruzzo. A walkway skirts the depiction of Adam and a duly contrite Eve being expelled from the Garden of Eden, but you can get a fine overview from the organ loft, reached by a spiral staircase near the ticket booth. ✉ *Piazza San Nicola, Anacapri* ☎ *081/8372396* 🌐 *www.chiesa-san-michele.com* 🎫 *€2* 🕑 *Closed Jan. and Feb.*

★ Santa Maria a Cetrella

RELIGIOUS BUILDING | Scenically perched on the slopes of Monte Solaro, this small sanctuary in late-Gothic style—with its older parts dating to the late 14th century—offers a truly picturesque frame for a panorama that takes in much of the island. It also marks the top of the second access route (Il Passetiello) used in ancient times, which linked Capri Town with Anacapri. Steep, slippery, and in spots still dangerous, this is the pathway that the Carthusian monks of San Giacomo would have used to reach their properties in the upper part of the island. Congregants were mainly fisherfolk whose boats were moored in the Marina Piccola directly below; they

Around Anacapri: A Good Walk

Axel Munthe's Masterpiece

From Anacapri's main square of Piazza Vittoria, take Via Capodimonte opposite the *seggiovia* (chairlift) to **Villa San Michele,** about a five-minute walk, past a formidable array of garish boutiques, bars, and liqueur factories, all vying to ensnare passersby.

As with many sites on the island, it's best to get to the villa shortly after it opens, or in the early evening when the day-trippers have moved through, to leisurely browse through its rooms and stroll through the gardens and the ecomuseum.

Siren Heights

Retrace your steps to Piazza Vittoria and make for the lower station of the Seggiovia to **Monte Solaro.** You'll soon be whisked out of town over white-washed houses and carpets of spring-flowering broom and rockrose to the viewing platform at the top of Solaro.

From here a path leads north downhill toward the sublimely picturesque church of **Santa Maria a Cetrella** through some of the most beautiful wooded countryside on Capri.

In spring and autumn watch for migrating birds. A splash of yellow combined with an undulating flight could be the golden oriole; the multicolor bee-eater also migrates via Capri in May and September.

On the way back down from Cetrella, follow the signs to Anacapri along Via Monte Solaro (downhill), passing close to the ruins of the **Castello Barbarossa** and then emerging close to the Villa San Michele.

Anacapri Town

If you have time and energy left over, make for Via Orlandi, a useful street for stocking up on provisions.

Pass the impressive **Casa Rossa** (Red House), on your right, and then take the next right turn (Via San Nicola) to Piazza San Nicola and the church of **San Michele.** Climb to the organ loft to savor its magnificent majolica-tile floor depicting the Garden of Eden, then head back to the Piazza Vittoria.

To the Sea

At this point choose between the Belvedere di Migliara and the Grotta Azzurra. A 40-minute walk to **Belvedere di Migliara** is rewarded with an iconic view as well as the world's first **Philosophical Park.** By mid- to late afternoon, the crowds will have vanished from the **Grotta Azzurra,** at the sea below Anacapri.

Catch the convenient bus that links the town with the grotto and enjoy this fabled sight around 4–5 pm, when connoisseurs swear that the light is best.

Timing

The walk takes approximately four hours, allowing at least one hour for the visit to Villa San Michele and its gardens, and a further two hours' leisurely amble on the round-trip. Add a half hour if visiting the Belvedere di Migliara, as it is off the beaten track.

If armed with a packed lunch, you're most likely to find a picnic site near Cetrella—in attempts to discourage low-spending day-trippers from the mainland, consumption of picnics is made fairly difficult on Capri.

A chairlift makes ascending Monte Solaro a breeze.

also used this clifftop aerie as a lookout against Saracen pirates. The church was substantially rebuilt by Franciscan monks in the early 17th century, when a sacristy was added. To reach Santa Maria, you can climb a path leading off Viale Axel Munthe (an hour-long walk); an alternative is to descend a path leading from the Monte Solaro chairlift for 20 minutes. The church is usually open on Saturday (10–3), but check at the chairlift. Mass is celebrated at dawn every Sunday in September, but the site remains unforgettable year-round. ✉ *Monte Solaro, Anacapri.*

Villa di Damecuta

RUINS | One of the best excursions from Anacapri is to the ruins of the Roman Villa di Damecuta. Sited strategically on a ridge with views sweeping across the Bay of Naples toward Procida and Ischia, the villa would have had its main access point at the landing stage right by the Grotta Azzurra at Gradola. This was probably one of the villas mentioned by Tacitus in his *Annals* as having been built by Tiberius: "Here on Capreae, in twelve spacious, separately named villas, Tiberius settled." Like Villa Jovis to the east, Villa di Damecuta was extensively plundered over the centuries prior to its proper excavation in 1937. Below the medieval tower (Torre Damecuta) there are two rooms (*domus* and *cubiculum*) that are thought to have been Tiberius's secret summer refuge. Affinities with Villa Jovis may be seen in the *ambulatio* (walkway) complete with seats and a stunning backdrop. To reach Villa Damecuta, get the bus from Anacapri to Grotta Azzurra and ask the driver to let you off at the proper stop. Alternatively, you can walk down from the center of Anacapri—from behind the Santa Sofia church take the well-marked network of virtually traffic-free little alleyways running parallel to the main road (about 30 minutes). ✉ *Via A. Maiuri, Capri* 🎫 *Free* ⏲ *Closed Mon.*

★ Villa San Michele

HISTORIC HOME | From Anacapri's Piazza Vittoria, picturesque Via Capodimonte leads to Villa San Michele, the charming former home of Swedish doctor and philanthropist Axel Munthe (1857–1949), and which Henry James called "the most fantastic beauty, poetry, and inutility that one had ever seen clustered together." At the ancient entranceway to Anacapri at the top of the Scala Fenicia, the villa is set around Roman-style courtyards, marble walkways, and atria. Rooms display the doctor's varied collections, which range from bric-a-brac to antiquities. Medieval choir stalls, Renaissance lecterns, and gilded statues of saints are all part of the setting, with some rooms preserving the doctor's personal memorabilia. A spectacular pergola path overlooking the entire Bay of Naples leads from the villa to the famous Sphinx Parapet, where an ancient Egyptian sphinx looks out toward Sorrento. ✉ *Viale Axel Munthe 34, Anacapri* ☎ *081/8371401* 🌐 *www.villasanmichele.eu* 🎫 *€10.*

Beaches

Lido del Faro

BEACH | The Lido del Faro, set amid rocks with a natural basin as a seawater swimming pool, is open from April to October during daylight hours. The sun usually beats down on this westerly headland all day while on summer nights the restaurant provides a unique setting for enjoying the freshest fish. The lido is easily accessible by bus from Anacapri. **Amenities:** food and drink; lifeguards; showers; toilets. **Best for:** snorkeling; swimming. ✉ *Località Punta Carena, Anacapri* ☎ *081/8371798* 🌐 *www.lidofaro.com* 🎫 *Approx. €50, includes locker and sun bed and €40 voucher for restaurant.*

Restaurants

Barbarossa

$$ | SOUTHERN ITALIAN | Take the staircase behind Piazza Vittoria's bus stop to the covered terrace of this ristorante-pizzeria with panoramic views of the Barbarossa castle and the sea. The no-frills ambience belies the quality of the a la carte *cucina*: besides *pizze* they specialize in local dishes—including risotto *con gamberi a limone* (shrimp with lemon). **Known for:** chef's semifreddi and other dessert specials; lively function room during events; authentic (certified) Vera Pizza Napoletana. 💲 *Average main: €17* ✉ *Piazza Vittoria 1, Anacapri* ☎ *081/8371483* 🌐 *www.ristorantebarbarossa.com.*

★ Da Gelsomina

$$$ | SOUTHERN ITALIAN | Amid its own terraced vineyards with inspiring views to the island of Ischia and beyond, this is much more than just a well-reputed restaurant. The owner's mother was a friend of Axel Munthe, and he encouraged her to open a food kiosk, which evolved into Da Gelsomina; today the specialties include *pollo a mattone,* chicken grilled on bricks, and locally caught rabbit. **Known for:** fresh produce and wine from their verdant gardens; chicken grilled on bricks; opened in the 1960s with family links to Axel Munthe. 💲 *Average main: €35* ✉ *Via Migliara 72, Anacapri* ☎ *081/8371499* 🌐 *www.dagelsomina.com* 🕓 *Closed Nov.–Mar.*

Il Cucciolo

$$ | SOUTHERN ITALIAN | Nestling in thick maquis high above the Grotta Azzurra and a five-minute walk from the Roman site of Villa Damecuta, this must be one of the most romantic locations in Capri, perfectly placed to catch the setting sun. The cucina is refreshingly inventive with fish being a specialty: ask for *pasta fresca con zucchini e gamberi* (fresh pasta with zucchini and shrimp). **Known for:** being family run; its fresh local cuisine; its magical setting. 💲 *Average main: €23* ✉ *Via La Fabbrica 52, Anacapri* ☎ *081/8371917* 🌐 *www.giorgioalcucciolo.com* 🕓 *Closed Nov.–Apr.*

Il Riccio Restaurant & Beach Club

$$$$ | SOUTHERN ITALIAN | Just above the Grotta Azzurra with a to-die-for view of the Sorrentine coast and Vesuvius, Il Riccio is a true Mediterranean experience. Chef Salvatore Elefante prepares

Did You Know?

Villa San Michele's original owner and guiding spirit, Axel Munthe, did not actually live in his ornate complex. He called the Torre di Materita, set higher on the island, his true home.

innovative takes on typical Neapolitan recipes, based mainly on seafood, that earned a Michelin star in 2013. **Known for:** stunning location; Michelin star; iconic dining. $ *Average main: €100* ✉ *Via Gradola 4, Anacapri* ☎ *081/8371380* 🌐 *www.capripalace.com* ⏲ *Closed Oct.–Easter.*

La Rondinella

$ | **SOUTHERN ITALIAN** | This is an airy ristorante-pizzeria opening onto the main road on one side and Anacapri's pedestrianized street on the other. In summer, make sure you reserve a table out on the popular terrace to feast on linguine *macchiavelle* (with capers and cherry tomatoes). **Known for:** family-run atmosphere; reasonable prices; informal setting. $ *Average main: €14* ✉ *Via Orlandi 295, Anacapri* ☎ *081/8371223* ⏲ *Closed Nov.–Feb., and Thurs. Oct.–May.*

Hotels

Biancamaria

$$ | **HOTEL** | This hotel, with its pleasing facade and whitewashed arches, lies in a traffic-free zone near the heart of Anacapri; front rooms have large terraces facing Monte Solaro, while those at the back are quieter and more private. **Pros:** friendly staff; Anacapri literally at your doorstep; inexpensive for Capri. **Cons:** no gardens; the breakfast is small; on the main pedestrian road. $ *Rooms from: €170* ✉ *Via G. Orlandi 54, Anacapri* ☎ *081/8371000* 🌐 *www.hotelbiancamaria.com* ⏲ *Closed mid-Oct.–Easter* 🛏 *25 rooms* 🍽 *Free Breakfast.*

★ **Caesar Augustus**

$$$$ | **HOTEL** | A favorite of the Hollywood set, this landmark villa hotel is a Caprese paradise thanks to its breathtaking perch atop a cliff; its grand gardens, terraces, and pool; and its charming, casual-chic rooms with their plump chairs and fragrant bouquets. **Pros:** serene terrace views; infinity pool; summer concerts on-site. **Cons:** pricey; no kids under 12 allowed; a bit far from the action for some. $ *Rooms from: €700* ✉ *Via G. Orlandi 4, Anacapri* ☎ *081/8373395* 🌐 *www.caesar-augustus.com* ⏲ *Closed Nov.–mid-Apr.* 🛏 *55 rooms* 🍽 *Free Breakfast.*

★ **Capri Palace Jumeirah**

$$$$ | **HOTEL** | For the cognoscenti, famous or otherwise, this is *the* place to stay in Anacapri, thanks to its spa, designer boutique, exceptional restaurants, suites with private pools, and rooms with art or film themes (ask for the Monroe, Callas, or Warhol). **Pros:** chic and stylish; the only medical spa on the island; Capri's only Michelin-star restaurant. **Cons:** a bit too close to the center of Anacapri; pricey; unattractive entrance. $ *Rooms from: €580* ✉ *Via Capodimonte 14, Anacapri* ☎ *081/9780111* 🌐 *www.capripalace.com* ⏲ *Closed Nov.–mid-Apr.* 🛏 *68 rooms* 🍽 *No Meals.*

San Michele

$$$ | **HOTEL** | Surrounded by luxuriant gardens, in a large cream-color villa, the San Michele offers solid comfort and good value, along with spectacular views from sky-high Anacapri. **Pros:** large pool; spectacular views; lovely gardens. **Cons:** the staff is not the friendliest; a bit run down; some rooms are tiny. $ *Rooms from: €220* ✉ *Via G. Orlandi 1–5, Anacapri* ☎ *081/8371427* 🌐 *www.sanmichele-capri.com* ⏲ *Closed Nov.–Mar.* 🛏 *61 rooms* 🍽 *Free Breakfast.*

Villa Eva

$$ | **HOTEL** | Popular with young *Wandervögel* (young German travelers) who have a laid-back approach to traveling, this unique option is noted for its artisanal style and picturesque architecture: most guest rooms are in tiny garden villas and often feature rotunda ceilings, toy fireplaces, and Caprese arts and crafts. **Pros:** rooms in small villas immersed in gardens; young energetic clientele; a paradise-island vibe. **Cons:** removed from the island's action; gardens can be a haven for mosquitoes; patchy cell phone reception. $ *Rooms from: €150* ✉ *Via*

La Fabbrica 8, Anacapri ☎ *081/8371549* 🌐 *www.villaeva.com* ⏲ *Closed mid-Oct.–Mar.* 20 rooms *Free Breakfast.*

Nightlife

La Lanterna Verde

LIVE MUSIC | Part of Hotel San Michele and open year round, this is the clubbing spot for thirtysomethings and older cognoscenti. ✉ *Hotel San Michele, Via G. Orlandi 1, Anacapri* ☎ *081/8371427* 🌐 *www.lanternaverdecapri.it.*

Maliblù

CAFÉS | For six days a week, this is a lively beach bar, but on Sunday evening it's *the* place to be for dance music and cocktails accompanying the sunset. ✉ *Punta Carena, Anacapri* ☎ *081/8372560* 🌐 *www.maliblusunset.com.*

Queen Pub & Disco

LIVE MUSIC | Anacapri cognoscenti of various ages gather here for the music and the beer. ✉ *Via Orlandi 259, Anacapri* ☎ *081/8373909.*

Shopping

Mariorita

MIXED CLOTHING | Lovers of fashion, both Italian and international, appreciate this hip boutique at the Capri Palace, which sells its own upscale items, as well as those by big labels such as Versace, Valentino, Missoni, Trussardi, and Hugo Boss. It also deals in fine ceramics and has a children's clothing section. ✉ *Piazza Vittoria, Anacapri* ☎ *081/9780540.*

Ischia

Although Capri leaves you breathless with its charm and beauty, Ischia (pronounced "EES-kee-ah," with the stress on the first syllable), also called the Isola Verde (Green Island)—not, as is often believed, because of its lush vegetation, but for its typical green tuff rock—takes time to cast its spell. In fact, an overnight stay is definitely not long enough; you have to look harder for the signs of antiquity, the traffic can be reminiscent of Naples, and the island displays all the hallmarks of rapid, uncontrolled urbanization. Ischia does have many jewels, though. There are the wine-growing villages beneath the lush volcanic slopes of Monte Epomeo, and unlike Capri, the island enjoys a life of its own that survives when the tourists head home. Ischia has some lovely hotel-resorts high in the hills, offering therapeutic programs and rooms with dramatic views. If you want to plunk down in the sun for a few days and tune out the world, go down to sea level: against the towering backdrop of Monte Epomeo with one of the island's inviting beaches—or natural hot baths—close at hand, you might wonder what Emperor Augustus could have been thinking when he surrendered Ischia to the Neapolitans in return for Capri.

Ischia is volcanic in origin, with thermal springs said to cure whatever ails you. Today the island's main industry, tourism, revolves around the more than 100 thermal baths, most of which are attached to hotels. In the height of summer, the island's population of 60,000 swells more than sixfold, placing considerable strain on local water resources and public transport facilities. However, most of the *confusione* is concentrated within the island's six towns and along its main roads, and it's relatively easy to find quiet spots even close to the beaten path.

Much of the 37 km (23 miles) of coastline are punctuated with a continuum of *stabilimenti balneari* (private bathing establishments) in summer. However, there are also lots of public beaches set against the scenic backdrop of Monte Epomeo and its verdant slopes. Most port traffic to the island—mainly ferries and hydrofoils from the mainland—is channeled into Ischia Porto with some arrivals at Casamicciola and Forio, burgeoning resorts and busy spa centers. The Castello Aragonese in Ischia Ponte, which is a vast medieval complex, is one of the island's main historic sights; Lacco Ameno, with its immense archaeological heritage and more upscale ambience, is a good base for exploring the north of the island; Forio is famous for the grand gardens of La Mortella and the Poseiden thermal baths. Buses between the main towns are frequent and cheap, though somewhat overcrowded.

GETTING HERE AND AROUND

Ischia is well-connected with the mainland in all seasons. The last boats leave for Naples and Pozzuoli at about 8 pm (though in the very high season there is a midnight sailing), and you should allow plenty of time for getting to the port and buying a ticket. Ischia has three ports—Ischia Porto, Casamicciola, and Forio (hydrofoils only)—so you should choose your ferry or hydrofoil according to your destination. Non-Italians can bring cars to the island relatively freely. Up-to-date schedules are published at 🌐 *www.traghetti-ischia.info*.

Ischia's bus network reaches all the major sites and beaches on one of its 17 lines. The principal lines are CD and CS, circling the island in clockwise and counterclockwise directions—in the summer months runs continue until after midnight. The main bus terminus is in Ischia Porto at the start of Via Cosca, where buses run by the company EAV radiate out around the island. There are also convenient *fermate* (stops) at the two main beaches—Citara and Maronti—with timetables displayed at the terminus. Tickets cost €1.50 per ride (€2 on board), €1.80 for 100 minutes, and €4.50 for 24 hours; note that conditions can get hot and crowded at peak beach-visiting times.

A number of car and scooter rental facilities are available. Note that police are vigilant about seat-belts, helmets, and parking violations.

FERRIES AND HYDROFOILS

Alilauro has roughly one hydrofoil per hour traveling from Beverello, Naples, to Ischia Porto (€21.20 to €23, travel time 50 minutes). From May through September, up to seven hydrofoils per day depart for Forio (€23, travel time 50 minutes). Caremar has six daily hydrofoil departures from Molo Beverello, Naples, to Ischia Porto (€17.90, travel time 45–60 minutes) and eight daily ferry departures from Calata Porta di Massa, Naples (€12.30, travel time 1 hour 30 minutes). Ferry departures are also available from Pozzuoli (€12, travel time 1 hour).

MedMar has up to six daily departures from Calata Porta di Massa, Naples (€12.40, travel time 1 hour 30 minutes), and up to 10 daily ferry departures from Pozzuoli, sometimes docking at Casamicciola (€12, travel time 1 hour). SNAV offers up to eight hydrofoils daily from Molo Beverello, Naples, to the marina of Casamicciola (€20.40-€21.40, travel time 50 minutes).

CONTACTS Alilauro. ☎ *081/4972238* 🌐 *www.alilauro.it.* **Caremar.** ☎ *081/18966690* 🌐 *www.caremar.it.* **MedMar.** ☎ *081/3334411* 🌐 *www.medmargroup.it.* **SNAV.** ☎ *081/4285555* 🌐 *www.snav.it.*

SCOOTERS AND BICYCLES

About 200 yards from Ischia Porto's ferry terminal, the company Del Franco, opposite Hotel Re Ferdinando, has a fair range of sturdy bicycles, both traditional (€12 per day) and electric (€25), as well as scooters (from €30).

Just to the left of the main bus stop, and with a branch also in Casamicciola, Mazzella has a fleet of new scooters from €20 per day and cars from €30.

CONTACTS Del Franco. ✉ *Via Alfredo De Luca 127, Ischia Porto* ☎ *081/991334* 🌐 *www.noleggiodelfrancoischia.com.* **Mazzella.** ✉ *Piazza Trieste e Trento 4, Ischia Porto* ☎ *081/991141* 🌐 *www.mazzellarent.it.*

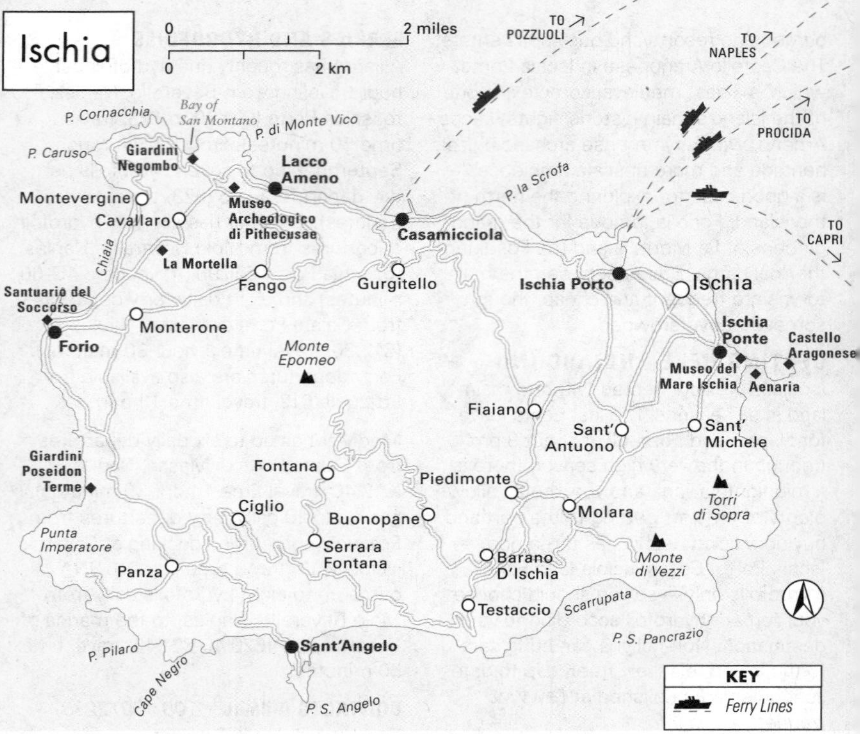

VISITOR INFORMATION

CONTACTS Azienda Autonoma di Cura, Soggiorno e Turismo. ✉ *Via Iasolino 7,* ☎ *081/5074211* 🌐 *www.agenziaturismo-campania.it.*

Ischia Porto

4 km (3 miles) east of Casamicciola.

Ischia Porto is the largest town on the island and the usual point of debarkation. It's not a workaday port, but a pretty resort town with plenty of hotels and low, flat-roofed houses on terraced hillsides above the water. Known by the Romans as Villa dei Bagni, its villas and gardens are framed by umbrella pines and locals mingle with tourists in the narrow streets.

The harbor area was originally a land-locked lake in a volcanic crater: the Bourbon king Ferdinand II had a channel cut to create an opening seaward, and then created a sheltered port (1854). As you walk into the town along the waterfront, note the grandiose facade of the municipal baths Ferdinand II used to visit, now used for town council offices and occasional art exhibitions.

GETTING HERE AND AROUND

Ferries and hydrofoils bring you here from Naples and Pozzuoli.

Restaurants

I Ricci

$ | SOUTHERN ITALIAN | Overlooking the boats at the end of the Riva Destra (Right Bank), this casual restaurant serves excellent fish in a convivial atmosphere.

Specialties include risotto *alla pescatore* (with shellfish) and linguine *all'aragosta* (with lobster), as well as an array of raw fish. **Known for:** friendly owner; sumptuous desserts; location on the Riva Destra. *Average main: €14* ✉ *Riva Destra, Via Porto 93, Ischia Porto* ☎ *335/5236383 mobile* 🌐 *iricciristorante.tumblr.com* ⏲ *Closed Mon. Nov.–Mar.*

Hotels

Hotel Aragona Palace

$$ | **HOTEL** | Dominating the entrance to the Riva Destra, Ischia's restaurant strip overlooking the port, this is the closest luxury hotel to the arriving hydrofoils. **Pros:** a hop, skip, and jump from the port; ferry-watching from the roof garden; friendly staff. **Cons:** rather far from the nearest beach; some noise from Riva outside; rooms have only showers with no baths. *Rooms from: €146* ✉ *Via Porto 12, Ischia Porto* ☎ *081/3331229* 🌐 *www.hotelaragona.it* *52 rooms* *Free Breakfast.*

Hotel La Villarosa Terme

$$ | **HOTEL** | In a villa and garden a short walk from the beach, this hotel has bright, airy guest rooms with charming antiques. **Pros:** view from roof garden; wonderful pool; in a semi-botanical garden. **Cons:** some rooms are more attractive than others; bathrooms small and a little run down; maybe too close to the town. *Rooms from: €180* ✉ *Via Giacinto Gigante 5, Ischia* ☎ *081/991316* 🌐 *www.dicohotels.it* ⏲ *Closed Nov.–Mar.* *37 rooms* *Free Breakfast.*

Nightlife

Nightlife on Ischia starts late in the evening and continues until the early hours. In some private gardens, occasional concerts and cultural events are offered during the summer months.

Ecstasy

DANCE CLUBS | Cocktails, snacks, and late-night dancing are on offer at this nightspot, which has an outdoor seating area and an indoor bar with a DJ. ✉ *Corso Vittoria Colonna 97, Ischia Porto* ☎ *081/982569* 🌐 *www.facebook.com/ischiaecstas.*

Valentino Club

DANCE CLUBS | In the center of Ischia Porto, this is the focal point for a clientele in its early twenties and above. Admission varies (€16–€25), depending on what's on offer. ✉ *Corso Vittorio Colonna 97, Ischia Porto* ☎ *081/982569* 🌐 *www.valentinoischia.eu/home.*

Ischia Ponte

2 km (1 mile) southeast of Ischia Porto.

The spectacular Castello Aragonese, towering atop an islet just off the main shore, landmarks Ischia Ponte. The town's name (Ischia Bridge) refers to the striking causeway built in the mid-15th century to connect it with the rest of Ischia. Although it has an amazing history, the castle also looms large in today's Ischia, as it becomes the appropriately cinematic setting for the Ischia Film Festival every July, with occasional exhibitions held in the Chiesa dell'Immacolata.

GETTING HERE AND AROUND

Take Bus No. 7 from Ischia Porto. If arriving by car or scooter, bear in mind that the access to the town is pedestrianized during peak hours (there is, however, a large car park).

Sights

Aenaria

RUINS | In 1972 local divers found two heavy lead ingots in the Bay of Cartaromana, just across from the castle, leading to the discovery of Aenaria, a metal-working Roman settlement destroyed in a volcanic eruption around

Ischia's Castello Aragonese sits on its own island, just offshore from Ischia Ponte.

150 AD (*aenum* is the Latin for metal), and referred to in records by Pliny the Elder. Ongoing excavations began in 2011, and Il Borgo del Mare organises a tour in a glass-bottom boat. ✉ *Via Luigi Mazzella 68, Ischia Ponte* ☎ *081/2304911* 🌐 *www.ilborgodimare.com* 🎫 *€30.*

★ Castello Aragonese

CASTLE/PALACE | The spectacular Castello Aragonese, towering atop an islet just off the main shore, landmarks Ischia Ponte. The little island was settled as early as the 5th century BC, when the tyrant Hiero of Syracuse came to the aid of Cumae in its power struggle against the Etruscans. This was his reward: an almost unassailable natural islet more than 300 feet high, on which he erected high watchtowers to monitor movements across the Bay of Naples. The island changed hands in the succession of centuries, with Greeks from Neapolis, Romans, Visigoths, Vandals, Ostrogoths, Saracens, Normans, Swabians, and Angevins successively modifying the fortifications and settlements. Ischia Ponte was where the population of Ischia sought refuge in 1301, when Epomeo's last eruption buried the town of Geronda on the other side of the causeway. The new influx of inhabitants led to a flurry of building activity, most notably the Cattedrale dell'Assunta, built above a preexisting chapel that then became its crypt. In the following century the Angevin castle was rebuilt by Alfonso of Aragon (1438), who gave it much of its present form. However, its turbulent history continued well into the 19th century, when it was seriously damaged by the English in their attempts to dislodge the French during the Napoleonic Wars (1809).

Two hours should be enough to give you a feel of the citadel, stroll along its ramparts, and visit its key religious sites. Don't miss the frescoed 14th-century crypt beneath the cathedral (Giotto school), although the ruined cathedral itself, with its noticeable 18th-century additions—such as the Baroque stucco work—is quite atmospheric. Occasional exhibitions are held in the Chiesa dell'Immacolata, and there are two bars. Access to the citadel is via an elevator from the base, and the various walks at the top are clearly signposted. While taking in the whole site, enjoy the stunning views from the various vantage points. ✉ *Castello Aragonese, Ischia Ponte* ☎ *081/992834* 🌐 *www.castelloaragoneseischia.it* 🎫 *€12.*

Museo del Mare Ischia

HISTORY MUSEUM | Housed in the Palazzo dell'Orologio, the town's Museo del Mare Ischia is dedicated to the daily life of fishermen. Ship models, archaeological finds, nautical instruments, and the stray modern art show make up the small holdings. ✉ *Via Giovanni Da Procida 3, Ischia Ponte* ☎ *333/7148020* 🎫 *€5* ⏲ *Closed Mon.*

Restaurants

Da Cocò

$$ | SOUTHERN ITALIAN | This inviting restaurant with a terrace is on the causeway that links the Aragonese castle to the rest of Ischia. It's renowned for its fresh seafood, which is highly prized by the Ischitani: shoreline classics dominate, including the antipasto *polipo con patate (octopus with potatoes)* and primo summer favorite *spaghetti allo scoglio.* **Known for:** good spot to just sit with an aperitivo and nibbles; deliciously light lemon and almond cake; magical setting near the castello. $ *Average main: €21* ✉ *Via Aragonese 1, Ischia Ponte* ☎ *081/981823* ⏲ *Closed Jan. and Feb.*

Coffee and Quick Bites

Ice da Luciano

$ | ITALIAN | A stop here for some gelato is a must upon arriving in Ischia Ponte. **Known for:** inexpensive prices; large selection; the best ice-cream on the island. $ *Average main: €2* ✉ *Via Luigi Mazzella 140, Ischia Ponte* ☎ *081/0123228* 🌐 *www.facebook.com/icedaluciano.*

Hotels

★ **Albergo Il Monastero**

$$ | HOTEL | The Castello Aragonese, on its own island, is the unrivaled location for this unique hotel with a peaceful ambience and simple but comfortable rooms overlooking the Mediterranean. **Pros:** stunning views and peaceful garden; great restaurant on terrace; situated inside the castle. **Cons:** some may not like the understated decor; perhaps too far from the town's action; a long way from the entrance to your room. $ *Rooms from: €150* ✉ *Castello Aragonese 3, Ischia Ponte* ☎ *081/992435* 🌐 *www.albergoilmonastero.it* ⏲ *Closed Nov.–late Apr.* *21 rooms* *Free Breakfast.*

Nightlife

Bar Calise

CAFÉS | Midway between Ischia Porto and Ischia Ponte, Bar Calise is allegedly "the biggest bar in Europe." Here you'll find everything you need for a good night out in one garden—you can choose between live music, a nightclub ('O Spasso), a piano bar, a restaurant-pizzeria, or a more traditional café. And if you have a hankering for a *cornetto* late at night, this is the only place on the island to find such pastry delicacies after midnight. Veteran Emiddio Calise runs this complex as well as two other bars and *pasticcerie* (try their specialty Monte Epomeo) around the island. ✉ *Piazza degli Eroi 69, Ischia* ☎ *081/991270* 🌐 *www.barcalise.com.*

Shopping

Imagaenaria

BOOKS | This bookshop seems to be from times long gone, with a large selection of rare volumes and limited editions, as well as the latest novels and a large English-language selection. ✉ *Via Luigi Mazzella 46–50, Ischia Ponte* ☎ *081/985632* 🌐 *www.imagaenaria.com.*

Panificio Boccia

FOOD | This bakery's oven has been functioning since 1938, fired up with dried local Mediterranean maquis. It's also a grocery store and an ideal place to grab a sandwich. ✉ *Via Giovanni da Procida 45, Ischia Ponte* ☎ *081/2134906* 🌐 *www.facebook.com/boccialievitatidautore.*

Casamicciola

2 km (1 mile) east of Lacco Ameno.

Known properly as Casamicciola Terme, this spa town has the largest concentration of thermal baths on the island and is where Giuseppe Garibaldi came to recover after the 1862 Battle of Aspromonte. The lower town revolves around the busy Piazza Marina with its large bust of the Italian king Vittorio Emanuele II and its marble plaque honoring Henrik Ibsen, who was inspired by the beauty of the area to write *Peer Gynt* here. Although much of the town was destroyed in an 1883 earthquake, with further damage in another quake in 2017, it has retained some charming examples of 19th-century architecture.

GETTING HERE AND AROUND

Take Bus No. 1, 2, or CS from Ischia Porto. Bus No. 3 climbs to the upper part of the town.

Sights

Other than a small 19th-century geophysical observatory, there are few sights in town. Most visitors head here to enjoy the famous spa hotels. Note the stunning, although now derelict, building on the left after you enter the town from Ischia: it is Pio Monte della Misericordia, opened in 1604 as a hospital that housed Europe's first spa.

Restaurants

Ristorante Pizzeria Corso

$ | PIZZA | Just behind the oddly named Topless Bar (it isn't), the lush gardens here are a haven from the bustle of Casamicciola's main thoroughfare. Authentic Neapolitan pizzas are made before your eyes under leafy trees and fresh fish, grilled meat, and, of course, Ischitan rabbit are also on the menu. **Known for:** its children's playground; typical Ischian food; its lovely back garden. [$] *Average main: €12* ✉ *Corso Luigi Manzi 107, Casamicciola Terme* ☎ *081/995481* 🌐 *www.corsoischia.it.*

Hotels

Albergo L'Approdo

$$ | HOTEL | A short walk from Casamicciola's port, spas, and town center, this small hotel has a fine array of facilities and guest rooms with private terraces. **Pros:** wonderful elevated views; pool perched above bay; great beauty treatments. **Cons:** showers are tiny; not quite in the town; the beach is across a busy road. [$] *Rooms from: €134* ✉ *Via Eddomade 29, Casamicciola Terme* ☎ *081/3330190* 🌐 *www.albergolapprodo.it* *38 rooms* 🍽 *Free Breakfast.*

Nightlife

Unico Café & More

CAFÉS | Elegant and modern, this place has a decidedly young soul, with DJs and local bands accompanying aperitivos and snacks. ✉ *Corso Luigi Manzi 5, Casamicciola Terme* ☎ *081/8435359* 🌐 *www.facebook.com/unicocafeemore.*

Shopping

Ischia Beauty

OTHER HEALTH & BEAUTY | If your visit to the spas makes you want more pampering, stop here for locally produced lotions, creams, and sprays. ✉ *Via T. Morgera*

17, Casamicciola Terme ☎ *081/996975* 🌐 *www.ischiacosmeticitermali.it.*

Lacco Ameno

6 km (4 miles) west of Ischia Porto, 3 km (2 miles) north of Forio.

Lacco Ameno was colonized by the Greeks as early as the 8th century BC, and the landscape here has remained epic: it was used as the backdrop for the barge scene in Elizabeth Taylor's *Cleopatra.* For all its famous visitors, the town does not have a jet-setty vibe and looks lackluster on first impression. But take a walk down the main road, which turns into the Corso Rizzoli along the seafront, and you will find a pedestrianized heaven: flanked by low-key shops, cafés, and restaurants and lined with cobblestones, the promenade runs for several idyllic blocks with the bay rarely out of sight. The Bay of San Montano, a brilliant blue-sapphire buckle along the coast, is the setting for the Giardini Negombo, the most stylish of the thermal complexes on the island. At sunset, Corso Rizzoli becomes a romantic's heaven.

GETTING HERE AND AROUND

Take Bus No. 1, 2 or CS from Ischia Porto.

Sights

The smallest of the six *comuni* (municipalities) on the island, Lacco Ameno is a mecca for some of Italy's rich and famous. Magnate Gianni Agnelli used to anchor his yacht every summer close to the Fungo, a most distinctive mushroom-shape rock in volcanic tuff sculpted by wave action in the small marina, now one of the most notable natural landmarks on Ischia. Luchino Visconti, the noted realist film director and opera designer, had his Villa La Colombaia nearby in the Bay of San Montano.

If you visit one of Ischia's many *terme,* or spa baths, you will not only be following a well-established tradition stretching back more than 2,000 years but also sampling one of the major contemporary delights of the island. You should allow at least half a day for this experience, but the better value is to get there early and indulge until sunset. If you do decide to restrict yourself to half a day, then go in the afternoon, when the hefty entrance fees are slightly lowered. The larger establishments have a plethora of pools offering natural hydromassage at different temperatures and in different settings, with a complement of bars and restaurants to enable customers to stay on the premises right through the day. Most terme are equipped with beauty centers, offering an unbelievably broad range of services, from mud-pack treatments and manicures to bioenergetic massage.

Giardini Negombo

HOT SPRING | For the ultimate Ischian spa escape, try the stylishly landscaped park of Giardini Negombo. Designed around a beach of the finest sand, by the scenic Bay of San Montano, it was created decades ago by Duke Luigi Camerini, a passionate botanist (who named his resort in honor of its resemblance to a bay in Sri Lanka). There are 12 saltwater or thermal pools here, plus facilities for hydromassage, a beauty center with sauna and Turkish bath, sports facilities for diving and windsurfing, a bar, restaurant, and, according to the brochure, "a boutique for irresponsible purchases." All this is set in gardens with 500 species of Mediterranean plants and several panoramic views. Everything here—modern stone waterfalls, elegant poolside tables with thatched-leaf umbrellas, sensitive landscaping—is in the finest taste. At night, the outdoor arena often hosts big-name concerts. The Hotel della Baia ($$) is also on-site. ✉ *Baia di San Montano, Lacco Ameno* ☎ *081/986152* 🌐 *www.negombo.it* 🎫 *From €23* 🕙 *Closed Nov.–mid-Apr.*

★ Museo Archeologico di Pithecusae

HISTORY MUSEUM | Lacco Ameno's archaeological importance—it rests below the first Greek settlement on Italian soil on the island, at Monte Vico—is amply reflected by the finds displayed in Ischia's top museum. The museum occupies much of the Villa Arbusto, built by Carlo d'Aquaviva in 1785 on top of a Bronze Age settlement. Inaugurated in 1999, with the directors of both the British Museum and the Louvre in attendance, its eight rooms house a wide range of Greek pottery unearthed at the ancient necropolis site near the Baia di San Montano, much of it dating to the earliest years of the Greek colony (late 8th century BC), including Nestor's Cup, the oldest known kotyle vase in existence. There is also a room dedicated to internationally renowned filmmaker Angelo Rizzoli, who once lived in the villa, as well as a section devoted to dolphins. Villa Arbusto combines musical *serate*, or evening soirées, in summer months with visits to the antiquities museum. ✉ *Villa Arbusto, Corso Angelo Rizzoli 210, Lacco Ameno* ☎ *081/996103, 081/3330288* 🌐 *www.pithecusae.it* 🎫 *€5, gardens free* ⏲ *Closed Mon.*

Restaurants

★ Indaco

$$$$ | **MEDITERRANEAN** | Part of the Regina Isabella and set beside a suggestive bay (the restaurant's name is inspired by the color of the sea just before nightfall), seafood features prominently at this Michelin-starred spot, which offers four degustazioni menus (€145) based on chef Pasquale Palamaro's inspired use of fresh local ingredients. Try the Ravioli with Genovese sauce, a typical onion-based Neapolitan dish, with red shrimps and pearls of tarragon and for desert, the *mio mare*, which looks like canned tuna. **Known for:** its fine dining; the chef's imaginative creations with local ingedients; its Michelin star. 💲 *Average main: €145* ✉ *Albergo della Regina Isabella, Piazza Santa Restituta 1, Lacco Ameno* ☎ *081/994322* 🌐 *www.reginaisabella.com* ⏲ *No lunch. Closed Nov.–mid-Apr.*

O' Padrone Dò Mare

$$ | **SOUTHERN ITALIAN** | In a gorgeous seaside location just off the pedestrian stretch, this is the ideal place to enjoy fresh seafood—the name, "owner of the sea," says it all. For more than 75 years, O' Padrone Dò Mare has been an institution on the island, and locals and visitors crowd the terrace. **Known for:** local institution; spot-on fritto misto di mare seafood medley; cracking harbor views. 💲 *Average main: €15* ✉ *Corso A. Rizzoli 6, Lacco Ameno* ☎ *081/900244* ⏲ *Closed Nov.–Mar.*

Hotels

★ Mezzatorre Resort & Spa

$$$$ | **HOTEL** | Far from the madding, sunburned crowds—in a sleekly renovated former fortress on Punta Cornacchia above the Bay of San Montano—this luxurious getaway tempts its privileged guests to stay put and *relax*, with a glamorous heated pool overlooking a storybook cove, fine restaurants, spa treatments, and hundreds of pretty pine and pomegranate trees. **Pros:** tranquil retreat with wonderful views; private bay; good restaurants and spa. **Cons:** far from the action; pricey; very isolated. 💲 *Rooms from: €680* ✉ *Via Mezzatorre 23, Forio* ☎ *081/986111* 🌐 *www.mezzatorre.it* ⏲ *Closed Nov.–Apr.* 🛏 *52 rooms* 🍽 *Free Breakfast.*

Regina Isabella – Resort Spa Restaurant

$$$$ | **HOTEL** | Built in the early 1960s, and home to Elizabeth Taylor and Richard Burton while they filmed *Cleopatra*, Ischia's largest luxury hotel is tucked away in an exclusive corner of the beach, where it pampers guests (some attending conventions) with its resort facilities and spa treatments. **Pros:** central location; considered by locals to be the top hotel on the island; Michelin-starred restaurant. **Cons:** rooms are fairly spartan; pricey; not the most elegant of facades. *Rooms from: €316 Piazza Santa Restituta 1, Lacco Ameno 081/994322 www.reginaisabella.com Closed Nov.–mid-Apr. 128 rooms Free Breakfast.*

Forio

9 km (6 miles) west of Ischia Porto.

Lying close to the main wine-producing area of the island, Forio is a busy seaside resort with beaches barely a minute's walk from its town center. Farther along are the small San Francesco and the larger Citara, two of the island's better-known beaches. At first glance, the town seems to provide sad evidence of suburban sprawl (there are more houses without planning permits here than with), and its natural setting of flat coastline is not the most alluring.

GETTING HERE AND AROUND

Take Bus No. 1, CS, or CD from Ischia Porto. Bus No. 2 continues to Citara beach and the popular Poseidon Gardens.

Sights

Giardini Poseidon Terme

HOT SPRING | FAMILY | The largest spa on the island has the added boon of a natural sauna hollowed out of the rocks. Here you can sit like a Roman senator on stone chairs recessed in the rock and let the hot water cascade over you. With countless thermally regulated pools, promenades, and steam pools, plus lots of kitschy toga-clad statues of the Caesars, Poseidon exerts a special pull on tourists, many of them grandparents shepherding grandchildren. On certain days, the place is overrun with people, so be prepared for crowds and wailing babies. *Citara Beach, Forio 081/9087111 www.giardiniposeidonterme.com €35 all day Apr.–June and Oct. and Nov., €40 July–Sept. Closed Nov.–mid-Apr.*

★ La Mortella

GARDEN | Two kilometers (1 mile) north of Forio is one of the most famous gardens in Mediterranean Italy, La Mortella. The garden was a labor of love designed in 1956 by the landscape architect Russell Page for Sir William Walton and his Argentine-born wife, Susana. The garden was created within a wide, bowl-shape, rocky valley, originally not much more than a quarry, overlooking the Bay of San Francesco and with spreading views toward Monte Epomeo and Forio. Lady Walton, who passed away in 2010, was a talented gardener in her own right, and first planted the trees of her childhood here (jacaranda, silk trees, erythrina, brugmansia) and then added tree ferns, palm trees, cycads, and rare bromeliads. Native wild plants were encouraged in the upper reaches of the gardens, with dainty vetches and orchids as well as myrtle, from which the garden got its name, La Mortella. Considering the volcanic valley out of which the gardens were sculpted, they are appropriately threaded with pathways of rocks hewn from Vesuvius. In homage to the hot springs of the island, the centerpiece is an elliptical pond with three small islands adorned with the immense boulders that once littered the grounds. Below, underground cisterns were excavated to catch natural drinking water.

Besides some soothing strolls among the well-labeled flower beds and landscaped rock gardens, try to spend some time in the museum dedicated to the life and works of the late English composer, William Walton. The gardens have excellent facilities, with a shop selling Sir William's music, a tea house for light refreshments, and a theater that hosts a concert series on most weekends; book well in advance for these tickets. *Via Francesco Calise 39, Forio*

☎ *081/986220* 🌐 *www.lamortella.org* 🎫 *€12; €20 for concert, includes visit to garden* ⏲ *Closed Mon., Wed., and Fri.; Nov.–Easter.*

★ **Santuario del Soccorso**

CHURCH | The 14th-century Santa Maria della Neve, better known as the Santuario del Soccorso, is the island's most picturesque church. Down at the harbor, the whitewashed church makes a good spot for a sunset stroll. Check out the wooden crucifix in the chapel on the left; it was washed up on the shore below the church in the 15th century. Restored in 2013, this is the oldest statue on the island. For an overview of the town go to the Torrione, one of 12 towers built under Aragonese rule in the 15th century to protect Forio's inhabitants from the ever-present threat of pirate raids. ✉ *Via Soccorso, Forio.*

Restaurants

Bar-Ristorante Bagno Teresa

$ | **SOUTHERN ITALIAN** | This unpretentious restaurant on Citara Beach offers a range of fresh, reasonably priced seafood served with lively local wine. If you want something light, this is the place to come—there's no need to order a full Mediterranean splurge. **Known for:** friendly staff; Thursday night parties; on-the-beach dining. $ *Average main: €10* ✉ *Baia di Citara, Forio* ☎ *081/908517* 🌐 *www.facebook.com/bagnoteresaforio* ⏲ *No dinner Sun.–Wed. Closed mid-Nov.–Mar.*

Cava dell'Isola

$$ | **MEDITERRANEAN** | Set on the beach that shares its name, this Forio dining favorite has a seaside terrace and a menu that offers a wide range of traditional Mediterranean cuisine, from classic Neapolitan pizza to fresh fish of the day. It's all accompanied by wonderful views; non-diners are welcome to sip a cocktail at the bar and partake of the vistas. **Known for:** large indoor and outdoor dining areas; the chef's imaginative takes on Mediterranean classics; spectacular sunsets. $ *Average main: €16* ✉ *Via G. Mazzella 31, Forio* ☎ *320/6557398 mobile* 🌐 *www.facebook.com/ristorantecavadelisola* ⏲ *Closed Nov.–Mar.*

★ **Umberto a Mare**

$$$ | **SOUTHERN ITALIAN** | This iconic eatery has occupied the space below the Santuario del Soccorso since 1936, when the original Umberto began to grill the local catch on the seafront. The setting is divine, with a terrace overlooking the Bay of Citara and the green tuff *scogli innamorati* (lovers' rocks). **Known for:** decades-long reputation for exquisite seafood; changing displays of artworks; breathtaking sunset sea views. $ *Average main: €26* ✉ *Via Soccorso 8, Forio* ☎ *081/997171* 🌐 *www.umbertoamare.it* ⏲ *Closed Nov.–Mar.*

Hotels

Hotel Semiramis

$$ | **HOTEL** | At this quiet family-run hotel—a short walk from Citara Beach and the crowded Giardini Poseidon spa—each of the tastefully decorated rooms has its own theme; the best and most expensive rooms take advantage of the hotel's panoramic views from the upper-terrace wing. **Pros:** great views; friendly staff; lovely pools. **Cons:** not much action in the evening; some rooms are a bit run down; a bit of a climb from the beach. $ *Rooms from: €140* ✉ *Via G. Mazzella 236, Spiaggia di Citara, Forio* ☎ *081/907511, 081/907511* 🌐 *www.hotelsemiramisischia.it* ⏲ *Closed Nov.–Mar.* 🛏 *33 rooms* 🍽 *Free Breakfast.*

Il Gattopardo

$$ | **HOTEL** | Surrounded by verdant Ischian maquis and a vineyard, this modern-style hotel has comfortable, airy rooms; a solarium with views of Citara Bay and Epomeo Mountain; and spa facilities with thermally heated pools, mud therapies, Finnish sauna, and massages. **Pros:**

The Giardini La Mortella was built by British composer Sir William Walton and his wife, Lady Susana.

indoor and outdoor swimming pools; friendly staff; great sunsets. **Cons:** some rooms are too close to the action; a little far from Forio town; the entrance is more akin to a sports club than hotel. *$ Rooms from: €180 ✉ Via G. Mazzella 196, Forio ☎ 081/997714 🌐 www.ilgattopardo.com ⏲ Closed Nov.–Mar. 72 rooms 🍽 Free Breakfast.*

La Scogliera

$$$ | HOTEL | Above the sea about a mile from Forio town—between the Bay of San Francesco and the crystal-clear waters of Chiaia—Hotel La Scogliera has tastefully furnished rooms done up in Mediterranean hues and bright tile flooring. **Pros:** direct access to beach; family atmosphere; large pool. **Cons:** some rooms look onto a wall; small breakfast; beach access not included in price. *$ Rooms from: €210 ✉ Via Aiemita 27, Forio ☎ 081/987651 🌐 www.hotel-lascogliera.it ⏲ Closed Nov.–Mar. 52 rooms 🍽 Free Breakfast.*

Sant'Angelo

6 km (3½ miles) south of Forio.

A sleepy fishing village out of season, Sant'Angelo, with La Roia promontory, has preserved its character remarkably well. The area has been spared much of the *speculazione edilizia* (speculative building, often without planning permission) that has hit the rest of the island, and the steep, winding path down to the sea is closed to traffic. Well connected by public transport, this is a perfect site for an early evening passeggiata: you can peek into local pottery shops or tasteful boutiques, and then settle into a café near the quayside for an aperitivo.

GETTING HERE AND AROUND

Take Bus No. 1, CS, or CD from Ischia Porto.

Restaurants

★ Ristorante dal Pescatore

$$ | **SOUTHERN ITALIAN** | Occupying Sant'Angelo's main square since the 1950s, this family-run institution has views of the beach and La Roia promonotory. Dine inside or out on creative pizzas (the *a fiori di zucchini* is a good bet) and seafood and pasta dishes, or simply drop by for house-made ice cream (often with unusual flavors, basil anyone?), liquors, or sumptuous desserts. **Known for:** wide variety; friendly owner; great location. *Average main: €20* ✉ *Piazzetta Sant'Angelo 7, Ischia* ☎ *081/999206* ⊕ *www.dalpescatore.info* ⊗ *No dinner Nov.–Mar. Closed mid-Jan.–Feb.*

Procida

Lying barely 3 km (2 miles) from the mainland and 10 km (6 miles) from the nearest port (Pozzuoli), Procida is an island of enormous contrasts. It's the most densely populated island in Europe—just more than 10,000 people crammed into less than 3½ square km (2 square miles)—and yet there are oases like Marina Corricella and Vivara, which seem to have been bypassed by modern civilization. The inhabitants of the island—the *procidani*—have an almost symbiotic relationship with the Mediterranean: many join the merchant navy, others either fish or ferry vacationers around local waters. And yet land traffic here is more intense than on any other island in the Bay of Naples.

In scenic terms this is the place to admire what the Italians call "Spontaneous," or folkloric Mediterranean, architecture: look for the tall archways on the ground floor, which signal places where boats could be stowed in winter, the outside staircases providing access to upper floors without cramping interior living space, and the delicate pastel colors of the facades contrasting with the deeper, bolder blues of the sea. Picturesquely scenic, it's no surprise that Procida, with its strong artistic traditions, and widely considered the painters' island par excellence, was chosen as Italy's Capital of Culture 2022.

GETTING HERE AND AROUND

Procida's ferry timetable caters to the many daily commuters who live on the island and work in Naples or Pozzuoli. The most frequent—and cheapest—connections are from the Port of Pozzuoli. Because of port fees, the ticket price is a few euro higher than to Ischia, the more distant island. After stopping at Procida's main port, Marina Grande (also called Sancio Cattolico), many ferries and hydrofoils continue on to Ischia, for which Procida is considered a halfway house. As with the other islands, buy a single ticket rather than a round trip (there's virtually no saving on a round-trip ticket, which is usually twice the single fare, and it ties you down to one operator on your return); up-to-date schedules are published on ⊕ *www.traghetti-ischia.info*. There are four main bus routes that will take you to practically every corner of the island as well as a fleet of microtaxis operating round-island tours and plying the route between the port and the Marina Chiaiolella, on the southwest of the island. To get to Vivara, a road climbs westward out of Chiaiolella, and motorized access is barred shortly before reaching the bridge linking the two islands. This island can only be visited on accompanied tours arranged through the Comune (⊕ *www.vivarariservanaturalestatale.it*).

The bus terminus in Procida is at the disembarkation point in Via Roma. Provided there's no traffic gridlock along the island's narrow streets, the buses run by the EAV Bus (☎ *081/991808*, ⊕ *www.eavsrl.it*) will get you to most destinations within about 10 minutes for €1.50. Chiaiolella is the most frequently served destination (about every 15 minutes) and timetables are displayed—and tickets bought—at a newsstand next to the hydrofoil ticket office.

In summer the bus service runs until about 1 in the morning. Tickets can be bought for €2 from the bus driver. Keep in mind that on-the-spot checks and hefty fines are frequently imposed on riders without a ticket.

Islanders are discovering the joys of electric bikes, but mopeds and scooters still prevail, which means the streets between the port and the center of the island are both noisy and loaded with pollutants, making casual strolling and window-shopping stressful. You can, however, walk the length of the island in under an hour.

Beaches can be reached by sea or land, with fishermen improvising as water-taxi drivers.

BICYCLES

Electric bikes are available at the port from €20 per day. Scooters can also be rented here from €30.

CONTACTS General Rental. ✉ *Via Roma 112, Procida* ☎ *081/8101132* 🌐 *www.generalrental.it.*

FERRIES AND HYDROFOILS

Caremar has four hydrofoils departing from Molo Beverello, Naples (€20.20, travel time 35 minutes), and up to seven ferry departures per day from Calata Porta di Massa, Naples (€15.90, travel time 1 hour). There are three ferries per day from Pozzuoli (€12.90, travel time 40 minutes). SNAV has four daily hydrofoils that leave from Molo Beverello, Naples (€21.20, travel time 35 minutes).

CONTACTS Caremar. ☎ *081/18966690* 🌐 *www.caremar.it.* **SNAV.** ☎ *081/4285555* 🌐 *www.snav.it.*

VISITOR INFORMATION

CONTACTS Info Point. ✉ *Via Roma (Stazione Marittima), Procida* ☎ *344/1162932* 🌐 *www.facebook.com/proloco.procida.3.*

Terra Murata and Abbazia di San Michele

Ferries pull into the main port, Marina Grande (Sancio Cattolico, or "safe place" in the local dialect), which is fetchingly adorned with pastel-hue houses and the church of Santa Maria della Pietà (1760). For your introductory look, hike up Via Principe Umberto on your way up to the Castello. For a fascinating glimpse of the traditional architecture, turn left at Piazza di Martiri and walk about 600 feet until you come to a tiny passageway that leads to the 16th-century Casale Vascello, originally a gated area of tumbling-down cottages. Continue up Via San Michele to the Chiesa Santa Margherita Nuova—almost at the highest point on the island—for magnificent views of the enchanting fishing village of the Marina della Corricella and beyond. An archway takes you to the old town of Terra Murata—a fascinating cluster of ancient buildings, including a church, palazzi, fortifications, ancient walls, and gateways, mostly in yellow-gray tuff stone. A Benedictine abbey was founded here in the 11th century, safely tucked away from mainland marauders, and the area became the focal point for the inhabitants of the island.

GETTING HERE AND AROUND

Take Bus C2 to get to this popular part of the island.

Sights

Abbazia di San Michele

RELIGIOUS BUILDING | Within Terra Murata is the Abbazia di San Michele. San Michele (St. Michael) is the island's patron saint and a key figure in its history and traditions. Legend has it that in 1535, when the sultan of Algeria's admiral laid siege to the island, San Michele appeared above the pirate force and put them to flight (the 17th-century painting depicting the scene is in the choir of the abbey's 17th-century church; one of the invaders' anchors can also be viewed). On the wall close to the church's richly coffered ceiling is another depiction of San Michele, attributed to the Tuscan Luigi Garzi (1699). As you walk around the church, note that the floor's marble flagstones have holes, which were, in effect, trapdoors through which bodies could be lowered to the underground crypt. The maze of catacombs (closed indefinitely) lead to a secret chapel. Mass is held every Sunday at 9:30 am, and the cultural association Millennium offers free guided tours by request. ✉ *Terra Murata, Procida* ☎ *081/8967612, 334/8514252 Millennium* 🌐 *www.abbaziasanmicheleprocida.it, www.associazionemillennium.it* 🎫 *Free* ⏲ *Closed Mon., Sun. afternoon; Nov.–mid-Apr.*

Palazzo d'Avalos

NOTABLE BUILDING | The easily distinguishable and now abandoned Palazzo d'Avalos—sometimes called Palazzo Reale or Il Castello—was the 17th-century residence of Innico d'Avalos, cardinal and mayor of Procida. The building was then used as a prison from the 1830s until 1988. Guided tours can be booked through the comune. ✉ *Via Terra Murata 33, Procida* ☎ *333/3510701 mobile* 🌐 *www.comune.procida.na.it* 🎫 *€10 (credit card only).*

Santa Margherita Nuova

CHURCH | The renovated 16th-century ex-convent of Santa Margherita Nuova is perched precariously at the top of a cliff facing the small bay of Corricella; a breathtaking view is guaranteed. ✉ *Salita Castello, Procida* ⏲ *Closed weekends.*

Shopping

Procida's best shopping area is at the port, with stores open year-round.

Fine House

CERAMICS | Although this shop specializes in Procida ceramics, its inventory includes lots of other items that would also make great gifts. It's affiliated with the store called La Controra in Corricella. ✉ *Via Roma 116, Procida* ☎ *081/8969593.*

L'Angolo

MIXED CLOTHING | If you haven't packed the right clothes, this store near the port carries brand-name casual clothing and beachwear. ✉ *Via Vittorio Emanuele 1, Procida* ☎ *081/8967023.*

Luigi Nappa Art Gallery

ART GALLERIES | Artist Luigi Nappa is behind all the creations for sale here, including clothing, art, furniture, and jewelry. ✉ *Via Roma 50, Procida* ☎ *081/8960561* 🌐 *luiginappa.com.*

Maricella

WOMEN'S CLOTHING | The women's clothing, jewelry, sandals, bags, and other accessories sold here include one-off pieces and island-inspired styles. ✉ *Via Roma 161, Procida* ☎ *081/19727274* 🌐 *www.facebook.com/maricellastore.*

Noi Due

CERAMICS | Shop here for fine ceramics and elegant linen clothing. There is also a branch at Chaiaolella. ✉ *Via Roma 51, Procida* ☎ *081/8967661.*

Rosso Corallo

JEWELRY & WATCHES | Luisa Izzo transforms coral into brooches, bracelets, and necklaces at this artisan boutique. ✉ *Via Vittorio Emanuele 6, Procida* ☎ *081/3775374* 🌐 *www.luisaizzorossocorallo.com.*

Sinergy Giangiulio

ELECTRONICS | A Procida institution since 1967, this store stocks electronics and ceramics. ✉ *Via Roma 62, Procida* ☎ *081/8967918* 🌐 *www.facebook.com/SinergyGiangiulio.*

Corricella

This sleepy fishing village, used as the setting for the waterfront scenes in the Oscar-winning film *Il Postino*, has been relatively immune to life in the limelight. Apart from a new restaurant and bar, there have been few changes, but the place comes alive at night.

GETTING HERE AND AROUND

Take Bus C2 from Marina Grande Sancio Cattolico to Terra Murata, then proceed on foot.

Sights

★ Marina Corricella

TOWN | FAMILY | Perched under the citadel of the Terra Murata, the Marina Corricella is Procida's most memorable sight. Singled out for the waterfront scenes in *Il Postino* (*The Postman*, the 1995 Oscar winner for Best Foreign Film), this fishermen's cove is one of the most eye-popping villages in Campania—a rainbow-hued, horizontal version of Positano, comprising hundreds of traditional Mediterranean-style stone houses threaded by numerous *scalatinelle* (staircase streets). ✉ *Procida.*

Restaurants

Graziella

$$ | SEAFOOD | This waterfront restaurant, family run since 1964, is as rustic as they come, with food served on plastic tables outside. For starters, try the bruschette and the seafood specialty (a selection of shellfish, octopus, and anchovies big enough for two); the *impepata di cozze* (mussels in pepper) is a must, as is the island's best *granita di limone* (lemon crushed ice), freshly made here everyday. **Known for:** informal atmosphere; imaginative use of lemons; its position in Corricella. [$] *Average main: €15* ✉ *Via Marina Corricella 14, Corricella* ☎ *081/8967479* ⏲ *Closed Dec.–Feb.*

La Conchiglia

$$ | SOUTHERN ITALIAN | A meal at this restaurant, on the beach about a half-mile east of Corricella, encapsulates Procida's seaside simplicity. Lapping waves and views of the marina and Capri form the backdrop for the fresh seafood and vegetable creations. **Known for:** boat trips and bathing nearby; freshest ingredients; beachside views and breezes through open windows. [$] *Average main: €20* ✉ *Via Pizzaco 10, Procida* ☎ *081/8967602* 🌐 *www.laconchigliaristorante.com* ⏲ *Closed mid-Nov.–Mar.*

Coffee and Quick Bites

Chiaro Di Luna

$ | ICE CREAM | Gelato made from local ingredients and a selection of cocktails make this bar a great place to stop at the Marina Corricella. **Known for:** the best ice cream on the island; great selection; stunning location. [$] *Average main: €2* ✉ *Via Marina Corricella 87, Corricella* ☎ *333/7700776* 🌐 *www.facebook.com/bargelateriachiarodiluna.*

Hotels

La Casa sul Mare

$$ | HOTEL | One of Procida's best boutique hotels is a great place to enjoy the sunshine, thanks to individually designed rooms, complete with antiques, traditional ceramics, and private terraces. **Pros:** stunning views; wonderful atmosphere; bright ceramic-filled decor. **Cons:** tiny bathrooms; four-night minimum stay in high season; an uphill climb. [$] *Rooms from: €180* ✉ *Via Salita Castello 13, Procida* ☎ *081/8968799* 🌐 *www.lacasasulmare.it* ⏲ *Closed Jan.* 🛏 *10 rooms* 🍽 *Free Breakfast.*

★ San Michele Boutique Hotel

$$$ | HOTEL | This oasis has stunning views of the Marina Corricella, with its terrace overlooking the pretty fishing village. **Pros:** light, airy rooms; great restaurant; a slice of paradise. **Cons:** pricey; usually booked out; a lot of steps. $ *Rooms from: €260 ✉ Via San Rocco 61bis, Corricella ☎ 081/2185208 🌐 www.san-micheleprocida.com ⇆ 12 rooms 🍽 Free Breakfast.*

Nightlife

Blu Bar

COCKTAIL LOUNGES | Once a boathouse for fishermen, this is the trendiest bar on the island. Sip a predinner cocktail at the pretty Marina Corricella accompanied by lounge music, or later in the evening, techno. ✉ *Marina Corricella, Corricella.*

Marina Chiaiolella

On the western coast of Procida, the small port of Marina Chaiolella is studded with a few hotels and bars and basically known as a port-of-call for all sorts of water activities, ranging from boating to scuba diving. Just beyond is the island of Vivara, a nature reserve with rich archaeological finds, reopened in 2016 after 14 years. It can only be visited as part of a guided tour.

GETTING HERE AND AROUND

Take Bus L1 or L2 from Marina Grande Sancio Cattolico to Marina Chiaiolella, then proceed on foot.

Sights

Isola di Vivara

ISLAND | The small crescent-shape island of Vivara, a terminal segment of a volcanic cone and Carlo III's 18th-century hunting lodge, is today a living museum of natural history with unsullied Mediterranean maquis vegetation. Reopened in 2016 after 14 years, visitors cross a causeway to a Napoleonic fort near the entrance gateway, then follow the path winding up to a cluster of abandoned settlements at the highest point of the island (357 feet above sea level). The main cultural interest lies in the island's rich archaeological finds dating to prehistoric times, especially the Bronze Age, as testified to by a wealth of Mycenaean pottery fragments. At its best in springtime, with most of its plants in flower and lots of birds on the move, admire the dense maquis on either side, growing unchecked for over 50 years, with characteristic plant species like tree heather, strawberry tree, and rockrose, the latter of which sports delicate pink flowers in spring. Although you'll hear birds—especially the blackcap—don't expect to see any of these skulking warblers except perhaps around the clearing at the center of the island. At migration times, watch for two of the Mediterranean's more exotic-looking summer visitors: the hoopoe, a bird that looks more in keeping with the African savanna, and the bee-eater, with a splash of unusually vivid colors. The only way to visit the island is by taking a guided tour booked in advance through the *comune.* ✉ *Procida ☎ 331/1723445 mobile 🌐 www.vivarariservanaturalestatale.it 🎫 €10 (credit card only).*

Hotels

La Tonnara

$$ | **HOTEL** | The closest hotel to Vivara, in the Marina Chiaiolella neighborhood, this inviting hotel in a former warehouse maintains the characteristics of its marine history while flaunting a sleek and modern decor. **Pros:** lovely setting; on the beach; the sunset. **Cons:** a bit spartan for a four-star; not much action at night; constant stream of beachgoers outside the gate. $ *Rooms from: €160 ✉ Via Marina Chiaiolella 51b, Corricella ☎ 081/8101052 🌐 www.latonnarahotel.it ⏲ Closed Nov-mid-Apr. ⇆ 14 rooms 🍽 Free Breakfast.*

Chapter 5

SORRENTO AND THE SORRENTINE PENINSULA

Updated by
Nick Bruno

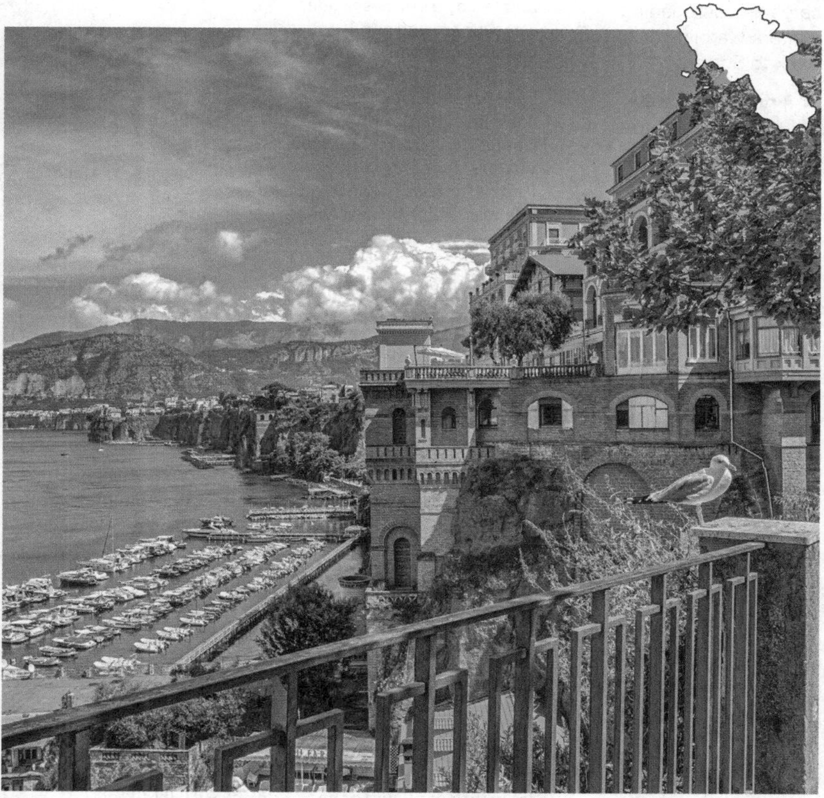

Sights ★★★★☆ | Restaurants ★★★★☆ | Hotels ★★★☆☆ | Shopping ★★☆☆☆ | Nightlife ★☆☆☆☆

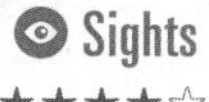

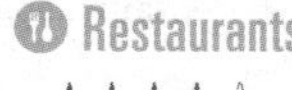

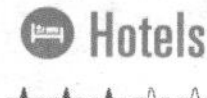

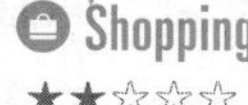

WELCOME TO SORRENTO AND THE SORRENTINE PENINSULA

TOP REASONS TO GO

★ **"Torna a Surriento":** Sorrento's old quarter is one of the most romantic places in Italy—be sure to linger beside the Sedile Dominova, a 16th-century frescoed loggia, which is a colorful backdrop for cafés and serenading waiters warbling "Come Back to Sorrento."

★ **A room with a view:** Splurge on Sorrento's grand Belle Époque hotels perched by the Bay of Naples.

★ **Shopping along Via San Cesareo:** Sorrento's regional goods are world-famous, and this charming street is just the place to find embroideries, inlaid wooden objects, music boxes, leather items, and lemon products.

★ **Passeggiare:** Join the passeggiata at Piazza Tasso and follow the locals as they make the rounds of Sorrento's historical center to gossip, strut, and see and be seen.

1 Sorrento. When Grand Tour-era literati sang Sorrento's praises, palatial hotels went up to accommodate the aristocrats who rushed to visit. Situated on a cliff across the bay from Naples, with Vesuvius front and center, it's easy to understand the allure. Today, Sorrento's verdant scenery is complemented by a buzzy seaside atmosphere and good transit links, making it a practical and beguiling base for exploring the coastline and Bay of Naples. It also offers many visitors their first taste of *il dolce far niente*: sweet idleness. This quintessential southern Italian trope—captured by movies in *costiera* romances and by glossy magazines in jet-set lifestyle photo spreads—led to a postwar tourism boom and today's focus on the hospitality industry. And yet, Sorrento maintains a genuine *contandino* peasant culture wrought by the hearty fisherfolk, subsistence farmers, and skilled craftspeople who long called this region home. A good place to experience this history—and the local passion for food, wine, and life—is the charming historic quarter centered on Piazza Tasso. Follow Via San Cesareo through a labyrinth of alleys to the Chiesa di San Francesco and the Villa Comunale for a panorama bay view.

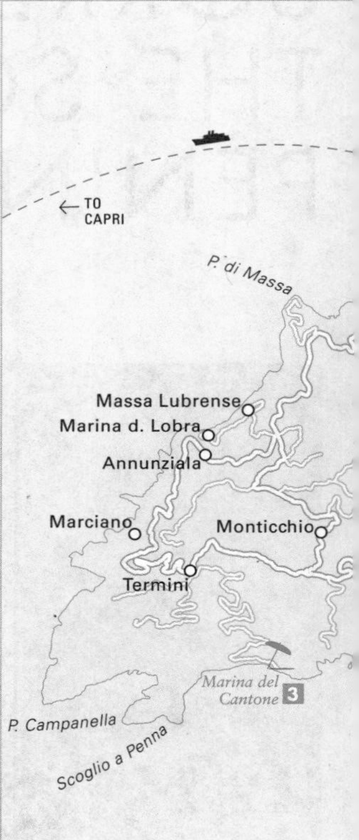

2 Sant'Agnello. If the crowds of Sorrento get too much, you can always get out of town. Northeast of the city, the route leads to Sant'Agnello, an aristocratic beauty spot hallowed by two historic hotels, the Cocumella and the Parco dei Principi (the latter with a famous botanical park).

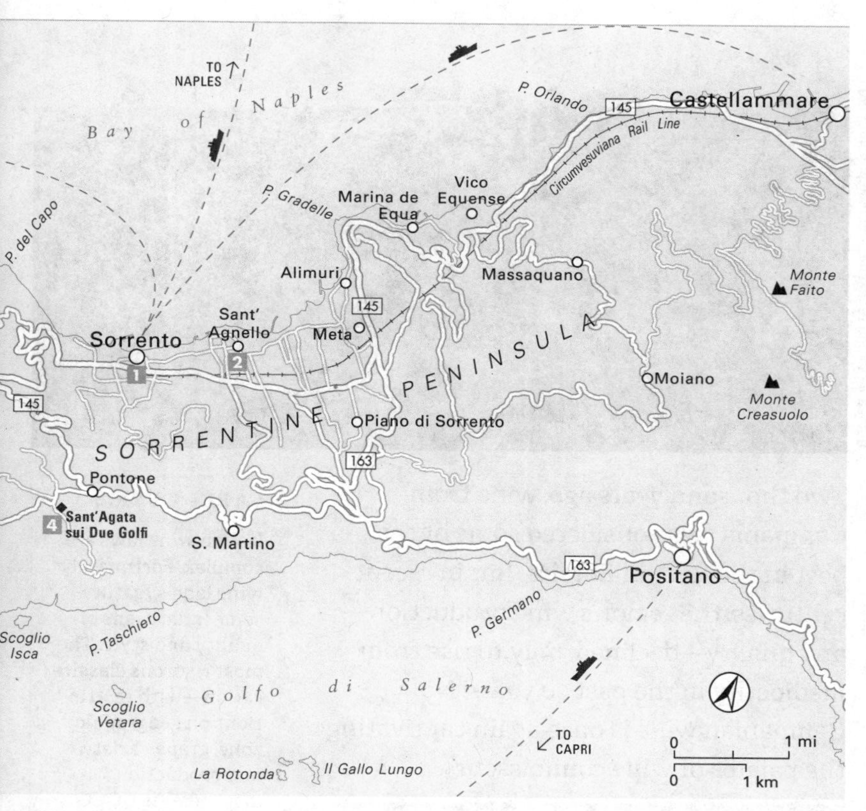

3 Marina del Cantone. Travel south along the peninsula and through the municipality of Massa Lubrense to reach the delightfully intimate and festive beach at Marina del Cantone. West of its chaise longues and seaside restaurants, three distinctive rocky headland peaks (Mortella, Mont'Alto and Penna) shelter the stunning Bay of Ieranto and the Punta Campanella marine reserve.

4 Sant'Agata sui Due Golfi. South of Sorrento, Sant'Agata sui Due Golfi crowns a peak that overlooks both the Bay of Naples and the Bay of Salerno. For the most sublime vistas, stretch your legs and test your lung capacity on a hike up to the serene tree-filled monastery grounds of Il Convento di San Paolo al Deserto.

CAMPANIA'S WINE RENAISSANCE

Campania's wine region has become popular with tourists.

Two thousand years ago, wine from Campania was considered some of the best in the Roman Empire. But in recent centuries, the region's wine production—and quality—declined, only to rise from mediocrity in the past 20 years. Now Campanian wine is once again captivating the palates of wine connoisseurs.

A vinous renaissance is underway: traditional grape varieties like Aglianico and Piedirosso (reds) and Fiano and Falanghina (whites) have halted the southward expansion of "foreign" (i.e., northern Italian) intruders like Sangiovese and Trebbiano. There is a new spirit of pride and achievement in the region, evidenced by the rapid increase in production of DOC (Controlled Denomination of Origin) wines, meaning they are recognized by Italy's system for ensuring quality. Like those in Tuscany to the north, wineries are increasingly opening their doors to the public.

LABEL TERMS

Italian wine laws are complex. Fortunately wine labels feature some indications of quality and style. The most rigorous classification—with restrictions on geographic zone, grape variety, and production methods—is DOCG (*Denominazione di Origine Controllata e Garantita*), followed by DOC (*Denominazione di Origine Controllata*), and IGT (*Indicazione Geografica Tipica*), which has the fewest restrictions.

AGLIANICO (TAURASI)

The most renowned regional red variety is Aglianico, which makes Taurasi near Avellino, the first-ever southern Italian wine to receive a DOCG label (1993). Taurasi has been called "the Barolo of the south" for its structure and ability to age. Aglianico yields full-bodied red wines with crisp acidity, robust tannins, and complex flavors of plum and spice. These wines are excellent with grilled steak, pizza, and pasta with meat ragù.

CODA DI VOLPE

This ancient full-bodied white grape is grown near Naples. Until recently, it was used as a blending grape with Falanghina and Greco (in the white Vesuvio DOC) or Fiano. Now it is possible to find the crisp, medium-bodied Coda di Volpe bottled by itself. The varietal is excellent with gently prepared (not grilled) shellfish dishes or panfried fish, as it is fairly neutral and can be overwhelmed by strongly flavored foods.

FALANGHINA

An ancient white grape that may have been a base for the fabled Falernum, Falanghina was the most highly prized wine of the Roman period. It is a full-bodied, fresh-tasting white wine with fruity notes. Falanghina can be found in many DOC wines by itself, and is blended with Greco and Biancolella to make Capri Bianco, the DOC white wine from the island of Capri. Falanghina is acidic enough to pair well with grilled and fried seafood dishes.

Renowned Aglianico red grapes.

A scenic Campania vineyard.

FIANO (FIANO DI AVELLINO)

This classical white grape shows best in the volcanic soils of Avellino, where it has garnered DOCG status. The wine expresses strong flavors of honey, spices, and nuts. It is excellent as an aperitivo, and pairs well with tough-to-match artichokes, as well as seafood linguine and most fish dishes.

GRECO (GRECO DI TUFO)

Greco is a Campanian variety that does best around the village of Tufo, where it has DOCG status. The soil there is a sulfurous soft rock called *tufo* (*tuffeau* in French). Greco is a light white wine that expresses ripe stone fruits, like peaches, with notes of almond and citrus. It is great served as an aperitivo and matched with cold antipasto.

PIEDIROSSO (AKA PER'E PALUMMO)

This late-ripening red grape variety produces a fruity wine with notes of cherries and herbs. It is the main grape in the red wines of Vesuvio DOC and Capri DOC. Piedirosso pairs well with pizza, cured meats, and grilled vegetables.

As a hub for visiting must-see sites—Pompeii and Naples to the north, Capri to the west, and the Amalfi Coast and Paestum to the south—the beautiful resort town of Sorrento is unequaled. The rest of the peninsula, with plains and limestone outcroppings, watchtowers and Roman ruins, groves and beaches, monasteries and villages, winding paths leading to isolated coves and panoramic views of the bays of both Naples and Salerno, remains relatively undiscovered.

Gently faded, Sorrento still exudes a robust appeal. Because it is relatively free of the urban grit found in Naples, the town's tourist industry that began centuries ago is still dominant, although the lords and ladies of bygone days have been replaced with tour groups and discretionary European vacationers (mainly Brits).

The Sorrentine Peninsula was first put on the map by the ancient Romans. Emperors and senators claimed the region for their own, crowning the golden, waterside cliffs of what was then called Surrentum with palatial villas. Modern resorts now stand where emperors once staked out vacation spots. Reminders of the Caesars' reigns—broken columns, capitals, and marble busts—lie scattered among the area's orange trees and terraces. Sorrento goes as far back as the Samnites and the Etruscans, the *bon vivants* of the early ancient world, and for much of Sorrento's existence it has remained focused, in fact, on pleasure. The Sorrentine Peninsula became a major stop on the elite's Grand Tour itineraries beginning in the late 18th century, and by the mid-19th century, grand hotels and wedding-cake villas had sprung up to welcome the flow of wealthy visitors.

Eons ago, when sea levels dropped during glaciations, the peninsula's tip and Capri were joined by an overland connection, and today it still seems you can almost make it in a single jump. Separating Sorrento from the Amalfi Coast, this hilly, forested peninsula provides the famed rivals breathing space, along with inviting restaurants and an uncrowded charm all its own.

MAJOR REGIONS

Sorrento is the most convenient base for exploring the region, especially for those relying on public transport. Not only is it equidistant from Pompeii and the Amalfi Coast, but it's also connected to Naples via the regular (though crowded and tatty) Circumvesuviana trains and to Capri and Amalfi via the ferries and hydrofoils that depart its Marina Piccola. Set high atop a bluff on the peninsula created by the Lattari Mountains, it has a stunning view of the Bay of Naples. Beyond the town lies a scenery-rich peninsula famous for fabulous restaurants, Edenic parks, and a popular beach at **Marina del Cantone.** Just to the northeast, **Sant'Agnello,** with its grand villas, is beloved by jet-setters, while lofty **Sant'Agata sui Due Golfi,** with its renowned monastery and spectacular views over the gulfs of Naples and Salerno, attracts photographers and history lovers. Gourmands come here, too, as it's home to Campania's most celebrated restaurant, established by slow food pioneer Don Alfonso.

Planning

When to Go

Summer is filled with festivities and offers the best weather for sunning and swimming, bringing dense crowds and higher prices, especially during the middle two weeks of August, when Italians vacation en masse. But no time is perfect: although April and May are sublime, Italian students are then on break and can overrun major sites. Horror stories of torrid days and humongous crowds have driven even more people to travel here during May and June and September and October, and the region is packed to the gills with travelers during those months. Many hotels close November–March.

Sheltered by the Lattari Mountains arcing east to west across the peninsula and inland from the Amalfi Coast, and exposed to cool breezes from two bays, the Sorrentine Peninsula enjoys a climate that is among the mildest in Italy; the temperature rarely falls below 10°C (50°F) in winter, or climbs above 31°C (90°F) in summer. Rain is rare, although weeklong storms can strike.

Planning Your Time

Sorrento has plenty of appeal in its own right, but its greatest virtue is its central location—it makes a fine base, putting you within day-trip distance of Pompeii, the Amalfi Coast, Naples, and the islands of the bay.

You should spend a day taking in Sorrento itself and the surrounding area, plus another leisurely day exploring the Sorrentine Peninsula, enjoying the best beaches and restaurants in the area or taking a rural hike. For day trips, an excursion along the Amalfi Drive is a rise-early, full-day excursion. You can easily get from Sorrento to the Amalfi Coast by bus, or ferry around the peninsula in the summertime. Other day-trip alternatives include an excursion to the archaeological sites around the Bay of Naples. The train from Sorrento will deposit you right in front of Pompeii, Villa Oplontis, a short distance from Herculaneum, or to Naples. Boat, ferry, and hydrofoil services also connect you with Naples and the surrounding area, plus the islands of Capri and Ischia, all valid day-trip alternatives.

Keep in mind that if you're driving, and you wind up not heading back to Sorrento until after dark, you should stick to the main roads. It's easy to get lost on back roads at night.

Getting Here and Around

BOAT

Many commercial ferries and hydrofoils run year-round (with more trips in high season). To get to smaller towns or to take private boats, you can make arrangements with private boat companies or independent fishermen. Seek out people who are recommended by the tourist office or your hotel. Ferries and hydrofoils go to and from Sorrento, with connections to Naples, Capri, Positano, and Amalfi. Check the local paper (*Il Mattino*) for timetables or go to 🌐 *www.naplesbayferry.com.*

CONTACTS Alilauro. ☎ *081/4972222* 🌐 *www.alilauro.it.* **Caremar.** ☎ *081/18966690* 🌐 *www.caremar.it.* **Gescab.** ☎ *081/8071812 Sorrento booking office, 081/4285555 Naples booking office* 🌐 *www.gescab.it.* **SNAV.** ☎ *081/4285555* 🌐 *www.snav.it.*

BUS

At around €3 (depending on destination) for a one-way *extraurbano* bus ticket from Sorrento to other locations on the peninsula—and some lines with departures every 20 minutes—the bus is a good way to get around quickly and cheaply. Municipal EAV bus lines radiate out from the Circumvesuviana station to most major destinations on the peninsula, while SITA buses go farther afield to Positano, Amalfi, and Naples. SITA also does a 24-hour CostieraSita Pass (€12) for unlimited bus travel across Sorrentine and Amalfi coastlines; their Costiera Terra e Mare (€15) ticket also adds a handy ferry trip with Terramar (🌐 *www.travelmar.it*).

Inform the driver of your destination when boarding to avoid missing your stop. If traveling up from the port of Sorrento at Marina Piccola, or the waterfront at Marina Grande, you'll need to get an EAV orange bus. The main orange bus stop in Sorrento is on Piazza De Curtis.

Tickets must be purchased in advance. Time-stamp your ticket in the machine at the front of the bus as you board. You can buy tickets at cafés, bars, tobacco shops, and newsstands area-wide.

CONTACTS SITA. ☎ *089/405145* 🌐 *www.sitasudtrasporti.it.*

CAR

All traffic from Naples to Sorrento is ultimately channeled onto the Statale 145, which must be one of the slowest state highways in southern Italy. The road is single lane all the way from the A3 Autostrada turnoff at Castellammare di Stabia.

Though you'll get some scenic vistas as you inch along the peninsula, it's only when you get beyond Sorrento, on the road to Massa Lubrense or Sant'Agata, that a car becomes more of a benefit than a liability. Don't expect excellent driving standards in the Sorrento area, and be especially careful of scooters, which tend to take considerable liberties. Avoid traveling from Naples to Sorrento on Saturday evenings and on fine Sunday mornings in summer. The same applies to the Statale 145 late on Sunday afternoons and evenings, when immense numbers of day-trippers and weekenders return home to the Naples area.

If you make a stop in Sorrento by car, head for one of the large parking lots: the municipal Parcheggio Achille Lauro (Correale) is in the very central Piazza Lauro. Another option is Ulisse (after the hotel of which it is a part): take a left turn into Via degli Aranci when you see the "no entry" signs as you enter Sorrento, pass under the railway bridge, and turn right at the roundabout. This road skirts the town center (to the right). At the stop sign on Corso Italia take a right turn, and turn right immediately down toward the Marina Grande. Those with deeper pockets (especially larger groups who can share the expense) should consider hiring a reputable driver from Sorrento Silver Star (🌐 *www.sorrentosilverstar.com*) for airport transfers and/or to explore the coastline.

TRAIN

The train stations on the Circumvesuviana line serving the Sorrentine Peninsula are Meta, Piano di Sorrento, Sant'Agnello, and Sorrento, in order of increasing distance from Naples. The main transport hub for cheap, efficient bus services radiating to destinations along the coast and inland is the Circumvesuviana station in Sorrento.

If heading to Sorrento from Naples, use the Stazione Centrale (Piazza Garibaldi), which is the second stop on the Circumvesuviana line as it departs from Naples. Follow the "Circumvesuviana" signs, which will take you through the ticket barriers down into the train stations.

Trains to Sorrento run every half hour from Naples; some trains are *direttissimo* (express), only stopping at major stations; they take half the time of local trains. Fares are €3.60 for Naples to Sorrento and €2.60 for Pompei Scavi–Sorrento. In Sorrento the train station is opposite Piazza Lauro and a five-minute walk from Piazza Tasso.

CONTACTS Circumvesuviana.
☎ *800/211388* 🌐 *www.eavsrl.it.*

Restaurants

With more tourism than Naples, the area around Sorrento has fewer cheap and cheerful restaurants for locals. The charming *trattorie* stay open right through August and serve excellent cuisine. As a rule of thumb, avoid set menus (often listed *menu turistico*) and go for whatever looks freshest to you. Remember that fish and steak prices on menus are often indicated by a price per 100 grams (that is, *prezzo per etto*). Look carefully if it seems suspiciously cheap and be careful as pricing per gram can add up!

Prices in the reviews are the average cost of a main course at dinner or, if dinner isn't served, at lunch. Restaurant reviews have been shortened. For full information, visit Fodors.com.

What It Costs in Euros

	$	$$	$$$	$$$$
RESTAURANTS				
	under €15	€15–€24	€25–€35	over €35

Hotels

Sorrento has a plethora of upper-range hotels with fin de siècle charm, perched on top of impressive tuff cliffs with balconies and terraces. For those traveling on a tighter budget, you can choose between a three-star accommodation or a B&B in the town center or a quieter hotel farther from Sorrento's hub and from the sea. If staying on the peninsula, don't assume you'll be a stone's throw from the shoreline: in places access to the sea is lengthy and arduous, and most of the coastline is rocky.

Hotel prices listed in the guide are for two people in a standard double room in high season. Hotel reviews have been shortened. For full information, visit Fodors.com.

What It Costs

	$	$$	$$$	$$$$
HOTELS				
	under €125	€125–€200	€201–€300	over €300

Tours

City Sightseeing Sorrento
BUS TOURS | FAMILY | A much better sightseeing alternative to driving yourself around (and driving yourself crazy in the process) is the double-decker tour bus operated by City Sightseeing Sorrento. Their Coast to Coast (€15) tour takes in nearby Sant'Agnello and also visits Positano and Amalfi. ✉ *Via degli Aranci 172* ☎ *081/18257088* 🌐 *www.city-sightseeing.it.*

Sami Private Day Tours
GUIDED TOURS | This reliable company offers several personalized tours around Sorrento and the Amalfi coast, including trips to the Pompeii and Herculaneum archaeological sites and vineyard/gastronomic excursions. ✉ *Via Giovanni d'Amalfi 50/A, Amalfi* ☎ *333/3668626* 🌐 *www.samiprivatetours.it.*

Visitor Information

CONTACTS Azienda Autonoma di Soggiorno Sorrento-Sant'Agnello. ✉ *Via L. De Maio 35* ☎ *081/8074033.*

Sorrento

Sorrento may have become a jumping-off point for visits to Pompeii, Capri, and Amalfi, but you can find countless reasons to love it for itself. The Sorrentine people are fair-minded and hardworking, bubbling with life and warmth. The cliff on which the town rests is spread over the bay, absorbing sunlight, while orange and lemon trees waft their perfume in spring.

Winding along a cliff above a small beach and two harbors, the town is split in two by a narrow ravine formed by a former mountain stream. To the east, dozens of hotels line busy Via Correale along the cliff—many have "grand" included in their names, and some indeed still are. To the west, however, is the historic sector, which still enchants. It's a relatively flat area, with winding, stone-paved lanes bordered by balconied buildings, some joined by medieval stone arches. The central piazza is named after the poet Torquato Tasso, born here in 1544. This part of town is a delightful place to walk through. Craftspeople are often at work in their stalls and shops and are happy to let you watch; in fact, that's the point. Music spots and bars cluster in the side streets near Piazza Tasso.

In the evening, people fill cafés to nibble, sip, and talk nonstop; then, arms linked, they stroll and browse through the maze of shop-lined lanes. It has been this way for centuries, ever since Sorrento became a prescribed stop for Grand Tour travelers, who savored its mild winters while sopping up its culture and history.

GETTING HERE AND AROUND

From downtown Naples, take a Circumvesuviana train from Stazione Centrale (Piazza Garibaldi), SITA bus from the Port (Varco Immacolatella), or hydrofoil from Molo Beverello. If you're coming directly from the airport in Naples, pick up a direct bus to Sorrento. By car, take the A3 Naples–Salerno highway, exiting at Castellammare, and then following signs for Penisola Sorrentina, then for Sorrento. The Parcheggio de Curtis parking area is conveniently close to the Circumvesuviana train station.

Sights

Basilica di Sant'Antonino
CHURCH | Gracing Piazza Sant'Antonino and one of the largest churches in Sorrento, the Basilica di Sant'Antonino honors the city's patron saint, St. Anthony the Abbot. The church and the portal on the right side date from the 11th century. Its nave and side aisles are divided by recycled ancient columns. A painting on the nave ceiling is signed and dated by

A Good Walk

The picturesque old town of Sorrento is festooned with palazzi, charming streets, and gorgeous landmarks, and seems custom-tailored for one of the most enjoyable promenades you will ever take.

Begin at Sorrento's historic center, **Piazza Tasso**, watched over by statues of the namesake poet. In the southwest corner of the piazza take a look at the noted **Palazzo Correale** (No. 24), whose 18th-century majolica courtyard, now a flower shop, overflows with charm. Follow Corso Italia until you reach the Largo Arcivescovado, site of the **Duomo dei SS Filippo e Giacomo.**

After viewing the cathedral, head for its campanile, then make a right off Corso Italia down Via Giuliani to enter Sorrento's most picturesque quarter.

Here, on Via San Cesareo, is the beautifully frescoed **Sedile Dominova**, the ancient, open-air site of civic discourse (at night illuminated for café sitters). Return to Piazza Tasso along Via San Cesareo, lit with 19th-century lanterns and the main shopping drag. When you arrive at the edge of Piazza Tasso, go left toward the bay, a block or so along Via De Maio, to pretty Piazza Sant'Antonino, the site of the 11th-century **Basilica di Sant'Antonino**. Past this piazza take Via Santa Maria delle Grazie and Via Donnorso to the church of **San Francesco** to feast your eyes on its legendary 14th-century "Paradise" cloister.

Relax in the adjoining **Villa Comunale** gardens and enjoy the Cinemascope-wide view of the Bay of Naples. Continue on Via Veneto to the **Piazza della Vittoria** to see the faded "Casa di Tasso" sign that marks the birthplace of the town's revered poet. Cross the piazza to the aristocratic Hotel Bellevue Syrene, whose fabulous garden belvedere is the most beautiful place to have drinks. Pass the hotel to exit the walls near the Porta Greca (Greek Gate) and take the stairway down to **Marina Grande** for dinner at a festive seafood restaurant. Catch a bus on the Via del Mare to return.

Giovan Battista Lama in 1734. The crypt, housing the saint's bones, is enriched by polychrome marble and votive offerings. In addition, a relic case contains two whale ribs, which commemorates one of the saint's miracles, when he saved a child from the cetacean. Directly opposite across the piazza is the turn-of-the-20th-century Municipio (town hall). ✉ *Piazza Sant'Antonino, Sorrento* ☎ *081/8781437* 🎫 *Free.*

Capo di Sorrento and the Bagno della Regina Giovanna

RUINS | Just 2 km (1 mile) west of Sorrento, turn right off Statale 145 toward the sea, and then park and walk a few minutes through citrus and olive groves to get to Capo di Sorrento, the craggy tip of the cape, with the most interesting ancient ruins in the area. They were identified by the Latin poet Publius Papinius Statius as the ancient Roman villa of historian Pollio Felix, patron of the great authors Virgil and Horace. Next to the ruins is Bagno della Regina Giovanna (Queen Joan's Bath). A cleft in the rocks allows the sea to channel through an archway into a clear, natural pool, with the water turning iridescent blue, green, and violet as the sunlight changes angles. The easiest way to see all this is to rent a boat at Sorrento; afterward, sailing westward will bring you to the

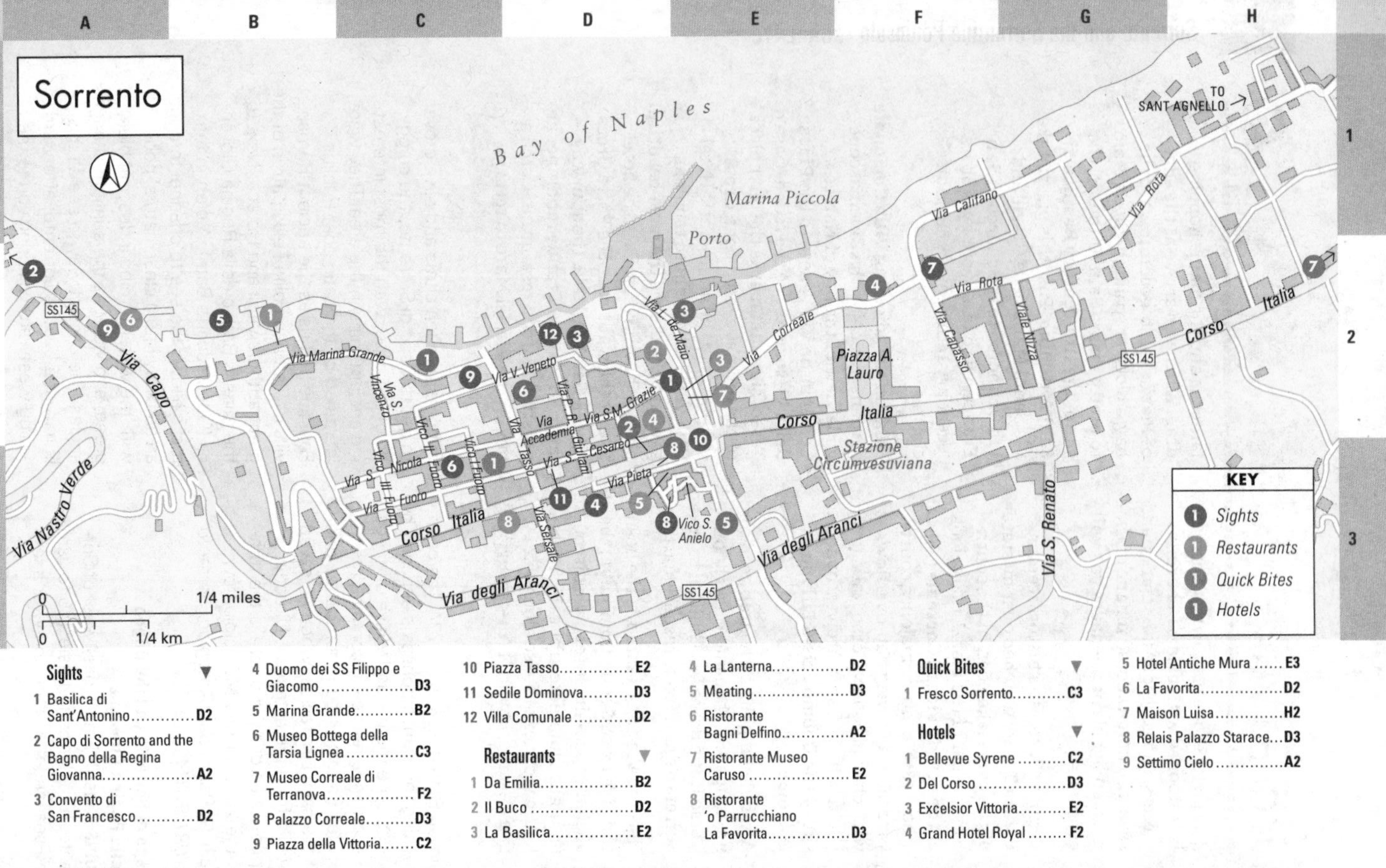

Sights

1 Basilica di Sant'Antonino............D2
2 Capo di Sorrento and the Bagno della Regina Giovanna..................A2
3 Convento di San Francesco............D2
4 Duomo dei SS Filippo e Giacomo...................D3
5 Marina Grande............B2
6 Museo Bottega della Tarsia Lignea..............C3
7 Museo Correale di Terranova..................F2
8 Palazzo Correale..........D3
9 Piazza della Vittoria.......C2
10 Piazza Tasso..............E2
11 Sedile Dominova..........D3
12 Villa Comunale...........D2

Restaurants

1 Da Emilia..................B2
2 Il Buco.....................D2
3 La Basilica................E2
4 La Lanterna................D2
5 Meating....................D3
6 Ristorante Bagni Delfino.............A2
7 Ristorante Museo Caruso....................E2
8 Ristorante 'o Parrucchiano La Favorita................D3

Quick Bites

1 Fresco Sorrento...........C3

Hotels

1 Bellevue Syrene..........C2
2 Del Corso.................D3
3 Excelsior Vittoria..........E2
4 Grand Hotel Royal........F2
5 Hotel Antiche Mura......E3
6 La Favorita................D2
7 Maison Luisa.............H2
8 Relais Palazzo Starace...D3
9 Settimo Cielo.............A2

fishermen's haven of Marina di Puolo, where you can lunch on fresh catch at a modest restaurant. ✉ *Sorrento.*

Convento di San Francesco

RELIGIOUS BUILDING | Near the Villa Comunale gardens and sharing its view over the Bay of Naples, the convent is celebrated for its 12th-century cloister. Filled with greenery and flowers, the Moorish-style cloister has interlaced pointed arches of tufa rock, alternating with octagonal columns topped by elegant capitals, supporting smaller arches. The combination makes a suitably evocative setting for summer concerts and theatrical presentations. The church portal is particularly impressive, with the 16th-century door (moved from a church across the road in 1947) featuring *intarsia* (inlaid) work. The interior's 17th-century decoration includes an altarpiece, by a student of Francesco Solimena, depicting St. Francis receiving the stigmata. The convent is now an art school, where students' works are often exhibited. ✉ *Piazza S. Francesco, Sorrento* ☎ *081/8781269* 🎫 *Free.*

Duomo dei SS Filippo e Giacomo

CHURCH | Ancient, but rebuilt from the 15th-century right up to 1924, the town's cathedral follows a Latin-cross design; its nave and two side aisles are divided by thick piers with round arches. A Renaissance-style door and artworks, including the archbishop's 16th-century marble throne and ceiling paintings attributed to the 18th-century Neapolitan school, are easily viewable. Twentieth-century marquetry ornaments the choir stalls with representations of the Stations of the Cross. Torquato Tasso, Sorrento's most famous native son, was baptized here in the 16th century (probably at the front in the first chapel on the right). The delightfully florid three-story campanile, topped by a clock and a belfry, has an open, arcaded base and recycled Roman columns. ✉ *At Corso Italia and Via S. Maria della Pietà 44, Largo Arcivescovado, Sorrento* ☎ *081/8782248* 🌐 *www.cattedralesorrento.it* 🎫 *Free.*

Marina Grande

MARINA/PIER | Close to the historic quarter (but not that close—many locals prefer to use the town bus to shuttle up and down the steep hill), the port, or *borgo,* of the Marina Grande is Sorrento's fishing harbor. In recent years it has become unashamedly touristy, with outdoor restaurants and cafés encroaching on what little remains of the original harbor. Most establishments down here are geared to the English-speaking market—expect a "good evening" rather than a "buona sera" as you enter. The marina still remains a magical location for an evening out on the waterfront, but if you're interested in a dip—given the dubious sea-water quality here and the cramped conditions—head out instead toward Massa Lubrense and Nerano. Don't confuse this harbor with Marina Piccola, at the base of the cliff, below Piazza Tasso and the Hotel Excelsior Vittoria; that's the area where ferries and hydrofoils dock. ✉ *Via del Mare, Sorrento.*

Museo Bottega della Tarsia Lignea (*Museum of Intarsia Work*)

OTHER MUSEUM | The 18th-century Palazzo Pomaranci Santomasi houses an assorted collection of the celebrated Sorrentine decorative art of intarsia, or *intarsi* (inlays), comprising mainly 19th-century furniture and some modern artistic creations. Also on view are 19th-century paintings, prints, and photographs of the Sorrentine Peninsula. ✉ *Via San Nicola 28, Sorrento* ☎ *081/8771942* 🌐 *www.museomuta.it* 🎫 *€8.*

Museo Correale di Terranova

ART MUSEUM | In an 18th-century villa with a lovely garden, on land given to the patrician Correale family by Queen Joan of Anjou in 1428, this museum is a highlight of Sorrento and a must for connoisseurs of the *seicento* (17th century). It has an eclectic private collection amassed by the count of Terranova and his brother—one of the finest devoted to Neapolitan paintings, decorative arts, and porcelains. Magnificent 18th- and 19th-century inlaid tables by Giuseppe Gargiulo, Capodimonte porcelains, and rococo portrait miniatures are reminders of the age when pleasure and delight were everything in wealthy circles. Also on view are regional Greek and Roman archaeological finds, medieval marble work, glasswork, old master paintings, and 17th-century majolicas—even the poet Tasso's death mask. The building itself is fairly charmless, with few period rooms, but the garden offers an allée of palm trees, citrus groves, floral nurseries, and an esplanade with a panoramic view of the Sorrento Coast. ✉ *Via Correale 50, Sorrento* ☎ *081/8781846* 🌐 *www.museocorreale.it* 💷 *€8, €13 with guide* ⏲ *Closed Mon.*

Palazzo Correale

NOTABLE BUILDING | Just off the southeast corner of Piazza Tasso, this palazzo was built in the 14th century in Catalan style but transformed into a Rococo-era show-stopper, thanks to its exquisite Esedra Maiolicata (Majolica Courtyard, 1772). This was one of the many examples of majolica and faienceware created in this region, a highlight of Campanian craftsmen. (The most notable example is the Chiostro delle Clarisse at Naples's Santa Chiara.) In 1610 the palazzo became the Ritiro di Santa Maria della Pietà and today remains private, but you can view the courtyard beyond the vestryway. Its back wall—a trompe l'oeil architectural fantasia—is entirely rendered in majolica tile. As you leave the palazzo, note the unusual arched windows on the palace facade, a grace note also seen a few doors away at Palazzo Veniero (No. 14), a 13th-century structure with a Byzantine-Arab influence. ✉ *Via Pietà 24, Sorrento.*

Piazza della Vittoria

PLAZA/SQUARE | Tree-shaded Piazza della Vittoria is book-ended by two fabled hotels, the Bellevue Syrene and the Imperial Hotel Tramontano, one wing of which was home to famed 16th-century writer Torquato Tasso. Set by the bayside balcony, the facade of the Casa di Tasso is all the more exquisite for its simplicity and seems little changed since his day. The poet's house originally belonged to the Rossi family, into which Tasso's mother married, and was adorned with beautiful gardens (Tasso wove gardens into many of his poems). The piazza itself is supposedly the site where a temple to Venus once stood, and the scattered Roman ruins make it a real possibility. ✉ *Piazza della Vittoria, Sorrento.*

Piazza Tasso

PLAZA/SQUARE | This was the site of Porta Catello, the summit of the old walls that once surrounded the city. Today it remains a symbolic portal to the old town, overflowing with cafés, Liberty Style buildings, people who congregate here day and night, and horse-drawn carriages. In the center of it all is Torquato Tasso himself, standing atop a high base and rendered in marble by sculptor Giovanni Carli in 1870. The great poet was born in Sorrento in 1544 and died in Rome in 1595, just before he was to be crowned poet laureate. Tasso wrote during a period when Italy was still recovering from devastating Ottoman incursions along its coasts—Sorrento itself was sacked and pillaged in 1558. He is best known for his epic poem *Jerusalem Delivered,* which deals with the conquest of Jerusalem during the First Crusade. At the northern edge of the piazza, where it merges into Corso Italia, is the church of Maria del Carmine, with a Rococo wedding-cake facade of gleaming white-and-yellow stucco. Step inside to note its wall of 18th-century tabernacles, all set, like a jeweler's display, in gilded cases, and the ceiling painting of the Virgin Mary. ✉ *Western end of Corso Italia and above Marina Piccola, at eastern edge of historic district, Piazzo Tasso, Sorrento.*

Did You Know?

The Sedile Dominova, an open-air loggia decorated with Baroque trompe-l'oeil frescoes, has been a meeting place for Sorrento residents since the 16th century.

The Majolica Courtyard is a highlight of the Palazzo Correale.

Sedile Dominova

NOTABLE BUILDING | Enchanting showpiece of the Largo Dominova—the little square that is the heart of Sorrento's historic quarter—the Sedile Dominova is a picturesque open loggia with expansive arches, balustrades, and a green-and-yellow-tile cupola, originally constructed in the 16th century. The open-air structure is frescoed with 18th-century trompe-l'oeil columns and the family coats of arms, which once belonged to the *sedile* (seat), the town council where nobles met to discuss civic problems as early as the Angevin period. Today Sorrentines still like to congregate around the umbrella-topped tables near the tiny square. ✉ *Largo Dominova, at Via S. Cesareo and Via P.R. Giuliani, Sorrento* 🎫 *Free.*

Villa Comunale

VIEWPOINT | The largest public park in Sorrento sits on a cliff top overlooking the entire Bay of Naples. It offers benches, flowers, palms, and people-watching, plus a seamless vista that stretches from Capri to Vesuvius. From here steps lead down to Sorrento's main harbor, the Marina Piccola. ✉ *Adjoining church of San Francesco, Sorrento.*

Restaurants

Da Emilia

$$ | **SOUTHERN ITALIAN** | Near the steps of the Marina Grande, this reliable choice for seafood (established in 1947) might not be Sorrento's most visually prepossessing place, but its homespun, family feel—complete with wooden tables and checked tablecloths—is a refreshing change from the town's (occasionally pretentious) elegance. **Known for:** family-run; harbor terrace above the rocks; tasty and fresh seafood combos like mussels with Sorrentine lemons. $ *Average main: €21* ✉ *Via Marina Grande 62, Sorrento* ☎ *081/8072720* 🌐 *www.daemilia.it* ⏲ *Closed Nov.–Feb.*

Il Buco

$$$ | **MODERN ITALIAN** | In the spirit of the "slow food" movement, this colorful contemporary restaurant just off Piazza Sant'Antonino uses only local and seasonal ingredients of the highest quality in its nouvelle creations. Ask your waiter what inventive sea and land dishes make up the day's specials. **Known for:** intimate outdoor rooms outside; choice of changing menus; exquisite, bite-size experimental dishes. *Average main: €35 Seconda Rampa di Marina Piccola 5, Sorrento 081/8782354 www.ilbucoristorante.it Closed Wed. and Jan. and Feb.*

La Basilica

$$ | **SOUTHERN ITALIAN** | Under the same ownership as the Ristorante Museo Caruso, this budget alternative—in a tiny alley between piazzas Tasso and St. Antonino—offers the same wine list (about 1,700 labels) plus a bountiful choice of hearty Italian dishes. Its main salon is decorated with modern paintings of an erupting Vesuvius (there's outdoor seating as well), but the smaller room on the opposite side of the road is more romantic, with a tiny balcony overlooking the tortuous road to the harbor. **Known for:** good choice of pizzas and meat dishes; homey, relaxed dining room; excellent wine list. *Average main: €22 Via S. Antonino 28, Sorrento 081/8774790 www.ristorantelabasilica.com.*

La Lanterna

$$ | **ITALIAN** | On the site of Roman thermal baths (you can see the ancient ruins under a glass section in the floor), this is a historic venue as well as a beloved eatery. Whether dining outdoors under the lanterns or indoors under the beamed ceiling and stucco arcades, you'll enjoy *cucina tipica, locale e nazionale* (traditional local and national cooking), including seafood and meat dishes as well as top-quality *vera pizza napoletana* (truly authentic Neapolitan pizza). **Known for:** intimate outside setting; occasional live music; excellent service. *Average main: €23 Via S. Cesareo 25, Sorrento 081/8781355 www.lalanternasorrento.it Closed Wed.*

Meating

$$ | **MODERN ITALIAN** | This steak house–pizzeria, with a stylish Spanish-theme dining area of fiery *toro* artwork and exposed brick, is a good alternative to Sorrento's many seafood-focused restaurants. As you'd expect from the name, it has plenty of meat dishes as well as a good selection of vegetarian and fish options. **Known for:** decent pizza; fried and grilled seafood; huge steaks. *Average main: €22 Via della Pietà, 20, Sorrento 081/8782891 www.meatingsorrento.com Closed weekdays in Jan.*

★ **Ristorante Bagni Delfino**

$$ | **SOUTHERN ITALIAN** | At this informal, waterside restaurant and snack bar, you won't see many locals—they're unlikely to be impressed by the four-language menus—but the seafood platters are fresh and flavorful, and you can eat alfresco in the sunshine or inside a glass-enclosed dining area with a nautical motif. You can even go for a swim (just please, wait an hour or so after eating!). **Known for:** great views of the Marina Grande and beyond; terrace beside a sunbathing/swimming jetty; bountiful portions. *Average main: €22 Via Marina Grande 216, Sorrento 081/8782038 www.ristoranteildelfinosorrento.com Closed Nov.–Mar.*

★ **Ristorante Museo Caruso**

$$$$ | **SOUTHERN ITALIAN** | Sorrentine favorites, including *acquerello* (fresh fish appetizer) and ravioli with crab and zucchini sauce, are tweaked creatively here. The staff is warm and helpful, the singer on the sound system is the long-departed "fourth tenor" himself, and the operatic memorabilia (including posters and old photos of Caruso) is displayed in a flattering blush-pink light. **Known for:** tasting menus and a few à la carte choices; Torna a Surriento and the Neapolitan

songbook; Caruso memorabilia aplenty. $ *Average main: €40 ✉ Via S. Antonino 12, Sorrento ☎ 081/8073156 🌐 www.ristorantemuseocaruso.com.*

Ristorante 'o Parrucchiano La Favorita
$$ | SOUTHERN ITALIAN | Opened in 1868 by an ex-priest (*'o parrucchiano* means "the priest" in the local dialect), this restaurant serves classic Sorrentine cuisine in an enchanting 19th-century setting: a sprawling, multilevel greenhouse, packed with tables and chairs amid fruit trees and enough tropical foliage to fill a Victorian conservatory. **Known for:** gorgeous setting but may disappoint food-wise; signature cannelloni created in 1870; fecund greenhouse and terrace foliage and fruit. $ *Average main: €24 ✉ Corso Italia 71, Sorrento ☎ 081/8781321 🌐 www.parrucchiano.com ⏲ Closed Wed. mid-Nov.–mid-Mar.*

Coffee and Quick Bites

★ Fresco Sorrento
$ | NEOPOLITAN | FAMILY | A popular gelateria run by a young couple offering lots of fresh house-made gelato flavors as well as interesting bubble tea options, granita, frappé, frullati, fresh fruit cups, and crepes. **Known for:** lemon granita slush and sorbetti; nutty pistachio and nocciola; fab ice-cream flavors. $ *Average main: €5 ✉ Via Fuoro 27, Sorrento ☎ 081/8772832 ⏲ Closed Jan.–Mar.*

Hotels

★ Bellevue Syrene
$$$$ | HOTEL | This luxurious retreat, magnificently set on a bluff high over the Bay of Naples, is one of Italy's most legendary hotels, complete with art deco touches throughout; lounges and salons decorated with avant-garde artwork and trompe-l'oeil frescoes; and guest rooms that range from sleekly modern to sumptuously fanciful. **Pros:** impeccable design elements; half board available; elegant common areas. **Cons:** small pool; parking is €25 a day; very expensive. $ *Rooms from: €550 ✉ Piazza della Vittoria 5, Sorrento ☎ 081/8781024 🌐 www.bellevue.it ⏲ Closed Jan.–Mar. 49 rooms Free Breakfast.*

Del Corso
$$ | HOTEL | This centrally located, family-run hotel close to Sorrento's major hub, Piazza Tasso, is homey and comfortable, with pleasant common areas, the occasional antique, fresh flowers, a solarium, a breakfast terrace, and basic rooms—some of which have courtyard entrances. **Pros:** open year-round; pleasant, accommodating staff; only 100 meters from the station. **Cons:** street noise in rooms overlooking the front, especially on lower floors; no parking; no pool. $ *Rooms from: €140 ✉ Corso Italia 134, Sorrento ☎ 081/8071016 🌐 www.hoteldelcorso.com ⏲ Closed Nov.–Feb. 27 rooms Free Breakfast.*

★ Excelsior Vittoria
$$$$ | HOTEL | Overlooking the Bay of Naples, this luxurious Belle Époque dream has been in the same family since 1834, which means that public spaces are virtual museums—with elegant Victorian love seats and *stile liberty* (Art Nouveau) ornamentation—and guest rooms are spacious, with soigné furnishings and balconies and terraces that overlook gardens or the bay. **Pros:** beyond the protected gates, you're in the heart of town; grand spaces and handsome furnishings; gardens buffer city noise. **Cons:** front desk can be cold; some rooms are comparatively small; not all rooms have sea views. $ *Rooms from: €746 ✉ Piazza Tasso 34, Sorrento ☎ 081/8777111 🌐 www.exvitt.it ⏲ Closed Jan.–Mar. 83 rooms Free Breakfast.*

Grand Hotel Royal
$$$$ | HOTEL | Lush, landscaped gardens surround this large hotel, an oasis of quiet and cool, where an elevator whisks you to and from sea level and a private beach, where the pool area practically leans out over the bay, and where there

are both indoor and alfresco dining options. **Pros:** centrally located; spacious lounge; friendly staff. **Cons:** some first-floor rooms have obstructed views; quality of the dining may disappoint; €25 parking fee per night. *$ Rooms from: €423 ✉ Via Correale 42, Sorrento ☎ 081/8073434 🌐 www.royalsorrento.com ⏲ Closed Nov.–Easter 96 rooms 🍽 Free Breakfast.*

Hotel Antiche Mura
$$$ | HOTEL | At this family-run hotel, the lobby's marble columns and ceramic tile make a lasting first impression, bright pastels make guest rooms feel comfortable and airy (despite the lack of views), and a citrus garden with sections of ancient city walls makes even the swimming pool feel classically elegant. **Pros:** central location; garden pool; friendly, helpful staff. **Cons:** lack of soundproofing; dated decor; no views from the guest rooms. *$ Rooms from: €250 ✉ Via Fourimura 7, Piazza Tasso, Sorrento ☎ 081/8073523 🌐 www.hotelantichemura.com ⏲ Closed Jan. and Feb. 51 rooms 🍽 Free Breakfast.*

La Favorita
$$$$ | HOTEL | The lobby might be a glamorous white-on-white extravaganza of Caprese columns, tufted sofas, shimmering crystal chandeliers, silver ecclesiastical objects, and gilded Baroque mirrors, but the charming staff ensure the vibe is elegantly casual, the guest rooms are well equipped and spacious, and the rooftop pool area has magnificent bay and Vesuvius vistas. **Pros:** central location; idyllic garden; beautiful terrace. **Cons:** rooms near the bar noisy after midnight; lack of decent air-conditioning and room thermostat control; no views to speak of from guest rooms. *$ Rooms from: €439 ✉ Via T. Tasso 61, Sorrento ☎ 081/8782031 🌐 www.hotellafavorita.com ⏲ Closed Jan.–Mar. 85 rooms 🍽 Free Breakfast.*

Maison Luisa
$$ | B&B/INN | Opened in 2018, this well-run B&B, in a striking burnished-yellow and Pompeiian red stile liberty palazzo, has spacious, high-ceilinged, whitewashed rooms with azure tiles; the two doubles have garden views, and the cavernous, three-person room has a mezzanine with an extra bed. **Pros:** recently refurbished and well maintained; spacious rooms; owners offer driving tours and airport transfers. **Cons:** on a busy road; minimum two-night stay; practical base may be unglamorous to some. *$ Rooms from: €125 ✉ Corso Italia 288/a, Sorrento ☎ 339/3888143 🌐 www.maisonluisasorrento.com 3 rooms 🍽 Free Breakfast.*

Relais Palazzo Starace
$$$ | B&B/INN | For those not requiring an elevator, this small, well-managed B&B—with simple but stylish, high-ceilinged rooms and a fabulous and funky breakfast setting overlooking Corso Italia—is a stand-out choice. **Pros:** great buzzy location; fabulous staff; hearty breakfast with great pastries. **Cons:** may be too noisy for some; no elevator; only street views. *$ Rooms from: €208 ✉ Via Santa Maria della Pietà 9, Sorrento ☎ 081/8072633 🌐 www.palazzostarace.com 5 rooms 🍽 Free Breakfast.*

Settimo Cielo
$$$ | HOTEL | Even if your wallet won't allow a stay at one of Sorrento's grand hotels, Settimo Cielo—although dated and a hike away on Capo Sorrento—provides gorgeous views, pretty gardens, and a swimming pool. **Pros:** plenty of parking; balcony options; wonderful sea and Vesuvio views. **Cons:** walls not soundproofed; basic, dated rooms and below-par breakfast; 15-minute walk along busy road into Sorrento. *$ Rooms from: €260 ✉ Via Capo 27, Sorrento ☎ 081/8781012 🌐 www.hotelsettimocielo.com 20 rooms 🍽 Free Breakfast.*

Nightlife

Banana Split Pub
PUBS | Friendly, family-run Irish pub opened since 1980 overseen by two labradors and serving an ample selection of beers, spirits (excellent gin choice) and cocktails (mojito by the jug). They also do decent food (classic pasta and pizza are mainstays) and show live tv sports. ✉ *Corso Italia 244, Sorrento* ☎ *081/8781040* 🌐 *ristopixel.com/bananasplit.*

Bollicine Wine Bar
WINE BARS | This intimate wine bar and eatery, with *osteria*-style dark wood interiors and a few seats outside, is a good choice for an aperitivo with *stuzzichini* (nibbles). ✉ *Via dell'Academia 7/9, Sorrento* ☎ *334/7657888* 🌐 *bollicinewinebar.it.*

Fauno Notte Club
DANCE CLUBS | Established in the 1950s, Sorrento's oldest nightclub hosts local DJs and has concerts between mid-April and October and every Saturday night in the winter. ✉ *Piazza Torquato Tasso 13, Sorrento* ☎ *8781821* 🌐 *www.faunonotte.it.*

Performing Arts

Teatro Armida
FILM | **FAMILY** | Opened in 1957, the Armida stages folk and traditional Neapolitan musical-performance dinners, including the Tarantella Show and Sorrento Show. It also has a cinema featuring family-friendly movies in Italian. ✉ *Corso Italia 219, Sorrento* ☎ *081/8781470* 🌐 *www.cinemateatroarmida.it.*

Villa Fiorentino
ARTS CENTERS | A 1930s villa, once the base for the Fiorentino family's embroidered-handkerchief enterprise, is now the base for a foundation that organizes frequent art exhibitions, musical performances, readings, and other cultural events. ✉ *Corso Italia 53, Sorrento* ☎ *081/8782284* 🌐 *www.fondazionesorrento.com.*

Shopping

Aromi di Sorrento-Mezzo Kilo
SOUVENIRS | Far from the tourist streets, this little shop is crammed with housewares, soaps and fragrances, delicious sweets, colorful ceramics, one-off Christmas decorations, and other local gift items. ✉ *Via Fuoro 62/A, Sorrento* ☎ *333/3718544.*

Autori Capresi
MIXED CLOTHING | Capri tailors produce high-class linen clothes for adults and children at this beautiful atelier. Nothing is left to chance in the handmade finishing on the classic white-and-beige linen and other more colorful creations. ✉ *Via Padre Reginaldo Giuliani 21, Sorrento* ☎ *081/8771717* 🌐 *autoricapresi.com.*

Biagio Barile
CRAFTS | The selection of gorgeous inlaid-wood boxes, coasters, and other objects on sale here includes those with colorful, modern, geometric patterns. ✉ *Vico S. Aniello 6, Traversa Via Pieta, Sorrento* ☎ *388/5321106* 🌐 *barileinlaidsorrento.com.*

Corium
SHOES | Choose a leather design from the hundreds of options on display, and the cobbler will custom-craft a pair of sandals for you. ✉ *Via degli Archi 20, Sorrento* ☎ *081/8071567* 🌐 *www.coriumsorrento.com.*

★ **Gargiulo Salvatore**
CRAFTS | A visit to this inlaid-wood shop, now in its third generation of Sorrentine craftsmen, takes you back in time. The jewelry, musical boxes, and wooden pictures are particularly fine. ✉ *Via Fuoro 33, Sorrento* ☎ *081/8782420* 🌐 *www.gargiuloinlaid.it.*

Gioielleria di Somma
JEWELRY & WATCHES | Tired of Sorrento's coral and cameos? A trendier alternative is this jewelry shop with classics by Pomellato, DoDo, Bulgari, and many others. ✉ *Corso Italia 114, Sorrento* ☎ *081/8073213* 🌐 *www.gioielleriadisomma.com.*

Leonard Jewels
JEWELRY & WATCHES | Vincenzo and his son Nicholas use both coral and lava to make distinguished jewelry. For those famous Sorrentine cameos, head to the mezzanine floor. ✉ *Via S. Cesareo 24, Sorrento* ☎ *081/8772923* 🌐 *www.leonardcoralcameos.com.*

★ **Libreria Tasso**
BOOKS | You won't run out of vacation reads thanks to this shop's browseworthy selection of English-language books. ✉ *Piazza Angelina Lauro 18/19, Sorrento* ☎ *081/8784703* 🌐 *www.facebook.com/libreria.sorrento.*

Limonoro
WINE/SPIRITS | The zesty local lemon liqueur, limoncello, is made and sold here, as are exquisite chocolates, baked goods like panettone and Neapolitan-style roasted coffee. Not only can you observe the production process in the back of the tiny white shop, but you can also watch the owners paint designs on the pretty bottles. ✉ *Via S. Cesareo 49/53, Sorrento* ☎ *081/8785348* 🌐 *www.ninoandfriends.it.*

Nonna Cristina
CHILDREN'S CLOTHING | The wearability and lovely style of these children's clothes in soft and extra-fine materials will have the little ones dressed in true Made-in-Italy fashion. ✉ *Piazza A. Lauro 13, Sorrento* ☎ *081/8072492.*

★ **Stinga Tarsia**
CRAFTS | Fine-quality marquetry and inlaid wood, coral, and cameos have been crafted and sold here since 1890. ✉ *Via L. De Maio 16, Sorrento* ☎ *081/8781165* 🌐 *www.stingatarsia.com.*

Terrerosse
CRAFTS | At this atelier-shop, two artists make unusual lamps, vases, paperweights, and other decorative objects from shell, ceramic, glass, wood, and stone. ✉ *Via Fuoro 73, Sorrento* ☎ *081/8073277.*

Vincenzo Piscopo
JEWELRY & WATCHES | This shop makes good use of silver and coral in its cameos, rings, necklaces, and bracelets. They also sell fancy designer watches. ✉ *Corso Italia 210 d, Sorrento* ☎ *081/8771777* 🌐 *www.piscopojewels.it.*

Sant'Agnello

2 km (1 mile) east of Sorrento.

Back in the 18th and 19th centuries, the tiny hamlet of Sant'Agnello was an address of choice. To escape Sorrento's crowds, Bourbon princes and exiled Russian millionaires vacationed here, some building sumptuous villas, others staying at the Hotel Cocumella, the oldest hotel on the Sorrentine Peninsula. On the quieter coastal side of town, Sant'Agnello still possesses a faintly ducal air. The 15th- to 16th-century parish church, Chiesa Parrocchiale di Sant'Agnello, is as lyrical as its name: swirls of lemon yellow and white, decorated with marble-gloss plasterwork. Nearby is a spectacular belvedere, the Terrazza Punta San Francesco, complete with café, which has breathtaking views of the Bay of Naples.

GETTING HERE AND AROUND

Take the A3 Napoli–Salerno highway to the Castellammare di Stabia exit. Take Statale 145 south and follow signs for "Penisola Sorrentina" and "Sant'Agnello." Note, though, that two-lane state roads in the region (i.e., 145 and 163) are often congested. By train, take the Circumvesuviana to the Sant'Agnello stop.
SITA buses run regularly throughout the peninsula from downtown Sorrento. They stop by request at official stops, which are frequent. Still, it's always best to be armed with a local timetable to avoid long waits at bus stops.

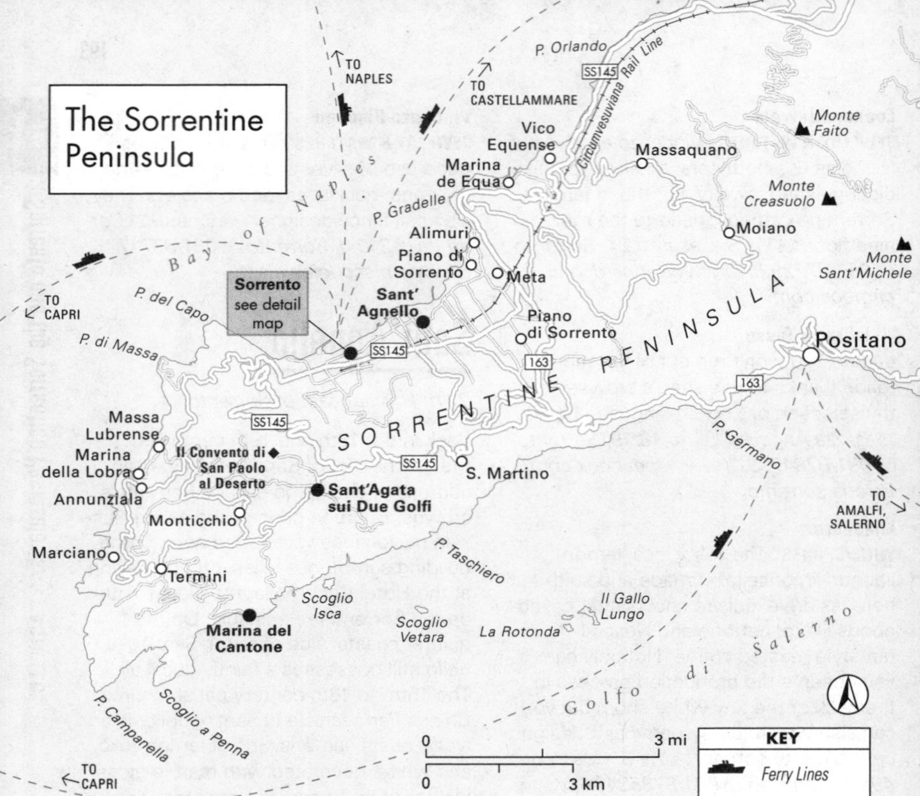

Sights

Parco dei Principi

NOTABLE BUILDING | Sant'Agnello's two most famous estates sit side by side. In the early 19th century, the Jesuit **Cocumella monastery** was transformed into a hotel, welcoming the rich and famous. Next door is the **Parco dei Principi,** a hotel built by Gio Ponti in 1962 surrounded by a botanical park laid out in 1792 by the Count of Siracusa, a cousin to the Bourbons. Traversed by a diminutive Bridge of Love, this was a favorite spot for Désireé, Napoléon's first *amour,* who came here often. Shaded by horticultural rarities, this park leads to the count's Villa di Poggio Siracusa, a Rococo-style iced birthday cake of a house perched over the bay. Green thumbs and other circumspect visitors can stroll through the romantic park, now part of the Hotel Parco dei Principi. It's notable for Ponti's alluring nautical design motifs and features, including a pool straight out of a David Hockey painting. ✉ *Via Bernardino Rota 44, Sant'Agnello* 🌐 *www.royalgroup.it/parcodeiprincipi.*

Restaurants

Anima e Pizza Trasaella

$ | **NEOPOLITAN** | **FAMILY** | To escape the pricey and sometimes ersatz-Italian eating experience, head up the hill to this gem of a pizzeria, which is loaded with local warmth and flavor. Don't be put off by the tattered building, with its peeling pink paint, no-frills interior, and TV invariably broadcasting a soccer match. **Known for:** panoramic terrace by a mini-chapel; arancio in fiore croquettes; great choice and value. $ *Average main: €10* ✉ *Via*

Trasaella 62, Sorrento ☎ 081/18492038 🌐 www.animaepizza.com ⏲ Closed Mon.

Hotels

Cocumella

$$$$ | HOTEL | In a clifftop garden overlooking the Bay of Naples, the Cocumella occupies a Baroque monastery, complete with frescoed ceilings, antique reliquaries, and a marble cloister; the lobby and grand suites (with stone fireplaces, Empire-style bureaus, and marble-clad bathrooms) have Italian-Victorian grace, but even the smaller rooms have their 19th-century charms. **Pros:** quiet location; verdant gardens; superb pool, spa and tennis court. **Cons:** car a necessity; breakfast options are limited; far from off-site restaurants. *$ Rooms from: €580 ✉ Via Cocumella 7, Sant'Agnello ☎ 081/8782933 🌐 www.cocumella.com ⏲ Closed Nov.–Mar. 50 rooms 🍴 Free Breakfast.*

Grand Hotel Parco dei Principi

$$$$ | HOTEL | This stylish 1960s hotel, designed by Giò Ponti, is all white walls and blue-glass accents; outside blooms the fabled Parco dei Principi, a lush 19th-century *giardino,* and paths lead to a romantic, bayside, Rococo villa—a splendiferous setting for the pool area. **Pros:** stunning garden; grand bay views; fun '60s decor. **Cons:** some might feel the design lacks warmth; can't use a clothes iron in rooms; rooms in roadside wing disappointing. *$ Rooms from: €450 ✉ Via Rota 44, Sorrento ☎ 081/8784644 🌐 www.grandhotelparcodeiprincipi.net 96 rooms 🍴 Free Breakfast.*

Hotel Mediterraneo

$$$$ | HOTEL | Combining understated old-world charm and contemporary chic and blessed with a garden with citrus trees, sweeping bay views (ask for a room with a balcony), and beach access, Hotel Mediterraneo seems worlds away from bustling Sorrento, though it's just a 1-km stroll from town. **Pros:** fab yacht excursions; free shuttle into town; bright and spacious rooms. **Cons:** some rooms on the small size; evening noise from the rooftop bar and road; expensive drinks and food. *$ Rooms from: €382 ✉ Via Crawford 85, Sant'Agnello ☎ 081/8781352 🌐 www.mediterraneosorrento.com ⏲ Closed Nov.–Mar. 70 rooms 🍴 Free Breakfast.*

Sant'Agata sui Due Golfi

7 km (4½ miles) south of Sorrento, 10 km (6 miles) east of Positano.

Because of its panoramic vistas, Sant'Agata was an end-of-the-line pilgrimage site for beauty lovers through the centuries, especially before the Amalfi Drive opened up the coast to the southeast. As its name suggests, this village 1,300 feet above sea level looks out over the bays of Naples and Salerno (Sant'Agata refers to a Sicilian saint, honored here with a 16th-century chapel), and it found its first fame during the Roman Empire as the nexus of merchant routes uniting the two gulfs. Now that the town has become slightly built up, you have to head to its outskirts to take in the vistas.

GETTING HERE AND AROUND

By car, take the A3 Napoli–Salerno highway to the Castellammare di Stabia exit. Take Statale 145 south and follow signs for "Penisola Sorrentina." Once you reach Piano di Sorrento, take Statale 163 (direction Positano), and after about 3 km (2 miles) turn back onto Statale 145, following signs for "Sant'Agata sui Due Golfi." By public transport, take the Circumvesuviana to Sorrento, then a SITA bus to Sant'Agata sui Due Golfi.

Sights

Il Convento di San Paolo al Deserto

VIEWPOINT | Sant'Agata's most famous vantage point is on the far north side of the hill, where an ancient Greek sanctuary is said—somewhat fancifully—to have been dedicated to the Sirens of legend. That choice location became Il Convento di San Paolo al Deserto, a monastery built by the Carmelite fathers in the 17th century and now occupied by an order of nuns. The monastery's famed belvedere—with panoramic views of the blue waters all around, and of Vesuvius, Capri, and the peninsula—was a top sight for Grand Tour–era travelers. To access the belvedere's tower, ring the bell at the monastery and ask for the key to open the gate. To get to the Deserto from the center of Sant'Agata, take the main road (Corso Sant'Agata) past the church of Santa Maria delle Grazie on your right, and keep walking uphill on Via Deserto for a little more than half a mile. *Via Deserto, Sant'Agata sui Due Golfi* *081/8780199* *Donations welcome.*

Santa Maria delle Grazie

CHURCH | Today's travelers head to Sant'Agata less for the sublime beauties of Il Deserto than for its lodging options and to dine at Don Alfonso 1890, one of the finest restaurants in Campania. Across the way from Don Alfonso on the town square is the beautiful 16th-century Renaissance church of Santa Maria delle Grazie. The shadowy, evocative interior features an exceptional 17th-century altar brought from the Girolamini church in Naples in 1843. Attributed to Florentine artists, it's inlaid with lapis, malachite, mother-of-pearl, and polychrome marble. *Corso Sant'Agata, Sant'Agata sui Due Golfi* *081/5339021.*

Restaurants

★ Antico Francischiello da Peppino

$$$ | **SOUTHERN ITALIAN** | Overlooking rows of olive trees that seem to run into the sea, this superb eatery is away from the throng, halfway between Sant'Agata and Massa Lubrense. Two huge, beamed dining rooms with brick archways, old chandeliers, antique mirrored sideboards, hundreds of mounted plates, and tangerine tablecloths make for an atmospheric place to dine. **Known for:** pork and lamb options; abundant seafood, including baccalà (cod); spectacular views from terrace. *Average main: €34* *Via Partenope 27, halfway between Sant'Agata and Massa Lubrense, Sorrento* *081/5339780* *www.francischiello.com* *Closed Wed. Nov.–Mar.*

★ Don Alfonso 1890

$$$$ | **SOUTHERN ITALIAN** | A gastronomic giant and pioneer in upscale farm-to-table cuisine (it even grows its own produce on a small farm nearby), Don Alfonso is considered one of Italy's best restaurants. It's a family affair, with mamma (Livia) handling the dining room, papà (former chef Alfonso Iaccarrino) tending to the organic plot, one son working as the current chef (preparing classic dishes alongside edgier creations), and the other serving as maître d'. **Known for:** Punta Campanella local garden produce; slow food pioneer; stellar tasting menus. *Average main: €160* *Corso Sant'Agata 13, Sant'Agata sui Due Golfi* *SITA Bus to via Nastro Verde or taxi from Sorrento.* *081/8780026* *www.donalfonso.com* *Closed Mon. and Tues. and Nov.–Apr. No lunch weekdays.*

Hotels

Sant'Agata

$$ | **HOTEL** | If you wish to stay in hilltop Sant'Agata sui Due Golfi, this efficiently run hotel provides airy and pleasant lodging and a good bed to fall into after a meal at Don Alfonso 1890 or a walk to the Deserto belvedere. **Pros:** helpful staff; easily accessible by SITA bus; nice pool. **Cons:** public areas a tad disappointing; flanked by noisy roads; far from the beach. *Rooms from: €130* *Via dei Campi 8/A, Sant'Agata sui Due Golfi* *081/8080800, 081/5330749* *www.hotelsantagata.com* *Closed Nov.–Feb.* *48 rooms* *Free Breakfast.*

Marina del Cantone

5 km (3 miles) southwest of Sant'Agata sui Due Golfi.

As the largest—yet still very intimate (pebble) beach on the Sorrentine Peninsula—Marina del Cantone attracts weekend sun worshippers and foodies drawn by the seaside restaurants here. To get to the beach, usually dotted with dozens of festive umbrellas, a slender road winds down to the sea through rolling vineyards and the small town of Nerano, ending at the Gulf of Positano near the Montalto watchtower. While enjoying Marina del Cantone's wonderful beach and laid-back village vibe, you'll also have a front-row seat to the geological spectacle that is the islets of Li Galli, which seems to follow you around as you drive up and down the Amalfi Coast. Other than Positano, Marina del Cantone is the best place to hire a boat to get closer to these tiny islands—Gallo Lungo, Castelluccia, and La Rotonda—which sit on the horizon to the east of the beach. They're also called Isole delle Sirene (Isles of the Sirens), after the mythical girl group that lured unwitting sailors onto the rocks.

GETTING HERE

By car, take the A3 Napoli–Salerno highway to the Castellammare di Stabia exit. Take Statale 145 south and follow signs for "Penisola Sorrentina." Once you reach Piano di Sorrento, take Statale 163 (direction Positano) and after about 3 km (2 miles), turn back onto Statale 145, following signs for Sant'Agata sui Due Golfi, then Metrano, then Nerano-Marina del Cantone. By public transport, take the Circumvesuviana to Sorrento, then a SITA bus to Nerano-Marina del Cantone. Check the latest timetable to avoid missing the last bus back to your accommodation.

Restaurants

★ Le Sirene

$$$ | SOUTHERN ITALIAN | With its sparkling *spiaggia* views and seafood freshly caught by local *pescatori*, it's hard not be lured by the siren charms of this prime place in Marina di Cantone. Expect lots of grilled fish, platefuls of small-bite *antipasti di casa*, and possibly the creamiest *spaghetti alla Nerano* on the planet. **Known for:** friendly servizo da famiglia; lovingly stirred lemon risotto; beautiful beach terrace atmosphere. *$ Average main: €26 ✉ Via Marina del Cantone, Marina del Cantone ☎ 081/8081771 ⊕ www.lesirenehotel.it.*

Taverna del Capitano

$$$ | SOUTHERN ITALIAN | The fascinating cuisine here is based on old recipes from the various cultures—Norman and Moorish among them—that loom large in regional history. You can rely on the knowledgeable maître d' for an absorbing commentary on the various seafood dishes and advice on the right wine from a siege-ready cellar. **Known for:** freshest seafood and produce; elegant presentation; fabulous beachside location and views. *$ Average main: €28 ✉ Piazza delle Sirene 10/11, Località Marina del Cantone, Massa Lubrense ☎ 081/8081028 ⊕ www.tavernadelcapitano.com ⏲ Closed Nov.–mid-Mar. and Mon. and Tues., except in summer.*

Hotels

Hotel Le Sirene

$$ | B&B/INN | Don't let the old-school *pensione* eccentricity fool you: this friendly, family-run hotel above a superb seafood restaurant offers oodles of value for such a gorgeous location—one that's complete with views of Marina del Cantone or Nerano's hills. **Pros:** family room options; restaurants galore below;

beach and boat facilities. **Cons:** only small balconies; sparse breakfast; feels a tad dated. *Rooms from: €150* ✉ *Piazza delle Sirene, via Marina del Cantone, Marina del Cantone* ☏ *081/8081771* 🌐 *www.lesirenehotel.it* *16 rooms* *Free Breakfast.*

Quattro Passi

$$$ | HOTEL | The focus at this hotel and Italian nouvelle restaurant is on both fine food and relaxation: the becalming Nerano environs and gorgeous rooms—all of them whitewashed with splashes of bold color and some of them with two-person whirlpool tubs—make it a pleasure to fall into bed. **Pros:** close to the beach; truly exceptional restaurant; cooking lessons on request. **Cons:** some may find the place pretentious; small fiddly dining portions; grounds can be a bit buggy in summer. *Rooms from: €230* ✉ *Via A. Vespucci 13N, Località Nerano, Massa Lubrense* ☏ *081/8082800* 🌐 *www.ristorantequattropassi.com* *Closed Wed., and Nov.–mid-Mar.* *7 rooms* *Free Breakfast.*

Activities

Nautica O Masticiello

BOATING | FAMILY | Based on the beautiful pebbly beach backed with swanky eateries, Nautica O Masticiello runs daily trips to Capri June–September, and regular tours along the Amalfi Coast including Li Galli, Amalfi, and Positano, weather permitting. They also offer a wide selection of boat rentals, with or without a captain. ✉ *Waterfront, Marina del Cantone* ☏ *081/2131742 office, 339/3142791 mobile* 🌐 *www.masticiello.com.*

Chapter 6

THE BAY OF NAPLES

Updated by
Nick Bruno

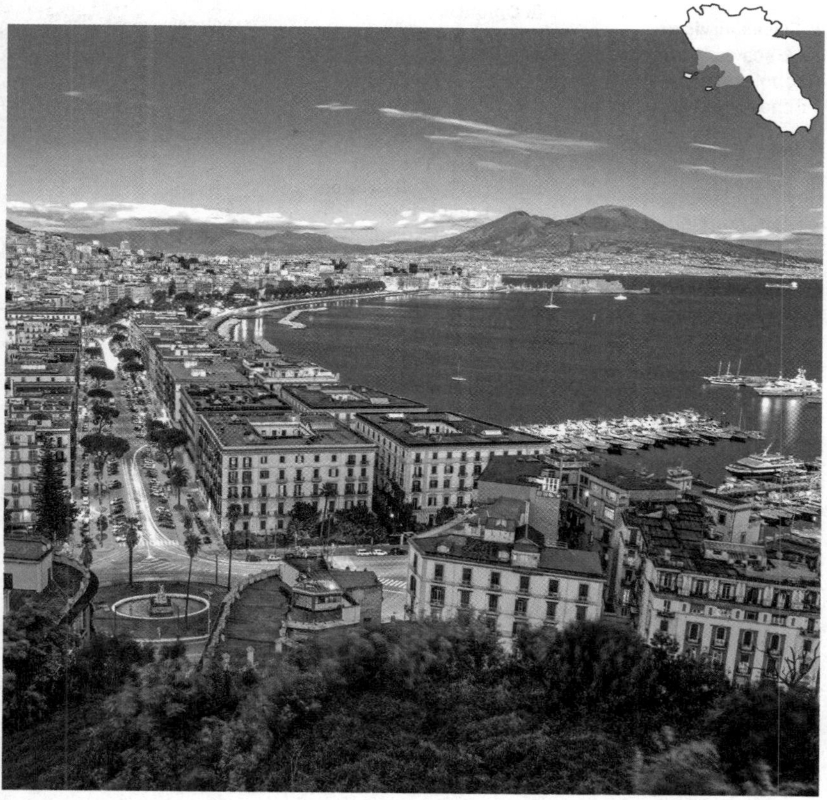

Sights	Restaurants	Hotels	Shopping	Nightlife
★★★★★	★★★★☆	★★☆☆☆	★☆☆☆☆	★☆☆☆☆

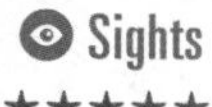

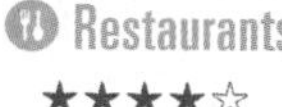

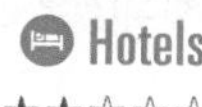

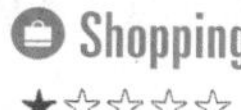

WELCOME TO THE BAY OF NAPLES

TOP REASONS TO GO

★ **Archaeological ruins:** Thanks to the destructive yet preserving powers of Vesuvius, you can visit Pompeii, Herculaneum, and other sites for a glimpse of ancient Roman life.

★ **Sweeping views:** Look seaward from the Acropolis at ancient Cumae for excellent views.

★ **Ancient gastronomy:** See how the Romans ate at restaurants in modern Pompei, or enjoy the day's catch on the waterfront at Pozzuoli.

★ **Old Roman homes:** As an alternative to the tourist bustle at other sites, head for Oplontis, a Roman villa with well-preserved frescoes.

★ **Mt. Vesuvius:** Geothermal energy has been trapped since time immemorial under the cone of Vesuvius—as you'll experience on a hike around the peak.

1 **Herculaneum (Ercolano).** The archaeological site of Herculaneum was once a wealthy seaside resort of learned and working citizens.

2 **Vesuvius.** Dominating the skyline southeast of Naples is the present cone form of the destructive Vesuvius caldera.

3 **Oplontis (Torre Annunziata).** The city of Torre Annunziata is home to the lavishly decorated Roman-era Oplontis Villa.

4 **Pompeii.** The most famous dig of all—the one that arguably kick-started archaeological studies and the Grand Tour—is Pompeii.

5 **Pozzuoli.** West of Naples lies Campi Flegrei—or Phlegraean Fields (meaning Fiery Fields), a volcanic landscape of craters, bubbling mud pits, and fumaroles. The region's hub is Pozzuoli.

6 **Baia.** The gorgeous bays of Baia were the playgrounds of the Roman elite.

7 **Cumae.** Farther along the coast from Baia, isolated Cumae is where Greek colonists first settled on mainland Campania: it's another of the Campi Flegrei's scenic archaeological sites.

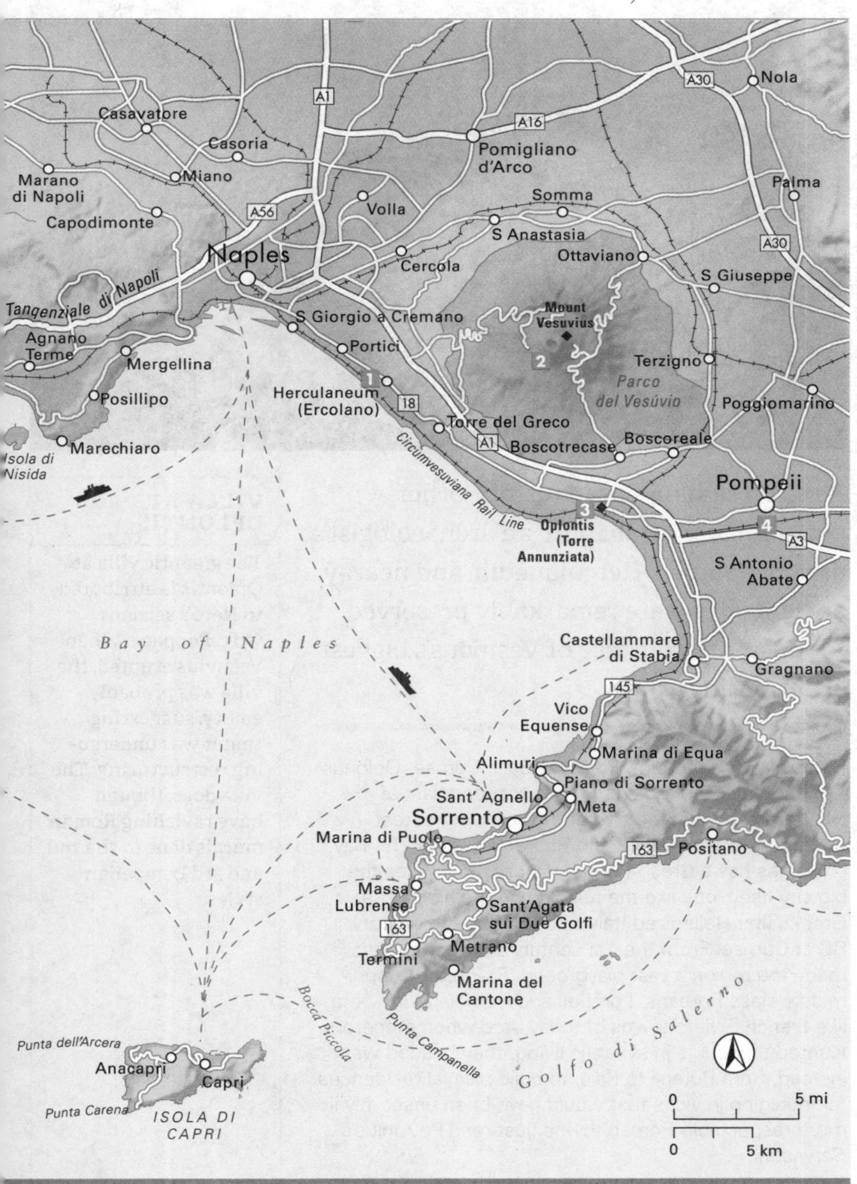
Casavatore
Casoria
Marano di Napoli
Miano
Capodimonte
Naples
Tangenziale di Napoli
Agnano Terme
Mergellina
Posillipo
Marechiaro
Isola di Nisida
Volla
Cercola
S Giorgio a Cremano
Portici
Herculaneum (Ercolano)
Torre del Greco
Circumvesuviana Rail Line
Pomigliano d'Arco
Somma
S Anastasia
Ottaviano
Mount Vesuvius
Parco del Vesúvio
Terzigno
Boscotrecase
Boscoreale
Oplontis (Torre Annunziata)
Nola
Palma
S Giuseppe
Poggiomarino
Pompeii
S Antonio Abate
Castellammare di Stabia
Gragnano
Vico Equense
Marina di Equa
Alimuri
Piano di Sorrento
Sant' Agnello
Meta
Sorrento
Marina di Puolo
Positano
Massa Lubrense
Sant'Agata sui Due Golfi
Metrano
Termini
Marina del Cantone
Bay of Naples
Bocca Piccola
Punta Campanella
Golfo di Salerno
Punta dell'Arcera
Anacapri
Capri
Punta Carena
ISOLA DI CAPRI
A1
A16
A30
A56
A3
18
145
163
0
5 mi
0
5 km

CAMPANIA'S ANCIENT TREASURES

The Museo Archeologico dei Campi Flegrei

As so often happens in history, other people's catastrophes are an archaeologist's dream: Pompeii, Herculaneum, and nearby ancient sites were remarkably preserved for posterity courtesy of Vesuvius's biggest eruption, in AD 79.

Pompeii, Herculaneum, Pozzuoli, Baia, Cumae, Oplontis ... no wonder the regions to the west and east of Naples are considered two of the world's greatest treasure troves of Greek and Roman antiquity. The Bay of Naples has a Greco-Roman history that makes the big city itself look like the new kid on the block. The Greeks first Hellenized Italy's boot in the 8th century BC at Cumae. From the 1st century BC, the Romans made the region a vast playground. Favored by upper-middle-class Romans, Pompeii and Herculaneum were like French Riviera towns of today. And when emperors wanted to indulge in sybaritic living, they headed west instead, from Puteoli to Baia, to build palatial residences for indulging in vices that would have been unseemly in more respectable Roman towns (just read Petronius's *Satyricon*).

VILLA AT OPLONTIS

The gigantic villa at Oplontis is attributed to Nero's second wife, Poppaea. When Vesuvius erupted, the villa was probably empty, suggesting that it was undergoing restructuring. The villa does, though, have ravishing Roman murals done in the 2nd and 3rd Pompeiian styles.

POMPEII

When it comes to Campania's overflowing basket of treasures of the ancient world, everyone starts with Pompeii, and rightly so. Rome's Forum might be more majestic, but for a cross-section of Roman everyday life, Pompeii is UNESCO World Heritage site number one.

Not only are the everyday people of the city commemorated, but in the Orchard of the Fugitives they are also preserved as death left them. In the Thermopolia, the day's takings were found in the till. On the walls of the thermal baths, houses, shops, theaters, and *lupanari* (brothels), graffiti abounds.

On the day you visit, some sections of Pompeii may be closed for restoration, but the place is so large that there's always more than enough to see.

HERCULANEUM

The excavations here are more compact than in Pompeii. The mix of mud and pyroclastic matter left much organic material eerily intact, down to a carbonized Roman boat given its own pavilion, along with spectacular frescoes and mosaics. To see it all come alive, visit the MAV Museum, whose exhibits include a computer re-creation of the fateful day in AD 79, when Vesuvius blew.

Roman ruins at Pozzuoli

Temple of Venus, Baia

BAIA

With its thermal springs, this bay of bays boasted antiquity's most extensive bath complex, where Rome's Great and the Good headed for leisure purposes. Much of the complex remains on the slopes, though part of one pleasure palace—Emperor Claudius's Nymphaeum—lies submerged, the highlight of a submarine area you can view on a glass-bottom boat.

CUMAE

Here Greeks established their first foothold on Italy's mainland, introducing the cult of Apollo whose priestess, the Cumaean Sibyl, prophesied for Aeneas the founding of Rome. Eight centuries later she was still in business, predicting, at least according to Robert Graves, to a young Claudius his future emperorship. Her "cave," one of the ancient wonders of the world, is actually part of a Roman military tunnel.

If you're lucky enough to travel to Naples by water, a peacock's tail of splendor unfolds before you as you enter the vast Golfo di Napoli, the Bay of Naples. This pulse-tingling vista offers a turquoise-rimmed crescent of isles, hills, azure sea, ancient cities, and modern villas, all arrayed around the bay to the east and west of Naples.

But on each side of the city the earth fumes and grumbles, reminding us that all this beauty was born of cataclysm. Along the coast to the west are the Campi Flegrei, the Phlegrean Fields of the ancients, where the crater of the Solfatara spews satisfyingly Dante-esque gases and where hills like Monte Nuovo have emerged seemingly overnight. Nearby are the dark, deep waters of Lago d'Averno (Lake Avernus), the lake that was allegedly the ancient doorway to the Underworld, realm of the pagan afterlife ruled over by the god Hades. To the southeast of Naples slumbers Vesuvius, the mother of all mounts, looking down from its 4,000-foot height at the coastal strip stretching from modern and ancient Pompeii all the way to Naples. With potential destruction ever at hand, it is no wonder that southern Italians—and in particular Neapolitans—obey to the letter Horace's precept: *carpe diem* (seize the day).

Even with the world's most famous volcano looming over the scene like a perpetual standby tombstone, visitors should feel relatively safe. The observatory on Vesuvius's slopes keeps its scientific finger on the subterranean pulse and will warn when signs of misbehavior become evident, so you need not worry about becoming an unwilling exhibit in some encore of Pompeii. You can simply concentrate on the memorable sights that fringe the spectacularly blue bay. The entire region is rife with legend and immortal names. Sixteen kilometers (10 miles) to the west of Naples lies an area where the emperors Claudius and Nero schemed and plotted in their villas, Virgil composed his poetry, and where, at Puteoli (now Pozzuoli), the Apostle Paul landed to spread the Gospel. Here, in and around what was called the Phlegrean (burning) Fields, are ancient sites like the Greeks' first colony in mainland Italy, the city of Cumae, home of the famed Cumaean Sibyl; the luxury-loving Baia, whose hot springs made it ancient Rome's most fashionable pleasure dome; and the amphitheater of Pozzuoli, whose subterranean galleries are better preserved than even those at Rome's Colosseum. Here are the Campi Flegrei—inspiration for Virgil's *Aeneid* and Dante's *Inferno*—and the sulfur-bound Solfatara. Leapfrogging over Naples and spread out east along the bay are the ancient noble villas at Oplontis and Stabiae and, in the shadow of Vesuvius, Herculaneum and

Pompeii—among the largest archaeological sites in Europe. Nowhere else in Italy is there a comparable mingling of natural vigor with the remains of antiquity.

MAJOR REGIONS

The Bay of Naples includes two main areas. Southeast from Naples are the *Comuni Vesuviani,* famed for wondrous archaeological sites pulverized, buried, and sealed by the eruption of Vesuvius of AD 79 and chronicled by Pliny the Younger across the Bay at Miseno in the Campi Flegrei. The sprawling unearthed ruins of **Pompeii** warrant many hours to explore, while the more compact Roman seaside resort of **Herculaneum** and nearby gorgeous villa at **Oplontis** require less legwork and contain better-preserved wooden artifacts and skeletons. Sandwiched between this awe-inspiring archaeological legacy there is paint-peeling, faded grandeur among Bourbon-era villas and an ugly 20th-century urban sprawl.

These contrasting ancient and modern sights are set against the fertile but threatening backdrop of 1,281-meter (4,203-foot) **Vesuvius,** worth visiting for its contorted magma rock-filled national park, vineyards, and produce-rich smallholdings. Starting from the western suburbs of Naples, the **Campi Flegrei** stretch in a coastal belt that includes the town of **Pozzuoli** and its impressive amphitheater, the scruffy but fascinating resort of **Baia,** and the atmospheric coastal Greco-Roman ruins at **Cumae.** Pockmarked with volcanic craters, this region is where Rome's vast naval fleet was based and where its senators and emperors let their hair down, tapping the geothermal energy to enhance their downtime in lavish villas with steam baths and swims between infamously salacious and cruel pursuits. It's no coincidence that this remains a favorite excursion for Neapolitans in the 21st century.

Planning

When to Go

This part of the Mediterranean is at its best in spring and fall, though you may encounter hordes of schoolchildren at archaeological sites. The weather is often chilly in winter, and roads on the upper slopes of Vesuvius can become dangerously icy. Spectacular summertime events take place at the ancient Roman baths at Baia and the ancient Roman theater at Pompeii. The verdant Campi Flegrei becomes a floral feast at springtime, and as late as June and July the north-facing slopes of Vesuvius remain awash with color.

Planning Your Time

Allow two full days for visiting the major sites of Herculaneum, best combined with a visit to Vesuvius. Likewise for Pompeii, which pairs well with a side trip to the more rarefied Oplontis. If traveling with children, spend some time at the Herculaneum's MAV museum where, thanks to cutting-edge computer technology, ruins are virtually restored to their original glory. In the Campi Flegrei, your top priorities should be the sites in Pozzuoli, the outlying site of Cumae, and the monumental archaeological park in Baia—all of which you can visit on a single ticket.

Getting Here and Around

BUS

All the main tourist sights east of Naples are well served by rail from the city, with more frequent departures and trips that take far less time than by bus. Travel west of Naples is best started by Cumana train, though for Baia and Cumae you will transfer to buses at either Fusaro or Lido Fusaro.

CAR

Pompeii is a short distance off the A3 Naples–Salerno Autostrada, but this major highway with only two lanes in each direction is often congested. A car can be useful for exploring the Campi Flegrei region, especially for sites like Cumae and Lake Avernus where public transportation is infrequent or nonexistent. From Naples, travel toward Pozzuoli on the Tangenziale—the Naples bypass—exiting at the appropriate junction.

Most archaeological sites are accessible by car. Use a *parcheggio custodito* (attended parking lot), particularly at Pompeii and Herculaneum, and avoid on-street unattended parking. Metered parking (look for the blue lines on the street) is scarce in most places.

Off the main highways, signposting is sometimes poor, with road signs competing with advertising placards. The westbound Tangenziale (Napoli–Pozzuoli) should be avoided on Saturday evening and on Sunday in summer (crowds heading out of Naples for nightlife or beaches). Road conditions are usually good, though surfaces near the top of Vesuvius can become icy in winter.

TRAIN

Stazione Centrale, in Naples's Piazza Garibaldi, is the hub for public transportation both east and west of Naples. The rather rundown and crowded Circumvesuviana connects Naples, Herculaneum, Torre del Greco, Torre Annunziata, Vesuvius, Pompeii, and Sorrento. For a more comfortable and faster ride with designated seats opt for the tourist-friendly, seasonal (mid-March through October) Campania Express which runs along the curve of the Bay of Naples from Naples to Sorrento. FS Metroplitana Linea 2 serves Pozzuoli *(see Pozzuoli)*. For the Phlegrean Fields to the west of Naples, take the Cumana aka linea 7, run by SEPSA, from the terminus at Piazza Montesanto near Montesanto Metropolitana station. Be prepared for delays and very scruffy trains.

■ TIP→ Confusion can be avoided by not taking every route map at face value. Baia, for instance, appears on some maps even though the station here vanished years ago. To reach Baia one needs to get down from the train at Fusaro and take a small red bus, waiting outside; likewise to get to Cumae.

CONTACTS Circumvesuviana and Cumana railway. ☎ *800/211388* 🌐 *www.eavsrl.it.*

Restaurants

Volcanoes might wreak disaster every millennium or so, but on a day-to-day basis they also guarantee the most fertile of soils. Wine, olives, vegetables—Naples and environs produce prize specimens, and in the cases of mozzarella and pizza can claim pride of origin. And, of course, there's the fruit of the sea, from the tiny and taste-packed anchovy to swordfish nearly a table long. Nowhere does the pride in tradition show more clearly than at Pompei's Il Principe. The restaurant's menu has some inventive dishes with flavor combinations that hark back to the era when Vesuvius was still the intact Monte Somma, the abode of the wine god Dionysus, whose image fittingly graces the wine list.

Prices in the reviews are the average cost of a main course at dinner or, if dinner isn't served, at lunch. Restaurant reviews have been shortened. For full information, visit Fodors.com.

What it Costs In Euros

$	$$	$$$	$$$$
RESTAURANTS			
under €15	€15–€24	€25–€35	over €35

Hotels

Although much of the Vesuvian area is embraced by the Vesuvius National Park, don't expect well-appointed *agriturismi*, or rustic lodgings—or, for that matter, hotels that have you sighing with pleasure when you throw open the shutters. But don't fear, you can find some good hotels east of Naples.

Prices in the reviews are the lowest cost of a standard double room in high season. Hotel reviews have been shortened. For full information, visit Fodors.com.

What it Costs In Euros			
$	$$	$$$	$$$$
HOTELS			
under €125	€125–€200	€201–€300	over €300

Tours

Vesuvius vs Pompeii runs tours to Vesuvius, Pompeii, Herculaneum, and other sights east and west of Naples. Sami Private Tours arranges all-day trips of Bay of Naples sights, or you can combine a trip up to Vesuvius with a visit to the Herculaneum ruins and a tasting at a vineyard on the volcanic slopes.

CONTACTS Drivinaples. ☎ *329/4214496* 🌐 *www.drivinaples.com.* **Sami Private Tours.** ✉ *Amalfi* ☎ *333/3668626* 🌐 *www.samiprivatetours.it.* **Vesuvius vs Pompei.** ☎ *333/6409000* 🌐 *www.vesuviusvspompeii.com.*

Visitor Information

In addition to the tourist offices listed in the various towns, the EPT office in Naples *(see Naples Planner, in Chapter 7)* is a good resource for touring and other information.

Herculaneum (Ercolano)

12 km (8 miles) southeast of Naples, 40 km (25 miles) northwest of Salerno.

A visit to the archaeological site of Herculaneum neatly counterbalances the hustle of its larger neighbor, Pompeii. Although close to the heart of busy Ercolano—indeed, in places right under the town—the ancient site seems worlds apart. Like Pompeii, Herculaneum was buried by Vesuvius's eruption in AD 79. Unlike Pompeii, it was submerged in a mass of volcanic mud that sealed and preserved wood and other organic materials including food (at Pompeii, most organic matter rotted away over time). Several villas have inlaid marble floors that evoke the same admiration as the mosaics in Naples's Museo Archeologico. Elsewhere it's possible to gauge how the less privileged lived: more remains of the upper stories than in Pompeii, so you can view the original stairs to the cramped, poorly lighted rooms that gave onto the central courtyard. There's also more of a sense of a small, living community than Pompeii conveys, but because only about the 20% of the town has been excavated, don't expect to find a forum and other public buildings like those offered by Pompeii.

GETTING HERE AND AROUND

To get to Herculaneum by car, take the A3 Naples–Salerno highway and exit at Ercolano. Follow signs for the "*Scavi*" (excavations). The Circumvesuviana railway *(see Bay of Naples Planner for contact info)* connects Herculaneum to Naples, Portici, Torre del Greco, Torre Annunziata, Pompeii, and Sorrento. The tourist-friendly, seasonal (mid-March through October) Campania Express is a more salubrious option.

VISITOR INFORMATION

The friendly staffers at the ticket office of the ruins provide advice and distribute copies of a helpful pamphlet and map of the ruins. The Campania Card (€32) gets you various transportation discounts as well as two included admission plus reduced entrance to key sights/activities including: Herculaneum and Villa Campolieto. You can buy it in advance at 🌐 *www.campaniartecard.it/artecard/en/card/ercolanovesuvio-card*.

Sights

Ad Cucumas

RUINS | The wall outside this ancient wine shop shows four jars (*cucumae*) of different colors and prices. Above the wine list is the god Sema Sancus, with the inscription Nola at the bottom, possibly an announcement of a show taking place in the town of Nola. ✉ *Insula VI, Herculaneum, Ercolano* 🌐 *www.ercolano.beniculturali.it*.

Antica Spiaggia

RUINS | Explore the ruins by the terrace of Marcus Nonius Balbus, where the town's great benefactor is buried, and the Suburban Baths (undergoing restoration). Directly below, on the onetime seafront, in the barrel arches, which were once storage for boats, 300 skeletons of escaping residents were found in 1980. ✉ *Ercolano* 🌐 *www.ercolano.beniculturali.it*.

★ Casa dei Cervi

RUINS | In antiquity, the Casa dei Cervi was one of the first houses that visitors to the town would have passed as they entered the city from the seaward side. As in most top-notch town residences, however, the entranceway is plain and leads into a *vestibulum,* a small vestibule, that opens onto an open courtyard called a *peristylium.* The showpiece in this particular house is the garden area, surrounded by a so-called *cryptoporticus* embellished with fine still life frescoes and terminating in a partially reconstructed gazebo. Of course, prior to the eruption, the house would have had a fine view over the Bay of Naples. ✉ *Insula IV, Herculaneum, Ercolano* 🌐 *www.ercolano.beniculturali.it* ⊗ *Closed 1st Mon. of month.*

Casa del Tramezzo di Legno

(*House of the Wooden Partition*)

RUINS | An outstanding example of carbonized remains is found in the Casa del Tramezzo di Legno, as it has been prosaically labeled by archaeologists. Following renovation work in the mid-1st century AD, the house was designed to have a frontage on three sides of Insula III and included a number of storerooms, shops, and second-floor habitations. This suggests that the owner was a wealthy *mercator,* a member of the up-and-coming merchant class who was starting to edge the patricians out of their privileged positions. The airy atrium has a lovely garden. Look closely at the *impluvium* (a basin to collect rainwater) and above the open *compluvium* roof with dog's-head spouts). You'll see the original flooring below, which was later replaced with marble, perhaps after a change of owners. Next to the impluvium is an elegant marble table, or *cartibulum,* while behind is the *tablinum* (reception room), partially screened off by a wooden partition that would also have had hooks for hanging *lucernae* (lamps). ✉ *Insula III, 11–12, Herculaneum, Ercolano* 🌐 *www.ercolano.beniculturali.it*.

★ Casa di Nettuno ed Anfitrite

(*House of Neptune and Amphitrite*)

RUINS | The ruin of this house takes its name from the mosaic in back that still sports its bright blue coloring and adorns the wall of the small, secluded *nymphaeum-triclinium* (a dining room with a fountain). The mosaic depicts the following scene: according to legend, in the time-honored fashion of the Olympians, Neptune (or Poseidon) saw Amphitrite dancing with the Nereids on the island of Naxos, carried her off, and married her. The adjacent wall, in similar mosaic style, has a hunting scene of a stag being pursued by a dog. Annexed to the same house is a remarkably preserved wine shop, where amphorae still rest on carbonized wooden shelves. ✉ *Insula V, on Cardo IV parallel to Cardo V, close to*

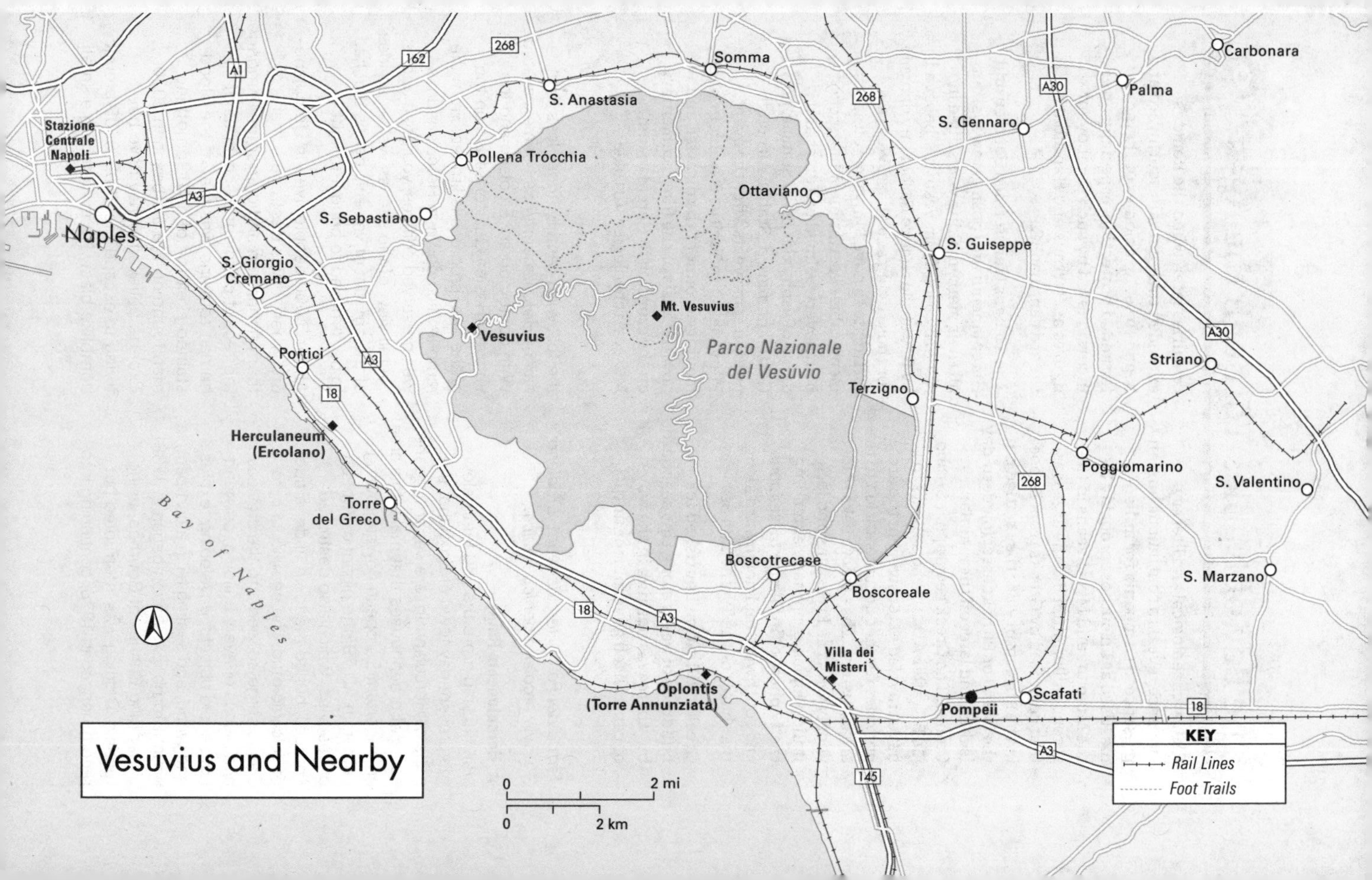
Vesuvius and Nearby
Naples
Stazione Centrale Napoli
S. Giorgio Cremano
Portici
Herculaneum (Ercolano)
Torre del Greco
Bay of Naples
S. Sebastiano
Pollena Trócchia
S. Anastasia
Somma
Vesuvius
Mt. Vesuvius
Parco Nazionale del Vesúvio
Ottaviano
S. Gennaro
Palma
Carbonara
S. Guiseppe
Terzigno
Striano
Poggiomarino
S. Valentino
S. Marzano
Boscotrecase
Boscoreale
Villa dei Misteri
Oplontis (Torre Annunziata)
Pompeii
Scafati
KEY
Rail Lines
Foot Trails
0
2 mi
0
2 km
A1
A3
A30
162
268
18
145

The Bay of Naples Through the Ages

Rich archaeological and literary evidence reveals a continuous human presence in Campania for millennia. Used as an outpost probably by the Minoans and Mycenaeans in the second millennium BC, the area was first colonized by Greeks from Euboea in the 8th century BC; they settled on the island of Pithekoussai (modern-day Ischia) and later on the mainland at Cumae. The Greek geographer Strabo (64 BC–after AD 21), who appears to have traveled extensively in the area, provides further documentation to the area's history. The early Greeks traded widely with the Etruscans and local Italic peoples, eventually extending their sphere of influence to Neapolis and southward and northward along the shores of the Tyrrhenian Sea.

Greek civilization flourished for hundreds of years along this seaboard, but there was nothing in the way of centralized government until centuries later, when the Romans extended their domain southward and began to set up colonies of their own for added protection, especially after incursions led by such flamboyant figures as Pyrrhus and Hannibal in the 3rd century BC.

The Romans transformed Pompeii and Herculaneum into posh getaways, but all their merrymaking was stilled in AD 79 by a jolt from Vesuvius, believed by few at the time to harbor any danger for those living at its base. We are fortunate to have Pliny the Younger's memorable description of his uncle being overwhelmed by fumes and dying of asphyxiation in Stabiae, now Castellammare di Stabia. Although written some years after the event, Pliny's letter to Tacitus is a unique and moving account of the disaster, and now the basis of the film commentary on the eruption in Herculaneum's Museo Archeologico Virtuale.

Terme del Foro, Herculaneum, Ercolano 🌐 *www.ercolano.beniculturali.it.*

★ **Herculaneum Ruins**

RUINS | Lying more than 50 feet below the present-day town of Ercolano, the ruins of Herculaneum are set among the acres of greenhouses that make this area an important European flower-growing center. In AD 79, the gigantic eruption of Vesuvius, which also destroyed Pompeii, buried the town under a tide of volcanic mud. The semiliquid pyroclastic surge seeped into the crevices and niches of every building, covering household objects, enveloping textiles and wood, and sealing all in a compact, airtight tomb. Excavation began in 1738 under King Charles of Bourbon, using tunnels. Digging was interrupted but recommenced in 1828, continuing into the following century. Today less than half of Herculaneum has been excavated. With contemporary Ercolano and the unlovely Resina Quarter sitting on top of the site, progress is limited. From the ramp leading down to Herculaneum's well-preserved edifices, you get a good overall view of the site, as well as an idea of the amount of volcanic debris that had to be removed to bring it to light.

About 5,000 people lived in Herculaneum when it was destroyed, many of them fishermen and craftsmen. Among the recent poignant discoveries of human remains was that of the blood-stained skeleton of a 40-something man found on the old beach in 2020. Experts believe he may have been trying to escape the 750F–950F atomic bomblike blast. He is clutching a small

Much better preserved than Pompeii, Herculaneum boasts houses with frescoes whose colors remain vivid.

leather bag with a wooden box, from which a ring is protruding.

Although Herculaneum had only one-third the population of Pompeii and has been only partially excavated, what has been found is generally better preserved. In some cases you can even see the original wooden beams, doors, and staircases. Unfortunately, the Villa dei Papiri (Villa of Papyri) is currently closed to the public—this excavation outside the main site was built by Julius Caesar's father-in-law (with a replica built by Paul Getty in Malibu almost 2,000 years later). The building is named for almost 2,000 carbonized papyrus scrolls dug up here in the 18th century, leading scholars to believe that this may have been a study center or library. Also worth special attention are the carbonized remains within the Casa del Tramezzo di Legno (House of the Wooden Partition).

Be sure to stock up on refreshments beforehand; there is no food at the archaeological site. At the entrance, pick up a free map showing the gridlike layout of the dig, which is divided into numbered blocks, or insulae. Splurge on an audio guide app via 🌐 *www.ercolano.tours* (€10; adult and children's versions): the standard audioguide (€8 for one, €13 for two) may be available for those without a smartphone. You can also join a group with a local guide (around €15 per person). Most of the houses are open, and a representative cross-section of domestic, commercial, and civic buildings can be seen. Check the website for the latest openings and news of recent excavation discoveries. ✉ *Corso Resina 6, Ercolano* ☎ *081/7777008* 🌐 *ercolano.beniculturali.it* 🎫 *€13* 🕐 *Closed Wed.*

Museo Archeologico Virtuale (MAV)

HISTORY MUSEUM | **FAMILY** | With dazzling "virtual" versions of Herculaneum's streets and squares and a multidimensional simulation of Vesuvius erupting, Herculaneum's 1st-century-meets-the-21st-century museum is a must for kids and adults alike. After stopping at the ticket office you descend, as in an excavation, to a floor below.

You'll experience Herculaneum's Villa dei Papiri before and (even more dramatically) during the eruption, courtesy of special effects: enter "the burning cloud" of AD 79; then emerge, virtually speaking, inside Pompeii's House of the Faun, which can be seen both as it is and as it was for two centuries BC. The next re-creation is again Villa dei Papiri. Then comes a stellar pre- and postflooding view of Baia's Nymphaeum, the now-displaced statues arrayed as they were in the days of Emperor Claudius, who commissioned them.

Visitors here are invited to take a front-row seat for "Day and Night in the Forum of Pompeii," with soldiers, litter-bearing slaves, and toga-clad figures moving spectrally to complete the spell; or to make a vicarious visit to the Lupanari brothels, their various pleasures illustrated in graphic virtual frescoes along the walls. A wooden model of Herculaneum's theater, its virtual re-creation, reminds us that it was here that a local farmer, while digging a well, first came across what proved to be not merely a single building, but a whole town. Equally fascinating are the virtual baths. There's also a 3D film of Vesuvius erupting, replete with a fatalistic narrative and cataclysmic special effects: the words of Pliny the Younger provide a timeless commentary while the floor vibrates under your feet.

MAV 5.0 enhances the visitor experience with more emphasis on interaction, AR (Augmented Reality) smartphone action and four new installations exploring artworks at Pompeii and Herculaneum. A curious, gesticulating humanoid robot called Pepper now dispenses information about the ancient world. ✉ *Via IV Novembre 44, Ercolano* ☎ *081/7776843* 🌐 *www.museomav.it* 🎫 *€10* 🕒 *Closed Mon. and Tues. Oct.–Feb.*

Palaestra

RUINS | No town would have been complete without its sports facilities, and Herculaneum was no exception. Just opposite the *thermopolium,* on Cardo V, is the entrance to the large Palaestra, where a variety of sports took place. Only a few of the peristyle columns here have been excavated, a reminder of how much of the ancient town remains buried under solidified volcanic mud. ✉ *Insula Orientalis II, Herculaneum, Ercolano* 🌐 *www.ercolano.beniculturali.it.*

Sacello degli Augustali (*Hall of the Augustals*)

RUINS | This site was where the emperor was worshipped. The frescoes on the walls represent Hercules, the mythical founder of the town. A marble inscription commemorates the politicians who donated funds for the building of the hall and offered a dinner here for the members of Herculaneum's ruling class. ✉ *Insula VI, Herculaneum, Ercolano* 🌐 *www.ercolano.beniculturali.it.*

Taverna di Priapo (*Priapus's Tavern*)

RUINS | This *thermopolium* (a place where hot food and drinks were served, hence the Greek name) was connected to the home of the owner and had the counter decorated with a Priapus (the god of fertility) to keep the evil eye at bay. ✉ *Insula IV, Herculaneum, Ercolano* 🌐 *www.ercolano.beniculturali.it.*

Terme del Foro (*Forum Baths*)

RUINS | These forum baths contained separate sections for men and women. Here you can see most of the architectural aspects of *thermae* (baths): the *apodyterium,* or changing room, with partitioned shelves for depositing togas and a low podium to use as seating space while in line to use the facilities; a round *frigidarium,* or a cool pool; a *tepidarium,* a semi-heated room; and a *calidarium,* or heated room with pool. For more attractive mosaics, go around into the women's baths, which had no frigidarium. The heating system in the tepidarium was also different—no hot air piped through or under, only braziers. Note the small overhead cubbies in which bathers stored their belongings. ✉ *Insula VI, Herculaneum, Ercolano* 🌐 *www.ercolano.beniculturali.it.*

Villa Campolieto and Ville Vesuviane

NOTABLE BUILDING | One of the Ville Vesuviane that were built during Bourbon rule, Villa Campolieto is on the so-called Miglio d'Oro (Golden Mile), now the scruffy traffic-ridden Corso Resina near Herculaneum. Although its rooms are empty, and it feels forlorn and neglected, it has some sumptuous paintings, a grand staircase, and vestiges of its formal gardens, making it worth a quick detour if time allows and you've purchased a Campania card. Check the website and *Il Mattino* newspaper for upcoming events, concerts, and tours of the more interesting villas: La Favorita and especially Villa Le Ginestre, where the tortured and dying 19th-century poet Leopardi contemplated his fate on a spectacular terrace looking up at the fuming Vesuvio. ✉ *Corso Resina 283, Ercolano* ☎ *081/7322134* 🌐 *www.villevesuviane.net* 🎫 *€5* ⏲ *Closed Mon.*

Restaurants

La Fornacella

$$ | **SOUTHERN ITALIAN** | Doing a brisk trade with both *stranieri* and *napoletani*—always a good sign—this restaurant and pizzeria on the roundabout near the Circumvesuviana station is a 10-minute walk from the excavations of Herculaneum. Dishes vary according to season but always draw on local recipes: pasta *e fagioli* (with beans) is a winter favorite, and richly garnished *schiaffoni* (flat tube pasta) with seafood is a summer stalwart. **Known for:** pizza with slow-proofed dough; grilled seafood; good value fixed-price options. [$] *Average main: €16* ✉ *Via IV Novembre 90–92, Ercolano* ☎ *081/7774861* 🌐 *www.lafornacella.it* ⏲ *Closed Mon.*

Hotels

Hotel Herculaneum

$ | **B&B/INN** | Across from the Herculaneum archaeological site, this decent, budget-friendly B&B has views of the ruins and the sea, is much quieter than its counterparts in Naples, and makes a good base for exploring nearby Pompeii and Oplontis as well as Herculaneum. **Pros:** convenient location; multiple meal plans, from breakfast-only to full board; free parking. **Cons:** tiny lift and need to use stairs for some rooms; echoey, noisy especially out front; rooms are on the smallish side. [$] *Rooms from: €84* ✉ *Corso Resina 230, Ercolano* ☎ *081/18556413* 🌐 *www.hotelherculaneum.com* *19 rooms* 🍽 *Free Breakfast.*

Miglio d'Oro Park Hotel

$ | **HOTEL** | The grand Vesuvian villas along the Golden Mile are normally just for visits, but you can actually stay in the magnificent pink and Pompeiian-red Miglio d'Oro, where spacious, high-ceilinged guest rooms are done in understated tones in fitting contrast to the sea view and vivid garden-green hues outside. **Pros:** five-minute walk from the Herculaneum ruins; rare "villa" experience; friendly reception. **Cons:** some corners neglected; can feel a bit like an institution when conferences staged here; limited breakfast choice. [$] *Rooms from: €100* ✉ *Corso Resina 296, Ercolano* ☎ *081/7399999* 🌐 *www.migliodoroparkhotel.it* *47 rooms* 🍽 *No Meals.*

★ **Il San Cristoforo**

$$ | **HOTEL** | **FAMILY** | Just out of town and immersed in gorgeous, blooming gardens, this grand, gleaming palazzo turned welcoming resort hotel (opened 2018) has sleek public areas and stylish guest rooms. **Pros:** great customer service; spacious contemporary rooms and marble bathrooms; family-friendly grounds. **Cons:** popular for weddings; infrequent shuttle bus service and tricky to reach without wheels; no gym or spa.

Rooms from: €145 ✉ *Via Benedetto Cozzolino 29/H, Ercolano* ☎ *081/7712292* 🌐 *www.ilsancristoforo.com* *30 rooms* *Free Breakfast.*

Vesuvius

16 km (10 miles) east of Naples, 8 km (5 miles) northeast of Herculaneum, 40 km (25 miles) northwest of Salerno.

Vesuvius may have lost its plume of smoke, but it has lost none of its fascination or threat—especially for those who live in the towns around the cone. They've now nicknamed it the "Sterminator." In centuries gone by, their predecessors would study the volcano for signs of impending destruction. "*Napoli fa i peccati e la Torre li paga,*" the residents of nearby Torre del Greco used to mutter—Naples sins and the Torre suffers. When reports of depraved behavior circulated about Neapolitans across the bay, chastisement was only to be expected. Today, the world continues to watch *'O Vesuvio* with bated breath.

GETTING HERE AND AROUND

Busvia del Vesuvio's guided tours (€22) depart from opposite the info point that's adjacent to Pompeii's Villa dei Misteri Circumvesuviana station. Vesuvio Express operates 10-seat minibuses (€10) from Ercolano Circumvesuviana station. The service is notoriously unreliable and brusque but apart from an expensive return taxi fare there's no regular transport option from Ercolano. Remember you need an extra €10 to get into the park itself, so the costs can mount. The vehicles thread their way rapidly up back roads, reaching the top in 20 minutes. Allow at least 2½ hours for the journey, including a 30-minute walk to the crater on a soft cinder track.

To arrive by car, take the A3 Napoli–Salerno highway exit "Torre del Greco" and follow Via E. De Nicola from the tollbooth. Follow signs for the Parco Nazionale del Vesuvio (Vesuvius National Park). Circumvesuviana railway (see Bay of Naples Planner for contact info) serves the main archaeological sites at the foot of Vesuvius. Trains leave from the Porta Nolana–Corso Garibaldi station in Naples and stop at the main terminal at Piazza Garibaldi 10 blocks away, taking in all the main archaeological sites on route. There are about two trains per hour, with a cost of €2.50 to Ercolano and Torre Annunziata, and €3.20 to Pompei Scavi–Villa dei Misteri).

CONTACTS Busvia del Vesuvio. 🌐 *www.busviadelvesuvio.com.* **Vesuvio Express.** ✉ *Piazzale Stazione Circumvesuviano 7,* ☎ *081/7393666* 🌐 *vesuvioexpress.info.*

Sights

Mt. Vesuvius

VOLCANO | Although Vesuvius's destructive powers are on hold, the threat of an eruption remains ever present. Seen from the other side of the Bay of Naples, Vesuvius appears to have two peaks: on the northern side is the steep face of Monte Somma, possibly part of the original crater wall in AD 79; to the south is the present-day cone of Vesuvius, which has actually formed within the ancient crater. The AD 79 cone would have been considerably higher, perhaps peaking at around 9,000 feet. The upper slopes bear the visible scars left by 19th- and 20th-century eruptions, the most striking being the lava flow from 1944 lying to the left (north side) of the approach road from Ercolano on the way up.

As you tour the cities that felt the volcano's wrath, you may be overwhelmed by the urge to explore Vesuvius itself, and it's well worth the trip. The view when

You'll be amazed at how Vesuvius looms over the entire region—even in Naples, 10 miles away, it remains a totally commanding presence.

the air is clear is magnificent, with the curve of the coast and the tiny white houses among the orange and lemon blossoms. When the summit becomes lost in mist, though, you'll be lucky to see your hand in front of your face. If you notice the summit clearing—it tends to be clearer in the afternoon—head for it. If possible, see Vesuvius after you've toured the ruins of buried Herculaneum to appreciate the magnitude of the volcano's power. Admission to the crater includes a compulsory guide, usually a young geologist who speaks a smattering of English. At the bottom you'll be offered a stout walking stick (a small tip is appreciated when you return it). The climb can be tiring if you're not used to steep hikes. Because of the volcanic stone you should wear athletic or sturdy shoes, not sandals. ☎ *081/7775720, 081/8653911* 🌐 *www.parconazionaledelvesuvio.it* 🎫 *€10* ☞ *Tickets in advance at vesuviopark.vivaticket.it.*

Museo dell'Osservatorio Vesuviano (*Museum of the Vesuvius Observatory*)

OBSERVATORY | In bygone ages, the task of protecting the local inhabitants from Vesuvius fell to the patron saint of Naples, San Gennaro, whose statue was often paraded through city streets to placate the volcano's wrath, but since the mid-19th century the Osservatorio Vesuviano has attentively monitored seismic activity. The original 1841 observatory, conspicuous with its Pompeian-red facade, has survived unscathed on the volcano's upper slopes and now serves as a conference center and small museum whose exhibits include a mineralogical display, landscape gouaches, and early seismographs. Informational panels describe the contributions of the observatory's directors and other staff to the development of volcano-monitoring instrumentation. ✉ *Via Osservatorio, Ercolano* ☎ *081/7777149, 081/6108483* 🌐 *www.ov.ingv.it* 🎫 *Free guided tours by appointment* 🕒 *Closed Aug. and several days in Dec. and Jan.*

Oplontis (Torre Annunziata)

20 km (12 miles) southeast of Naples, 5 km (3 miles) west of Pompeii.

Surrounded by the fairly drab 1960s urban landscape of Torre Annunziata, Oplontis justifies its reputation as one of the more mysterious archaeological sites to be unearthed in the 20th century. The villa complex has been imaginatively ascribed—from a mere inscription on an amphora—to Nero's second wife, Poppaea Sabina. Her family was well known among the landed gentry of neighboring Pompeii, although, after a kick in the stomach from her emperor husband, she died some 15 years before the villa was overwhelmed by the eruption of AD 79. As Roman villas go, Poppaea's Villa, or Villa A, as it's called by archaeologists, is way off the top end of the scale.

GETTING HERE AND AROUND

By car, take the A3 Napoli–Salerno highway to the "Torre Annunziata" exit. Follow Via Veneto west, then turn left onto Via Sepolcri for the excavations. By train take the Circumvesuviana railway to Torre Annunziata, the town's modern name (€3.20 from Naples).

Sights

Oplontis

RUINS | For those overwhelmed by the throngs at Pompeii, a visit to the site of Oplontis offers a chance for contemplation and intellectual stimulation. What has been excavated so far of the Villa of the Empress Poppaea covers more than 7,000 square meters (75,000 square feet), and because the site is bound by a road to the west and a canal to the south, its full extent may never be known.

Complete with porticoes, a large peristyle, a pool, baths, and extensive gardens, the villa is thought by some to have been a school for young philosophers and orators. You have to visit to appreciate the full range of Roman wall paintings; one highlight is found in Room 5, a sitting room that overlooked the sea. ✉ *Via Sepolcri 1, Torre Annunziata* ☎ *081/8575347* 🌐 *www.pompeiisites.org* 🎟 *From €5* ⏲ *Closed Tues.*

Pompeii

Mention Pompeii and most travelers think of ancient Roman villas, prancing bronze fauns, writhing plaster casts of Vesuvius's victims, and the fabled days of the emperors. Millions of culture seekers worldwide continue to head for ancient Pompeii every year, but a similar number of Italian pilgrims converge on the new town's 19th-century basilica, the Santuario della Madonna del Rosario, as a token of faith—joining processions, making ex-voto offerings, or just honoring a vow. Wealthy Neapolitans come to make their donations to help the church carry out its good deeds. New car-owners even come to get their vehicles blessed—and given driving standards in these parts of the world, insurance coverage from on high is probably a sensible move.

Caught between the hammer and anvil of cultural and religious tourism, the modern town of Pompei has shaken off its rather complacent approach and is now endeavoring to polish up its act. In attempts to ease congestion, parts of the town have been made pedestrian-friendly and parking restrictions tightened. Departing from the rather sleazy reputation of previous years, several hotels have filled the sizable niche in the market for quality deals at affordable prices. As for recommendable restaurants, if you deviate from the archaeological site and make for the center of town, your choices will include two long-established top-notch family-run favorites among a very mixed bag of eateries. The modern town may be a circus, but the center ring

Pompeii Prep

Pompeii inspires under any circumstances, but it comes alive if you do some preparation before your visit.

First, read up—there are many good books on the subject, including these engaging, jargon-free histories: *Pompeii: The Day a City Died*, by Robert Etienne; *Pompeii: Public and Private Life*, by Paul Zanker; *The Lost World of Pompeii*, by Colin Amery; and *Pompeii: Life of a Roman Town*, by Mary Beard. For accurate historical information woven into the pages of a thriller, pick up *Pompeii: A Novel*, by Robert Harris.

Second, be sure to visit the Museo Archeologico Nazionale in Naples, where most of the finest art from Pompeii now resides. The highlights include the epic Alexander fresco, which once decorated the House of the Faun, and, in the Museum's "Gabinetto Secreto," louche frescoes advertising services on offer in the Lupari brothels. The museum is a rewarding stop even if Pompeii isn't in your plans. Over at the Herculaneum Museo Archeologico Virtuale (MAV), through virtual reconstructions, ancient structures come alive before your eyes, and even the occasional animated figure to match.

is always the splendors and wonders of ancient Pompeii itself.

GETTING HERE AND AROUND

To get to Pompeii by car, take the A3 Napoli–Salerno highway to the "Pompei" exit and follow signs for the nearby "Scavi" excavations. There are numerous guarded car parks near the Porta Marina, Piazza Essedra, and Anfiteatro entrances where you can leave your vehicle for a fee.

Pompeii has two central Circumvesuviana railway stations served by two separate train lines. The Naples–Sorrento train stops at "Pompei Scavi–Villa dei Misteri," 100 yards from the Porta Marina ticket office of the archaeological site, while the Naples–Poggiomarino train stops at Pompei Santuario, more convenient for the Santuario della Madonna del Rosario and the hotels and restaurants in the modern town center. A third Ferrovie della Statale (FS) train station south of the town center is only convenient if arriving from Salerno or Rome. The tourist-friendly, seasonal (mid-March–October) Campania Express is a more salubrious option.

If you're planning to visit all the Pompeii circuit sites and have a ticket, there's a free shuttle bus Pompeii Arte Bus (Wednesday–Monday April–early July) from Piazza Esedra: 🌐 *pompeiisites.org/en/visiting-info/pompeii-arte-bus-timetables-and-methods*.

VISITOR INFORMATION

You can pick up a free map at the Ufficio Informazione booth located at the entrance to the archaeological site. The staffers can tell you which sites can't be visited on the day you've arrived, saving you unnecessary walking. You can also join a guided group tour.

If you're planning to visit all the sites in the Pompeii circuit (Pompeii, the Villa of Poppaea/Oplontis, the Antiquarium of Boscoreale and Villa Regina, the Stabian Villas and the Libero D'Orsi Archaeological Museum/the Royal Palace of Quisisana) consider the €35 **My Pompeii Card.** It's valid for a year and includes special events and exhibitions too, and alongside all Pompeii tickets can be purchased at 🌐 *www.ticketone.it*.

CONTACTS Ufficio informazioni Porta Marina. ✉ *Piazza Porta Marina Inferiore, Pompei* ☎ *081/8575347* 🌐 *www.pompeiisites.org*.

Sights

★ Pompeii

RUINS | Petrified memorial to Vesuvius's eruption in 79 AD, Pompeii is the largest, most accessible, and most famous excavation anywhere. Ancient Pompeii had a population of 10,000–20,000 and covered about 170 acres on the seaward end of the Sarno Plain. Today it attracts more than 2 million visitors every year, but if you come in the quieter late afternoon, you can truly fall under the site's spell. Highlights include the Foro (Forum), which served as Pompeii's cultural, political, commercial, and religious hub; homes that were captured in various states by the eruption of Vesuvius, including the Casa del Poeta Tragico (House of the Tragic Poet), a typical middle-class residence with a floor mosaic of a chained dog, and the Casa dei Vettii (House of the Vettii), the best example of a wealthy merchant's home; the Villa dei Misteri (Villa of the Mysteries), a palatial abode with many fresco-adorned rooms; and the Anfiteatro (Amphitheater), built around 70 BC. Consider renting an €8 audio guide and opt for one of the three itineraries (two hours, four hours, or six hours) available at Porta Marina. If hiring a guide, agree beforehand on the length of the tour and the price. *Pompei* *081/8575347* *www.pompeiisites.org* *From €16* *Tickets available online at www.ticketone.it/en/artist/scavi-pompei/.*

Restaurants

Il Principe

$$ | **ITALIAN** | Il Principe's owner, Gian Marco Carli, inherited his parents' 30-year research into ancient Roman cuisine; Famiglia Carli may not have fed Roman emperors, but they have cooked for at least three U.S. presidents. Their quality meat and fish dishes, and sumptuous tasting menus honor the past, while delivering exquisitely presented, modern plates of food. **Known for:** grand interior, informal outdoor dining area; excellent cheese and wine choice; summer outdoor dining events staged amid Pompeii's ruins. *Average main: €22* *Via Colle San Bartolomeo 8, Pompei* *081/8505566* *www.ilprincipe.com.*

★ Ristorante President

$$$ | **SOUTHERN ITALIAN** | Carrying on a tradition of top-quality cuisine started by his father, chef Paolo Gramaglia and his wife Laila—the pastry chef and sommelier—run this Michelin-starred restaurant that consistently ranks among Campania's best. The presentation of every dish is beautiful, and service is impeccable; what's more, the restaurant sometimes hosts Roman-inspired banquets with musical accompaniment. **Known for:** extensive wine list; Roman-inspired bread; unusual, themed tasting menus. *Average main: €33* *Piazza Schettini 12, Pompei* *081/8507245* *www.ristorantepresident.it.*

Coffee and Quick Bites

Pasticceria De Vivo

$ | **NEOPOLITAN** | **FAMILY** | Opened in 1955 this popular pastry parlor and gelateria is a reliable spot to pick up a coffee with a cornetto, sfogliatella, or krapfen doughnut. Their delicious gelato comes in colorful *cone cialde* waffle cones. **Known for:** breakfast and savory snack pitstop near the ruins; colombia cakes and small semifreddi treats; boozy babà al rhum. *Average main: €8* *Via Roma 36, Pompei* *081/8631163* *www.lapasticceriadevivo.it.*

Continued on page 226

ANCIENT POMPEII
TOMB OF A CIVILIZATION

The site of Pompeii, petrified memorial to Vesuvius's eruption in AD 79, is the largest, most accessible, and probably most famous of excavations anywhere.

A busy commercial center with a population of 10,000–20,000, ancient Pompeii covered about 170 acres on the seaward end of the fertile Sarno Plain. Today Pompeii is choked with both the dust of 25 centuries and more than 2 million visitors every year; only by escaping the hordes and lingering along its silent streets can you truly fall under the site's spell. On a quiet backstreet, all you need is a little imagination to picture life in this ancient town. Come in the late afternoon when the site is nearly deserted and you will understand the true pleasure of visiting Pompei.

A FUNNY THING HAPPENS ON THE WAY TO THE FORUM as you walk through Pompeii. Covered with dust and decay as it is, the city seems to come alive. Perhaps it's the familiar signs of life observed along the ancient streets: bakeries with large ovens just like those for making pizzas, *thermopolia* (snack bars) tracks of cart wheels cut into the road surface, graffiti etched onto the plastered surfaces of street walls. But a glance up at Vesuvius, still brooding over the scene like an enormous headstone, reminds you that these folks—whether imagined in your head or actually wearing a mantle of

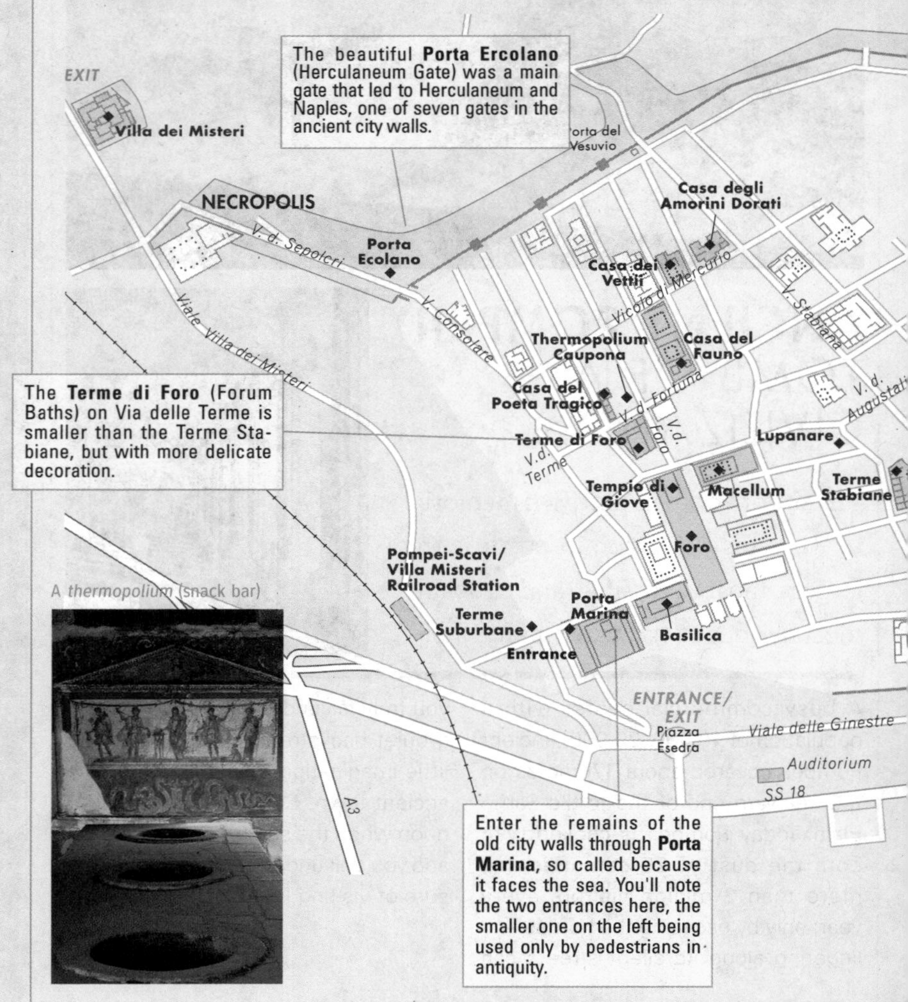

A *thermopolium* (snack bar)

Pompeii's cemetery, or Necropolis

lava dust—have not taken a breath for centuries. The town was laid out in a grid pattern, with two main intersecting streets. The wealthiest took a whole block for themselves; or built a house and rented out the front rooms, facing the street, as shops. There were good numbers of tabernae (taverns) and thermopolia on almost every corner, and frequent shows at the amphitheater.

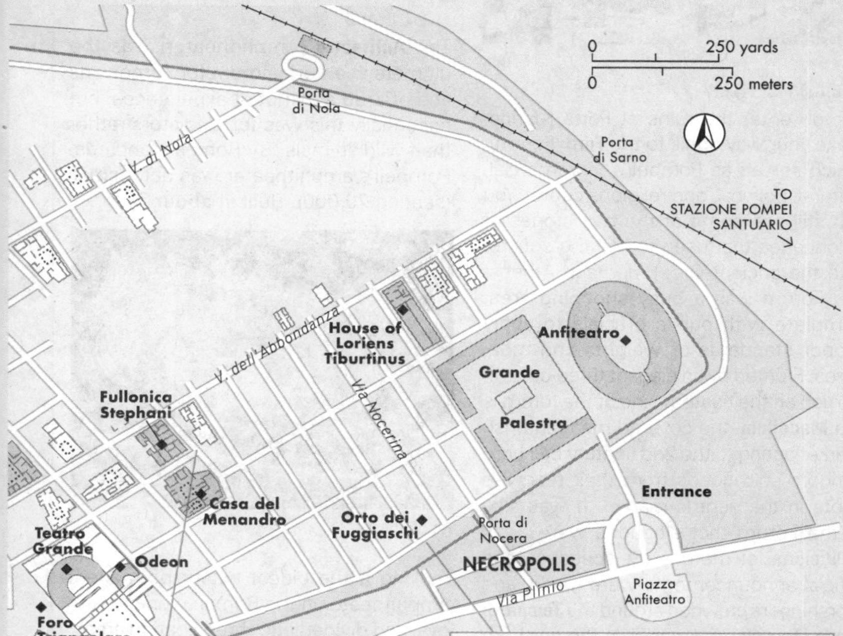

0 250 yards
0 250 meters
Porta di Nola
V. di Nola
Porta di Sarno
TO STAZIONE POMPEI SANTUARIO
V. dell'Abbondanza
House of Loriens Tiburtinus
Anfiteatro
Grande Palestra
Via Nocerina
Fullonica Stephani
Casa del Menandro
Orto dei Fuggiaschi
Entrance
Porta di Nocera
NECROPOLIS
Teatro Grande
Odeon
Foro Triangolare
Via Plinio
Piazza Anfiteatro
Porta di Stabia
Via Plinio

Togas, the required Roman attire, were washed and wool was dyed at . Urine was used to bleach and clean garments.

The **Orto dei Fuggiaschi** (Garden of the Fugitives) contains poignant plaster casts of those overwhelmed by the eruption in AD 79 and left *in situ*. Many of the victims were claimed a day after the initial eruption not by the rain of lapilli and ash but by the first surge—a dense cloud of vapor, ash, and other solids that swept down the slopes of the volcano like a boiling avalanche at 40–50 miles per hour.

PUBLIC LIFE IN ANCIENT POMPEII

Forum

THE CITY CENTER

As you enter the ruins at Porta Marina, make your way uphill to the **Foro** (Forum), which served as Pompeii's commercial, cultural, political, and religious center. You can still see some of the two stories of colonnades that used to line the square. Like the ancient Greek *agora* in Athens, the Forum was a busy shopping area, complete with public officials to apply proper standards of weights and measures. Fronted by an elegant three-column portico on the eastern side of the forum is the **Macellum**, the covered meat and fish market dating to the 2nd century BC; here vendors sold goods from their reserved spots in the central market. It was also in the Forum that elections were held, politicians let rhetoric fly, speeches and official announcements were made, and worshippers crowded around the **Tempio di Giove** (Temple of Jupiter), at the northern end of the forum.

Basilica

On the southwestern corner is the **Basilica**, the city's law court and the economic center. These rectangular aisled halls were the model for early Christian churches, which had a nave (central aisle) and two side aisles separated by rows of columns. Standing in the Basilica, you can recognize the continuity between Roman and Christian architecture.

THE GAMES

The **Anfiteatro** (Amphitheater) was the ultimate in entertainment for Pompeians and offered a gamut of experiences, but essentially this was for gladiators rather than wild animals. By Roman standards, Pompeii's amphitheater was quite small (seating 20,000). Built in about 70 BC,

Amphitheater

making it the oldest extant permanent amphitheater in the Roman world, it was oval and divided into three seating areas. There were two main entrances—at the north and south ends—and a narrow passage on the west called the Porta Libitinensis, through which the dead were probably dragged out. A wall painting found in a house near the theater (now in the Naples Museum) depicts the riot in the amphitheater in AD 59 when several citizens from the nearby town of Nocera were killed. After Nocerian appeals to Nero, shows were suspended for three years.

Fresco of Pyramus and Thisbe in the House of Loreius Tiburtinus

BATHS AND BROTHELS

In its day, Pompeii was celebrated as the Côte d'Azur, the Fire Island of the ancient Roman empire. Evidence of a Sybaritic bent is everywhere—in the town's grandest villas, in its baths and rich decorations, and murals reveal ing a worship of hedonism. Satyrs, bacchantes, hermaphrodites, and acrobatic couples are pictured.

The first buildings to the left past the ticket turnstiles are the **Terme Suburbane** (Suburban Baths), built—by all accounts without permission—right up against the city walls. The baths have eyebrow-raising frescoes in the *apodyterium* (changing room) that strongly suggest that more than just bathing and massaging went on here.

On the walls of **Lupanari** (brothels) are scenes of erotic games in which clients could engage. The **Terme Stabiane** (Stabian Baths) had underground furnaces, the heat from which circulated beneath the floor, rose through flues in the walls, and escaped through chimneys. The sequence of the rooms is standard: changing room (apoditerium), tepid (tepidarium), hot (calidarium), and cold (frigidarium). A vigorous massage with oil was followed by rest, and conversation.

Thanks to those deep layers of pyroclastic deposits from Vesuvius that protected the site from natural wear and tear over the centuries, graffiti found in Pompeii provide unique insights into the sort of things that the locals found important 2,000 years ago. A good many were personal and lend a human dimension to the disaster that not even the sights can equal.

At the baths: **"What is the use of having a Venus if she's made of marble?"**

At the entrance to the front lavatory at a private house: **"May I always and everywhere be as potent with women as I was here."**

On the Viale ai Teatri: **"A copper pot went missing from my shop. Anyone who returns it to me will be given 65 bronze coins."**

In the Basilica: **"A small problem gets larger if you ignore it."**

PRIVATE LIFE IN ANCIENT POMPEII

The facades of houses in Pompeii were relatively plain and seldom hinted at the care and attention lavished on the private rooms within. When visitors arrived they passed the shops and entered an atrium, from which the occupants received air, sunlight, and rainwater, the latter caught by the *impluvium*, a rectangular-shaped receptacle under the sloped roof. In the back was a receiving room, the *tablinum*, and behind was another open area, the peristyle. Life revolved around this uncovered inner courtyard, with rows of columns and perhaps a garden with a fountain. The atrium was surrounded by *cubicula* (bedrooms) and the *triclinium* (dining area). Interior floors and walls were covered with colorful marble tiles, mosaics, and frescoes.

House of Paquius Proculus

Several homes were captured in various states by the eruption of Vesuvius, each representing a different slice of Pompeiian life. The **Casa del Fauno** (House of the Faun) displayed wonderful mosaics, now at the Museo Archeologico Nazionale in Naples. The **Casa del Poeta Tragico** (House of the Tragic Poet) is a typical middle-class house. On the floor is a mosaic of a chained dog and the inscription *cave canem* ("Beware of the dog"). The **Casa degli Amorini Dorati** (House of the Gilded Cupids) is an elegant, well-preserved home with original decorations. Many paintings and mosaics were executed at **Casa del Menandro** (House of Menander), a patrician's villa named for a fresco of the Greek playwright. Two blocks beyond the Stabian Baths you'll notice on the left the current digs at the **Casa dei Casti Amanti** (House of the Chaste Lovers). A team of plasterers and painters were at work here when Vesuvius erupted, redecorating one of the rooms and patching up the cracks in the bread oven near the entrance—possibly caused by tremors a matter of days before.

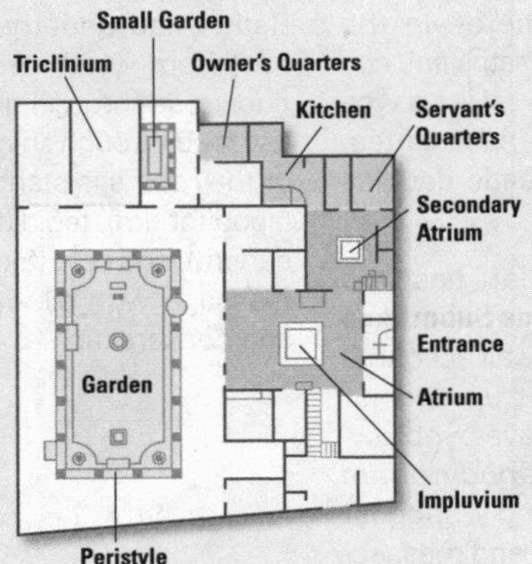

CASA DEI VETTII

The **House of the Vettii** (temporarily closed for restoration) is the best example of a house owned by wealthy *mercatores* (merchants). It contains vivid murals—a magnificent pinacoteca (picture gallery) within the very heart of Pompeii. The scenes here—except for those in the two wings off the atrium—were all painted after the earthquake of AD 62. Once inside, look at the delicate frieze around the wall of the (on the right of the peristyle garden as you enter from the atrium), depicting cupids engaged in various activities, such as selling oils and perfumes, working as goldsmiths and metalworkers, acting as wine merchants, or performing in chariot races. Another of the main attractions in the Casa dei Vettii is the small cubicle beyond the kitchen area (to the right of the atrium) with its faded erotic frescoes now protected by Perspex screens.

UNLOCKING THE VILLA DEI MISTERI

Villa dei Misteri

There is no more astounding, magnificently memorable evidence of Pompeii's devotion to the pleasures of the flesh than the frescoes on view at the **Villa dei Misteri** (Villa of the Mysteries), a palatial abode 400 yards outside the city gates, northwest of Porta Ercolano. Unearthed in 1909, this villa had many beautiful rooms painted with frescoes; the finest are in the *triclinium*. Painted in the most glowing Pompeiian reds and ochers, the panels may relate the saga of a young bride (Ariadne) and her initiation into the mysteries of the cult of Dionysus, who was a god imported to Italy from Greece and then given the Latin name of Bacchus. The god of wine and debauchery also represented the triumph of the irrational—of all those mysterious forces that no official state religion could fully suppress.

Pompeii's best frescoes, painted in glowing reds and oranges, retain an amazing vibrancy.

The Villa of the Mysteries frescoes were painted circa 50 BC, most art historians believe, and represent the peak of the Second Style of Pompeiian wall painting. The triclinium frescoes are thought to have been painted by a local artist, although the theme may well have been copied from an earlier cycle of paintings from the Hellenistic period. In all there are 10 scenes, depicting children and matrons, musicians and satyrs, phalluses and gods. There are no inscriptions (such as are found on Greek vases), and after 2,000 years historians remain puzzled by many aspects of the triclinium cycle. Scholars endlessly debate the meaning of these frescoes, but anyone can tell they are among the most beautiful paintings left to us by antiquity. In several ways, the eruption of Vesuvius was a blessing in disguise, for without it, these masterworks of art would have perished long ago.

Planning for Your Day in Pompeii

Getting There

The archaeological site of Pompeii has its own stop (Pompei–Villa dei Misteri) on the Circumvesuviana line to Sorrento, close to the main entrance at the Porta Marina, which is the best place from which to start a tour. If, like many visitors every year, you get the wrong train from Naples (stopping at the other "Pompei" station), all is not lost. There's another entrance to the excavations at the far end of the site, just a seven-minute walk to the Amphitheater.

Admission

Single tickets cost €16 (€10 reduced afternoon admission fee from 3:30 pm) and are valid for one full day. The site is open April–October, daily 9–7 (last admission at 5:30; although check ahead as it's closed Monday from early autumn through early June); and November–March, daily 9–5 (last admission at 3:30). For more information call ☎ *081/8575347* or visit 🌐 *www.pompeiisites.org*.

What to Bring

The only restaurant inside the site is both overpriced and busy, so bring along water and snacks. There are some shady, underused picnic tables outside the Porta di Nola, to the northeast of the site. Luggage is not allowed in the site.

Timing

Visiting Pompeii does have its frustrating aspects: many buildings are blocked off by locked gates, and enormous group tours tend to clog up more popular attractions. But the site is so big that it's easy to lose yourself. To really see the site, you'll need four or five hours, a bit less if you hire a guide.

To get the most out of Pompeii, rent an audio guide and opt for one of the three itineraries (two hours, four hours, or six hours). If hiring a guide, make sure the guide is registered for an English tour and standing inside the gate; agree beforehand on the length of the tour and the price, and prepare yourself for sound bites of English mixed with dollops of hearsay. For a higher-quality (and more expensive) full-day tour, try Context Travel (🌐 *www.contexttravel.com*).

Hotels

Hotel Diana

$ | **HOTEL** | **FAMILY** | This small family-run hotel is a good base for budget travelers wishing to be within striking distance of Pompeii's ruins. **Pros:** charming courtyard garden and playground for children; near Pompeii's archaeological site; good for travelers using public transportation. **Cons:** noisy when fully booked; smallish rooms; no pool. 💲 *Rooms from: €70* ✉ *Vico Sant'Abbondio 12, Pompei* ☎ *081/8631264* 🌐 *www.pompeihotel.com/en* 🛏 *32 rooms* 🍽 *Free Breakfast.*

MGallery Habita79

$$ | **HOTEL** | **FAMILY** | Opened in 2021, this impressive Neoclassical building near the santuario now houses a well-thought-out hotel that fuses comfortable contemporary design with historic decorative touches. **Pros:** smart Nuxe spa, treatments, and gym; fabulous terrace and solarium with views; green design credentials including geothermal energy.

Cons: some may find the decor too clinical; can be busy for conferences and events; restaurant food not top-notch. *Rooms from: €130* ✉ *Via Roma 10, Pompei* ☎ *081/5959625* 🌐 *www.habita79.it* *79 rooms* *Free Breakfast.*

Villa Diomede Hotel

$ | HOTEL | A practical choice near Pompeii's archaeological site, this hotel run by a friendly staff has a pleasant sun terrace and spacious, ultramodern rooms, five with kitchens and cooking utensils. **Pros:** good for families; convenient location; affiliated with nearby Vesuvio Tours tram bus to Mt. Vesuvius. **Cons:** some train noise can be heard; lack of facilities in the area; decor is pleasant but not luxurious. *Rooms from: €90* ✉ *Via Diomede 9, Pompei* ☎ *081/5362753* 🌐 *www.hotelvilladiomede.it* *16 rooms* *Free Breakfast.*

Pozzuoli

8 km (5 miles) west of Naples.

Legendary spirits populate Pozzuoli. St. Paul stepped ashore at the harbor here in AD 61 en route to Rome; his own ship had been wrecked off Malta, and he was brought here on the *Castor and Pollux,* a grain ship from Alexandria carrying corn from Egypt to Italy. Not far from the harbor esplanade, San Gennaro, patron saint of Naples, earned his holy martyrdom by being thrown to the lions at an imperial gala staged in the town's enormous amphitheater, constructed by the Flavian emperors (the wild beasts were said to have torn the rags from Gennaro's body but to have left him unharmed—at which point he was taken to the Solfatara volcanic vent and there decapitated). More recently, that latter-day goddess Sophia Loren was raised in a house located on a backstreet of the town.

Today's Pozzuoli is a well-connected, busy town of about 80,000 inhabitants mainly employed by its fisheries, docks, and the tourism industry. Built on geologically unstable land, the area near the port was partially evacuated in the early 1980s due to a phenomenon known as *bradyseism,* or the rise and fall of the land surface. Since then it has been gradually recolonized and partially gentrified; many of the buildings in the Centro Storico have been given a face-lift, the main park (Villa Avellino) has become a mecca for open-air summer festivals, and the town's reputation as a center for gastronomy has been firmly established. Pozzuoli has also capitalized on its strategic position close to two of the islands in the Bay of Naples: Procida and Ischia.

Another selling point is its main arena—Puteoli was the only place in the empire to boast two amphitheaters—offering glimpses into the life of *panem et circenses* (bread and circuses) in classical times, when Puteoli was one of the busiest ports in the Mediterranean and easily eclipsed Neapolis (today's Naples).

GETTING HERE AND AROUND

By car take the Tangenziale (bypass) from Naples toward Pozzuoli and get off at the Pozzuoli–Via Campana exit. At the roundabout, follow the signs for "Porto" to get to the port and the town center. There are subsequent signs for the "Anfiteatro" (amphitheater) and the "Volcano Solfatara." To get to Lake Avernus take the Pozzuoli–Arco Felice exit and follow the "Lago d'Averno" signs. The FS (state-run) Metropolitana Linea 2 from Naples (Piazza Garibaldi, Mergellina, Cavour, and Montesanto stations) stops at Pozzuoli–Solfatara near the Anfiteatro. For the town center get off at the main Pozzuoli station, which is nearer the sea. It's a 1-km (½-mile) walk uphill from Pozzuoli's Metropolitana station to the Solfatara (or take Bus P9; no extra fare necessary).

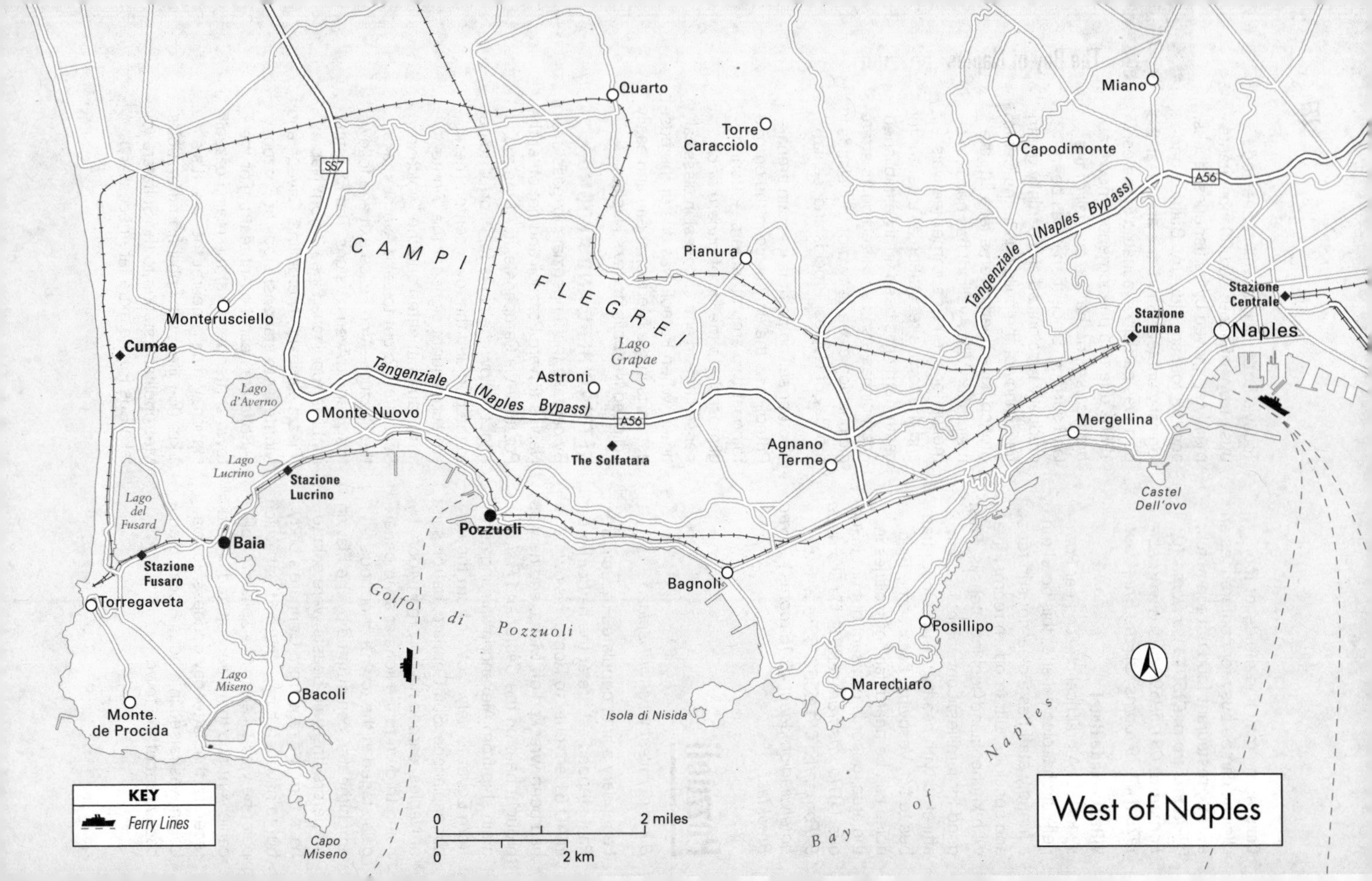
West of Naples
KEY
Ferry Lines
0
2 miles
0
2 km
Quarto
Torre Caracciolo
Miano
Capodimonte
SS7
A56
CAMPI FLEGREI
Pianura
Tangenziale (Naples Bypass)
Stazione Centrale
Stazione Cumana
Naples
Monterusciello
Cumae
Lago Grapae
Astroni
Lago d'Averno
Monte Nuovo
Mergellina
Agnano Terme
The Solfatara
Lago Lucrino
Stazione Lucrino
Castel Dell'ovo
Lago del Fusard
Pozzuoli
Baia
Stazione Fusaro
Bagnoli
Torregaveta
Golfo di Pozzuoli
Posillipo
Lago Miseno
Bacoli
Marechiaro
Monte de Procida
Isola di Nisida
Bay of Naples
Capo Miseno

Sights

Anfiteatro Flavio (*Flavian Amphitheater*)
RUINS | Despite the wear and tear of the millennia and the loss of masonry during the Middle Ages, this site is one of the Campi Flegrei area's Roman architectural marvels. The amphitheater (seating capacity, 40,000) was probably built under Vespasian (AD 70–AD 79), although some historians maintain that work started under Nero (AD 54–AD 69) and was merely completed later. As you approach, note the exterior's combination of volcanic stone masonry, arranged in a net-shape pattern, and horizontal bands of brick. This technique, typical of the late 1st and early 2nd centuries, was designed to reduce stress and minimize damage during seismic events. Despite this precaution, much of the superstructure has been lost: the outside part consisted of three stories surmounted by a decorative attic, while the sitting area would have had a portico above the top row of seats, decorated with statues and supported by columns. A surviving passageway near the ticket office leads into a complex underground network of *carceres* (cells), which is well worth a visit.

In classical times, the entertainment here consisted mainly of animal hunts, public executions, and gladiator fights. The hunts often involved lions, tigers, and other exotic animals imported from far-flung corners of the Roman Empire. The *fossa,* or large ditch in the arena's middle, may have contained the permanent stage setting, which could be raised when necessary to provide a scenic backdrop. According to tradition, several early Christians—including the Naples protector St. Januarius, or San Gennaro—were condemned to be savaged by wild beasts here under the Fourth Edict, passed in AD 304 by Diocletian, but the sentence was later commuted to a less spectacular decapitation, carried out farther up the hill in the Solfatara. The amphitheater is near the Pozzuoli Metropolitana railway station and a 15-minute walk from the Solfatara: the bubbling volcanic crater has been closed to the public since the tragic death of a family there in 2017. The Pozzuoli tourist office has event and other information. ✉ *Anfiteatro Grande, Via Terracciano 75, Pozzuoli* ☎ *081/5266007, 081/5262419 for Pozzuoli tourist office* 🎫 *€4; €8 includes 4 sights of the Circuit Flegreo: Anfiteatro Flavio, Cumae and Museo Archeologico dei Campi Flegrei, and site of Baia* Ⓜ *Pozzuoli.*

Lago d'Averno (*Lake Avernus*)
NATURE SIGHT | Regarded by the ancients as the doorway to the Underworld, the fabled lake was well known by the time the great poet Virgil settled here to write the *Aeneid.* Forested hills rise on three sides of the lake, and the menacing cone of Monte Nuovo looms on the fourth. Its name comes from the Greek *Aornos* ("without birds," *Avernus* in Latin). The water is "black," the smell of sulfur sometimes hangs over the landscape, and blocked-off passages lead into long-abandoned caves into which Virgil might well have ventured. Not far away is the spring that was thought to flow directly from the River Styx. It was there that Aeneas descended into the Underworld with the guidance of the Cumaean Sibyl, as famously recounted in the *Aeneid.* ✉ *Via Lago Averno Lato Destro, off Via Italia, Pozzuoli.*

Restaurants

Bobò
$$$ | **SEAFOOD** | A meal at this stylish but *simpatico* seafood restaurant across from the ferry terminal is a fitting way to round out a day in the Campi Flegrei. The exquisite antipasti, delicately garnished pasta, and *pesce* straight off the boats make this a favorite with the locals. **Known for:** choice of seafood antipasti; elegant presentation; tasting menu for a special occasion. $ *Average main: €26* ✉ *Via C. Colombo 20, Pozzuoli* ☎ *081/5262034* 🌐 *www.ristorantebobo.com* 🕓 *Closed Tues., 2 wks in Aug., and 1 wk at Christmas. No dinner Sun.*

The Anfiteatro Flavio is a marvel of ancient Roman architecture.

Da Don Antonio 2.0

$$ | **SEAFOOD** | Despite its unflattering location on a *vicolo* (alley) one block from the Pozzuoli waterfront, this restaurant (est. 1946) is admired in Neapolitan circles for its fresh seafood, ample portions, and reasonable prices. Spaghetti with clams, octopus salad, grilled and fried fish, and seafood risotto are among the longtime favorites prepared here. **Known for:** rustic, nautical-theme dining room; warm, family-run atmosphere; seafood straight off Pozzuoli's fleet. *Average main: €23* ✉ *Vico Magazzini 20, off Piazza San Paolo, Pozzuoli* ☎ *081/5267941* ⏲ *Closed Tues.*

La Cucina di Ruggiero

$$ | **SOUTHERN ITALIAN** | The celebrated site of oyster beds and fish farms in ancient times, Lake Lucrino is now the setting for this rustic trattoria. Quirky Ruggiero runs the dining room with a whimsical charm—don't be shocked if he addresses you through his megaphone or warmly embraces you when you leave—and his wife, Maria, lovingly prepares specialties from land, sea, and lake, much to the delight of the locals who tend to pack the place. **Known for:** very intimate dining room; reasonable prix-fixe options; convivial atmosphere. *Average main: €24* ✉ *Via Intorno al Lago 3, Pozzuoli, loc. Lucrino, Pozzuoli* ☎ *081/8687473* ⏲ *Closed Mon. and Tues. No lunch Wed.–Fri. No dinner Sun.*

Coffee and Quick Bites

Casa Infante

$ | **NEOPOLITAN** | With a Neapolitan street food pedigree—the Infante made famed taralli on Via Foria back in the 19th century—this is a reliable spot for ice cream, drinks, and snacks from breakfast to midnight Sweet-tooths may be tempted by their indulgent babà in bicchiere while for those seeking savory there's bruschetta, filled pannini, and cold cuts and cheese platters, among many snacks. **Known for:** 36-plus gelato flavors to choose from; pastries galore including babà and cannoli; buzzy evenings of aperitivi and snacks. *Average main: €9* ✉ *Piazza della*

Repubblica 81, Pozzuoli ☎ *081/0108092* 🌐 *www.casainfante.it.*

Hotels

Villa Avellino

$$ | **HOTEL** | With commanding views over Pozzuoli's seafront, this beautifully renovated villa—once owned by a famous archaeologist—offers stylish contemporary accommodations that range from junior suites to palatial apartments with rooftop terraces. **Pros:** modern decor; apartments with kitchenettes; bistro and restaurant. **Cons:** pricey food; breakfast in room only; maintenance could be improved. *Rooms from: €136* ✉ *Via Carlo Maria Rosini 21–29, Pozzuoli* ☎ *081/3036812* 🌐 *www.villaavellino.it* *18 rooms* *Free Breakfast.*

Villa Luisa

$ | **RESORT** | A stay at Villa Luisa might not put you in the lap of luxury, but its location—near Lake Lucrino and the Stufe di Nerone thermal baths—as well as its spa facilities, beachside lido, and sun terrace make it a good-value option. **Pros:** lots of area restaurants; nearby beach and pool; good base for the Campi Flegrei and Pozzuoli port. **Cons:** uninspiring decor; sparse continental breakfast; no on-site pool or lift. *Rooms from: €85* ✉ *Via Tripergola 50, Pozzuoli* ☎ *081/8042870* 🌐 *www.villaluisaresort.it* *37 rooms* *Free Breakfast.*

Baia

12 km (7 miles) west of Naples, 4 km (2½ miles) west of Pozzuoli.

Now largely under the sea, ancient Baia was once the most opulent and fashionable resort area of the Roman Empire, the place where Sulla, Pompey, Cicero, Julius Caesar, Tiberius, and Nero built their holiday villas. It was here that Cleopatra was staying when Julius Caesar was murdered on the Ides of March (March 15) in 44 BC; here that Emperor Claudius built a great villa for his third wife, Messalina (who is reputed to have spent her nights indulging herself at local brothels); and near here that Agrippina (Claudius's fourth wife and murderer) is believed to have been killed by henchmen sent by her son Nero in AD 59. Unfortunately, the Romans did not pursue the custom of writing official graffiti—"Here lived Crassus" would help—so it's difficult to assign these historical events to specific locations. Consequently, conjecture is the order of the day: Julius Caesar's villa is now thought to be at the top of the hill behind the archaeological site and not near the foot of the Aragonese castle, though we cannot be absolutely certain. We do know, however, that the Romans found this area staggeringly beautiful. A visit to the site can only confirm what Horace wrote in one of his epistles: *Nullus in orbe sinus Baiis praelucet amoenis* (No bay on Earth outshines pleasing Baia).

GETTING HERE AND AROUND

To arrive by car, take the Tangenziale from Naples and exit at Pozzuoli–Arco Felice and follow the indications for Baia. By train, take the Cumana railway (leaving every 20 minutes from Montesanto in Naples, travel time 30 minutes, nearest stop Fusaro), followed by an EAV bus for the last 3 km (2 miles). Where the bus stops in the square outside the Baia station, cross the disused railway line on a footbridge. Continue upward for about five minutes until you reach the entrance to the site (limited parking is available). The same EAV bus also stops at the Museo Archeologico dei Campi Flegrei.

Sights

BaiaSommersa

NAUTICAL SIGHT | **FAMILY** | From the small modern-day port of Baia you can board Cymba, a boat with glass panels on its lower deck and view part of the *città sommersa,* the underwater city of ancient Baia. The guided tour—usually in Italian, but given in English if arranged well in advance—lasts about 75 minutes and is best undertaken in calm conditions, when you can get good glimpses of Roman columns, roads, villa walls, and mosaics. Peer through fish-flecked plexiglass at statues of Octavia Claudia (Claudius's sister) and of Ulysses, his outstretched arms and mollusk-eaten head once a part of the nymphaeum since sunk into the deeps after an outbreak of bradyseism. (Note that these statues are actually replicas. The originals are up the hill in the Castle museum.) ✉ *Baia* ☎ *349/4974183 mobile* 🌐 *www.baiasommersa.it* 🎫 *€12.*

★ **Museo Archeologico dei Campi Flegrei**
OTHER MUSEUM | The Castle of Baia, which commands a 360-degree view eastward across the Bay of Pozzuoli and westward across the open Tyrrhenian, provides a fittingly dramatic setting for the Archaeological Museum of Campi Flegrei. Though the castle's foundation dates to the late 15th century, when Naples was ruled by the House of Aragon and an invasion by Charles VIII of France looked imminent, the structure was radically transformed under the Spanish viceroy Don Pedro de Toledo after the nearby eruption of Monte Nuovo in 1538. Indeed, its bastions bear a striking resemblance to the imposing Castel Sant'Elmo in Naples.

The museum has been reorganized to describe in detail the history of Cumae, Puteoli, Baiae, Misenum, and Liternum. Sculptures, architectural remains, pottery, glass, jewelry, and coins are displayed in the ex-dormitories of the soldiers. Of the various exhibitions, the first on the suggested itinerary consists of plaster casts from the Roman period found at the Baia archaeological site. This gives valuable insights into the techniques used by the Romans to make copies from Greek originals in bronze from the Classical and Hellenistic periods. Pride of place goes to the *sacellum,* or small sanctuary, transported from nearby Misenum and tastefully displayed inside the Aragonese tower, the Torre Tenaglia. Standing about 20 feet high, the sacellum has been reconstructed, with two of its original six columns (the rest in steel) and a marble architrave with its dedicatory inscription to the husband-and-wife team who commissioned the sanctuary's restoration in the 2nd century AD. The beneficent couple is depicted above this. Another highlight is the marble splendor of the Ninfeo Imperiale di Punta Epitaffio, or Nymphaeum of Emperor Claudius, which was discovered in 1969 some 23 feet below the waters of the Bay of Pozzuoli. Note that although this museum is poorly maintained and staffed it's well worth visiting, given that it's not often you find yourself alone among such fascinating ancient artifacts. ✉ *Via Castello 39, Baia* ☎ *081/5233797* 🌐 *www.coopculture.it* 🎫 *€4; €8 Phlegreaen Circuit ticket including Cumae, Parco Archeologico di Baia, and Anfiteatro Flavio* ⏲ *Closed Mon.*

Parco Archeologico e Monumentale di Baia
(*Monumental and Archaeological Park of Baia*)
HISTORIC SIGHT | In antiquity this whole area was the Palatium Baianum (the Palace of Baia), dedicated to *otium* (leisure) and the residence of emperors from Augustus to as late as Septimius Severus in the 3rd century AD. At the park's ticket office, you should receive a small site map, and information panels in English are posted at strategic intervals. The first terrace, the Villa dell'Ambulatio, is one of the best levels from which to appreciate the site's topography: the whole hillside down to the level of the modern road near the waterfront has been modeled into flat terraces, each sporting different architectural features.

While up on the first terrace look for the depictions of dolphins, swans, and cupids in the *balneum* (thermal bathing, Room 13), and admire the theatrical motifs in the floor mosaic in Room 14. Below the balneum and inviting further exploration is a nymphaeum shrine, which can be reached from the western side. Make sure you get down to the so-called Temple of Mercury, on the lowest level, which has held much fascination for travelers from the 18th century onward. It has been variously interpreted as a frigidarium and as a *natatio* (swimming pool) and is the oldest example of a large dome (50 BC–27 BC), predating the cupola of the Pantheon in Rome. (Test the rich echo in the interior.) In summer the site often provides an unusual backdrop for evening concerts and opera performances. ✉ *Parco Archeologico e Monumentale di Baia, Via Sella di Baia 22, Baia* ☎ *081/8687592* 🌐 *www.coopculture.it* 🎫 *€4, €8 Phlegraean Circuit ticket also includes Cumae, Museo Archeologico dei Campi Flegrei in Baia, and Anfiteatro Flavio in Pozzuoli* ⏲ *Closed Mon.*

Restaurants

A' Casa 'e Tobia

$$ | NEOPOLITAN | Come here for the rare experience of dining within a 10,000-year-old volcanic crater (thankfully extinct). Sit back in the homey dining area crammed with bizarre knickknacks, and enjoy a cornucopia of tasting dishes, many made with produce grown in the fertile volcanic soil outside. **Known for:** seasonal selections; nouvelle vegetarian dishes; rustic place in an interesting setting. $ *Average main: €18* ✉ *Fondi di Baia 12, Bacoli* ☎ *081/5235193* 💳 *No credit cards* ⏲ *Closed Mon. and Tues. No dinner Sun.*

Da Lucullo

$$$ | NEOPOLITAN | The whitewashed chalet on stilts above the beach at Bacoli is a fab spot for a seafood odyssey. Book a table by the picture windows, and let the staff guide you through the specials, including the *pescato del giorno* (catch of the day). **Known for:** friendly staff; frittura di mare (fried seafood medley); gorgeous seaside location. $ *Average main: €26* ✉ *Via Montegrillo 8, Bacoli* ☎ *081/8687606* ⏲ *Closed Mon. No dinner Sun.*

Hotels

Cala Moresca

$$ | HOTEL | This contemporary, white-washed hotel makes a great beach and Campi Flegrei sightseeing base thanks to a superb pool and whirlpool tub, a chic bar, and grand views of Capo Miseno, Bacoli, and beyond. **Pros:** serene, elevated position; excellent restaurant and cocktail bar; breakfast in panoramic room. **Cons:** weddings disrupt use of restaurant; uninspiring room decor; books up early. $ *Rooms from: €129* ✉ *Via Faro 44, Bacoli* ☎ *080/5235595* 🌐 *www.calamoresca.it* *27 rooms* 🍽 *Free Breakfast.*

La Rada B&B

$ | B&B/INN | The views here rival any of those at a five-star hotel: two rooms look out onto the bay of bays (this is a great spot for divers), while another room takes in the world's largest Roman bath complex; both are tastefully furnished, with wardrobes and other fittings from Florence. **Pros:** large rooms; lots of personal touches; wonderful views. **Cons:** breakfast in nearby bar or room; local bar can be noisy at night; steep stairs to first floor. $ *Rooms from: €100* ✉ *Via Violo di Baia 9, Baia* ☎ *339/2692258* 🌐 *www.laradadibaia.com* *3 rooms* 🍽 *Free Breakfast.*

Villa Gervasio

$ | HOTEL | From its soothing rooms and suites to its chic, panoramic breakfast room/restaurant and whitewashed terraces, this hilltop retreat and self-styled boutique hotel offers oodles of contemporary, minimalist style with dashes of bling. **Pros:** breathtaking terrace views; gorgeous grounds; large showers. **Cons:** some might find the decor lacking warmth; a hike to the beach; wedding venue, so can get busy. $ *Rooms*

Did You Know?

In the Cave of the Cumaean Sibyl, ancient generals, aristocrats, and commoners alike would consult the oracle for guidance on everything from military campaigns to affairs of the heart.

from: €100 ✉ Via Bellavista 176, Bacoli ☎ 081/8687892 🌐 www.villagervasio.it 🛏 7 rooms 🍽 Free Breakfast.

Cumae

16 km (10 miles) west of Naples, 5 km (3 miles) north of Baia.

Perhaps the oldest Greek colony on mainland Italy, Cumae (Cuma in Italian) overshadowed the Phlegrean Fields and Neapolis in the 7th and 6th centuries BC, because it was home to the Antro della Sibilla, the fabled Cave of the Cumaean Sibyl—one of the three greatest oracles of antiquity—who is said to have presided over the destinies of men. In about the 6th century BC, the Greeks hollowed the cave from the rock beneath the ridge leading up to the present ruins of Cumae's acropolis. Today you can walk—just as Virgil's Aeneas did—through a dark, massive 350-foot-long stone tunnel that opens into the vaulted Chamber of the Prophetic Voice, where the Sibyl delivered her oracles. Standing here in one of the most venerated sites of ancient times, the sense of the *numen*—of communication with invisible powers—is overwhelming. "This is the most romantic classical site in Italy," claimed the famed travelogue writer H. V. Morton, referring to Cumae.

GETTING HERE AND AROUND

If driving, take the Cumae Exit 13 from the Naples Tangenziale and proceed along Montenuovo Licola Patria, following signs for Cumae. At the first major intersection, take a left onto Via Arco Felice Vecchio, pass under the arch, and make a right at the next intersection; after about 400 yards, turn left into the site. There is a free parking lot. There is no train station in Cumae, so to arrive from Naples, take the Cumana railway to Fusaro, then the EAV Miseno–Cumae bus to Cumae.

Sights

Parco Archeologico di Cuma

RUINS | Allow at least two hours to soak up the ambience of the ruins of Cumae, founded by Greek colonists late in the 8th century BC. Centuries later Virgil wrote his epic of the *Aeneid,* the story of the Trojan prince Aeneas's wanderings, partly to give Rome the historical legitimacy that Homer had given the Greeks. On his journey, Aeneas had to descend to the underworld to speak to his father, and to find his way in, he needed the guidance of the Cumaean Sibyl. Virgil did not dream up the Sibyl's Cave or the entrance to Hades—he must have actually stood both in her chamber and along the rim of Lake Avernus. When he described the Sibyl's Cave in Book VI of the *Aeneid* as having "*centum ostia*" (a hundred mouths), and depicted the entrance to the underworld on Lake Avernus so vividly, "*spelunca alta...tuta lacu nigro nemorum tenebris*" (a deep cave...protected by a lake of black water and the glooming forest), it was because he was familiar with this bewitching landscape. In Book VI of the *Aeneid*, Virgil describes how Aeneas, arriving at Cumae, sought Apollo's throne—remains of the Temple of Apollo can still be seen—and "the deep hidden abode of the dread Sibyl / An enormous cave..."

Although Cumae never achieved the status of Delphi, it was the most important oracular center in Magna Graecia (Great Greece), and the Sibyl would have been consulted on a whole range of matters. Governments consulted the Sibyl before mounting campaigns. It was the Sibyl's prophecies that ensured the crowds here, prophecies written on palm leaves and later collected into the corpus of the Sibylline books.

Explore the fascinating Sibyl Chamber, a long trapezoidal corridor where light filters through shafts cut into the tufa rock. Steep steps climb above the Cave and lead to the Sacred Road; before reaching the remains of Apollo's temple that Virgil described as *immanea templa* (spacious temples), you can stop at the terrace overlooking the sea. From the temple of the God of the Sun, the via Sacra reaches the highest part of the acropolis, where the remains of the temple of Jupiter can be seen. This Greek temple was transformed by the Romans and than became a Christian basilica with a baptismal font still visible. Unlike in Greek and Roman times, when access to Cumae was through a network of underground passages, an aboveground EAV bus service leaves outside Fusaro station at regular intervals. (See 🌐 *www.eavsrl.it* for times.) ✉ *Via Acropoli 1, Baia* ☎ *081/848800288* 🌐 *www.coopculture.it* 🎫 *€4, €8 Phlegraean Circuit ticket also includes Museo Archeologico dei Campi Flegrei, Parco Archeologico di Baia, and Anfiteatro Flavio in Pozzuoli* ⏲ *Closed Tues.*

Chapter 7

NAPLES

Updated by
Fergal Kavanagh

Sights ★★★★★ | Restaurants ★★★★★ | Hotels ★★★★☆ | Shopping ★★★★☆ | Nightlife ★★★★☆

WELCOME TO NAPLES

TOP REASONS TO GO

★ **A Spaccanapoli stroll:** For perfect people-watching, walk along this historic street, whose bustling crowds, pungent aromas, and sonorous hawking offer all the energy, chaos, and beauty that make this the most operatic of cities.

★ **A seafront with a view:** Walk, skate, or bike in this gorgeous traffic-free area, and enjoy a meal with Vesuvius, the Sorrentine coast, and Capri in the background.

★ **A Baroque extravaganza:** Explore the city's 17th-century churches, whose swirling gilt naves offer stunning examples of Baroque architecture.

★ **A museum of treasures:** All the excavated finds from Pompeii and Herculaneum ended up in Naples's Museo Archeologico Nazionale, the finest treasure trove of ancient art.

★ **Pizza:** There are hundreds of restaurants that specialize in pizza in Naples, and the best of these make nothing else. This is where the classic Margherita was invented, after all.

1 Centro Storico. Dubbed an open-air museum by the United Nations, the Centro Storico (historic center) is one of the most exquisitely packed neighborhoods on earth, still populated by locals and teeming with vibrant street life, art, and history. The grid layout is virtually unchanged since Greco-Roman times.

2 Piazza Garibaldi. Bustling and grimy, the train station and bus stations are here, so it's almost unavoidable. Things have improved recently, thanks to a major overhaul of the square, but there is no need to spend more time than necessary here.

3 Museo Archeologico Nazionale, La Sanità, and Capodimonte. A stone's throw from the Centro Storico, La Sanità and the Museo neighborhood houses a large portion of Naples's riches, with Italy's premier archaeological museum, marble-filled Baroque churches, ancient frescoed catacombs, monumental palaces, and a buzzing street market. Capodimonte, the upper neighborhood of ancient Naples, is home to a palace-turned-museum that holds Spanish and Dutch masterworks.

4 Toledo and the Port. The central Toledo district contains the sumptuous apartments of the Palazzo Reale and the broad open space of Piazza Plebiscito. The pedestrianized shopping street Via Toledo borders the grid of Quartieri Spagnoli. Work is ongoing on the Piazza Municipio Metro station, under the majestic gaze of Castel Nuovo—the station will display a selection of

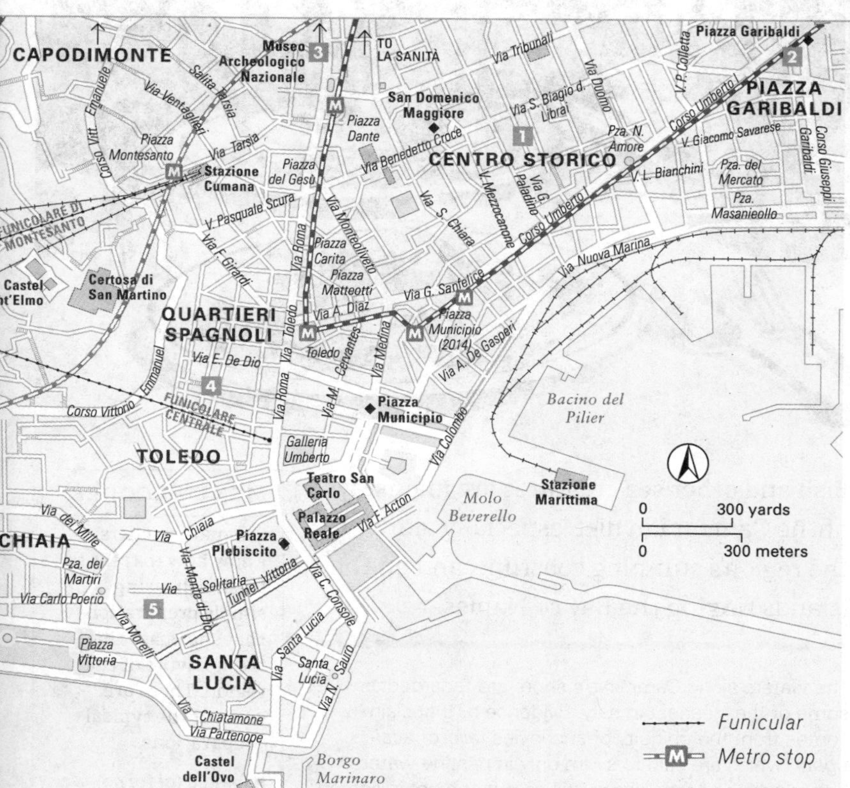

findings from the Roman port unearthed during excavations.

5 Chiaia, Santa Lucia, and Nearby. The area along the harbor south of Toledo consists of two quarters, Santa Lucia and Chiaia. Both are geared to *la dolce vita*; in Santa Lucia you can expect serenades from street musicians over dinner, while the *baretti* (bars) in Chiaia are where to be seen, sipping an *aperitivo* with the young and beautiful Neapolitans.

6 Vomero. The Vomero hill, connected to the city below by three funiculars, boasts the Certosa di San Martino. This monastery-turned-museum-complex is a highlight, with magnificent works of art, wraparound views of Naples, and gardens fit for contemplation.

7 Mergellina and Posillipo. Private boats bob in the harbor of Mergellina, with the hill of Posillipo offering breath-taking views and a unique archaeological park reached via a 2,500-foot tunnel. Swimmers and sun-worshippers will find small beaches here, with entry (and a sunbed) for around €10 a day.

CAMPANIA'S SEAFOOD BOUNTY

Campania is known for its outstanding seafood.

Fish and other sea creatures are mainstays of the Campanian diet, especially along the region's stunning coastline, and on the islands ringing the Bay of Naples.

The waters along Campania's shore are regarded as some of the cleanest in Italy. Evidence of that claim comes from the ubiquity of anchovies (*alici* or *acciughe*), which are said to swim only in pristine waters. Fishermen in some villages still go out at night in lighted fishing boats to attract and net anchovies, which are cooked fresh or cured with salt.

The Mediterranean Sea's bounty extends far beyond alici. Gustatory explorers eating their way down the coastline might also encounter these sea creatures: *aguglie* (needle fish); *calamari* (squid); *cicale* (mantis shrimp); *mazzancolle* (a type of prawn); *orata* (sea bream or daurade); *pesce spada* (swordfish); *seppia* (cuttlefish); *scorfano di fondale* (ocean perch); *scorfano rosso* (scorpion fish); and *scampi* (langoustines).

MENU DECODER

Campanian chefs know how to treat fresh fish, using simple preparations that showcase the fresh flavors of the region. These are some of the typical preparations.

- baked (*al forno*)
- baked in a paper pouch (*al cartoccio*)
- cured (*salato*)
- fried (*fritto*)
- grilled (*alla griglia*)
- marinated (*marinato*)
- poached (*affogato*)
- raw (*crudo*)
- roasted (*arrostito*)

ALICI OR ACCIUGHE (ANCHOVY)
Highly flavored, small fish that may be served fresh or cured. Grilled or fried anchovies have a milder taste than the cured fish, which can be quite pungent. Fried anchovies are a popular snack along the coast.

BACCALÀ (SALT COD)
Cod that has been dried and cured in salt. Before use, the dried *baccalà* fillet is soaked repeatedly in water to reduce saltiness and reconstitute the flesh. Common dishes include sautéed baccalà with potatoes, and baccalà baked in spicy tomato sauce.

BRANZINO (EUROPEAN SEA BASS)
A medium-size fish with lean, flaky white meat and a slightly sweet, mild flavor. May also be called *spigola*. It is often grilled and served with potatoes, or baked *al cartoccio*.

COZZE (MUSSELS)
Extremely popular in the region since Roman times, these fat yellow delights are more likely than not to be farmed, as natural resources have been severely depleted.

GALLINELLA (GURNARD)
A meaty white fish that may also be called *mazzole* or tub fish. Gallinella *all'acqua pazza* is cooked in "crazy water" (oil mixed with water and flavored with tomatoes and herbs). A related fish is *cappone gallinella* (red gurnard).

A fresh selection at a Naples fish market.

Expect octopus (polpo) on local menus.

POLPO (OCTOPUS)
The firmly textured, gently flavored octopus may be boiled in simple soups, stewed (*polpi in cassuola*), or simply sautéed with garlic and olive oil, among myriad preparations. *Polpetto* is the term used for little octopi.

SARDE (SARDINES)
Sardines are considered *pesce azzurro*—small blue fish that swim near the surface of the sea—along with the anchovy and *cecinelli* (smelt). These fish typically appear in seafood *fritto misto*, a mixture of small fried fish.

TOTANI (FLYING SQUID)
These squid closely resemble calamari, and likewise are a popular snack when cut into rings and deep-fried. They may be stuffed with diced vegetables, fried as a snack, or boiled and served cold in salads.

TRIGLIA (RED MULLET)
Small bony fish with moderately fatty flesh and delicate flavor. It is often featured in fish stews and may also be served sautéed, baked, or roasted.

Located under the shadow of Vesuvius, Naples is the most vibrant city in Italy—a steaming, bubbling, reverberating minestrone in which each block is a small village and everything seems to be a backdrop for an opera not yet composed.

It's said that northern Italians vacation here to remind themselves of the time when Italy was *molto Italiana—really* Italian. In this respect, Naples (Napoli in Italian) doesn't disappoint: Neapolitan rainbows of laundry wave in the wind over alleyways, mothers caress children, men break out into impromptu arias at sidewalk cafés, and street scenes offer Fellini-esque slices of life. Everywhere contrasting elements of faded gilt and romance, grandeur and squalor form a pageant of pure *Italianità*—Italy at its most Italian.

As the historic capital of the region known as Campania, Naples has been perpetually and tumultuously in a state of flux. Neapolitans are instinctively the most hospitable of people, and they've often paid a price for being so, having unwittingly extended a warm welcome to wave after wave of invaders. Lombards, Goths, Normans, Swabians, Spanish vice-roys and kings, and Napoleonic generals arrived in turn; most of them proved to be greedy and self-serving. Still, if these foreign rulers bled the populace dry with taxes, they left the impoverished city with a rich architectural inheritance.

Much of that inheritance is on display in the Centro Storico neighborhood, where the Piazza del Gesù Nuovo and the surrounding blocks are a showplace for the city's most beloved churches. In recent years tourism has become an established industry, with both CNN and the *New York Times* listing Naples as a must-see destination in 2022. You will, however, find yourself becoming a native very quickly if you spend enough time wandering through the gridlike narrow streets of the old center.

Planning

When to Go

High seasons in Naples are the so-called shoulder seasons elsewhere—April–June and September and October. Nativity scenes are a Neapolitan specialty, so Christmas and New Year are also busy times. Book well in advance if visiting then. From July into September the entire area surrounding Naples—including the Amalfi Coast and Capri—fills up with local Italian holidaymakers, pushing up prices. Many shops close during August, but tourism ensures sights and restaurants remain open, although the summer humidity can be oppressive for many.

Planning Your Time

Three to four days should be enough to give you a taste of the city and see you through the main monuments, as well as factor in a breather to one of the islands in the bay. Always make a contingency plan for each day. Naples can be fraying on the nerves and tiring in terms of legwork, so head for one of the city parks (Villa Comunale, Floridiana, or Capodimonte) for a well-earned break in between doses of culture. You may need a rest after touring the Centro Storico, which, thanks to the original Greek street plan, is wonderfully compact, with more culture packed into a square mile or two than almost anywhere else in the world.

Sightseeing days should begin no later than 9, as most churches are usually open only from 7:30 until noon or 12:30, reopening only after the afternoon siesta, from 4 or 4:30 until about 7. Most museums have extended hours, with a few even open in evenings. Note that government-run sites are free on the first Sunday of each month—good for those on a budget, but less so for avoiding crowds. The **Campania Artecard** entitles users to free or discounted admission to about four dozen museums and monuments in Naples and beyond. These are the main passes: Naples, three days (€21) has three sights included and a fourth at up to 50% off, plus transportation; Campania region, three days (€32), including Pompeii and other Bay of Naples sights and Ravello and Paestum with two sights included and a third at up to 50% off, plus transportation; Campania region, seven days (€34) with five sights included and a sixth for up to 50% off, but no transportation. Other benefits (which vary depending on the pass) include discounts on audio guides, theater and ferry tickets, city tours, and other activities, and visitors age 18–24 receive generous discounts. Your hotel or the tourist office can give you more information, or visit the Campania Artecard website (🌐 *www.campaniartecard.it*).

Getting Here and Around

Public transportation in Naples is decent, and includes two subway lines, four funiculars, and a multitude of buses. Tickets cost €1.10 per journey (€1.30 on Metro Linea 2), but a Ticket Integrato Campania costs €1.60 and is valid for 90 minutes on all transport for as far as Bagnoli to the west and Portici to the east; €4.50 buys a *biglietto giornaliero* (all-day ticket). Buy your ticket at newsagents or tobacconists, or download the Unico Campania app.

CONTACTS Unico Campania. ✉ *Naples* ☎ *081/5513109* 🌐 *www.unicocampania.it.*

BICYCLE

The Lungomare (also known as Via Partenope) is closed to car traffic, making bike travel along the waterfront safe and pleasant. Kiosks by the Villa Comunale rent bicycles for one, two, or even six, for adults and children, as well as skateboards and skates. Electric bikes are available at NeapoliSolare in the Centro Strorico for €5 per hour, as well as bike tours.

CONTACTS NeapoliSolare. ✉ *Via Domenico Capitelli 31, Centro Storico* ☎ *081/0127430* 🌐 *www.neapolisolare.it* Ⓜ *Dante.*

BUS

Bus service has become viable over the last few years, especially with the introduction of larger buses on the regular routes. Electronic signs display wait times at many stops.

CAR

Car travel within Naples is not recommended: it's difficult, parking is a nightmare, and theft of cars parked on the street is a persistent threat. If you come to Naples by car, find a garage, agree on the cost, and leave it there for the duration of your stay. The garages listed here are safe and centrally located. A car rental could be useful if you want to explore the Amalfi Coast, though you need to leave plenty of time to spare for your return because traffic along the coast can be heavy and slow moving. Expect to pay €55 per day for a compact manual vehicle.

Quick Morelli, hewn from the tuff under the Pizzafalcone hill, was awarded the World's Coolest Car Park in 2018.

CONTACTS Petraglia. ✉ *Via Ferraris 42, Piazza Garibaldi* ☎ *081/3602840* 🌐 *www.garagepetraglia.it* Ⓜ *Garibaldi.* **Quick Morelli.** ✉ *Via Domenico Morelli 40, Chiaia* ☎ *081/19130220* 🌐 *www.quick-parking.it.*

SUBWAY

Now with a couple of art-decorated stations (Toledo and Università) recently voted among Europe's most attractive, Naples's Metropolitana provides fairly frequent service and can be the fastest way to get across the traffic-clogged city. Linea 1, Metropolitana Collinare, links the hill area of the Vomero and beyond with the National Archaeological Museum and Piazza Municipio near the port, as well as Stazione Centrale. The older Linea 2 stretches from the train station to Pozzuoli. Trains on both lines run 6 am–10:30 pm.

TAXI

You may be able to hail a taxi if you see one driving, but your best bet is to call Radio Taxi or ask someone at your hotel to book one. Taxi ranks can be found outside the central Piazza Garibaldi train station and the port (Molo Beverello), as well as throughout the city. Watch out for overcharging at three locations: the airport, the railway station, and the hydrofoil marina. The fixed rate (be sure to ask for it!) from the airport to the central station is €18, which covers three people, two large pieces of luggage, and two small pieces. City Airport Taxis offers a private service. Some destinations have a fixed tariff—you should ask for this, as drivers don't always suggest it. Trips around the city should cost €8–€13. You can, of course, request that the meter is switched on; this often results in your paying less. Taxis charge approximately €3.50 initially (more on Sunday, holidays, and after 10 pm), then €0.05 per 65 meters or 10 seconds of idling. An information sheet about fees to destinations within and near Naples must be displayed in every cab. Other options besides Radio Taxi include Consorttaxi (☎ *081/2222*), Partenope (☎ *081/0101*), and La 570 (☎ *081/5707070*). In summer, many cabs in Naples have no air-conditioning—which the city's buses and metro do have—and you can bake if caught in a traffic jam.

CONTACTS City Airport Taxis. ✉ 🌐 *www.city-airport-taxis.com.* **Radio Taxi Napoli.** ☎ *081/8888* 🌐 *www.taxinapoli.it.*

TRAIN

The main train station in Naples is Stazione Centrale, where all trains from the capital arrive. Piazza Garibaldi shares the same building, on the lower level, and Mergellina and Campi Flegrei, now Metro stops rather than mainline stations, are to the west. ⇨ *For more information about traveling by train to Naples and for station and railroad contacts, see Train Travel in this book's Travel Smart chapter. For information about train travel to Mt. Vesuvius, Pompeii, and other areas just outside Naples, see the Planner section of the Bay of Naples chapter.*

Restaurants

Naples has a wide choice of naturally elegant restaurants, but some Neapolitans will go out of town for a high-end restaurant meal, heading to gastronomic enclaves in the Pozzuoli area or on the Sorrentine Peninsula, or opting for a feast at one of the private dining clubs the Neapolitan aristocracy favors. If you stay in town, you're likely to be pleasantly

Beyond First Impressions

If you're arriving in Naples by train, you might not be instantly charmed. Piazza Garibaldi, which is home to the Stazione Centrale, the main railroad terminal, has had an extensive makeover and has somewhat improved, but it continues to be a battered labyrinth—crowded, messy, and inhospitable, with buses and taxis vying for space at a tangle of intersections. Longtime home to street sharks and souvenir hawkers, the piazza is now also a meeting point for Eastern European guest workers, who have become a growing presence in the city.

When you make your way beyond Piazza Garibaldi, first impressions begin to mellow: Delightfully and unforgettably, Naples reveals itself as a cornucopia of elegant boulevards, treasure-stocked palaces, the world's greatest museum of classical antiquities, the stage-set Centro Storico, and scores of historic churches. Naples becomes *Napoli la bella*, a city that centuries of romantics have deemed one of the most beautiful in the world.

surprised. Wherever you go, be prepared to deviate from the menu (locals rarely ask for one), and ask the waiter for the chef's special *piatto* (dish). At the lower end, service may be rough and ready, but then you don't expect to be served by liveried waitstaff when your restaurant sits at the end of an alley. The increase in tourism in recent years has resulted in the opening of numerous pizzerias and local food restaurants, some of which are better than others. Note that many restaurants in Naples close for at least a week around August 15 to celebrate the Ferragosto holiday.

Appropriately, the monumental city center—the area around **Piazza Municipio** and **Toledo**—contains the city's' most iconic restaurants. The nearby **Centro Storico** is now one of the evening locations where *buona cucina* (good food) meets low- and high-brow culture after 9 pm, offering excellent value. The upscale area of **Chiaia** is a favorite with locals and discerning expatriates and will likely be a little more expensive, while next-door **Santa Lucia** is a classic choice for its chic but touristy fish restaurants with that just-how-you-imagined-Naples sea view. The ritzy bayside suburbs of **Mergellina** and **Posillipo** host some of the Naples area's most panoramic restaurants. Several occupy space on secluded waterfront culs-de-sac, so unless you have your own wheels, taking a taxi will be the most convenient option. Atop a hill, the wealthy and residential **Vomero** doesn't seem like a place to dine, but if you've been shopping on Via Scarlatti or taking in the Castel Sant'Elmo, this isn't a bad place to grab a nontouristy bite. The **Piazza Garibaldi** area is known for fine no-nonsense eating, mostly from traditional restaurants offering varying value for the money. If returning to your base after dark, stick to well-lighted main roads or ask a restaurant staffer to order a taxi.

Prices in the reviews are the average cost of a main course at dinner or, if dinner isn't served, at lunch. Restaurant reviews have been shortened. For full information, visit Fodors.com.

What it Costs In Euros

	$	$$	$$$	$$$$
RESTAURANTS	under €15	€15–€24	€25–€35	over €35

Hotels

The **Centro Storico** is Naples's most picturesque quarter, so if you're looking for classic Neapolitan atmosphere, this is the place to roost. The flip side of the coin is the nearby **Piazza Municipio/Toledo** area; it's the bustling heart of the modern city, and it has a collection of upscale, large-capacity business hotels, along with some quirky finds in historic buildings. **Santa Lucia** and the Lungomare offer visitors an unsurpassed view of the Bay of Naples, all the more so for being traffic-free. This area has the city's greatest concentration of luxury hotels, although more reasonable lodging is available on the side streets. Adjacent **Chiaia** is the ritziest residential neighborhood in town, studded with 19th-century mansions and containing an elegant shopping district. The **Vomero** hill rises above the city, offering great bay vistas. The bay-side atmosphere continues at **Mergellina,** set at the far western end of the Riviera di Chiaia, and beyond at the suburban coastal district of **Posillipo.** North of the city center in gritty La Sanità is a B&B that's part of a 17th-century church complex. Also noisy and edgy is the **Piazza Garibaldi** area. It's handy if you have to catch an early morning train, but otherwise you're better off putting some distance between you and the central station; the area is relatively unsafe (and unpleasant) for evening strolls after 8:30 pm.

Don't be alarmed if your bill is a little larger than anticipated; the city imposes a *tassa di soggiorno* (tourist tax) of between €1.50 and €5 per person per night, depending on the hotel category. Another amenity that might cost you more is air-conditioning—Naples hotels offer some of the strongest air-conditioning around—so when making reservations, be sure to inquire if there's an additional charge. The peak visiting times are April–June and September and October, as well as Christmastime; book well in advance if visiting then

Prices in the reviews are the lowest cost of a standard double room in high season. Hotel reviews have been shortened. For full information, visit Fodors.com.

What it Costs In Euros

	$	$$	$$$	$$$$
HOTELS	under €125	€125–€200	€201–€300	over €300

Nightlife

Nightlife in Naples begins well after the sun has gone down. If you're going to a club, don't even think about turning up before 11, and don't plan on going to bed much before 3. Yet if you're willing to stay up late enough, and prepared to hang around outside places—with the rest of the *perdi-tempo* ("time wasters")—where there's sometimes more going on in the street than in the clubs themselves, Naples offers distractions for night owls of all persuasions. The designer-clad young and not-so-young hang out in the area around Chiaia; a more artsy postgrad crowd congregates around Piazza Bellini; the rawer, punkier edge prefers to hang around on Piazza del Gesù or Piazza San Domenico. Clubs tend to open and close or change name, style, or ownership with bewildering rapidity, so be sure to check locally before planning a night out. The best way to find out what's going on is to keep your eyes on the posters that cover the Centro Storico.

If chaotic nightlife is more than you can take after a day experiencing the all-too-chaotic daylife of Naples, there's the civilized option of the *enoteca,* not exactly a wine bar, but a place where you can stop for a drink or meet up with friends without having to shout over the music or hang around on the street outside for hours, and have something more substantial to eat than peanuts and pretzels.

Performing Arts

Lively and energetic yet chaotic and often difficult to follow, the cultural scene in Naples reflects the city's charming yet frustrating character. Event schedules are published in daily newspapers, particularly *Il Mattino, La Repubblica,* and *Corriere della Sera,* or advertised on websites such as 🌐 *www.napolitoday.it.* Bear in mind, though, that they can't be relied on to reveal everything that is happening or the frequent last-minute changes of program or venue. Word of mouth (hotel staffers are often good sources) is your best source of information, and keep your eyes peeled for the theater and concert posters that wallpaper much of the city center. Neapolitans take their cinema seriously; several cinemas run "cineforums" one day a week to cater to discerning cinemagoers, and from the end of June to mid-September, the *comune* funds an open-air cinema to provide aficionados with a chance to catch up on movies missed during the year.

TICKET AGENCIES

Box Office. ✉ *Galleria Umberto I 17, Piazza Municipio* ☎ *081/5519188* Ⓜ *Municipio.* **Concerteria.** ✉ *Via Schipa 23, Chiaia* ☎ *081/7611221* 🌐 *www.concerteria.it.*

Tours

Many companies run tours and excursions within Naples proper and to Vesuvius, Pompeii, the Amalfi Coast, and other places. Vesuvius Vs Pompeii has local tours to the top sights in Naples, for instance, or you can combine a city tour with one to Pompeii. The company will also work with you to create a custom itinerary tailored to your interests.

City Sightseeing

BUS TOURS | FAMILY | Close to the port, beside the main entrance to Castel Nuovo, is the terminal for double-decker buses belonging to City Sightseeing. For €23 you can take two different excursions, giving you reasonable coverage of the downtown sights and outlying attractions like the Museo di Capodimonte. ✉ *Piazza Municipio, Naples* ☎ *055/961237, 39/3248114807 WhatsApp/Cellphone* 🌐 *www.city-sightseeing.it/naples.*

Lino Tour

GUIDED TOURS | Lino Tour offers tailor-made tours of the attractions in and around Naples. ✉ *Naples* ☎ *081/8772244* 🌐 *www.linotourcarservice.com.*

Tramvia

GUIDED TOURS | Providing daily transfers to Pompeii, Vesuvius, and the Amalfi Coast, as well as eight daily hop-on, hop-off tours of Naples for €10, which depart from the port. ✉ *Naples* ☎ *081/7772347* 🌐 *www.tramvianapoli.com* Ⓜ *Municipio.*

Vesuvius vs Pompeii

GUIDED TOURS | In addition to Pompeii tours, this company provides many other guided tours including ones to Capri and the Amalfi Coast. ☎ *333/6409000* 🌐 *www.vesuviusvspompeii.com.*

Visitor Information

You can pick up a free map and the latest Art in Campania brochure listing key venues and possible savings through the Campania Artecard at temporary information points dotted around the city, or at the tourist office in Piazza del Gesù. The helpful inStazione agency has an office with lounge on the lower level of Stazione Centrale and Ki Point near Platform 2 provides left-luggage (€6 for five hours, open 8–8) and porter services.

CONTACTS | Naples. ✉ *Piazza del Gesù 7, Centro Storico* ☎ *081/5512701* 🌐 *www.inaples.it.* **inStazione.** ✉ *Stazione Centrale, Naples* 🌐 *www.instazione.it.*

Centro Storico

To experience the true essence of Naples, you need to explore the Centro Storico, an unforgettable neighborhood that is the heart of old Naples. This is the Naples of peeling building facades and hanging laundry, with small alleyways fragrant with fresh flowers laid at the many shrines to the Blessed Virgin. Here the cheapest pizzerias in town feed the locals like kings, and the raucous street carnival of Neapolitan daily life is punctuated with oases of spiritual calm. All the contradictions of Naples—splendor and squalor, palace and slum, triumph and tragedy—meet here and sing a full-throated chorale. But the Centro Storico is not simply picturesque. It also contains some of Naples's most important sights, including a striking conglomeration of churches—Lombard, Gothic, Renaissance, Baroque, Rococo, and Neoclassical. There are the majolica-adorned cloister of Santa Chiara; the sumptuous Church of the Gesù Nuovo; two opera-set piazzas; the city duomo (where the Festa di San Gennaro is celebrated every September); the Museo Cappella Sansevero; the greatest painting in Naples—Caravaggio's *Seven Acts of Mercy* altarpiece—on view at the museum complex of Pio Monte; and Via Gregorio Armeno, where shops devoted to *Presepi* (Nativity scenes) make every day a rehearsal for Christmas. And even though this was the medieval center of the city, the city's flagship museum of modern art, the Museo Madre, is here and night owls will find that many of Naples's most cutting-edge clubs and bars are hidden among its nooks and alleys. For soccer fanatics, there is even a shrine to Diego Maradona.

Because many churches open at 7:30 and close for the afternoon around 1, it's imperative to get an early start to fit in as many sights as possible before the midday break. Many shops close for three hours, from 1:30 to 4:30. By 4 many of the churches reopen. Plan on a good two hours to walk this route, plus some time for each of the principal churches you decide to visit. But since the Centro Storico is the most memorable part of Naples, take a full day if you can, and wear comfortable shoes.

The almost mile-long Spaccanapoli cuts through the heart of the largely pedestrianised Centro Storico. Start at Piazza del Gesù Nuovo (approachable from all directions but easily reachable from Via Toledo by heading eastward from Piazza Carità through the pedestrianized Piazza Monteoliveto and then up Calata Trinità Maggiore), then head east toward the Duomo, returning along Via dei Tribunali.

Sights

Complesso Museale Santa Maria delle Anime del Purgatorio ad Arco

RELIGIOUS BUILDING | Once a tavern, this building was rebuilt by the Monte di Pietà charity in 1616 as a church, and its two stories are fascinatingly complementary. As bare as the upper Church is lavish, the altar below-stairs is a stark black cross against a peeling gray wall. The nave covers what was a 1656 plague pit now set off by chains with four lamps to represent the flames of Purgatory. As the pit filled up, to accommodate more recent dead the skulls of earlier plague victims were placed on the central floor. So was born the cult of *le anime pezzentelle* (wretched souls). By praying for them, the living could accelerate these souls' way to Heaven, at which point the pezzentelle could intercede on behalf of the living.

During the 20th century, World War II left many Neapolitans with missing relatives. Some families found consolation by adopting a skull in their loved ones' stead. The skulls would be cleaned, polished, and then given a box-type *altarino.*

If all this verges on the pagan, the Catholic Church thought likewise, and in 1969 the practice was banned. The *altarini* were blocked off and eventually abandoned. In 1992 the church reopened and most of the skulls were taken to Cimitero delle Fontanelle. Some still remain, like that of one Lucia, princess of skulls and patron of *amore infelice* (unhappy love). ✉ *Via Tribunali 39, Centro Storico* ☎ *081/440438* 🌐 *www.purgatorioadarco.it* 🎫 *€6, upper church free* ⏲ *Closed Sun. and afternoons* Ⓜ *Dante, Cavour.*

Duomo

CHURCH | Hemmed in on three sides, this cathedral is a trip through the city's history. Although the cathedral was established in the 1200s, the building you see was erected a century later and has since undergone radical changes—especially during the Baroque period. Inside, ancient columns salvaged from pagan buildings rise to the 350-year-old richly decorated false wooden ceiling (the original Gothic ceiling is 6 meters higher). Off the left aisle, step down into the 4th-century church of **Santa Restituta,** which was incorporated into the cathedral. Though Santa Restituta was redecorated in the late 1600s in the prevalent Baroque style, the **Battistero** (Baptistery) is the oldest in the Western world, with what some claim to be the most beautiful mosaics in Italy.

On the right aisle of the cathedral, in the **Cappella del Tesoro di San Gennaro,** multicolor marbles and frescoes honor Saint Januarius, the miracle-working patron saint of Naples, whose altar and relics are encased in silver. Three times a year—on September 19 (his feast day); on the Saturday preceding the first Sunday in May, which commemorates the transfer of his relics to Naples; and on December 16—his dried blood, contained in two sealed vials, is believed to liquefy during rites in his honor; the rare occasions on which it does not liquefy portend ill, as in 1980, the year of the Irpinia earthquake. The most spectacular painting on display is Ribera's *San Gennaro in the Furnace* (1647), depicting the saint emerging unscathed from the furnace while his persecutors scatter in disarray. These days large numbers of devout Neapolitans offer up prayers in his memory. The **Museo del Tesoro di San Gennaro** houses a rich collection of treasures associated with the saint. Paintings by Solimena and Luca Giordano hang alongside statues, busts, candelabras, and tabernacles in gold, silver, and marble by Cosimo Fanzago and other 18th-century Baroque masters. ✉ *Via Duomo 149, Centro Storico* ☎ *081/449097 Duomo, 081/294980* 🌐 *www.museosangennaro.it* 🎫 *Cappella del Tesoro di San Gennaro €4; museum and chapel €10* Ⓜ *Duomo, Cavour.*

Gesù Nuovo

CHURCH | A stunning architectural contrast to the plain Romanesque frontage of other nearby churches, the oddly faceted stone facade of this elaborate Baroque church dates to the late 16th century. Originally a palace, the building was seized by Pedro of Toledo in 1547 and sold to the Jesuits with the condition the facade remain intact. Recent research has revealed that the symbols on the stones out front are Aramaic musical notes that produce a 45-minute concerto. Behind the entrance is Francesco Solimena's action-packed *Heliodorus' Eviction from the Temple.* The bulk of the interior decoration took more than 40 years and was completed only in the 18th century. You can find the work of familiar Baroque sculptors (Naccherino, Finelli) and

Continued on page 254

Sights

1 Complesso Museale Santa Maria delle Anime del Purgatorio ad Arco C3
2 Duomo E2
3 Gesù Nuovo B5
4 LAPIS Museum C4
5 The Madonna and Pistol E3
6 Madre D1
7 Monumento Nazionale dei Girolamini D3
8 Museo Cappella Sansevero C4
9 Museo Civico Gaetano Filangieri E4
10 Museo Diocesano Napoli E1
11 Napoli Sotterranea D3
12 Pio Monte della Misericordia E3
13 San Domenico Maggiore C4
14 San Gennaro Mural E4
15 San Giuseppe dei Ruffi D2
16 San Gregorio Armeno D3
17 San Lorenzo Maggiore D3
18 San Paolo Maggiore D3
19 San Severo al Pendino E4
20 Santa Chiara B5
21 Sant'Angelo a Nilo C5
22 Santi Apostoli E1

Restaurants

1 Amico Bio - Sorriso Integrale B4
2 Biancomangiare- La Vecchia Cantina A5
3 Di Matteo D3
4 Gino Sorbillo C3
5 La Campagnola C3
6 La Cantina di Via Sapienza B3
7 La Taverna dell'Arte C5
8 Le Sorelle Bandiera D3
9 L'Etto B3
10 Lombardi a Santa Chiara B5
11 O' Munaciello A5
12 Osteria da Carmela A3
13 Palazzo Petrucci Pizzeria C5
14 Pizzeria Giuliano A5
15 Ristorante Bellini B4
16 Tandem C5

Quick Bites

1 Bar Nilo D5
2 Scaturchio C5
3 Vaco 'e Press A4

Hotels

1 Caravaggio Hotel E2
2 Costantinopoli 104 .... B3
3 Decumani Hotel de Charme C5
4 Ecumano Space C5
5 Hotel Neapolis C3
6 Hotel Palazzo Decumani E4

WALKING SPACCANAPOLI

Spaccanapoli is the informal designation given to the long, straight street running down the middle of Naples's Centro Storico (historic center). The Centro Storico is the very essence of Naples, it's chaotic, vibrant, edgy, colorful, noisy, mysterious, and very beautiful. A walk along Spaccanapoli takes you past peeling palaces, artisans' workshops, many churches and street shrines, stores of all sorts, bars, and people young and old.

left, Via San Gregorio Armeno; top right, church of Gesú Nuovo; bottom right, a presepe shop window

A STROLL THROUGH THE HEART OF NAPLES

Santa Chiara

Frescoes, Santa Chiara

Morning is the best time to make this walk—many of the churches are closed in the afternoon. The route is a mile and a half long; done at a leisurely pace, with numerous stops along the way, it will take a full morning.

❶ **Start at Piazza Gesù Nuovo.** At this point Spaccanapoli goes by the name Via Benedetto Croce. The Guglia dell'Immacolata, an extravagant carved-stone spire honoring the Virgin Mary, stands in the middle of the district's largest square. The forbidding 15th-century facade of the church of Gesù Nuovo suits the building's original function as a fort; it was converted into the city's most extravagant baroque church by the Jesuits in the 18th century.

❷ **Cross the road and enter the church of Santa Chiara.** Originally built by Robert of Anjou in the early 1300s and reconstructed after a direct hit from a bomb in 1943, the church is light, airy, and spacious. Look for the traces of the Giotto frescoes behind the altar. A side entrance leads to a delightful vine-laden cloister decorated with hundreds of majolica tiles, an unexpected outbreak of peace in noisy Naples.

❸ **Head east on Spaccanapoli.** You'll cross Via San Sebastiano, a street filled with music shops frequented by students from the nearby conservatory; it can be a veritable symphony in the morning. **Palazzo Filomarino**, former home of philosopher Benedetto Croce and now the site of his library, is on the left as you continue. Next on your right is architect Cosimo Fanzago's **Palazzo Carafa della Spina**; coachmen once used the mouths of the gargoyles at the entrance to tamp out their torches.

Piazza Gesú Nuovo

❹ **Continue east to Piazza San Domenico Maggiore.** The rear of the church of San Domenico Maggiore, the Palazzo Cori-

Piazza San Domenico Maggiore

Chapel of San Gennaro

Capella Sansevero

Street uppet theater

gliano (today part of the university), and another spire contribute to one of Naples's most charming squares. Outdoor cafés (including Scaturchio, one of Naples's most celebrated pastry shops) give the piazza the feel of an open-air living room. Heading up the right-hand side of the piazza, swing right onto Via Francesco de Sanctis, where you find the fascinating **Cappella Sansevero**, the tomb-chapel of the Sangro di San Severo family.

❺ **Return to Spaccanapoli on Via Nilo.** Where the two streets intersect you pass a statue of the Egyptian river god Nile reclining on a pedestal. (A few steps beyond, Spaccanapoli's street name changes to Via San Biagio dei Librai.) Several blocks down is the storefront Ospedale delle Bambole (Doll Hospital).

❻ **Turn left (north) when you reach Via Duomo.** The next main intersection is Via Tribunali, the other great thoroughfare of the district. Take a right to reach the **Pio Monte della Misericordia**, which contains one of the greatest 17th-century altarpieces in Europe, Caravaggio's Seven Acts of Mercy. Return to the Via Duomo to visit the **Duomo di San Gennaro** and its spectacular chapel.

❼ **Head west on Via dei Tribunali.** After a short block you'll reach one of the street's many imposing churches, the gigantic **San Lorenzo Maggiore.** Its 18th-century facade hides a Gothic-era nave and—surprise—one of the most interesting archaeological sites in the city.

❽ **Turn left onto Via San Gregorio Armeno.** This may be the most charming street in Naples. The towering campanile of the Rococo church of **San Gregorio Armeno** arches over the street, which is lined with presepe (crèche) stores.

❾ **Continue west along Via Tribunali.** Stop to note the curious brass skulls outside the church of **Purgatorio ad Arco** on your right—touch them to bring good luck. At the end of Via Tribunali, turn right into Piazza Bellini and stop for a drink at one of the leafy square's many cafés.

Murder in the Cathedral?

Most of the frescoes of the San Gennaro chapel are by the Bolognese artist Domenichino, but his compatriot Guido Reni was originally hired to paint the frescoes, and thereby hangs a tale.

When he arrived in Naples, Reni found himself so harassed and threatened by jealous local artists, who were indignant that the commission had been given to an outsider, that he gave up the job and fled town. Ultimately he was replaced by the great Domenichino, who came to Naples only after the viceroy himself guaranteed his protection.

Domenichino started painting under armed guard beginning in 1630 and had almost completed the work in 1641 when he died suddenly; poisoning was suspected. The committee charged with finding his replacement pointedly refused to consider a Neapolitan painter, instead selecting the Roman Giovanni Lanfranco, who bravely (and quickly) finished the dome. It was Lanfranco who painted the dome's frescoed vision of paradise. The most spectacular painting of all, however, is on the right—Ribera's depiction of the saint emerging from the furnace unscathed.

painters inside. The gracious *Visitation* above the altar in the second chapel on the right is by Massimo Stanzione, who also contributed the fine frescoes in the main nave: they're in the presbytery (behind and around the main altar).

Don't miss the votive chapel dedicated to the surgeon and university teacher Saint Giuseppe Moscato, along with a re-creation of his studio. Here hundreds of tiny silver images have been hung on the walls to give thanks to the saint, who was canonized in 1987, for his assistance in medical matters. On the opposite far left corner a smaller chapel similarly gives thanks to San Ciro (Saint Cyrus), also a doctor. Farther down are impressive statues of David and Jeremiah by Fanzago. Left of the altar the wooden heads of various saints are aligned like gods in an antique theater. ✉ *Piazza Gesù Nuovo, Centro Storico* ☎ *081/5578111* Ⓜ *Dante.*

★ LAPIS Museum

RUINS | FAMILY | The beautifully restored 17th century Basilica di Pietrasanta, a Cosimo Fanzago Baroque masterpiece built on the site of the Roman Temple of Diana, hosts regular multimedia exhibitions, but the star attraction here is the underground visit to a section of Naples's oldest aqueduct. Four tours a day descend 40 meters below the busy Via dei Tribunali to large lavishly illuminated cisterns hewed from excavated tuff 2 millennia ago, still filled with running water (thanks to a collaboration with the city's waterworks). A quarter-mile stroll east through the tunnels takes you to where up to a thousand Neapolitans at a time huddled when the air raid sirens sounded during World War II, often returning to the surface to find their houses destroyed by Allied or German bombs. Nowadays there's a lift—the only archaeological elevator in Naples—to whisk you back up to the 21st century. ✉ *Piazzetta Pietrasanta 17/18, Centro Storico* ☎ *081/19230565* 🌐 *www.lapismuseum.com* 🎟 *€10* Ⓜ *Dante.*

The Madonna and Pistol

PUBLIC ART | This piece is by controversial street artist Banksy. Located on the wall of the birthplace of 17th-century philosopher Giambattista Vico, a stencilled *La Madonna con la Pistola* sits beside a religious shrine to the Virgin Mary. Fans of street art can take a tour of the city's other interesting graffiti by contacting Napoli Paint Stories. ✉ *Piazza Gerolomini, Naples* 🌐 *www.napolipaintstories.it* Ⓜ *Cavour.*

Madre (*Museum of Contemporary Art Donnaregina*)

ART GALLERY | With 8,000 square meters (86,111 square feet) of exhibition space, a host of young and helpful attendants, and occasional late-night events, the Madre is one of the most visited museums in Naples. Most of the artworks on the first floor were installed in situ by their creators, but the second-floor gallery exhibits works by international and Italian contemporary artists. The museum also hosts temporary shows by major international artists. ✉ *Via Settembrini 79, San Lorenzo, Centro Storico* ☎ *081/19978017* 🌐 *www.madrenapoli.it/en* 🎫 *€8* 🕓 *Closed Tues.* Ⓜ *Cavour.*

Monumento Nazionale dei Girolamini

RELIGIOUS BUILDING | *I Girolamini* is another name for the Oratorians, followers of St. Philip Neri, to whom the splendid church I Girolamini is dedicated. The church is part of a larger complex managed as the Monumento Nazionale dei Girolamini. The Florentine architect Giovanni Antonio Dosio designed I Girolamini, which was erected between 1592 and 1619; the dome and facade were rebuilt (circa 1780) in the most elegant neoclassical style after a design by Ferdinando Fuga. Inside the entrance wall is Luca Giordano's grandiose fresco (1684) of Christ chasing the money-changers from the temple. The intricate carved-wood ceiling, damaged by Allied bombs in 1943, has now been restored to its original magnificence.

The Oratorians also built the Casa dei Padri dell'Oratorio (House of the Oratorio Fathers). Step through its gate to see the two cloisters, from the 16th and the 17th centuries, the latter designed by Dosio and other Florentine architects. The gallery in this section contains 16th- and 17th-century paintings by Ribera, Reni, and other Baroque masters. One of Europe's most gloriously decorated 18th-century libraries, the Biblioteca dei Girolamini (Girolamini Library: closed for restoration) helped make this an intellectual nexus during the Renaissance and Baroque periods. Ongoing restoration works mean that visits are only via prebooked tours so contact ahead for upcoming dates and times. ✉ *Via Duomo 142, Centro Storico* ☎ *081/294444* 🌐 *www.bibliotecadeigirolamini.beniculturali.it* 🎫 *€8* Ⓜ *Cavour.*

★ **Museo Cappella Sansevero** (*Sansevero Chapel Museum*)

NOTABLE BUILDING | The dazzling funerary chapel of the Sangro di Sansevero princes combines noble swagger, overwhelming color, and a touch of the macabre—which expresses Naples perfectly. The chapel was begun in 1590 by Prince Giovan Francesco di Sangro to fulfill a vow to the Virgin if he were cured of a dire illness. The seventh Sangro di Sansevero prince, Raimondo, had the building modified in the mid-18th century and is generally credited for its current Baroque styling, the noteworthy elements of which include the splendid marble-inlay floor. A larger-than-life figure, Prince Raimondo was believed to have signed a pact with the devil allowing him to plumb nature's secrets. He commissioned the young sculptor Giuseppe Sanmartino to create numerous works, including the chapel's centerpiece, the remarkable *Veiled Christ,* which has a seemingly transparent marble veil. If you have the stomach for it, take a look in the crypt, where some of the anatomical experiments conducted by the prince are gruesomely displayed. ✉ *Via Francesco de Sanctis 19, off Vicolo Domenico Maggiore, Centro Storico* ☎ *081/5518470* 🌐 *www.museosansevero.it* 🎫 *€8* 🕓 *Closed Tues.* Ⓜ *Dante.*

Museo Civico Gaetano Filangieri
ART MUSEUM | Housed in a 15th-century palazzo, this museum was opened in 1888 by Gaetano Filangieri, prince of Satriano, to house his large and varied collection of paintings, sculptures, porcelain, weapons, and manuscripts. The arched ceiling of the armory features a glittering golden mosaic that bears the family's coat of arms, and the Sala Agata upstairs, with its wooden tiers and majolica floor, is a museum piece in and of itself. The archive stores letters from Benjamin Franklin to Filangieri's grandfather, author of *The Science of Legislation* (1780); it's said that the book and its mention of the pursuit of happiness inspired the U.S. Declaration of Independence. In the 1870s, the impressive Palazzo Como became known locally as *o palazzo ca cammina* (the walking building), when it was moved back 65 feet, brick by brick, to widen Via Duomo. ✉ *Via Duomo 288, Naples* ☎ *081/203175* 🌐 *www.filangierimuseo.it* 🎟 *€5* Ⓜ *Duomo.*

Museo Diocesano Napoli
(*Diocesan Museum of Naples*)
RELIGIOUS BUILDING | This impressive museum exhibits brilliantly restored works by late-Gothic, Renaissance, and Neapolitan Baroque masters. It incorporates the Baroque church of Santa Maria Donnaregina Nuova, which was started in 1617 and consecrated 50 years later for Franciscan nuns (les Clarisses), and the Gothic Donnaregina Vecchia, which was damaged by an earthquake. In more modern times the building was used as legal offices before being closed completely, and becoming prey to the occasional theft as well as bomb damage during World War II. In 2008 the space was officially reborn as a museum.

The last two works of Luca Giordano, *The Wedding at Cana* and *The Multiplication of Loaves,* both from 1705, are displayed on either side of the church's altar, which was moved from the original church. The central painting focuses on the life of the Virgin Mary, while the first chapel on the left houses French painter Charles Mellin's beautiful *Immaculate Conception* (1646). To the left of the nave is a space rich in Gothic and Renaissance statuary from the former church. Take the elevator upstairs to where the nuns once attended Mass, concealed from the congregation by screens. The works on display there follow the theme of life as an Imitation of Christ. There is also the chance to see Francesco Solimena's 17th-century roof frescoes close up, with floodlights showing off their restoration to maximum effect. ✉ *Largo Donna Regina, Centro Storico* ☎ *081/5571365* 🌐 *www.museodiocesanonapoli.it* 🎟 *€7* ⏲ *Closed Tues.* Ⓜ *Cavour.*

Napoli Sotterranea (*Underground Naples*)
HISTORIC SIGHT | FAMILY | Fascinating 90-minute tours of a portion of Naples's fabled underground city provide an initiation into the complex history of the city center. Efforts to dramatize the experience—amphoras lowered on ropes to draw water from cisterns, candles given to navigate narrow passages, objects shifted to reveal secret passages—combine with enthusiastic English-speaking guides to make this particularly exciting for older children.

A short descent delivers you to a section of a 400-km (249-mile) system of quarries and aqueducts used from Greek times until the 1845 cholera epidemic, including a highly claustrophobic 1-km (½-mile) walk with only your mobile phone to light your way. At the end of the aqueduct, you come first to a Greek and then a much larger Roman cistern. Near the entrance is the War Museum, which displays uniforms, armed transportation vehicles, and weapons from World War II. Returning aboveground your guide leads you to a small apartment where you step down to a section of an amphitheater where Nero famously performed three times. During one of his performances an earthquake struck and—so Suetonius relates—the emperor forbade the 6,000

Napoli Sotterranea (Naples Underground) is an extensive network of tunnels, caverns, and aqueducts.

spectators to leave. The rumbling, he insisted, was only the gods applauding his performance. A room at the end of the tour contains examples of that most Neapolitan of art forms, *il presepe* (the crib). Be prepared on the underground tour to go up and down many steps and crouch in very narrow corridors. Temperatures in summer will be much lower below than at street level, so bring a sweater. ✉ *Piazza San Gaetano 68, along Via dei Tribunali, Centro Storico* ☎ *081/296944* 🌐 *www.napolisotterranea.org* 🎫 *€10* Ⓜ *Dante, Cavour.*

★ Pio Monte della Misericordia

RELIGIOUS BUILDING | One of the Centro Storico's defining sites, this octagonal church was built around the corner from the Duomo for a charitable institution seven noblemen founded in 1601. The institution's aim was to carry out acts of Christian charity like feeding the hungry, clothing the poor, nursing the sick, sheltering pilgrims, visiting prisoners, and burying the indigent dead—acts immortalized in the history of art by Caravaggio's famous altarpiece depicting the *Sette Opere della Misericordia* (*Seven Acts of Mercy*). In this haunting work, the artist has brought the Virgin, borne atop the shoulders of two angels, down into the streets of Spaccanapoli, populated by figures in whose spontaneous and passionate movements the people could see themselves. The original church was considered too small and was destroyed in 1658 to make way for a new church that was designed by Antonio Picchiatti and built between 1658 and 1672. Pride of place is given to the great Caravaggio above the altar, but there are other important Baroque paintings on view here. Some hang in the church—among them seven other works of mercy depicted individually by Caravaggio acolytes—while other works, including a wonderful self-portrait by Luca Giordano, are in the adjoining *pinacoteca* (picture gallery). **TIP→ Step into the choral chamber for a bird's-eye view of the Sette Opere della Misericordia.** ✉ *Via Tribunali 253, Centro Storico* ☎ *081/446973*

Caravaggio's Seven Acts of Mercy

The most unforgettable painting in Naples, Michelangelo Merisi da Caravaggio's *Sette Opere della Misericordia* (*Seven Acts of Mercy*) takes centerstage in the Church of Pio Monte della Misericordia, as well as in nearly all of southern Italy, for its emotional spectacle and unflinching truthfulness.

The Painting

Painted in 1607, it combines the traditional seven acts of Christian charity in sometimes-abbreviated form in a tight, dynamic composition under the close, compassionate gaze of the Virgin. Borne by two angels, she flutters down with the Christ child into a torch-lighted street scene.

Illuminated in the artist's landmark chiaroscuro style (featuring pronounced contrasts of light, *chiaro*, and deep shadow, *scuro*), a corpse is being carried away for burial, a nude beggar is being clothed, and—this artist never pulled any punches—a starving prisoner suckles a woman.

The Artist

Caravaggio, as with most geniuses, was a difficult artist and personality. His romantic bad-boy reputation as the original bohemian, complete with angry, nihilistic, rebel-with-a-cause sneer and roistering lifestyle, has dominated interpretations of his revolutionary oeuvre, undermining its intense religiosity, in which the act of painting almost becomes an act of penance.

This is perhaps understandable—most of the documents pertaining to his life relate to his problems with the law and make for a good story indeed (he came to Naples after killing a man in a bar brawl in Rome, where his cardinal patrons could no longer protect him). But in spite of (or perhaps because of) his personal life, Caravaggio painted some of the most moving religious art ever produced in the West, whittling away all the rhetoric to reveal the emotional core of the subject.

His genuine love of the popular classes and for the "real" life of the street found expression in his use of ordinary street folk as models—he modeled the face of the Virgin in the *Seven Acts of Mercy* on a local prostitute. If his art seems to surge directly from the gut, his famous "objectivity" of observation and reduced palette have clear antecedents in paintings from his home region in northern Italy. The simplicity and warts-and-all depictions of his characters show a deeply original response to the Counter-Reformation writings on religious art by Carlo Borromeo, a future saint, also from Lombardy.

The Legacy

The *Seven Acts of Mercy*, the first altarpiece commissioned for the new church of the charitable institution, has been called "the most important religious painting of the 17th century" by the great 20th-century Italian art critics Roberto Longhi and Giuliano Argan. This astonishing painting immediately inspired the seven imitative Acts of Mercy individually depicted by other Neapolitan artists on the remaining seven walls of the same chapel, and the painting could lay claim to having kick-started the Neapolitan Baroque, with visual relations being expressed purely in terms of dramatic light and shadow, further exalting the contrasts of human experience.

Did You Know?

The notorious bad boy of Italian painting, Caravaggio (1571–1610) is considered one of the greatest painters of all time. He is celebrated for his dramatic use of light and shadow.

🌐 *www.piomontedellamisericordia.it* 🎫 *€8* ⏲ *Closed Sun. afternoon* Ⓜ *Cavour, Duomo.*

San Domenico Maggiore

RELIGIOUS BUILDING | One of the Centro Storico's largest churches, this Dominican house of worship was originally constructed by Charles I of Anjou in 1238. Legend has it that a painting of the crucifixion spoke to St. Thomas Aquinas when he was at prayer here. Three centuries later a fire destroyed most of this early structure, and in 1850 a neo-Gothic edifice rose in its place, complete with a nave of awe-inspiring dimensions. In the second chapel on the right (if you enter through the north door) are remnants of the earlier church—14th-century frescoes by Pietro Cavallini, a Roman predecessor of Giotto. Note the depiction of Mary Magdalene dressed in her own hair, and, in front, the crucifixion of Andrew as a devil strangles his judge, the Prefect Aegeas, just below. Along the side are some noted funerary monuments, including those of the Carafa family, whose chapel, to the left of Cosimo Fanzago's 17th-century altar, is a beautiful Renaissance-era set-piece. The San Carlo Borromeo chapel features an excellent *Baptism of Christ* (1564), by Marco Pino, a Michelangelo protégé. Other interesting works are the unusual *Madonna di Latte,* in the Cappella di S. Maria Maddalena, and a beautiful Madonna by Agostino Tesauro in the Cappella San Giovanni. A Ribera painting in the San Bartolomeo chapel depicts the saint's martyrdom. Near the back of the church, looking like a giant gold peacock's tail, is the so-called Machine of 40 Hours, a devotional device for displaying the sacrament for the 40 hours between Christ's burial and resurrection.

Adjacent to the church is its brilliantly restored Dominican monastery, where Saint Thomas Aquinas studied and taught. Virtual photographs outside the Chapter Hall show how the monastery, parts of which date to the 13th century, would have looked before the suppression of monasteries under Napoleon. The hall itself contains a significant fresco of the Crucifixion by the late 17th-century Sicilian painter Michele Ragolia, and the ubiquitous Baroque master Fanzago is responsible for the stuccowork. Note the false windows, a work of optical illusion common to the period.

The standout work in the nearby **Grand Refectory** is Domenico Vaccaro's *Last Supper* mural, in which Christ comforts John while Judas, clutching a moneybag, glares at something else. Another mural in the Refectory depicts a famous incident from Saint Thomas Aquinas's life here. Christ is shown directing at Thomas the words, *Bravo Tommaso che parlasti bene di me.* (Well done, Thomas, for speaking well of me.) Visible in the Refectory are the remains of the stations where the monks would wash their hands before eating, but more recently it served as a law court. Two Camorra bosses—Raffaele Cutolo and Pupetta Maresca—were sentenced here as late as the 1990s.

Also of note are the cloisters, originally for about a hundred monks, now less than five remain. It was here that Thomas Aquinas lived and studied and taught from 1272 to 1274. A magnificent doorway by Marco Bottiglieri marks his cell, now a chapel that can be visited as part of the guided tour. ✉ *Piazza San Domenico Maggiore 8, Centro Storico* ☎ *081/459188* 🌐 *www.museosandomenicomaggiore.it* 🎫 *Church free, museum from €5* Ⓜ *Dante.*

San Gennaro Mural

PUBLIC ART | Internationally renowned Neapolitan-Dutch street artist Jorit completed this 50-foot mural in September 2015 to honor the feast-day of the city's patron saint on the 19th. Where Spaccanapoli meets Via Duomo, politicized Jorit depicts the martyr wearing a backpack in homage to the immigration crisis and, in a nod to Caravaggio, used the face of a factory-worker friend. Jorit also has murals, including Diego Maradona and Che Guevara, in the Parco dei Murales in San Giovanni di Teduccio, 3 miles to the east, and in Vomero. ✉ *Via Vicaria Vecchia, Centro Storico* 🌐 *www.jorit.it* Ⓜ *Duomo.*

San Giuseppe dei Ruffi

CHURCH | Every morning at 7:30 am (and 9:30 on Sunday), the Perpetue Adoratrici (Sacramentine nuns) beautifully sing early mass beneath Francesco de Mura's *The Paradise,* inside this late-17th-century church. Dressed in immaculate white and red habits, the nuns, at the end of the celebration, prostrate themselves before the altar, which stretches upward with layer after Baroque layer of Dionisio Lazzari's sumptuous gold and marble (1686), topped by the putti and the figures of Hope and Charity by Matteo Bottigliero (1733). Upon entering or exiting, take note of San Giuseppe dei Ruffi's dramatically Baroque facade, designed, as was the interior, by Lazzari, a renowned architect and sculptor. Hearing the nuns sing is a unique, if little known, Naples experience, and well worth rising early for. ✉ *Piazza San Giuseppe dei Ruffi 2, half block from Duomo, Centro Storico* ☎ *081/449239* Ⓜ *Cavour.*

San Gregorio Armeno

CHURCH | This convent is one of the oldest and most important in Naples. Set on Via San Gregorio Armeno, the street lined with Naples's most adorable presepi, the convent is landmarked by a picturesque campanile. The nuns who lived here, often the daughters of Naples' richest families, must have been disappointed with heaven when they arrived—banquets here outrivaled those of the royal court, hallways were lined with paintings, and the church was filled with gilt stucco and semiprecious stones. Described as "a room of Paradise on Earth" by Carlo Celano and designed by Niccolò Tagliacozzi Canale, the church has a highly detailed wooden ceiling, uniquely decorated choir lofts, shimmering organs, illuminated shrines, and important Luca Giordano frescoes of scenes of the life of St. Gregory, whose relics were brought to Naples in the 8th century from Byzantium. The newly restored Baroque fountain with Matteo Bottiglieri's 17th-century Christ and the Samaritan Woman statues is in the center of the convent's cloister (entrance off the small square up the road). You can gain access from here to the nuns' gallery shielded by 18th-century jalousies and see the church from a different perspective, as well as to the Salottino della Badessa—generally not on view, as this is still a working convent—and other areas preserved as magnificent 18th-century interiors. ✉ *Piazzetta San Gregorio Armeno 1, Centro Storico* ☎ *081/5520186* 🎫 *Cloister €4* Ⓜ *Cavour, Duomo.*

★ **San Lorenzo Maggiore**

RELIGIOUS BUILDING | One of the city's unmissable sights has a travel-through-time descent to the Roman and Greek eras, as well as the grandest medieval church of the Decumano Maggiore. The Archaeological Area explores the original streets below the bustling Centro Storico, first with the Roman law courts and then down a level to the streets, markets, and workshops on the *cardo* (north–south road) crossing the *decumani* (east–west road) of the 1st century BC Neapolis.

The church of San Lorenzo features a very unmedieval facade of 18th-century splendor. Due to the effects and threats of earthquakes, the church was reinforced and reshaped along Baroque lines in the 17th and 18th centuries. Begun by Robert d'Anjou in 1270 on the site of a previous 6th-century church, the church has a single, barnlike nave that reflects the Franciscans' desire for simple spaces with enough room to preach to large crowds. A grandiose triumphal arch announces the transept, and the main altar (1530) is the sculptor Giovanni da Nola's masterpiece; this is a copy of the original, now disappeared, pedestal. Also found here is the church's most important monument: the tomb of Catherine of Austria (circa 1323), by Tino da Camaino, among the first sculptors to introduce the Gothic style into Italy.

The apse, designed by an unknown French architect of great caliber, is pure French Angevin in style, complete with an ambulatory of nine chapels covered by a magnificent web of cross arches. The left transept contains the 14th-century funerary monument of Carlo di Durazzo and yet another Cosimo Fanzago masterpiece, the Cappellone di Sant'Antonio.

Tickets to the excavations also give access to the Museo dell'Opera di San Lorenzo, installed in the 16th-century palazzo around the *torre campanaria* (bell tower). In Room 1 ancient remains from the Greek agora beneath combine with modern maps to provide a fascinating impression of import and export trends in the 4th century BC. The museum also contains ceramics dug up from the Swabian period, many pieces from the early Middle Ages, large tracts of mosaics from the 6th-century basilica, and helpful models of how the ancient Roman forum and nearby buildings must have looked. An app is available to do further justice to a place that exists in several historical dimensions. ✉ *Via dei Tribunali 316, Centro Storico* ☎ *081/2110860* 🌐 *www.laneapolissotterrata.it* 🎫 *Excavations and museum €9* Ⓜ *Cavour, Dante.*

San Paolo Maggiore

RELIGIOUS BUILDING | Like the nearby Santi Apostoli, this church was erected for the Theatin fathers in the late 16th century (from 1524), the period of their order's rapid expansion. This was another instance where Francesco Grimaldi, the (ordained) house architect, erected a church on the ruins of an ancient Roman temple, then transformed it into a Christian basilica. Spoils from the temple survive in the present incarnation, especially the two monumental Corinthian columns on the facade. An earthquake knocked down the original facade in 1688, and damage during World War II, coupled with decades of neglect, led to further deterioration that has since been reversed. Two large murals by Francesco Solimena in the sacristy have been restored. In the first, Simon Magus is depicted flying headlong down to Earth as biblical and Neapolitan figures ignore him. Similarly spectacular is the fresco depicting the imminent conversion of Saul: illuminated by a light-projecting cloud, the future Saint Paul tumbles off a horse in the picture's center. The richly decorated Santuario di San Gaetano is below the church, housing Saint San Gaetano's remains. ✉ *Piazza San Gaetano, Centro Storico* ☎ *081/454048* Ⓜ *Cavour, Duomo.*

San Severo al Pendino

CHURCH | Erected in the 16th century atop a previous church, this building has evolved many times—from the church of San Severo into a private palace, a monastery later suppressed by Napoleon, a state archive, a World War II bomb shelter, and an earthquake-damaged relic—before a long and painstaking renovation restored its luster. To the right of the nave, high above a door, rests the tomb of Charles V's general—and original church benefactor—Giovanni Bisvallo. In addition to its aesthetic highlights, the complex also provides a telling lesson on mortality. Aboveground one can view the grandeur of monuments to the dead. Less grandly, a brief excursion downstairs reveals the *scolatoi*; these are draining holes where the recently deceased, seated upright and left to be drained of bodily fluids, were visited daily by Dominican monks seeking to reinforce their sense of the fragility of human existence. ✉ *Via Duomo 286, Centro Storico* 🌐 *www.comune.napoli.it* 🎫 *Free* Ⓜ *Duomo.*

The unique majolica-decorated cloister at Santa Chiara serves as a tranquil oasis amid the hectic Centro Storico.

Sant'Angelo a Nilo

CHURCH | Amid this church's graceful interior is the earliest evidence of the Renaissance in Naples: the funerary monument (1426–27) of Sant'Angelo's builder, Cardinal Brancaccio, sculpted by the famous Donatello and the almost-as-famous Michelozzo. The front of the sarcophagus bears Donatello's contribution, a bas-relief *Assumption of the Virgin*; upheld by angels, the Virgin seeming to float in air. Built in the late 1300s, the church was redesigned in the 16th century by Arcangelo Guglielmelli. ✉ *Piazzetta Nilo, along Via San Biagio dei Librai, Centro Storico* ☎ *081/2110860* 🎫 *Free* Ⓜ *Università*.

★ Santa Chiara

RELIGIOUS BUILDING | Offering a stark and telling contrast to the opulence of the nearby Gesù Nuovo, Santa Chiara is the leading Angevin Gothic monument in Naples. The fashionable house of worship for the 14th-century nobility and a favorite Angevin church from the start, the church of St. Clare was intended to be a great dynastic monument by Robert d'Anjou. His second wife, Sancia di Majorca, added the adjoining convent for the Poor Clares to a monastery of the Franciscan Minors so she could vicariously satisfy a lifelong desire for the cloistered seclusion of a convent. This was the first time the two sexes were combined in a single complex. Built in a Provençal Gothic style between 1310 and 1328 (probably by Gagliardo Primario) and dedicated in 1340, the church had its aspect radically altered, as did so many others, in the Baroque period. A six-day fire started by Allied bombs on August 4, 1943, put an end to all that, as well as to what might have been left of the important cycle of frescoes by Giotto and his Neapolitan workshop. The church's most important tomb towers behind the altar. Sculpted by Giovanni and Pacio Bertini of Florence (1343–45), it is, fittingly, the tomb of the founding king: the great Robert d'Anjou, known as the Wise. Nearby are the tombs of Carlo, duke of Calabria, and his wife, Marie de Valois, both by Tino da Camaino.

Around the left side of the church is the Chiostro delle Clarisse, the most famous cloister in Naples. Complemented by citrus trees, the benches and octagonal columns comprise a light-handed masterpiece of painted majolica designed by Domenico Antonio Vaccaro, with a delightful profusion of landscapes and light yellow, azure, and green floral motifs realized by Donato and Giuseppe Massa and their studio (1742). ✉ *Piazza Gesù Nuovo, Centro Storico* ☎ *081/5516673* 🌐 *www.monasterodisantachiara.it* 🎫 *Museum and cloister €6* ⏲ *Closed Sun. afternoon* Ⓜ *Dante, Università.*

Santi Apostoli

CHURCH | This Baroque church in a basic Latin-cross style with a single nave shares the piazza with a contemporary art school in a typically anarchic Neapolitan mix. The church, designed by the architect Francesco Grimaldi for the Theatin fathers and erected between 1610 and 1649, replaced a previous church, itself constructed on the remains of a temple probably dedicated to Mercury. Santi Apostoli is worth a quick peek for its coherent, intact Baroque decorative scheme. Excellent paintings (circa 1644) by Giovanni Lanfranco each narrate a different martyrdom, and there are works by his successors, Francesco Solimena and Luca Giordano. An altar in the left transept by Francesco Borromini is the only work in Naples by this noted architect whose freedom from formality so inspired the exuberance of the Baroque. ✉ *Largo Santi Apostoli 9, Centro Storico* ☎ *081/299375* 🎫 *Free* Ⓜ *Cavour.*

Restaurants

Amico Bio - Sorriso Integrale

$ | **VEGETARIAN** | A vegetarian's paradise in a leafy courtyard, the menu here changes with every meal, depending on the season's produce. All ingredients are organic, as are the wines; try the grilled setan or the fried pumpkin in the late summer. **Known for:** quiet courtyard location; a respite from pasta and pizza; fine vegetarian fare. $ *Average main: €9* ✉ *Vico San Pietro a Majella 6, Piazza Bellini, Centro Storico* ☎ *081/455026* 🌐 *www.sorrisointegrale.com* Ⓜ *Dante.*

Biancomangaire-La Vecchia Cantina

$ | **NEOPOLITAN** | On a rather dark side street in the scruffier section of the Centro Storico, this place is well worth seeking out for its combination of old-style Neapolitan hospitality and attention to the quality of its food and wine. The place is run as a family affair, much like a typical Neapolitan household, and everyone who comes here seems to know each other. **Known for:** Neapolitan hospitality; vast wine list; convivial atmosphere. $ *Average main: €11* ✉ *Via S. Nicola alla Carità 13–14, Centro Storico* ☎ *081/5520226* ⏲ *No dinner Sun.* Ⓜ *Dante.*

★ **Di Matteo**

$ | **PIZZA** | Every pizzeria along Via dei Tribunali is worth the long wait—and trust us, all the good ones will be jam-packed—but just one can claim to have served a U.S. President: Bill Clinton enjoyed a margherita here when the G8 was held in Naples in 1994. **Known for:** top value, including filling pizza fritta (fried); funny pics of Clinton and the "Pizzaiolo del Presidente" Ernesto Cacialli in 1994; functional decor and pizzaioli working at front. $ *Average main: €6* ✉ *Via Tribunali 94, Centro Storico* ☎ *081/455262* 🌐 *www.pizzeriadimatteo.com* Ⓜ *Cavour, Dante.*

Gino Sorbillo

$ | **PIZZA** | **FAMILY** | There are a few restaurants called Sorbillo along Via dei Tribunali; this is the one with the crowds waiting outside and is world-renowned. Order the same thing the locals come for: a basic Neapolitan pizza (try the unique pizza al pesto or the stunningly simple marinara—just tomatoes and oregano). **Known for:** head honcho Gino is a celebrity and pizza ambassador; leave your name at the door and listen to be called;

the crowd waiting outside. $ *Average main: €10* ✉ *Via dei Tribunali 32, Centro Storico* ☎ *081/446643* 🌐 *www.sorbillo.it* ⏲ *Closed Sun.* M *Dante.*

La Campagnola

$ | **SOUTHERN ITALIAN** | This well-known trattoria–wine shop sees everyone from foodies to students and professors from the nearby university. The menu on the wall's blackboard changes daily, but there is always a good selection of pastas, meat, fish, and vegetable side dishes. **Known for:** efficient service; pleasing pastel decor; no-nonsense dining. $ *Average main: €9* ✉ *Via Tribunali 47, Centro Storico* ☎ *081/459034* M *Dante, Cavour.*

La Cantina di Via Sapienza

$ | **SOUTHERN ITALIAN** | With a balanced array of mainly land-based cuisine, owner-manager Gaetano's unpretentious eatery attracts students and young professionals, mainly regulars from the school of medicine around the corner. It's busy and small (expect to share a table—and if your fellow diners are not shy, why should you be?), but the prices can't be beat and the daily selection of a good dozen vegetable side plates merits a detour of its own, even if you're not a vegetarian. **Known for:** seasonal dishes with lots of veggies; simple, home-cooked meals; delicous pasta e patate. $ *Average main: €9* ✉ *Via Sapienza 40, Centro Storico* ☎ *081/459078* 🌐 *www.cantinadiviasapienza.it* ⏲ *Closed Sun., and Aug. No dinner* M *Dante.*

La Taverna dell'Arte

$$ | **SOUTHERN ITALIAN** | As its name suggests, this gracious trattoria atop a flight of steps on a small side street near Naples's main university is popular with actors, but it manages to remain welcomingly low-key. Warmed with touches of wood, it prides itself on its fresh interpretations of Neapolitan classics: excellent salami, mozzarella, and frittura among the appetizers, cabbage soup fragrant with good beef stock, and meat and fish grilled over wood. **Known for:** old-school surroundings; Neapolitan cuisine; thespian atmosphere. $ *Average main: €15* ✉ *Rampe San Giovanni Maggiore 1/a, Port* ☎ *081/5527558* 🌐 *www.tavernadellarte.it* ⏲ *Closed Sun., and last 2 wks in Aug. No lunch* M *Universtà.*

L'Etto

$ | **SOUTHERN ITALIAN** | The premise of this innovative eatery is to weigh the delicacies diners choose from the adventurous buffet and charge by the pound. In recent times they have introduced a menu of fixed-price bowls, a Neapolitan variation of Hawaiian poke—the *squisita* (exquisite) includes rice, octopus, onions and cherry tomatoes, and there is also a vegan option. **Known for:** selling meals by the pound; communal eating area; Neapolitan poke. $ *Average main: €14* ✉ *Via Santa Maria di Costantinopoli 102, Centro Storico* ☎ *081/19320967* 🌐 *www.ettoexperience.it* ⏲ *No dinner Thurs.* M *Dante, Museo.*

Le Sorelle Bandiera

$ | **PIZZA** | For a mere €8, you can eat under a bust of Queen Margherita herself, otherwise known as the Pizza Queen, whose name inspired the traditional pizza. The dough here is kept in a tufa-stone area, allowing the restaurant to claim it is "geo-thermal." The slightly upmarket pizza is served on tables, which are set with majolica tiling unearthed during the excavation of the historic San Paolo convent, which was once located on the same corner as the restaurant, thus bolstering the sense of authenticity. **Known for:** outside seating area; geo-thermal pizza; lovely majolica-tiled tables. $ *Average main: €8* ✉ *Vico Cinquesanti 33, Centro Storico* ☎ *081/19503535* 🌐 *www.lesorellebandiera.com* M *Cavour, Dante.*

Lombardi a Santa Chiara

$ | **PIZZA** | Opposite the Palazzo Croce, home to the philosopher and historian Benedetto Croce, this is one of the city's most famous pizzerias, packed night after night. The young crowd heads down into the more boisterous basement, while the atmosphere upstairs is calmer and more congenial to conversation at standard decibel levels. **Known for:** lively basement; outside seating on Spaccanapoli; pizza-making tradition. $ *Average main: €8* ✉ *Via Benedetto Croce 59, Centro Storico* ☎ *081/5520780* 🌐 *www.lombardisantachiara.it* Ⓜ *Dante.*

O' Munaciello

$ | SOUTHERN ITALIAN | Right on Piazza Gesù, this restaurant is a good place to sit outside, relax, and people-watch after a tour around Spaccanapoli. It caters to diverse palates and budgets: pizzas are served here at lunchtime. **Known for:** good location on Piazza del Gesù; wide variety of menu options; all-day pizza. $ *Average main: €9* ✉ *Piazza del Gesù Nuovo 26–27, Centro Storico* ☎ *081/5521144* 🌐 *omunaciello.it* Ⓜ *Dante.*

Osteria da Carmela

$ | ITALIAN | Conveniently close to the archaeological museum, yet surprisingly off the tourist beat, this small eatery is patronized by *professori* from the nearby Academy of Fine Arts and theatergoers from the Teatro Bellini next door. A specialty here is the blend of seafood with vegetables—try the *tubettoni con cozze e zucchini* (tube-shape pasta with mussels and zucchini) or *paccheri al baccalà* (large pasta with codfish). **Known for:** wine list; friendly staff; location beside Teatro Bellini. $ *Average main: €11* ✉ *Via Conte di Ruvo 11–12, Centro Storico* ☎ *081/5499738* 🌐 *www.osteriadacarmela.it* ⏲ *Closed Sun.* Ⓜ *Dante.*

Palazzo Petrucci Pizzeria

$ | PIZZA | In a 17th-century mansion facing the grand Piazza San Domenico Maggiore, Palazzo Petrucci doesn't lack for dramatic settings for dining—under the vaulted ceiling of the former stables, near the pizzaiolo and oven action, outside in the piazza, or on the roof terrace at *giuglia* (obelisk) di San Domenico level. Expect classic *pizze, pizze fritte,* and some unusual topping combinations, alongside heaped salads and antipasti. **Known for:** craft beer, pizze fritte, and vegan options; atmospheric views and sounds over the piazza; grandest palazzo venue for a pizza feast. $ *Average main: €10* ✉ *Piazza San Domenico Maggiore 5–7, Centro Storico* ☎ *081/5512460* 🌐 *www.palazzopetruccipizzeria.it* ⏲ *Closed 2 wks in Aug.* Ⓜ *Dante.*

Pizzeria Giuliano

$ | PIZZA | A favorite haunt of students from the adjacent school of architecture, Giuliano has an old-style glass cabinet where the *arancini* are kept. These fried rice balls are the size of tennis balls, and you'll also find deep-fried pizzas, filled with mozzarella, tomato, prosciutto, or ricotta, which can fill that yawning void in your stomach—even if you have to sit down on the steps in the square afterward to recover. **Known for:** wide range of fried goodies; bustling atmosphere; no-nonsense pizzas. $ *Average main: €6* ✉ *Calata Trinità Maggiore 31–33, Centro Storico* ☎ *081/5510986* 🌐 *www.pizzeriagiuliano.com* Ⓜ *Dante.*

Ristorante Bellini

$ | NEOPOLITAN | Set on a proud perch on the corner of the chicly bohemian Piazza Bellini for more than 70 years, this spot is worth visiting just to observe the waiters, who all seem to have just stepped off the stage of a Neapolitan comedy. But if the neighborhood remains scruffy, this staple Neapolitan restaurant proudly retains its old-world feel. **Known for:** choice of pizza or pasta dishes; efficient staff; location in Piazza Bellini. $ *Average main: €13* ✉ *Via Santa Maria di Costantinopoli 79, Centro Storico* ☎ *081/459774* ⏲ *Closed Aug. No dinner Sun.* Ⓜ *Dante, Museo.*

Tandem

$ | ITALIAN | Come here to taste traditional Neapolitan *ragù,* a meat-based sauce generally served with pasta and prepared from cuts of beef and pork. At Tandem, local cervellatine sausages are included in the sauce. **Known for:** traditional cooking; outside seating; old school ragù.

Naples is for Coffee Lovers

Espresso was invented here and is still considered by the Neapolitans to be an essential and priceless part of their cultural patrimony (the word *espresso*, by the way, should probably be understood here in its meaning "pressed out," rather than the more common interpretation of "quick"). Italian bars (meaning coffee bars) are generally tied to a coffee roaster–distributor, as English pubs once were with brewers. The sponsoring brand is indicated with a sign on the outside, so you can choose your bar by looking for the sign of your favorite brand. Brands tend to be highly regional; the most widely advertised Neapolitan brand is Kimbo, but Borbone, Moreno, Caffè Nero, and Tico are considered superior by those in the know.

You won't find any double low-fat mochas with extra vanilla, although there are certain permitted variations: *corretto*, with a shot of grappa or the local moonshine thrown in; *al vetro*, in a glass; *macchiato*, "stained" with a burst of steamed milk; and, of course, cappuccino. Ask for *amaro* so the barman doesn't add a generous spoon of sugar and a *tazza fredda* (cold cup) to avoid burning your lips on the cup plucked from a sanitizing basin of boiling water. You will be given a glass of water (*bicchiere d'acqua*) to drink before your shot, to clean the palate.

On the whole, coffee is a Neapolitan sacred ritual with precise rules. Cappuccino, for instance, is essentially a breakfast beverage, accepted in the afternoon with a pastry but looked strangely at after a meal (some claim it's bad for the liver). Coffee is perhaps the one feature of life in which Neapolitans don't gild the lily. As with so much about the traditional cuisine here, why fix what works?

Average main: €8 Via Paladino 51, Centro Storico 081/19002468 www.tandemnapoli.it Dante.

Coffee and Quick Bites

Bar Nilo

$ | **CAFÉ** | Stop in for one of the best coffees in town opposite the Roman marble statue of Egyptian river god Nile and marvel at the Pop Art masterpiece homemade shrine to football giant Diego Maradona. Appropriately bearing the colors of Argentina's flag, Napoli's adopted hero is flanked by San Gennaro and Nuestra Senora de Lujan, a clipping from *La Gazzetta dello Sport* (Sports Gazette), and an ampoule containing tears from the fateful year (1991) when the champion left Naples and his team's winning streak promptly ended. **Known for:** Sacro Cappella di Diego Maradona; great coffee; bustling atmosphere. *Average main: €1 Bar Nilo, Via S. Biagio dei Librai 129, Centro Storico 081/5517029 Dante.*

Scaturchio

$ | **CAFÉ** | This is the quintessential Neapolitan pastry shop. Although the coffee is top-of-the-line and the ice cream and pastries are quite good—including the specialty, the *ministeriale*, a pert chocolate cake with a rum-cream filling—it's the atmosphere that counts here. **Known for:** convivial atmosphere; delicious pastries; a Neapolitan institution. *Average main: €2 Piazza San Domenico Maggiore 19, Centro Storico 081/5516944 www.scaturchio.it Dante.*

Vaco 'e Press

$ | **CAFÉ** | This is the perfect place to stop before or after your visit to the Museo Archeologico, a five-minute walk away.

The busy eatery is close to the metro station in Piazza Dante and has a wide variety of hot meals, pizzas, vegetable pies, and rolls. **Known for:** perfect for a quick bite; food outside lunch hour; self-service efficiency. *$ Average main: €5 ✉ Piazza Dante 87, Centro Storico ☎ 081/5499424 Ⓜ Dante.*

Hotels

Caravaggio Hotel

$$ | **HOTEL** | In a 17th-century palazzo on a tiny square opposite the chapel of Pio Monte della Miseriacordia, this place takes its name from the painter of the amazing *Sette Opere della Misericordia* altarpiece. **Pros:** great base for sightseeing; historic setting; nice lounge bar. **Cons:** neighborhood might be too rough around the edges for some travelers; Wi-Fi not available in all rooms; small rooms. *$ Rooms from: €130 ✉ Piazza Riario Sforza 157, Centro Storico ☎ 081/2110066 🌐 www.caravaggiohotel.it 16 rooms Free Breakfast Ⓜ Cavour, Duomo.*

Costantinopoli 104

$$ | **HOTEL** | An oasis of what Italians call *stile liberty* (Art Nouveau style), with impressive stained-glass fittings and striking artwork, this serene, elegant hotel is well placed for touring the Museo Archeologico Nazionale and the Centro Storico. **Pros:** pool (a rarity in Neapolitan hotels) and garden; convenient Centro Storico location; pleasant service. **Cons:** some rooms suffer from nightlife disturbance from Piazza Bellini; can be difficult to find; rooms getting dated. *$ Rooms from: €184 ✉ Via Costantinopoli 104, Centro Storico ☎ 081/5571035 🌐 costantinopoli104.it 19 rooms Free Breakfast Ⓜ Museo.*

Decumani Hotel de Charme

$$ | **HOTEL** | The 19th-century residence of Cardinal Sisto Riario Sforza, this charming hotel is an authentic grand palazzo experience. **Pros:** former home of a catholic cardinal; over-the-top breakfast room; central location. **Cons:** street facing rooms can be noisy; narrow staircase to first floor; can be hard to find. *$ Rooms from: €160 ✉ Via San Giovanni Maggiore Pignatelli 15, Centro Storico ☎ 081/5518188 🌐 www.decumani.com 39 rooms Free Breakfast Ⓜ Università.*

Ecumano Space

$$ | **HOTEL** | A modern hotel in the heart of the historic center, Ecumano opened in 2018 primarily as a leisure center and gym. **Pros:** the largest pool in the center; close to everything; parking on-site. **Cons:** the smell of chlorine; a lot of outside visitors to the gym; too modern for the Centro Storico. *$ Rooms from: €130 ✉ Vico Pallonetto Santa Chiara, Centro Storico ☎ 081/5802152 🌐 www.ecumano-space.hotel-naples.com 13 rooms Free Breakfast Ⓜ Dante.*

Hotel Neapolis

$ | **HOTEL** | On a narrow alley off the humming Via Tribunali, close to Piazza Bellini, this hotel looks out over the 13th-century Pietrasanta bell tower. **Pros:** great location in the historic center; data ports in every room; near lots of sights. **Cons:** small breakfast; on the third floor of a building with a tiny lift; street noise can be loud. *$ Rooms from: €110 ✉ Via Francesco Del Giudice 13, Centro Storico ☎ 081/4420815, 081/4420819 🌐 www.hotelneapolis.com 18 rooms Free Breakfast Ⓜ Dante.*

★ Hotel Palazzo Decumani

$$ | **HOTEL** | This contemporary upscale hotel near the Centro Storico's major sights occupies an early-20th-century palazzo, but you won't find heavy, ornate furnishings—the emphasis is on light and space, both in short supply in old Naples. **Pros:** guests-only lounge-bar; service on par with fancier hotels; large rooms and bathrooms. **Cons:** soundproofing not the best; some may find decor a tad sparse; can be hard to find—follow signs from Corso Umberto. *$ Rooms from: €180 ✉ Piazzetta Giustino Fortunato 8, Centro*

Storico ☎ *081/4201379* 🌐 *www.palazzodecumani.com* 28 rooms Free Breakfast Ⓜ Duomo.

 Nightlife

Nightlife in Naples begins well after the sun has gone down. If you're going to a club, don't even think about turning up before 11, and don't plan on going to bed much before 3. Yet if you're willing to stay up late enough, and prepared to hang around outside places—with the rest of the *perdi-tempo* ("time wasters")—where there's sometimes more going on in the street than in the clubs themselves, Naples offers distractions for night owls of all persuasions. The designer-clad young and not-so-young hang out in the area around Chiaia and Mergellina; a more artsy poststudent crowd congregates around Piazza Bellini; the rawer, punkier edge prefers to hang around on Piazza Dante or Piazza San Domenico. Clubs tend to open and close or change name, style, or ownership with bewildering rapidity, so be sure to check locally before planning a night out. The best way to find out what's going on is to keep your eyes on the flyers that cover the Centro Storico.

Many dance clubs issue a drink card (prices vary, €15 is average) at the door that must be returned when you leave, stamped to show you've consumed at least one drink. After the first or second drink, other drinks usually run less (about €5).

If chaotic nightlife is more than you can take after a day experiencing the all-too-chaotic daylife of Naples, there's the civilized option of the *enoteca,* not exactly a wine bar, but a place where you can stop for a drink or meet up with friends without having to shout over the music or hang around on the street outside for hours, and have something more substantial to eat than peanuts and pretzels.

BARS

Alter Ego

COCKTAIL LOUNGES | The most fashionable lounge bar in the Centro Storico caters to young trendsetters. ✉ *Via Constanipoli 105, Centro Storico* ☎ *081/19807771* 🌐 *www.facebook.com/alteregonapoli* Ⓜ *Museo.*

Caffè Intramoenia

CAFÉS | The granddaddy of all the boho bars in Piazza Bellini was set up as a bookstore in the late 1980s and still has its own small publishing house with a variety of interesting titles, historic prints, and photos. Seats in the heated veranda are at a premium in winter, though many customers sit outside year-round. ✉ *Piazza Bellini 70, Centro Storico* ☎ *081/451652* 🌐 *www.intramoenia.it* Ⓜ *Dante, Museo.*

Ex-Salumeria

BARS | This onetime delicatessen now serves its own flavored rum. Be sure to try the cinnamon-honey mix. ✉ *Via Candelora 1, Centro Storico* 🌐 *www.ronespeciado.com* Ⓜ *Università.*

Kestè

LIVE MUSIC | The cool chrome furnishings at Kestè contrast with the old arched ceiling inside, but try to get a table out in the beautiful square in front of the Orientale University, and mingle with the city's students. A DJ spins tunes, and there's live music on the tiny stage on weekends. ✉ *Largo S. Giovanni Maggiore 26, Centro Storico* ☎ *081/7810034* 🌐 *www.keste.it* Ⓜ *Università.*

Libreria Berisio

BARS | On a street populated by bookstores, this one is turned into a bar at night, serving wine and cocktails to the sound of live jazz or the DJ's chilled selections. ✉ *Via Port'Alba 28–29, Centro Storico* ☎ *081/5499090* 🌐 *www.facebook.com/Berisio* Ⓜ *Dante.*

Nea

BARS | A beautiful café and contemporary art gallery, Nea is a highly atmospheric spot to just hang out on student-filled Piazza Bellini, especially in fine weather at the tables outside or on the steps of the gorgeous university library. ✉ *Via Costantinopoli 53, Centro Storico* ☎ *081/451358* 🌐 *www.spazionea.it* Ⓜ *Museo, Dante.*

Portico 340

BARS | The first to open under the now throbbing *portici*on Via dei Tribunali, join in the fun as the owner offers free drinks in spot-games of *tombola*, a traditional Neapolitan raffle. ✉ *Via Tribunali 340, Centro Storico* ☎ *081/19518847* Ⓜ *Dante.*

Shanti 4rt Mu5ik Bar

BARS | Tucked behind the newspaper kiosk in Piazza Nilo, this Indian-styled outdoor bar is adorned with colorful hanging lanterns and dreamcatchers. By day sip a fresh fruit cocktail, but by night try something a little stronger. ✉ *Via G. Paladino 56/57, Centro Storico* ☎ *081/5514979* 🌐 *shanticlub.tumblr.com* Ⓜ *Dante.*

Superfly

BARS | Via Cisterna dell'Olio hosts the tiny but agreeably funky Superfly, with classic jazz on the speakers and a huge collage of punters' favorite albums lining the wall. ✉ *Via Cisterna Dell'Olio 12, Centro Storico* ☎ *347/1272178* 🌐 *www.facebook.com/soulbar.superfly* Ⓜ *Dante.*

MUSIC CLUBS

Bourbon Street

LIVE MUSIC | This small club in the historic district books jazz musicians and hosts jam sessions and live DJ sets. The cocktails are as good as the music. ✉ *Via Bellini 52, Centro Storico* ☎ *338/8253756* 🌐 *www.bourbonstreetjazzclub.com* Ⓜ *Dante.*

Volver

LIVE MUSIC | You can play board games while having a drink at Volver, a lounge that hosts live music, tango (you can take classes), and other events. ✉ *Via Bellini 56, Centro Storico* ☎ *081/0606630* 🌐 *www.volvercafe.it* Ⓜ *Dante.*

 Performing Arts

Lively and energetic yet also chaotic and often difficult to follow, the cultural scene in Naples reflects the city's charming yet frustrating character. Event schedules are published in daily newspapers, particularly *Il Mattino, La Repubblica,* and *Corriere della Sera,* or advertised on websites such as 🌐 *www.napolitoday.it*. Bear in mind, though, that they can't be relied on to reveal everything that is happening or the frequent last-minute changes of program or venue. Word of mouth (hotel staffers are often good sources) is your best source of information, and keep your eyes peeled for the theater and concert posters that wallpaper much of the city center. Neapolitans take their cinema seriously; several cinemas run "cineforums" one day a week to cater to discerning cinemagoers, and from the end of June to mid-September, the *comune* funds an open-air cinema to provide aficionados with a chance to catch up on movies missed during the year.

Modernissimo

FILM | This Italian-style multiplex is in the historical center of town, and shows films in their original language on Thursday nights. ✉ *Via Cisterna dell'Olio 59, Centro Storico* ☎ *081/5800254* 🌐 *modernissimo.stellafilm.stellafilm.it* Ⓜ *Dante.*

Teatro Bellini

CONCERTS | A gilded Belle Époque theater, the Teatro Bellini presents plays and concerts of a more traditional flavor. ✉ *Via Conte di Ruvo 14, Centro Storico* ☎ *081/5491266* 🌐 *www.teatrobellini.it* Ⓜ *Dante.*

Shopping

ART GALLERIES

Fondazione Morra Greco

ART GALLERIES | The influential collector Maurizio Morra Greco mounts shows by emerging artists in the recently renovated 15th-century Palazzo Caracciolo di Avellino. ✉ *Largo Avellino 17, Centro Storico* ☎ *081/210690* 🌐 *www.fondazionemorragreco.com* Ⓜ *Cavour.*

Lello Esposito

CRAFTS | Neapolitan artist Lello Esposito has his workshop here, just across the courtyard from what is more of a museum than a store. Renowned for his renderings of a popular puppet named Pulcinella (the prototype for Punch of Punch & Judy), you can see a statue of his creation at the top of Vico del Fico al Purgatorio, just off Via dei Tribunali. Lello also has an atelier in Brooklyn and has created works for Obama. ✉ *Palazzo Sansevero, Vico San Domenico Maggiore 9, Centro Storico* ☎ *081/5514171* 🌐 *www.lelloesposito.com* Ⓜ *Dante.*

BOOKS AND PRINTS

Colonnese

BOOKS | The antique wooden cabinets and tables at this old-fashioned bookstore are laden with volumes about art, local history, and esoterica. ✉ *Via San Pietro a Maiella 32/33, Centro Storico* ☎ *081/459858* 🌐 *colonnese.it* Ⓜ *Dante.*

Libreria Neapolis

BOOKS | A small store with many books about Neapolitan art and history, this place stocks a few English titles and has a wide selection of music CDs. ✉ *Via Duomo 80, Centro Storico* ☎ *081/5514337* 🌐 *www.librerianeapolis.it* Ⓜ *Cavour.*

CLOTHING AND ACCESSORIES

Oblomova

MIXED CLOTHING | The club set heads to perky Oblomova for vintage and handmade clothing and accessories, but also for books, vinyl, CDs, and even cassettes. ✉ *Via San Sebastiano 20, Centro Storico* ☎ *081/4420855* Ⓜ *Dante.*

CRAFTS AND GIFTS

Egraphe

STATIONERY | A tiny hole in the wall, Egraphe is crammed with notebooks of every style and size, different kinds of handmade papers, and unusual pens and pencils. ✉ *Piazza L. Miraglia 391, Centro Storico* ☎ *081/446266* 🌐 *www.egraphe.it* Ⓜ *Dante.*

Ferrigno

CRAFTS | Shops selling Nativity scenes cluster along the Via San Gregorio Armeno off Spaccanapoli, and they're all worth a glance. The most famous is Ferrigno. Although Maestro Giuseppe Ferrigno died in 2008, the family business continues, still faithfully using 18th-century techniques. ✉ *Via San Gregorio Armeno 8, Centro Storico* ☎ *081/5523148* 🌐 *www.arteferrigno.it* Ⓜ *Cavour, Duomo.*

Gallucci

CHOCOLATE | A small alleyway leading off the side of the Gesù Nuovo toward Via Toledo hides a little-known jewel that is worth the detour: Gallucci, founded in 1890, specializes in fruit-filled chocolates (cherry and grape are memorable) and a delightfully original local cult item: chestnuts filled with marsala. It also produces the most fantastically packaged Easter eggs—all with huge silver or gold bows—that you are ever likely to see. ✉ *Via Cisterna dell'Olio 6, Centro Storico* ☎ *081/5513148* 🌐 *www.galluccicisternadellolio.it* Ⓜ *Dante.*

Gay-Odin

CHOCOLATE | Chocolate lovers will be relieved to know that Gay-Odin, Naples's most famous *cioccolateria,* has nine stores around town, all recognizable by their inviting dark-wood Art Nouveau decor; try the signature chocolate forest cake (*foresta*) or the unusual "naked" chocolates (*nudi*), a suave mixture of chestnuts and walnuts, some with a whole coffee bean wrapped in the center. ✉ *Via Benedetto Croce 61, Centro Storico* ☎ *081/5510794* 🌐 *www.gay-odin.it* Ⓜ *Dante.*

Il Mosaico Artistico

CRAFTS | The art of mosaic making is still practiced in Naples, and can be seen in this tiny workshop. ✉ *Strada dell'Anticaglia 22, Centro Storico* ☎ *081/0332409* 🌐 *www.ilmosaicoartistico.it* Ⓜ *Cavour.*

La Scarabattola

CRAFTS | The store's Scuotto family creates Nativity scenes in both classic Neapolitan and contemporary styles, donating the *Presepe Favoloso* to the Basilica di Santa Maria in Sanità in 2021. Past customers include the Spanish royal family. ✉ *Via Tribunali 50, Centro Storico* ☎ *081/291735* 🌐 *www.lascarabattola.it* Ⓜ *Dante.*

Liuteria Calace

CRAFTS | Since 1825, several generations of the Calace family have contributed to this prestigious shop's reputation for exquisitely made mandolins. This is an active workshop, so phone ahead for an appointment. ✉ *Palazzo Sansevero, Vico San Domenico Maggiore 9, Centro Storico* ☎ *081/5515983* 🌐 *www.calace.it* Ⓜ *Dante.*

Ospedale delle Bambole

TOYS | **FAMILY** | In the courtyard of the 16th-century Palazzo Marigliano is this world-famous hospital for dolls. In business since 1850, it's a wonderful place to take kids (and their injured toys). It's closed Sunday. ✉ *Via San Biagio dei Librai 39, Centro Storico* ☎ *081/18639797* 🌐 *ospedaledellebambole.com* Ⓜ *Duomo.*

LEATHER GOODS

Bottega 21

LEATHER GOODS | Crafted bags and purses are made here while you watch. ✉ *Vico San Domenico Maggiore 21, Centro Storico* ☎ *081/0335542* 🌐 *www.bottega21.it* Ⓜ *Dante.*

MARKETS

Mercatino della Pignasecca

MARKET | The best place in the city for fruit and vegetables, this market can be found several blocks northwest of Piazza Carità off Via Toledo. ✉ *Centro Storico* Ⓜ *Montesanto.*

Piazza Garibaldi and Nearby

The first place many see in Naples thanks to the city's main train station, the Piazza is not a lot to hold your attention here. Recently completely rebuilt, it now features a swanky new underground shopping mall based around the train station, but is still a gathering point for street sellers and hawkers and is best avoided at night. The surrounding area has some notable churches as well as the famed Porta Capuana, one of the historic gates to the city walls.

The city's transport hub, this is where you will arrive if you travel by train or bus. A departure point for Pompeii and Sorrento, both metro lines stop here and it is also easily reached, and explored, on foot. Head southwest along Corso Umberto towards the Centro Storico, or northwest along Via Poerio for Porta Capuana and, a mile or so beyond, the botanical gardens.

Sights

Orto Botanico

GARDEN | Founded in 1807 by Joseph Bonaparte and Prince Joachim Murat as an oasis from hectic Naples, this is one of the largest of all Italian botanical gardens, comprising some 30 acres. Nineteenth-century greenhouses and picturesque paths hold an important collection of tree, shrub, cactus, and floral specimens from all over the world. Next to the Orto Botanico, with a 1,200-foot facade dwarfing Piazza Carlo III, is one of the largest public buildings in Europe, the Albergo dei Poveri, built in the 18th and 19th centuries to house the city's destitute and homeless; it's now awaiting an ambitious restoration scheme. The gardens can be visited on weekday mornings. ✉ *Via Foria 223, Carlo III* ☎ *081/2533937* 🌐 *www.ortobotanico.unina.it* 🎟 *Free* ⏲ *Closed weekends.*

Porta Capuana

NOTABLE BUILDING | Occupying a rather unkempt pedestrianized piazza, this elegant ceremonial gateway is one of Naples's finest landmarks of the Renaissance era. Ferdinand II of Aragon commissioned the Florentine sculptor and architect Giuliano da Maiano to build this white triumphal arch—perhaps in competition with the Arco di Trionfo found on the facade of the city's Castel Nuovo—in the late 15th century. As at Castel Nuovo, this arch is framed by two peperino stone towers, here nicknamed Honor and Virtue, while the statue of Saint Gennaro keeps watch against Mt. Vesuvius in the distance. Across Via Carbonara stands the medieval bulk of the Castel Capuano, once home to Angevin and Aragonese rulers until it was transformed in 1540 by the Spanish viceroy into law courts, a function it fulfilled until just a few years ago. On Sunday this is a meeting place for Naples's *extracomunitari* (immigrants), who chat in their native tongues—from Ukrainian and Polish to Twi and Igbo. ✉ *Piazza San Francesco, Carlo III* Ⓜ *Garibaldi.*

San Giovanni a Carbonara

CHURCH | An engaging complex of Renaissance architecture and sculpture, this church is named for its location during medieval times near the city trash dump, where refuse was burned and carbonized. The church's history starts in 1339, when the Neapolitan nobleman Gualtiero Galeota donated a few houses and a vegetable garden to Augustinian monks who ministered to the poor neighborhood nearby.

San Giovanni's dramatic piperno-stone staircase, with its double run of elliptical stairs, was modeled after a 1707 design by Ferdinando Sanfelice similar to other organ-curved stairways in Rome, such as the Spanish Steps. Cross the courtyard to the left of the main entrance and enter the rectangular nave. The first thing you see is the monument to the Miroballo family, which is actually a chapel on the opposite wall, finished by Tommaso Malvito and his workshop in 1519 for the Marchese Bracigliano; the magnificent statues in the semicircular arch immediately set the tone for this surprising repository of first-class Renaissance sculpture.

Dominating the skeletal main altar, which has been stripped of its 18th-century Baroque additions, is the 59-foot-tall funerary monument of King Ladislaus and Joan II, finished by Marco and Andrea da Firenze in 1428. A door underneath this monument leads to the Ser Caracciolo del Sole chapel, with its rare and beautiful original majolica pavement. The oldest produced in Italy, from a workshop in Campania, it shows the influence of Arab motifs and glazing technique.

The dating of the circular Caracciolo di Vico chapel, to the left of the altar, is the subject of debate. Usually given as 1517, with the sculptural decor complete by 1557, the design (often attributed to Tommaso Malvito) may go back to 1499 and thus precede the much more famous Tempietto in Rome, by Bramante, which it so resembles. Hanging to the right of the altar is the impressively restored 16th-century *Crucifixion* by Giorgio Vasari, and in the back chapel, some brightly colored frescoes by an anonymous 16th-century master, as well as an intriguing sculpture of a knight taking a nap in his armor. Because this great church is off the path of tour groups, you can absorb the ordered beauty of the decoration in peace. ✉ *Via San Giovanni a Carbonara 5, Decumano Maggiore* ☎ *081/295873* Ⓜ *Cavour.*

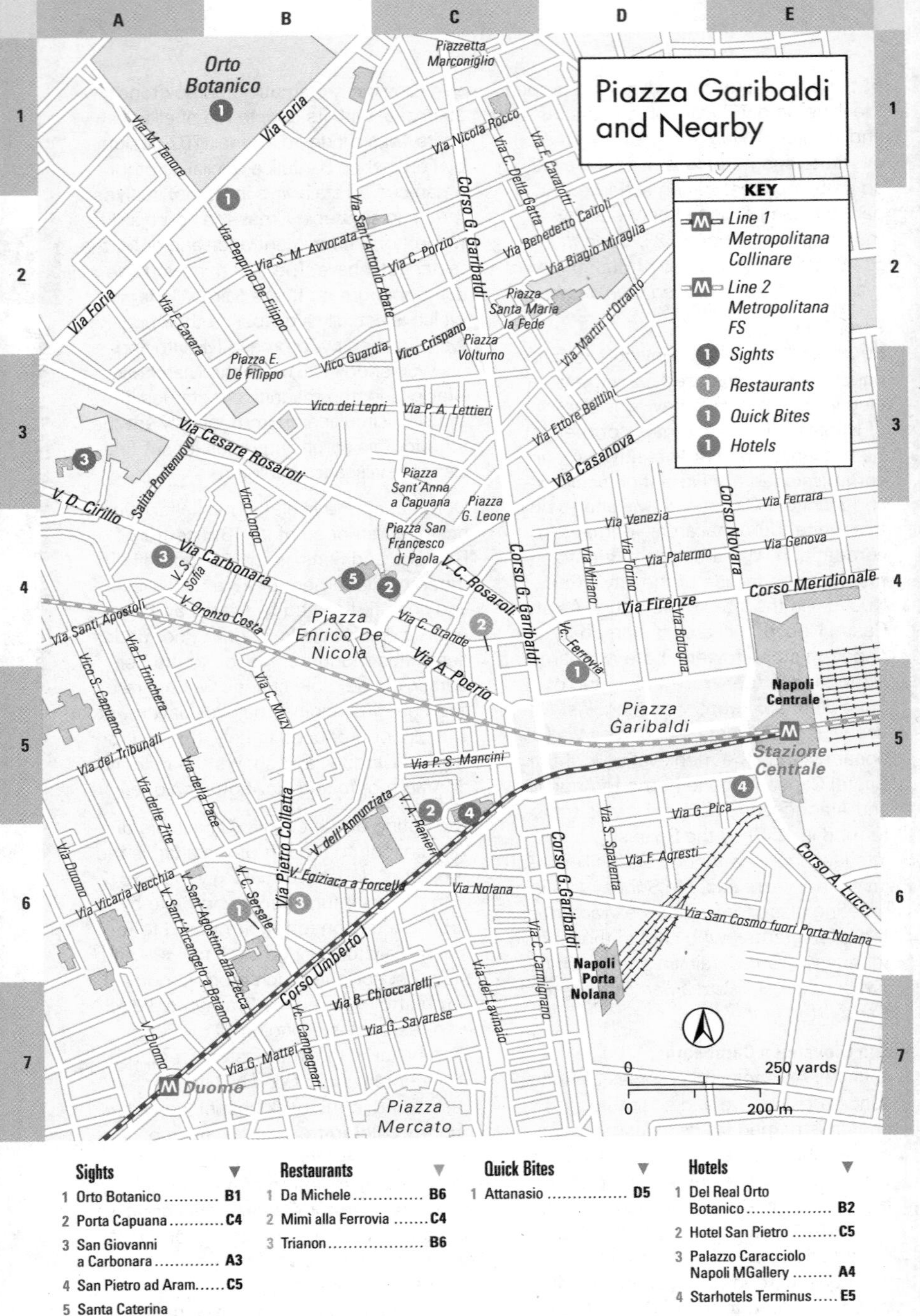

Sights		**Restaurants**		**Quick Bites**		**Hotels**	
1 Orto Botanico	B1	1 Da Michele	B6	1 Attanasio	D5	1 Del Real Orto Botanico	B2
2 Porta Capuana	C4	2 Mimì alla Ferrovia	C4			2 Hotel San Pietro	C5
3 San Giovanni a Carbonara	A3	3 Trianon	B6			3 Palazzo Caracciolo Napoli MGallery	A4
4 San Pietro ad Aram	C5					4 Starhotels Terminus	E5
5 Santa Caterina a Formiello	B4						

San Pietro ad Aram

CHURCH | On the site of Naples's oldest church, it contains an altar where Saint Peter supposedly preached while in Naples. Enter by the side door on Corso Umberto I, and you'll find the altar in the vestibule at the back, along with a 16th-century fresco depicting the preaching scene. The church also houses two canvases by Luca Giordano. Descend into the labyrinthine crypt on Monday and Wednesday afternoons and Sunday mornings, where the first Christian community in Europe was founded and the first six saints of Naples are buried. ✉ *Via Santa Candida 4, Piazza Garibaldi* Ⓜ *Garibaldi.*

Santa Caterina a Formiello

CHURCH | With museum-worthy paintings and sculptures on display, this church is a must-see of Naples. The Formiello in the name refers to the *formali,* the nearby underground aqueduct, which, according to history, the Aragonese also used to capture the town. The church and its dark piperno stone was designed for the Dominicans by the Tuscan architect Romolo Balsimelli, a student of Brunelleschi.

The side chapels are as interesting for their relics as they are for their art. In the Orsini chapel, are the elaborately framed remains of St. Vincent Martyr and other Dominican saints, while the fourth chapel displays some 20 skulls of the martyrs of Otranto, brought to Naples by King Alfonso in 1490 after the Ottoman sack of Otranto in 1480, when 813 Christians were executed for refusing to renounce their faith. This event is in the rather surrealistic altar painting of the beheading of Antonio Primaldo, whose decapitated body, through the strength of faith, stands upright to confound his Ottoman executioner.

In the fifth chapel, a cycle of paintings by Giacomo del Po depicts the life and afterlife of St. Catherine, while in the vault Luigi Garzi depicts the same saint in glory. Up in the faded dome painted by Paolo di Mattei, Catherine, together with the Madonna, implores the Trinity to watch over the city. ✉ *Piazza Enrico de Nicola 49, Porta Capuana* ☎ *081/444297* Ⓜ *Garibaldi.*

Restaurants

Da Michele

$ | PIZZA | You may recognize Da Michele from the movie *Eat Pray Love,* but for more than 140 years before Julia Roberts arrived, this place was a culinary reference point. Despite offering only two types of pizza—marinara (with tomato, garlic, and oregano) and Margherita (with tomato, mozzarella, and basil)—plus a small selection of drinks, it still manages to draw long lines. **Known for:** long lines outside the humble, historic HQ; marinara and Margherita only; pizza purists' favorite. $ *Average main: €6* ✉ *Via Sersale 1/3, off Corso Umberto, between Piazza Garibaldi and Piazza Nicola Amore, Piazza Garibaldi* ☎ *081/5539204* 🌐 *www.damichele.net* ⏲ *Closed Sun. and 2 wks in Aug.* Ⓜ *Garibaldi, Duomo.*

Mimì alla Ferrovia

$$ | NEOPOLITAN | Patrons of this Neapolitan institution have included the filmmaker Federico Fellini and that truly Neapolitan comic genius and self-styled aristocrat, Totò. It's in a fairly seedy area so take a taxi, especially at night, but it's worth it to sample Mimì's classics such as pasta e fagioli and the sea bass *al presidente,* baked in a pastry crust and enjoyed by visiting Italian presidents. **Known for:** fresh fish on display from the market; classic Neapolitan dishes; crammed with washed-out photos of Italian VIPs. $ *Average main: €18* ✉ *Via A. D'Aragona 19/21, Piazza Garibaldi* ☎ *081/5538525* 🌐 *www.mimiallaferrovia.it* ⏲ *Closed Sun. and last wk in Aug.* Ⓜ *Garibaldi.*

Trianon

$ | **PIZZA** | Across the street from its archrival Da Michele—but without its lines stretching outside—this is a classic pizzeria with a simple yet upscale Art Nouveau ambience expressed in soothing tile and marble. More relaxed and upmarket than its rival, Trianon does the classics (Margherita, marinara) in an exemplary manner, but you can also feast on pizza with sausage and broccoli greens. **Known for:** multitopping specialties; efficient service; almost 100 years of pizza making. *Average main: €8 Via P. Coletta 46, Piazza Garibaldi 081/5539426 www.pizzeriatrianon.it Garibaldi, Duomo.*

Coffee and Quick Bites

Attanasio

$ | **SOUTHERN ITALIAN** | For a hot-out-of-the-oven *sfogliatella,* Naples's tasty ricotta-filled pastry, try the justifiably famous Attanasio. You can grab one as soon as you get off the train; this place is hidden away off Piazza Garibaldi. **Known for:** oven-to-palate service; a great spot for a quick bite; tastiest sfogliatelle in town. *Average main: €1 Vico Ferrovia 2, Piazza Garibaldi 081/285675 www.sfogliatelleattanasio.it Closed Mon. Garibaldi.*

Hotels

Del Real Orto Botanico

$ | **HOTEL** | Opposite Naples's noted botanical gardens, this 18th-century building has been turned into a spacious hotel whose owner's attention to detail makes the place stand out. **Pros:** eight-minute taxi ride from the airport; short bus ride from city center; some rooms overlook the botanical gardens. **Cons:** noisy location; not a great area at night; far from other attractions. *Rooms from: €80 Via Foria 192, Piazza Garibaldi 081/4421528 www.hotelrealortobotanico.it 36 rooms Free Breakfast.*

Hotel San Pietro

$$ | **HOTEL** | A recent addition to the Naples lodging scene, this pleasant boutique hotel is tucked behind the beginning of Corso Umberto I. The soothing lobby and large bar area are filled with plush sofas, antiques, and Art Nouveau works. **Pros:** charming staff; wonderful roof garden; a hop, skip, and jump from the station. **Cons:** rooms are small; not the most pleasant of neighborhoods; a little far from the main sites. *Rooms from: €139 Via San Pietro ad Aram 18, Piazza Garibaldi 081/286040 www.sanpietrohotel.it 35 rooms Free Breakfast Garibaldi.*

Palazzo Caracciolo Napoli MGallery

$$ | **HOTEL** | Sleek, soigné, and swank, this hotel set in the majestic palace of the very majestic Caracciolos (one of the most gilded names in Neapolitan history) is definitely a diamond in the rough—the rough being its immediate neighborhood, which is a bit far from the tourist or historic quarters. **Pros:** multilingual receptionists; complimentary shuttle to Centro Storico; contemporary room decor. **Cons:** a bit far away from sights; not a lot going on nearby in the evening; rough neighborhood. *Rooms from: €149 Via Carbonara 111, Piazza Garibaldi 081/0160111 www.palazzocaracciolo.com 146 rooms Free Breakfast Garibaldi.*

Starhotels Terminus

$$ | **HOTEL** | A pastel oasis of calm amid hectic Piazza Garibaldi, this sleek, clean, and stylish hotel has up-to-date, comfortable rooms. **Pros:** clean and spacious; good for business travelers; next to train station. **Cons:** area can be dangerous at night; far from the port or the city center; Piazza Garibaldi is noisy, dirty, and ugly. *Rooms from: €140 Piazza Garibaldi 91, Piazza Garibaldi 081/7793111, 081/206689 www.starhotels.com 169 rooms Free Breakfast Garibaldi.*

Performing Arts

Made In Cloister

ARTS CENTERS | In the renovated cloister of the church of Santa Caterina a Formiello, this sleek gallery opened in 2014 with an exhibition of Laurie Anderson's paintings. They organize regular film screenings and music performances, with Patti Smith playing here in 2017. They're closed Sunday and Monday. ✉ *Piazza Enrico de Nicola 48, Piazza Garibaldi* ☎ *081/447252* 🌐 *www.madeincloister.com* 🎫 *€5* Ⓜ *Garibaldi.*

Teatro Trianon

CONCERTS | An old cinema refurbished to provide a "home for Neapolitan song," this theater mixes showings of classic Neapolitan movies with local comedies and comedy acts, and frequent concerts by traditional Neapolitan musicians. ✉ *Piazza Calenda 9, Piazza Garibaldi* ☎ *081/2258285* 🌐 *www.teatrotrianon.org.*

Shopping

MARKETS

Mercatino di Poggioreale

MARKET | Open four days a week (Friday–Monday), this market is a little farther out than most, but it has a vast selection of shoes in all styles and sizes, and at uniformly low prices. Clothes, antiques, and other items are also for sale. Some locals insist that the best bargains can be found on Friday. ✉ *Via Nuova Poggioreale, Piazza Garibaldi* 🌐 *www.facebook.com/Mercatocaramanico.*

Museo Archeologico Nazionale, La Sanità, and Capodimonte

It's only fitting that the Museo Archeologico Nazionale—the single most important and remarkable museum of Greco-Roman antiquities in the world (in spite of itself, some observers say)—sits in the upper *decumanus,* or neighborhood, of ancient Neapolis, the district colonized by the ancient Greeks and Romans. Happily, it's open all day (its core collection, that is). But if two hours are your limit for gazing at ancient art, nearby you can discover some of the lesser-known delights of medieval and Renaissance Naples. Churches here are repositories for magnificent 15th- and 16th-century art and sculpture.

If you're feeling intrepid you might like to deviate into La Sanità, one of Naples's most densely populated and once an uncomfortably lawless neighborhood, but now a go-to area for locals in the know, studded with legendary palaces and gilded churches as well as the fascinating, closed-at-time-of-writing, Cimitero delle Fontanelle.

The Bosco di Capodimonte is the crowning point of the vast mountainous plain that slopes down through the city to the waterfront area. Nearly 3 km (2 miles) removed from the crowds in the Centro Storico, the park is enjoyed by locals and visitors alike as a favored escape from the overheated city center. With picture-perfect views over the entire city and bay, it was first founded in the 18th century as a hunting preserve by Charles of Bourbon. Before long, partly to house the famous Farnese collection that he had inherited from his mother, he commissioned a spectacular Palazzo Reale for

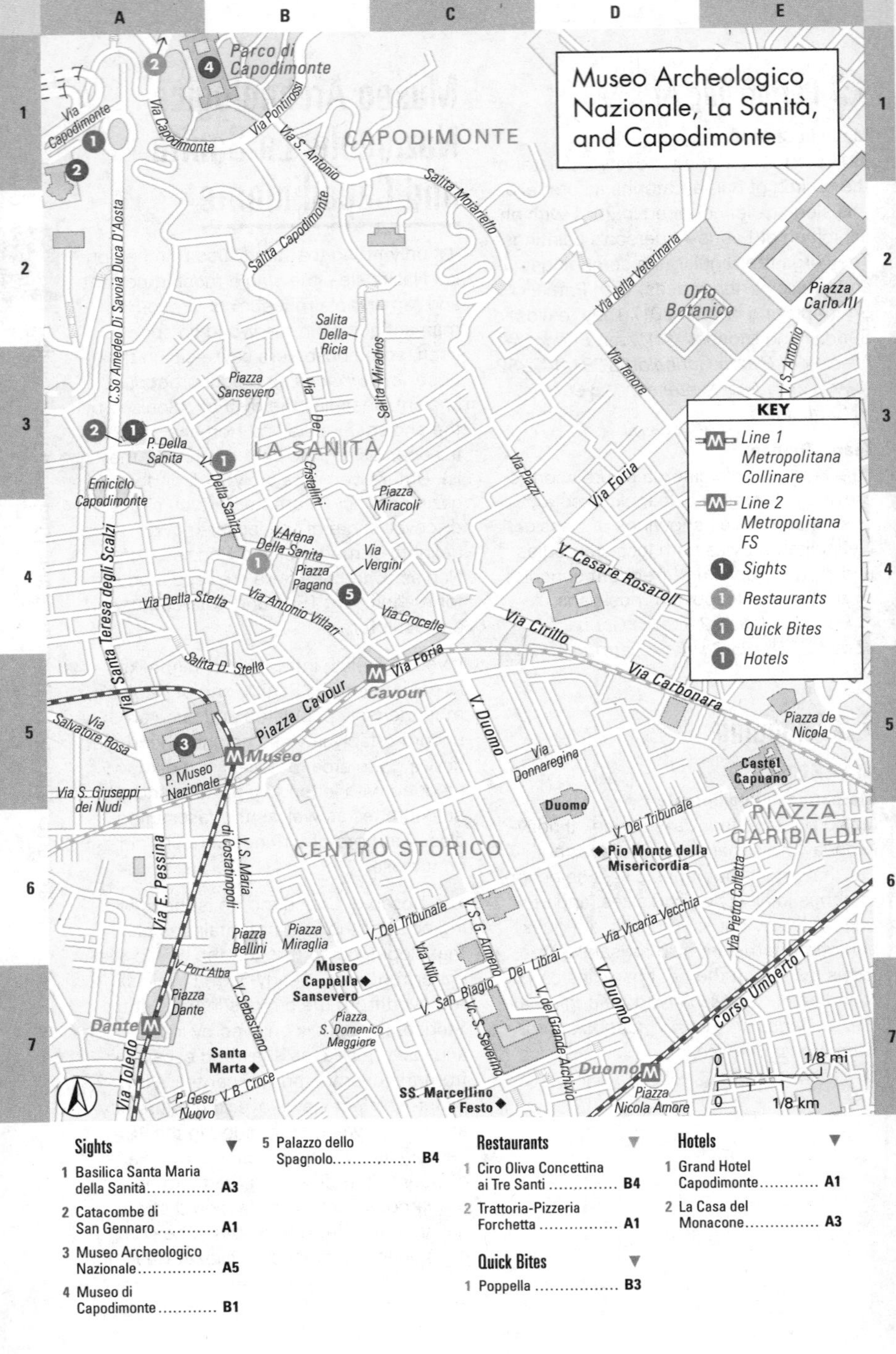

Museo Archeologico Nazionale, La Sanità, and Capodimonte
A
B
C
D
E
1
2
3
4
5
6
7
Parco di Capodimonte
Via Capodimonte
Via Capodimonte
Via Pontirossi
Via S. Antonio
CAPODIMONTE
Salita Moiariello
Salita Capodimonte
C.So Amedeo Di Savoia Duca D'Aosta
Via della Veterinaria
Orto Botanico
Piazza Carlo III
Salita Della Ricia
Salita Miradios
Via Tenore
V. S. Antonio
Piazza Sansevero
Via Dei Cristallini
P. Della Sanità
LA SANITÀ
V. Della Sanità
Emiciclo Capodimonte
Via Piazzi
Piazza Miracoli
Via Foria
V.Arena Della Sanità
Via Vergini
Piazza Pagano
Via Santa Teresa degli Scalzi
Via Della Stella
Via Antonio Villari
Via Crocelle
V. Cesare Rosaroll
Via Cirillo
Salita D. Stella
Via Foria
Piazza Cavour
Cavour
Via Carbonara
V. Duomo
Via Salvatore Rosa
Museo
P. Museo Nazionale
Via Donnaregina
Piazza de Nicola
Castel Capuano
Via S. Giuseppi dei Nudi
Duomo
V. Dei Tribunale
PIAZZA GARIBALDI
CENTRO STORICO
Pio Monte della Misericordia
Via E. Pessina
V.S. Maria di Costatinopoli
Via Pietro Colletta
V. Dei Tribunale
V.S.G. Armeno
Via Vicaria Vecchia
Piazza Bellini
Piazza Miraglia
Via Nilo
V. Port'Alba
Museo Cappella Sansevero
Dei Librai
V. Duomo
Corso Umberto I
Piazza Dante
V. Sebastiano
V. San Biagio
Vc. S. Severino
V. del Grande Archivio
Dante
Piazza S. Domenico Maggiore
Santa Marta
Via Toledo
P. Gesu Nuovo
V. B. Croce
SS. Marcellino e Festo
Duomo
Piazza Nicola Amore
0
1/8 mi
0
1/8 km
KEY
Line 1 Metropolitana Collinare
Line 2 Metropolitana FS
Sights
Restaurants
Quick Bites
Hotels
Sights
1 Basilica Santa Maria della Sanità A3
2 Catacombe di San Gennaro A1
3 Museo Archeologico Nazionale A5
4 Museo di Capodimonte B1
5 Palazzo dello Spagnolo B4
Restaurants
1 Ciro Oliva Concettina ai Tre Santi B4
2 Trattoria-Pizzeria Forchetta A1
Quick Bites
1 Poppella B3
Hotels
1 Grand Hotel Capodimonte A1
2 La Casa del Monacone A3

the park. Today this palace is the Museo di Capodimonte, which contains among its treasures the city's greatest collection of Old Masters paintings.

GETTING HERE AND AROUND

The metro stops Museo and Piazza Cavour take you to the museum and La Sanità. Bus 3M, known as the 3 Museums route, connects the lower city with the Catacombes of San Gennaro and Capodimonte. The more crowded routes C63, 168, and 178 also regularly climb the hill.

Sights

Basilica Santa Maria della Sanità

CHURCH | Dominican friars commissioned this Baroque, Greek cross–shape basilica, replete with majolica-tiled dome, in the early 17th century. The church acts as a small museum of the era's Counter-Reformation art—the most flagrantly devotional school of Catholic art—and includes no less than five Luca Giordano altarpieces. Note Giovan Vincenzo Forli's 17th-century *Circumcision* on the left. Elsewhere, the richly decorated elevated presbytery, complete with a double staircase, provides a note of color in the mostly gray-and-white decoration. The stairs to the right of the crypt provide access to the Catacombe di San Gaudioso, with visits every hour 10 am–1 pm, which includes a visit to the *Presepe Favoloso*, an elaborate Nativity scene donated to the church by renowned artisans the Scuotto brothers in 2021. ✉ *Via della Sanità 124, Sanità* ☎ *081/7443714* 🌐 *www.catacombedinapoli.it* 🎫 *Catacombs €9, includes visit to nearby Catacombe di San Gennaro* Ⓜ *Cavour.*

Catacombe di San Gennaro

RUINS | These catacombs—designed for Christian burial—date back at least as far as the 2nd century AD. This was where St. Gennaro's body was brought from Pozzuoli in the 5th century, after which the catacombs became a key pilgrimage center. The 45-minute guided tour of the two-level site takes you down a series of vestibules with frescoed niche tombs. Looming over the site is the imposing bulk of the early-20th-century Madre del Buon Consiglio church, whose form was apparently inspired by St. Peter's in Rome. Under the general site name of Catacombe di Napoli, these catacombs are now linked ticketwise with the Catacombe di San Gaudioso, in the Sanità district. ✉ *Via Capodimonte 13, next to Madonna del Buon Consiglio church, Capodimonte* ☎ *081/7443714* 🌐 *www.catacombedinapoli.it* 🎫 *€9, includes visit to Catacombe di San Gaudioso* 🕑 *Closed Sun. afternoon.*

★ **Museo Archeologico Nazionale** (*National Museum of Archaeology*)

HISTORY MUSEUM | Also known as MANN, this legendary museum has experienced something of a rebirth in recent years. Its unrivaled collections include world-renowned archaeological finds that put most other museums to shame, from some of the best mosaics and paintings from Pompeii and Herculaneum to the legendary Farnese collection of ancient sculpture. The core masterpiece collection is almost always open to visitors, while seasonal exhibitions feature intriguing cultural events, collaborations, and contemporary artists. Some of the newer rooms, covering archaeological discoveries in the Greco-Roman settlements and necropolises in and around Naples, have helpful informational panels in English. ✉ *Piazza Museo 19, Centro Storico* ☎ *081/4422111* 🌐 *mannapoli.it* 🎫 *€15* 🕑 *Closed Tues.* Ⓜ *Museo.*

★ **Museo di Capodimonte**

ART MUSEUM | The grandiose, 18th-century, Neoclassical, Bourbon royal palace houses fine and decorative art in 124 rooms. Capodimonte's greatest treasure is the excellent collection of paintings displayed in the Galleria Nazionale, on the palace's first and second floors. Aside from the artwork, part of the royal

The Salone della Meridiana, on the top floor of the Museo Archeologico, is one of the largest rooms in Europe.

apartments still has a collection of beautiful antique furniture (most of it on the splashy scale so dear to the Bourbons) and a staggering range of porcelain and majolica from the various royal residences. Note that due to ongoing renovation works, the royal apartments will be without air-conditioning until 2022. The main galleries on the first floor are devoted to the Farnese collection, as well as work from the 13th to the 18th century, including many pieces by Dutch masters, as well as an El Greco and 12 Titian paintings. On the second floor look for stunning paintings by Simone Martini (circa 1284–1344) and Caravaggio (1573–1610). For a contrast, don't miss the contemporary art collection, including Warhol's iconic version of Vesuvius. The palace is in the vast Bosco di Capodimonte (Capodimonte Park), which served as the royal hunting preserve and later as the site of the Capodimonte porcelain works. Covering 331 acres, it's the largest green area in Naples and was declared Italy's most beautiful garden in 2014. ✉ *Via Miano 2, Capodimonte* ☎ *081/7499111, 848/800288* 🌐 *capodimonte.cultura.gov.it, www.amicidicapodimonte.org* 🎟 *€14* ⏲ *Closed Wed.*

Palazzo dello Spagnolo

HISTORIC HOME | Built in 1738 for the Neapolitan aristocrat Marchese Moscati, this palazzo is famed for its external "hawk-winged staircase," believed to follow the design of star architect Ferdinando Sanfelice and decorated with sumptuous stucco and a bust and panel at the top of each flight. The palace was at one point owned by a Spanish nobleman, Don Tommaso Atienza, thus the name "dello Spagnolo." In the left corner of the courtyard in the back, a nondescript metal door leads to a tunnel running all the way to Piazza Carlo III—another example of the Neapolitan underground. The palace was immortalized in *Passione,* John Turturro's excellent film about Naples and music. ✉ *Via Vergini 19, Sanità* Ⓜ *Cavour.*

Worth the Trip

Reggia di Caserta. Located 16 miles northeast of the city, the palace known as the Reggia shows how Bourbon royals lived in the mid-18th century. Architect Luigi Vanvitelli devoted 20 years to its construction under Bourbon ruler Charles III, whose son, Ferdinand IV (1751–1825), moved in when it was completed in 1774. Both king and architect were inspired by Versailles, and the rectangular palace was conceived on a massive scale, with four interconnecting courtyards, 1,200 rooms, and a vast park. Though the palace is not as well maintained as its French counterpart, the main staircase puts the one at Versailles to shame, and the royal apartments are sumptuous. It was here, in what Eisenhower called "a castle near Naples," that the Allied High Command had its headquarters in World War II, and here that German forces in Italy surrendered in April 1945. There's a museum of items relating to the palace and the region. Most enjoyable are the gardens and parks, particularly the Cascades, adorned with sculptures of the goddess Diana and her maidens, and the landscaped English Garden at the far end. A shuttle bus will help you cover the 3-km (2-mile) path from the palace to the end of the gardens. You can also rent a bicycle just inside the park. Take the frequent—but slow—train service from Stazione Centrale. The palace is just across from the station. By car, leave the Naples-Caserta motorway at Caserta Sud and follow signs to the Reggia. Park in the underground lot opposite the palace. ✉ *Viale Douhet 2/a, Caserta* ☎ *0823/448084* 🌐 *reggiadicaserta.cultura.gov.it* 🎫 *Gardens €9, gardens and apartments €14* ⏲ *Closed Tues.*

Restaurants

Ciro Oliva Concettina ai Tre Santi

$ | **PIZZA** | In the 1954 film *L'Oro di Napoli* Sofia Loren sold fried pizza from a *basso* (a street-level room), something Concettina Flessigno Oliva had already been doing since three years earlier. Now one of Naples's most highly acclaimed pizzerias, her great-grandson's menu includes all the usual culprits as well as pizza wedges based on local in-season ingredients. **Known for:** a Neapolitan institution; waiting outside for a table; great pizza. [$] *Average main: €7* ✉ *Via Arena della Sanità 7 Bis, Sanità* ☎ *081/290037* 🌐 *www.pizzeriaoliva.it* ⏲ *No dinner Sun.* [M] *Cavour.*

Trattoria-Pizzeria Forchetta

$ | **SOUTHERN ITALIAN** | Just 50 yards from the main Capodimonte gate, this no-nonsense eatery has photos of its dishes prominently framing its entrance. Favored by locals as well as day trippers to the park and museum, the friendly owners will talk you through the day's specialities, as well as offering an inexpensive set menu. **Known for:** quick service; good value; close to the park. [$] *Average main: €8* ✉ *Via Miano 35, Capodimonte* ☎ *081/7410829.*

Coffee and Quick Bites

Poppella

$ | **SOUTHERN ITALIAN** | Famed for its *fiocco di neve* (snowflake), the deliciously creamy pastry ball was created in 2015 by this century-old pasticceria. **Known for:** fiocco di neve; mixing with the locals; a new Naples tradition. [$] *Average main: €1* ✉ *Via Arena alla Sanità, 28/29, Sanità* ☎ *081/455309* 🌐 *www.pasticceriapoppella.com* [M] *Cavour.*

Hotels

Grand Hotel Capodimonte
$ | **HOTEL** | Housed in a 19th-century Stigmatine Sisters convent, time seems to have stopped at this charming hotel at the base of the Capodimonte hill. **Pros:** sleep in an ex-convent; convenient to the motorway; good price. **Cons:** many rooms are noisy; off-site parking, €10; entrance on very busy road. *Rooms from: €80* *Via Capodimonte 3, Capodimonte* *081/3653494* *www.grandhotelcapodimonte.it* *34 rooms* *Free Breakfast.*

La Casa del Monacone
$ | **B&B/INN** | It's not every day you can be a "guest" of a famed 17th-century church, but this distinctive B&B was once part of the giant complex of Santa Maria della Sanità, the main landmark of the Rione Sanità quarter. **Pros:** practically inside the church; beautiful terrace; dynamic and friendly staff. **Cons:** hard to locate; terrace under a busy road; small bathrooms. *Rooms from: €65* *Via Sanità 124, Sanità* *081/7443714* *www.casadelmonacone.it* *6 rooms* *Free Breakfast* *Cavour.*

Nightlife

Antica Cantina Sepe
WINE BARS | This fourth-generation wine shop began a weekly evening aperitivo in 2016, with local and international bands performing for the gathered masses. This is the place to be on Thursday. *Via Vergini 55, Sanità* *081/454609* *Cavour.*

Shopping

Mercatino dei Vergini
MARKET | Groceries and household items are sold at this popular street market. *Via Vergini, Sanità* *Cavour.*

Toledo and the Port

Naples's setting on what is possibly the most beautiful bay in the world has long been a boon for its inhabitants—the expansive harbor has always brought great mercantile wealth to the city—and, intermittently, a curse. Throughout history, a who's who of Greek, Roman, Norman, Spanish, and French despots has quarreled over this gateway to Campania. Each set of conquerors recognized that the area around the city harbor—today occupied by the Molo Beverello hydrofoil terminal and the 1928 Stazione Marittima—functioned as a veritable welcome mat to the metropolis and consequently should be a fitting showcase of regal and royal authority. This had become imperative because of explosive population growth, which, by the mid-16th century, had made Naples the second-largest city in Europe, after Paris. With the mass migration of the rural population to the city, Naples had grown into a capricious, unplanned, disorderly, and untrammeled capital. Thus, the central aim of the ruling dynasties became the creation of a *Napoli nobilissima*—a "most noble" Naples.

The monuments they created remain prominent features of the city center: one of the most magnificent opera houses in Europe, a palace that rivals Versailles, an impregnable *castello* (castle), a majestic church modeled on Rome's Pantheon, and a 19th-century shopping galleria are landmarks that characterized the shifts among the ruling powers, from the French Angevins to the Spanish Habsburgs and Bourbons and, later, the postunification rise of the bourgeoisie and the regime of Mussolini. In contrast to the intense intimacy of the Centro Storico, the official center of Naples unrolls its majesty with great pomp along its spacious avenues and monumental piazzas.

Visited by Boccaccio and Giotto, massive Castel Nuovo sits near the shore of the Bay of Naples and once protected the heart of the medieval city.

GETTING HERE AND AROUND

The metro stops Toledo and Municipio bring you to the heart of this area, where all sights are within walking distance.

 Sights

★ Castel Nuovo

CASTLE/PALACE | Known to locals as Maschio Angioino, in reference to its Angevin builders, this imposing castle is now used more for marital than military purposes—a portion of it serves as a government registry office. A white four-tiered triumphal entrance arch, ordered by Alfonso of Aragon after he entered the city in 1443 to seize power from the increasingly beleaguered Angevin Giovanna II, upstages the building's looming Angevin stonework. At the arch's top, as if justifying Alfonso's claim to the throne, the Archangel Michael raises his right arm to slay a demon.

Across the courtyard within the castle, up a staircase, is the Sala Grande, also known as the Sala dei Baroni, which has a stunning vaulted ceiling 92 feet high. In 1486, local barons hatched a plot against Alfonso's son, King Ferrante, who reacted by inviting them to this hall for a wedding banquet, which promptly turned into a mass arrest. (Ferrante is also said to have kept a crocodile in the castle as his pet executioner.) You can also visit the Sala dell'Armeria, where a glass floor reveals recent excavations of Roman baths from the Augustan period, with resin plaster casts of the skeletons also found here (the originals are in storage in the Museo Archeologico Nazionale). In the next room on the left, the Cappella Palatina, revolving exhibitions (some free) adorn the walls along with a few tiny remaining fragments of the famous Giotto pictures described by Petrarch.

Before climbing to the castle's first-floor gallery, with its beautiful Renaissance-era masterpieces, check out the magnificent 16th-century Cappella delle Anime del Purgatorio and its richly decorated gold-plated altar.

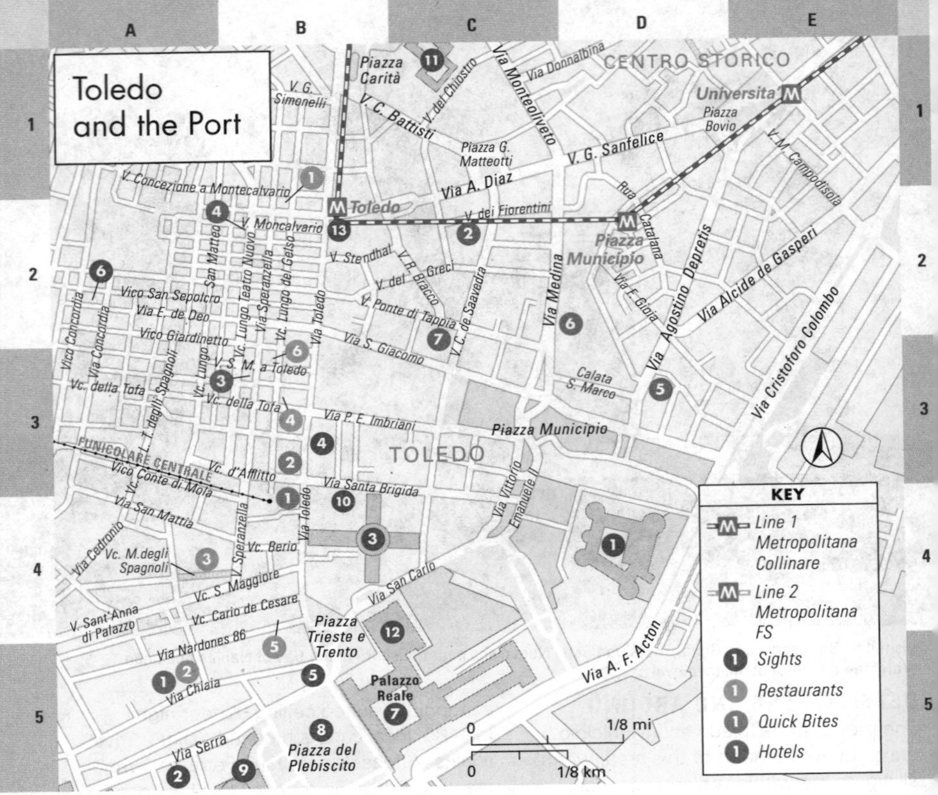

Sights

1 Castel Nuovo............ **D4**
2 Galleria Borbonica **A6**
3 Galleria Umberto I...... **B4**
4 Gallerie d'Italia.......... **B3**
5 Gran Caffè Gambrinus............... **B5**
6 Maradona Mural........ **A2**
7 Palazzo Reale **B5**
8 Piazza del Plebiscito.... **B5**
9 San Francesco di Paola **B5**
10 Santa Brigida........... **B4**
11 Sant'Anna dei Lombardi.................. **C1**
12 Teatro San Carlo and MeMus Museum **B4**
13 Toledo Metro Station... **B2**

Restaurants

1 A Pignata **B2**
2 Brandi..................... **A5**
3 'Ntretella.................. **A4**
4 7 Soldi..................... **B3**
5 Trattoria San Ferdinando **B4**
6 Valù....................... **B3**

Quick Bites

1 L.u.i.s.e. **B4**
2 Pintauro.................. **B3**

Hotels

1 Chiaja Hotel de Charme............... **A5**
2 Golden Hotel **C2**
3 Hotel Il Convento **B3**
4 Hotel Toledo............. **B2**
5 Mercure Napoli Angioino **D3**
6 Palazzo Turchini......... **D2**
7 Renaissance Naples Hotel Mediterraneo **C2**

Napoli: A Good Walk

The Piazza

In a day filled with monarchist grandeur, it's fitting to start out at **Gran Caffè Gambrinus**, in the very center of Naples on Piazza Trieste e Trento, between Piazza Plebiscito and Piazza Municipio. This ornate café was once the rendezvous for Italian dukes, prime ministers, and the literati, including Oscar Wilde. Treat yourself to a cappuccino and a pastry, then step outside into the grand **Piazza Plebiscito**, which makes an imposing setting for **San Francesco di Paola**, the domed 19th-century church built by Ferdinand I.

Palazzo Reale and Teatro San Carlo

From there, head directly across the piazza to take in the facade of the **Palazzo Reale**, before walking up the grand staircase of its Scalone d'Onore, and touring the spectacular 18th- and 19th-century salons of the Museo dell'Appartmento Reale. To visit the adjacent **Teatro San Carlo**, head back down to the piazza and make a right turn in the Piazza Trieste e Trento. Guided English-language tours of the theater take place daily; you can book them in advance at the theater's website (🌐 *www.teatrosancarlo.it*).

Galleria Umberto I, Santa Brigida, and Castel Nuovo

Across from the theater is the vast, elegant **Galleria Umberto I**, an ancestor of the shopping mall. Walk through it to Via Santa Brigida and tour the Church of **Santa Brigida**. Head back through the Galleria and then gently downhill on the Via San Carlo and the Via Vittorio Emanuele III; you'll come to the usually light-drenched Piazza Municipio with the impressive Fontana di Nettuno (Fountain of Neptune). Above the piazza rises the imposing fortress of the **Castel Nuovo**. From the outside, study its sculpted triumphal arch of Alfonso of Aragon; inside, explore the museum and the spidery-roofed Hall of the Barons, plus giant photos of the Roman ships unearthed when the metro tube outside was being dug.

Via Monteoliveto and Via Toledo

Head across Piazza Municipio to Via Medina until you reach the 20th-century post office and police station at Piazza Matteotti. Then trip across the centuries by continuing up Via Monteoliveto, passing the Tuscan-influenced rusticated facade of Palazzo Gravina, to the pedestrianized piazza on the left, where you can find the quiet church of **Sant'Anna dei Lombardi**.

Make a left leaving Sant'Anna dei Lombardi and head over to Piazza Carità, then take the 10 or so blocks down pedestrianized Via Toledo (the main thoroughfare of the area, often referred to as Via Roma) back to the Piazza Trieste e Trento; along the way, take in the vast fascist style facade of the **Gallerie d'Italia**, do some window-shopping, and pick up a hot, flaky *sfogliatella* pastry at Pintauro. You'll arrive back at Piazza Trieste e Trento in time to seek out a leisurely lunch.

Timing

Not including stops at the Palazzo Reale and Castel Nuovo museums, this walk will take about three hours.

At the back of the courtyard are giant photographs of three Roman ships, wood amazingly intact, unearthed during recent digging of the nearby metro station and now hidden away for restoration. A few tour itineraries are offered, including one of the underground prisons and the terrace with its unrivaled views of Piazza Muncipio's Roman excavations. ✉ *Piazza Municipio, Toledo* ☎ *081/7957722* 🌐 *castelnuovo.comune.napoli.it, www.timelinenapoli.it* 🎫 *From €6, tours €10* ⏲ *Closed Sun.* Ⓜ *Municipio.*

Galleria Borbonica

TUNNEL | Following a revolution in 1848 Ferdinando II decided to build an escape route from the Palazzo Reale to the sea, under the Pizzofalcone hill, with work beginning five years later. The death of the king and political changes (leading to Garibaldi's unification of Italy in 1861) meant the project was never completed and the tunnel lay abandoned for almost a century until World War II, when it was used as a bomb shelter. The visit begins with a descent of 90 steps to a series of large tuff chambers, excavated for building work in the 18th century and then used as water cisterns. A short passageway leads to the tunnel itself, which after the war was used as a pound for stolen cars and motorbikes, many of which are still here. The more adventurous can book a tour of the cisterns on a ramp. Note, the tour begins on Vico del Grottone 4, just off Via Gennaro Serra behind Piazza Plebsicito. ✉ *Via D. Morelli 61, Naples* ☎ *081/7645808* 🌐 *www.galleriaborbonica.com* 🎫 *€10* ⏲ *Closed Mon.–Thurs.* Ⓜ *Chiaia.*

Galleria Umberto I

NOTABLE BUILDING | The galleria was erected during the "cleanup" of Naples following the devastating cholera epidemic of 1884, part of a massive urban-renewal plan that entailed the destruction of slum areas between the Centro Storico and the Palazzo Reale. With facades on Via Toledo—the most animated street in Naples at the time—the structure, built between 1887 and 1890 according to a design by Emanuele Rocco, had a prestigious and important location. As with its smaller predecessor, the Galleria Vittorio Emanuele II in Milan, the Galleria Umberto Primo exalts the taste of the postunification commercial elite in a virtuoso display of late-19th-century technology clothed in traditional style. Here are the iron-ribbed glass barrel vault and 188-feet-high dome by Paolo Boubée, which represented the latest advance in modern form yet was layered over with the reassuring architectural ornament of the 14th century (another era when the bourgeoisie triumphed in Italy). ✉ *Entrances on Via San Carlo, Via Toledo, Via Santa Brigida, and Via Verdi, Toledo* Ⓜ *Toledo.*

Gallerie d'Italia

ART GALLERY | Once the headquarters of the Banco di Napoli, this vast 20th-century building houses a small museum that's worth seeking out for its outstanding collection of 17th- and 18th-century paintings. Relocated from the nearby 17th-century Palazzo Zevallos Stigliano in 2022, the star attraction is Caravaggio's last work, *The Martyrdom of Saint Ursula.* The saint here is, for dramatic effect, deprived of her usual retinue of a thousand followers. On the left, with a face of pure spite, is the king of the Huns, who has just shot Ursula with an arrow after his proposal of marriage has been rejected. Free lunchtime concerts are sometimes held in the atrium of the palazzo. ✉ *Via Toledo 177, Toledo* ☎ *800/454229* 🌐 *www.gallerieditalia.com* 🎫 *€5* ⏲ *Closed Mon.* Ⓜ *Toledo.*

Gran Caffè Gambrinus

RESTAURANT | The most famous coffeehouse in town is the Caffè Gambrinus, diagonal to the Palazzo Reale across the Piazza Trieste e Trento. Although its glory days as an intellectual salon are well in the past, the rooms inside, with mirrored walls and gilded ceilings, make

Did You Know?

The French Enlightenment philosopher Montesquieu declared the Palazzo Reale's Scalone d'Onore the finest staircase in Europe.

this an essential stop. It was here that Oscar Wilde, down on his luck, would, for the price of a cup of tea, amaze Anglophone visitors with his still-intact wit. Disappointingly, it's not the best coffee in town. ✉ *Via Chiaia 1/2, Toledo* ☎ *081/417582* 🌐 *www.grancaffegambrinus.com* Ⓜ *Toledo, Municipio.*

★ Palazzo Reale

CASTLE/PALACE | A leading Naples showpiece created as an expression of Bourbon power and values, the Palazzo Reale dates from 1600. Renovated and redecorated by successive rulers and once lorded over by a dim-witted king who liked to shoot his hunting guns at the birds in his tapestries, it is filled with salons designed in the most lavish 18th-century Neapolitan style. The Spanish viceroys originally commissioned the palace, ordering the Swiss architect Domenico Fontana to build a suitable new residence for King Philip III, should he ever visit Naples. He died in 1621 before ever doing so. The palace saw its greatest moment of splendor in the 18th century, when Charles III of Bourbon became the first permanent resident. The flamboyant Naples-born architect Luigi Vanvitelli redesigned the facade, and Ferdinando Fuga, under Ferdinand IV, created the Royal Apartments, sumptuously furnished and full of precious paintings, tapestries, porcelains, and other objets d'art.

To access these 30 rooms, climb the monumental Scalone d'Onore (Staircase). On the right is the Court Theater, built by Fuga for Charles III and his private opera company. Damaged during World War II, it was restored in the 1950s; note the resplendent royal box. Pass through three regal antechambers to Room VI, the Throne Room, the ponderous titular object dating to sometime after 1850.

In the Ambassadors' Room, choice Gobelin tapestries grace the beige fabric walls and the ceiling honors Spanish military victories, painted by local artist Belisario Corenzio (1610–20). Room IX was bedroom to Charles's queen, Maria Cristina. The brilliantly gold private oratory has beautiful paintings by Francesco Liani (1760).

The Great Captain's Room has ceiling frescoes by Battistello Caracciolo (1610–16); all velvet, fire, and smoke, they reveal the influence of Caravaggio's visit to the city. A wall-mounted, jolly series by Federico Zuccari depicts 12 proverbs.

Room XIII was Joachim Murat's writing room when he was king of Naples; brought with him from France, some of the furniture is courtesy of Adam Weisweiler, cabinetmaker to Marie Antoinette. The huge Room XXII, painted in green and gold with kitschy faux tapestries, is known as the Hercules Hall, because it once housed the *Farnese Hercules,* an epic sculpture of the mythological Greek hero. Pride of place now goes to the Sèvres porcelain.

The Palatine Chapel, also known as the Royal Chapel, redone by Gaetano Genovese in the 1830s, is gussied up with an excess of gold, although it has a stunning multicolor marble intarsia altar transported from a now-destroyed chapel in Capodimonte (Dionisio Lazzari, 1678). Also here is a Nativity scene with pieces sculpted by Giuseppe Sammartino and others. Another wing holds the Biblioteca Nazionale Vittorio Emanuele III. Starting out from Farnese bits and pieces, it was enriched with the papyri from Herculaneum found in 1752 and opened to the public in 1804. The sumptuous rooms can still be viewed, and there's a tasteful terrace that looks onto Castel Nuovo.

The newly opened Galleria del Tempo is a multimedia trip through the history of Naples, in the Bourbon stables. ✉ *Piazza Plebiscito, Toledo* ☎ *081/5808255, 848/082408 schools and guided tours* 🌐 *www.palazzorealedinapoli.org* 🎫 *€6* ⏲ *Closed Wed.* Ⓜ *Toledo, Municipio.*

Piazza del Plebiscito

PLAZA/SQUARE | After spending time as a parking lot, this square was restored in 1994 to one of Napoli Nobilissima's most majestic spaces, with a Doric semicircle of columns resembling Saint Peter's Square in Rome. The piazza was erected in the early 1800s under the Napoleonic regime, but after the regime fell, Ferdinand, the new King of the Two Sicilies, ordered the addition of the Church of San Francesco di Paola. On the left as you approach the church is a statue of Ferdinand and on the right one of his father, Charles III, both of them clad in Roman togas. Around dusk, floodlights come on, creating a magical effect. A delightful sea breeze airs the square, and most days one corner becomes an improvised soccer stadium where local youths emulate their heroes. ✉ *Piazza Plebiscito, Toledo* Ⓜ *Toledo, Municipio.*

Maradona Mural

PUBLIC ART | This small square 300 yards up the hill from Via Toledo is a shrine to to Napoli's all-time favorite soccer player, Diego Maradona. "The hand of God, the head of Maradona," quoth the famous Argentina-born superstar after scoring a much-disputed World cup goal against England. This sentiment and its ability to mix the earthly and fallible with the divine is also peculiarly Neapolitan. The south wall is dominated by a mural of the Argentine giant featuring his original Swarovski diamond earring. Painted by fan Mario Filardi in 1990 when Napoli won their second league title, it was given an overhaul in 2016 with the face subsequently retouched by Argentine street artist Francisco Bosoletti (whose mural *Iside*, inspired by Pudicizia del Corradini in the Cappella Sansevero, is on the west wall). When Maradona passed away in 2020, fans gathered here to pay their respects, as well as at the city's stadium (now renamed *Stadio Maradona*), and the square has now transformed from a crammed parking lot to a colourful museum for the footballing hero, with pilgrims leaving photos, scarves and gadgets in tribute. There is another giant mural of Maradona in the eastern suburb of San Giovanni a Teduccio, painted by Neapolitan-Dutch artist Jorit in 2017. ✉ *Via Emanuele de Deo 60, Toledo* Ⓜ *Toledo.*

San Francesco di Paola

CHURCH | Modeled after Rome's Pantheon, this circular basilica is the centerpiece of the Piazza Plebiscito and remains one of the most frigidly voluptuous examples of the Stile Empire, or Neoclassical style, in Italy. Commissioned by Ferdinand I to fulfill a vow he had made in order to enlist divine aid in being reinstated to the throne of the Kingdom of the Two Sicilies, it rose at one end of the vast parade ground built several years earlier by Joachim Murat. Completed in the late 1840s after 30 years of construction, it managed to transform Murat's inconveniently grandiose colonnade—whose architect was clearly inspired by the colonnades of St. Peter's in Rome—into a setting for restored Bourbon glory. Pietro Bianchi from Lugano in Switzerland won a competition and built a slightly smaller version of the Pantheon, with a beautiful coffered dome and a splendid set of 34 Corinthian columns in gray marble; but the overall lack of color (so different from the warm interior of the Pantheon), combined with the severe geometrical forms, produces an almost defiantly cold space. Art historians find the spectacle of the church to be the ultimate in Neoclassical *grandezza* (greatness); others think this Roman temple is only suitable to honor Jupiter, not Christ. In any event, the main altar, done in gold, lapis lazuli, and other precious stones by Anselmo Caggiano (1641), was taken from the destroyed Church of the Santi Apostoli and provides some relief from the oppressive perfection of the setting. On a hot summer day, the church's preponderance of marble guarantees sanctuary from the heat outside, with a temperature drop of 10 or more degrees. ✉ *Piazza Plebiscito, Toledo*

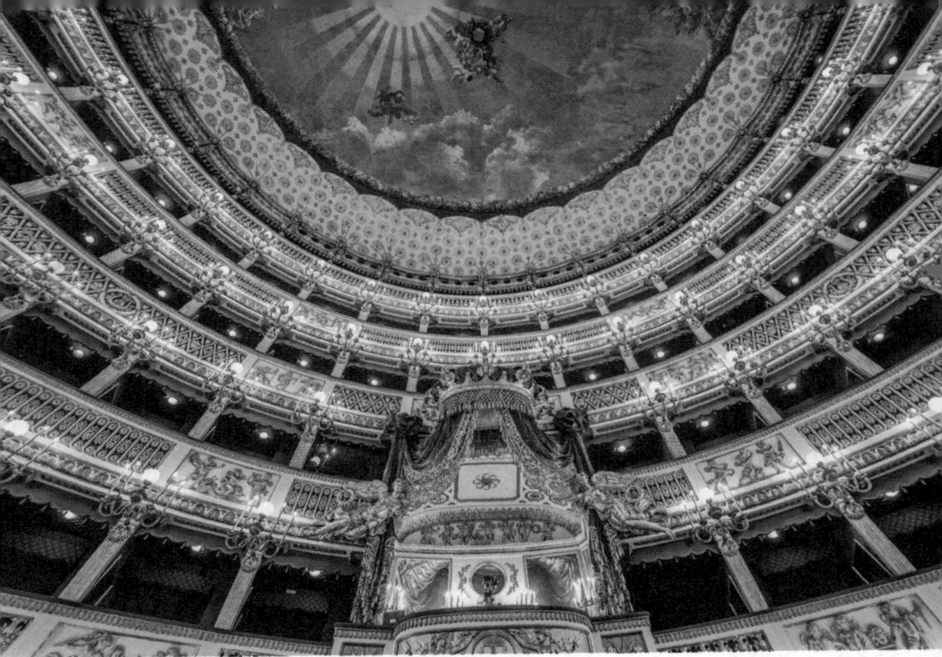

Awash in gold and red velvet, the interior of the Teatro San Carlo, Naples's grand opera house, is almost more spectacular than its stage presentations.

☎ *081/7645133* 🌐 *www.facebook.com/basilicasanfrancescodipaola* Ⓜ *Toledo, Municipio.*

★ **Sant'Anna dei Lombardi**

CHURCH | Long favored by the Aragonese kings, this church, simple and rather anonymous from the outside, houses some of the most important ensembles of Renaissance sculpture in southern Italy. Begun with the adjacent convent of the Olivetani and its four cloisters in 1411, it was given a Baroque makeover in the mid-17th century by Gennaro Sacco. This, however, is no longer so visible because the bombs of 1943 led to a restoration favoring the original *quattrocento* (15th-century) lines. The wonderful coffered wooden ceiling adds a bit of pomp. Inside the porch is the tomb of Domenico Fontana, one of the major architects of the late 16th century, who died in Naples after beginning the Palazzo Reale.

On either side of the original entrance door are two fine Renaissance tombs. The one on the left as you face the door belongs to the Ligorio family (whose descendant Pirro designed the Villa d'Este in Tivoli) and is a work by Giovanni da Nola (1524). The tomb on the right is a masterpiece by Giuseppe Santacroce (1532) done for the del Pozzo family. To the left of the Ligorio Altar (the corner chapel on the immediate right as you face the altar) is the Mastrogiudice Chapel, whose altar contains precious reliefs of the Annunciation and *Scenes from the Life of Jesus* (1489) by Benedetto da Maiano, a great name in Tuscan sculpture. On the other side of the entrance is the Piccolomini Chapel, with a *Crucifixion* by Giulio Mazzoni (circa 1550), a refined marble altar (circa 1475), a funerary monument to Maria d'Aragona by another prominent Florentine sculptor, Antonello Rossellino (circa 1475), and on the right, a rather sweet fresco of the Annunciation by an anonymous follower of Piero della Francesca.

The true surprises of the church are to the right of the altar, in the presbytery and adjoining rooms. The chapel just to the right of the main altar, belonging to the Orefice family, is richly decorated in pre-Baroque (1596–98) polychrome marbles and frescoes by Luis Rodriguez; from here you continue on through the Oratory of the Holy Sepulchre, with the tomb of Antonio D'Alessandro and his wife, to reach the church's showpiece: a potently realistic life-size group of eight terra-cotta figures by Guido Mazzoni (1492), which make up a Pietà; the faces are said to be modeled from people at the Aragonese court. Toward the rear of the church is Cappella dell'Assunta, with a fun painting in its corner of a monk by Michelangelo's student Giorgio Vasari, and the lovely Sacrestia Vecchia (Old Sacristy), adorned with one of the most successful decorative ensembles Vasari ever painted (1544) and breathtaking wood-inlay stalls by Fra' Giovanni da Verona and assistants (1506–10) with views of famous buildings. ✉ *Piazza Monteoliveto 15, Toledo* ☎ *081/4420039* 🌐 *www.santannadeilombardi.com* 🎫 *Side chapels, oratory, and sacristy €6* 🕑 *Side chapels, oratory, and sacristy closed Sun. morning* Ⓜ *Dante.*

Santa Brigida

CHURCH | The Lucchesi fathers built this church around 1640 in honor of the Swedish queen and saint who visited her fellow queen, Naples's unsaintly Giovanna I, in 1372 and became one of the first people to publicly denounce the loose morals and overt sensuality of the Neapolitans. The height of the church's dome was limited to prevent its interfering with cannon fire from nearby Castel Nuovo, but Luca Giordano, the pioneer painter of the trompe-l'oeil Baroque dome, effectively opened it up with a spacious sky serving as the setting for an *Apotheosis of Saint Bridget* (1678), painted (and restored in 2018) in exchange for his tomb space, marked by a pavement inscription in the left transept. Don't miss the sacristy with its ceiling fresco from the Giordano school. ✉ *Via Santa Brigida 68, Toledo* ☎ *081/5523793* 🌐 *www.santabrigida.net* Ⓜ *Toledo, Municipio.*

Teatro San Carlo and MeMus Museum

PERFORMANCE VENUE | Out of all the Italian opera houses, La Scala in Milan is the most famous, but San Carlo is more beautiful, and Naples is, after all, the most operatic of cities. The neoclassical structure, designed by Antonio Niccolini, was built in a mere nine months after an 1816 fire destroyed the original. Many operas were composed for the house, including Donizetti's *Lucia di Lammermoor* and Rossini's *La Donna del Lago*. In the theater, nearly 200 boxes are arranged on six levels, and the 1,115-square-meter (12,000-square-foot) stage permits productions with horses, camels, and elephants, and even has a backdrop that can lift to reveal the Palazzo Reale Gardens. Above the rich red-and-gold auditorium is a ceiling fresco by Giuseppe Cammarano representing Apollo presenting poets to Athena. Performance standards are among Europe's highest—even the great Enrico Caruso was hissed here. If you're not attending an opera, you can still see the splendid theater on a 30-minute guided tour and visit MeMus (Museo Memoria e Musica): San Carlo's theatrically lit museum and archive has props, costumes, stage sets, and multimedia and documents galore. English-language tours, which take place daily except on holidays, can be booked in advance on the theater's website. ✉ *Via San Carlo 101–103, Toledo* ☎ *081/7972331 ticket office, 081/7972412 tours, 081/7972449 MeMus* 🌐 *www.teatrosancarlo.it* 🎫 *From €6* 🕑 *MeMus closed Wed. and Aug.* Ⓜ *Municipio.*

★ **Toledo Metro Station**

TRAIN/TRAIN STATION | Designed by Catalan architect Oscar Tusquets Blanca and opened in 2012, this is the most impressive of the numerous Stazioni dell'Arte on the city's Metro Linea 1. First archaeological remains, then mosaics by William

One of the most frigidly voluptuous examples of the Neoclassical style, the church of San Francesco di Paola was designed to emulate Rome's Pantheon.

Kentridge, lead to a 165-foot escalator descending below Robert Wilson's glittering oval *Crater de Luz*. A 560-foot corridor, connecting the station to the Quartieri Spagnoli, is lined with light-boxes depicting *Razza Umana* (Human Race) by Oliviero Toscani. Lauded by both CNN and Britain's *Telegraph,* it also won a prestigious ITA Tunneling Award in 2015. Information on guided tours, and detailed descriptions of artworks in the Linea 1 and 6 stations can be found on the station's website. ✉ *Via Toledo, Toledo* ☎ *800/568866* 🌐 *metroart.anm.it* 🎫 *€2* Ⓜ *Toledo.*

Restaurants

A Pignata

$ | SOUTHERN ITALIAN | A hidden gem in the Quartieri Spagnoli, A Pignata is a favorite with locals for its typical Neapolitan cooking. The antipasta is a meal in itself but save space for the grilled *calamari* or *Baccalà alla Siciliana*, made with potatoes, tomatoes, olives and capers. **Known for:** sumptuous local dishes; a favorite with locals; relaxed atmosphere. $ *Average main: €12* ✉ *Vico Lungo del Gelso 110/112, Toledo* ☎ *081/413526* 🌐 *www.trattoriapignata.it* ⏲ *Closed Mon.* Ⓜ *Toledo.*

Brandi

$$ | PIZZA | Considered the birthplace of pizza Margherita, it's also one of the most picturesque restaurants in Italy. Set on a cobblestone alleyway just off chic Via Chiaia, with an elaborate presepe in the window, it welcomes you with an enchanting wood-beam salon festooned with 19th-century memorabilia, saint shrines, gilded mirrors, and bouquets of flowers, beyond which you can see the kitchen and the pizzaioli at work. **Known for:** atmosphere is better than the food; historical; the birthplace of pizza. $ *Average main: €15* ✉ *Salita Sant'Anna di Palazzo 1, Toledo* ☎ *081/416928* 🌐 *www.brandi.it* Ⓜ *Chiaia.*

★ 'Ntretella

$ | **SOUTHERN ITALIAN** | Named for Neapolitan character Pulcinella's girlfriend, this gem is in the one-time oratory of the adjoining church, which became a sawmill in the early twentieth century. The high tufo arches and period fittings have been maintained, and the food is to-die-for—pizza is the popular choice, with an adventurous menu, and there is also a selection of pasta dishes. **Known for:** delicious pizza; friendly service; a step back in time. *Average main: €8 Vico Maddalenella degli Spagnoli 19, Toledo 081/427970 www.pizzeriantretella.it Closed Wed. Toledo.*

7 Soldi

$ | **SOUTHERN ITALIAN** | Just off Via Toledo, this simple restaurant with outside tables in summer serves good pizza and other southern Italian favorites. Try the *gamberoni alla Posillipo* (prawns in a seafood sauce made with cherry tomatoes) or the *pignatiello di mare* (octopus, calamari, prawns, and other seafood on fried bread). **Known for:** lively outside seating area; convivial atmosphere; choice of pasta or pizza. *Average main: €12 Vico Tre Re a Toledo 6, Toledo 081/418727 www.facebook.com/7Soldi Toledo.*

Trattoria San Ferdinando

$$$ | **SOUTHERN ITALIAN** | This cheerful trattoria seems to be run for the sheer pleasure of it, and chatting locals give it a buzzy Neapolitan atmosphere. Try the excellent fish or the traditional (but cooked with a lighter modern touch) pasta dishes, especially those with *verdure* (fresh leafy vegetables) or with *patate con la provola* (potatoes and smoked mozzarella). **Known for:** near Teatro San Carlo; popular with locals in the evening, so reserve ahead; excellent, fresh seafood specialties. *Average main: €25 Via Nardones 117, Toledo 081/421964 www.trattoriasanferdinando.com Closed Sun. and last 3 wks of Aug. No dinner Sat. and Mon. Toledo, Municipio.*

Valù

$ | **ITALIAN** | Fans of rice will be spoiled for choice at this *risotteria,* the only one of its kind in the city. The menu offers 20 dishes, including vegetarian and gluten-free options. **Known for:** friendly staff; expansive wine-list; good alternative to pizza and pasta. *Average main: €12 Vico Lungo del Gelso 80, Toledo 081/0381139 www.valu.it Closed Mon. No dinner Sun. Toledo.*

Coffee and Quick Bites

L.u.i.s.e.

$ | **SOUTHERN ITALIAN** | At this perfect place for a lunchtime snack, you point to what you want in the tempting glass counter, and pay for it at the cash desk. Among the specialties are the usual frittura, tangy cheese pies (*sfoglino al formaggio*), pizza *scarola* (an escarole pie with black olives), and slices of omelets stuffed with spinach, peppers, or onions. **Known for:** efficient service; lots of variety on the menu; quick bite. *Average main: €6 Via Toledo 266–269, Toledo 081/415367 Toledo.*

Pintauro

$ | **SOUTHERN ITALIAN** | The classic address for sfogliatelle is Pintauro, which rarely disappoints. Try one of these fresh from the back-room oven. **Known for:** oven-to-palate service; perfect grab-and-go spot; tasty pastries. *Average main: €1 Via Toledo 275, Toledo 081/417339 Toledo.*

Hotels

Chiaja Hotel de Charme

$ | **HOTEL** | This 18th-century palazzo has a great location and its apartments, all on the first floor, have plenty of atmosphere. **Pros:** good location near Piazza del Plebiscito and the Palazzo Reale; some

Continued on page 298

NEAPOLITAN
Baroque

Even charitable observers would say that excess, fake opulence, and exaggeration are typical Neapolitan qualities. It's not surprising, then, that the baroque, an artistic style that revels in details added to swirls added to flourishes added to twists—a style that is playful, theatrical, dynamic, and seems permanently about to burst its bonds—should find one of its most spectacular showcases in Naples.

The very word "baroque" derives from a Portuguese word describing an impressive-looking but worthless type of pearl, and was originally used as an insult to describe the flagrantly emotional, floridly luxurious style that surfaced in Europe around 1600. Critics now use baroque to describe a style more than a period.

It's a style that found immediate favor in a city of volcanic passions. Like the city itself, the decorative scheme is diffuse and disjunctive, with little effort to organize everything into an easily understood scheme.

Contradictions still abound in Naples: plenty with want; grandeur with muddle; beauty with decay; the wide bay, lush countryside, and peaceful sky harboring the dense, chaotic city, sheltered by the ever-present threat of the slumbering Mount Vesuvius. In this context, the vivid, dramatic baroque style feels right at home.

NAPLES AND BAROQUE: A MATCH MADE FOR HEAVEN

At the beginning of the 17th century, thanks to the Counter-Reformation, the Catholic Church was busy making an overt appeal to its congregants, using emotion and motion to get its message across—and nowhere was this more blatant than in Naples, which, as the most populous city in Italy at the time, had more clerics (some 20,000) than even Rome. Baroque artists and architects, given an open invitation to indulge their illusionistic whims on church cupolas and the like, began arriving in Naples to strut their aesthetic stuff.

The most representative practitioner of Neapolitan baroque was **Cosimo Fanzago (1591–1678).** A Lombard by birth, he traveled to Naples to study sculpture; even when decorating a church, he usually covered it head to toe with colored and inlaid marbles, as in his work at the Certosa di San Martino atop the Vomero hill.

Preceding Fanzago by two decades was **Caravaggio (1571–1610),** who moved to Naples from Rome. This great painter took the city by storm, with an unflinching truthfulness and extroverted sensuality in his work. Experts will continue to argue to what degree Caravaggio was or wasn't a baroque painter, but certainly his use of chiaroscuro, a quality common in baroque art, can be seen dramatically in his Neapolitan paintings *The Flagellation of Christ* and *The Seven Acts of Mercy.*

(preceding page) The dome of Gesú Nuovo; (top) *St Bruno* by Cosimo Fanzago; (bottom) Caravaggio

BAROQUE TECHNIQUES: TRICKS OF THE TRADE

MEMENTO MORI. Lest all the sumptuous decoration should appeal too directly to the senses, the Church (as the major sponsor of the baroque) felt it was necessary to remind people of their ultimate message: *memento mori*—"remember that you will die." Don't be surprised if, in the midst of the most delicate and beautiful inlaid marble floor, you find leering skulls. In the tiny church of **Purgatorio ad Arco** ❶ in Spaccanapoli, a winged skull by Fanzago awaits salvation.

DOMES: LOOK UP! If there was one thing baroque architects loved, it was a dome—Exhibit One being the **Duomo di San Gennaro** ❷. Domes offered space and height and lots of opportunities for trompe trompe l'oeil oeil. Even in the tightly packed old center of Naples, domes manage to make you feel as if you are in an enormous, heavenly space. This is in part due to their acoustic qualities, which reduce the city and its noisy inhabitants to swirling whispers and echoes.

MARVELOUS MARBLE. Making the most of the large quantities of marble quarries in Italy, baroque architects outdid their Renaissance predecessors. They used softer kinds of stone and developed intricate, interlaced patterns of different colored marble, such as seen in the **Certosa di San Martino** ❸.

KEEPING IT (HYPER)REAL. Getting solid marble or stone to "move" was one of the skills of any baroque sculptor worth his chisel. Giuseppe Sammartino, who sculpted the **Veiled Christ** ❹ in the Capella Sansevero, was so good at his craft that it was rumored (falsely) his boss had him blinded so he couldn't repeat his genius anywhere else. In

4

5

6

Gesù Nuovo a dead Christ lies near the entrance in a glass case, often giving visitors cause to stop momentarily as they think they've stumbled across a real person. It is common to find saints' marble effigies still dressed in real period clothes.

OUT OF THE SHADOWS. Chiaroscuro ("light-dark") is the word most often used to describe baroque painting, with its mixture of bright shafts of light and thick shadows. Figures loom out of the dark while the main action is highlighted by dazzling beams of light—as in Ribera's ***Apollo and Marsyas*** ❺ at the Museo di Capodimonte.

TROMPE L'OEIL. Literally "tricking the eye," trompe l'oeil is a method of painting that creates an optical illusion of three dimensions. Angels lean over balconies and out of paintings, walls become windows, and skylights bestow views into heaven itself, as grandly displayed in Luca Giordano's ***Triumph of Judith*** ❻ at the Certosa di San Martino. There is something very baroque in trompe l'oeil's sense of trickery, of something being built upon nothing.

STAIRWAYS TO HEAVEN. The principles of movement and ascension naturally conveyed by a staircase appealed to baroque architects. Staircases can often be seen with winged banisters, as if those simply climbing the steps were on a journey into a higher realm. The staircase in the entrance of the Royal Palace in Naples splits and divides and splits again, its movement magnified and reflected dizzyingly by the windows and mirrors surrounding it. At the Palazzo della Spagnola in the Sanità neighborhood, the M.C. Escher–esque staircase boasts steps wide enough to ride a horse up them—which is precisely what they were used for in the 17th century.

ON STAGE. If some of the more extravagant interiors of Neapolitan churches remind you of theater sets, you're not far off. Many designers crossed over into ecclesiastical work, usually having first been noticed in the theater. Many arches over altars are made from a reinforced form of papier-mâché, originally used in theatrical productions.

Attenzione! How to Cross Naples' Streets

Long considered a threatened species, the Naples pedestrian is gradually being provided with a friendlier environment. Once Piazza Garibaldi has been negotiated, traffic in much of Naples is no more off-putting than in other Italian cities. (Accident rates involving pedestrians are higher in Rome.) In fact, large tracts of Naples are open to pedestrians only. That's the case for the sea-hugging Via Partenope, and also for most of Via Toledo. Leading off it is the fashionable Via Chiaia, a destination for posh shopping and the birthplace of the pizza Margherita. Piazza Plebiscito, reduced to a parking lot until the 1990s, is also now an ideal space to stroll through, touched by a pleasant sea breeze.

That being said, crossing major thoroughfares in Naples still takes some savvy. In a city where red traffic lights may be blithely ignored, especially by two-wheelers, walking across a busy avenue can be like a game of chess—if you hesitate, you capitulate. Some residents just forge out into the unceasing flow of traffic, knowing cars invariably slow down to let them cross. Look both ways even on one-way streets, as there may be motorcyclists riding against the flow. Areas where you have to be particularly vigilant—and cross at the lights—are around the Archaeological Museum and on Via Marina outside the port, as well as the ever-challenging Piazza Garibaldi.

antiques in guest rooms; on a bustling pedestrian-only street. **Cons:** entrance up a flight of stairs; even with a/c, some rooms get hot in summer; no views in a town with some great ones. *$ Rooms from: €89 ✉ Via Chiaia 216, Chiaia ☎ 081/415555 ⊕ www.hotelchiaia.it 33 rooms Free Breakfast Ⓜ Chiaia.*

Golden Hotel

$$ | **HOTEL** | At this "techno-style" hotel, one of the most plugged-in lodgings in Naples, minimal-chic guest rooms are done up in steel grays, night blacks, and rich purples, and the large flat-screen TVs (with foreign channels available) compensate for the lack of a view. **Pros:** Wi-Fi connection in every room; ideal for visiting the city on foot; in the middle of things yet out of the whirlwind. **Cons:** might be too hip for some; some rooms are small; rooms lack views. *$ Rooms from: €140 ✉ Via dei Fiorentini 51, Toledo ☎ 081/2514192 ⊕ www.goldenhotel.it 13 rooms Free Breakfast Ⓜ Toledo, Municipio.*

Hotel Il Convento

$ | **HOTEL** | A 17th-century palazzo in the Quartieri Spagnoli contains this hotel whose small but elegant guest rooms have original architectural features such as arched or beamed ceilings. **Pros:** close to cafés and shops; free Internet access; warm Neapolitan reception. **Cons:** church bells may wake you in the morning; just off the busy Via Toledo; neighborhood can be a bit rough. *$ Rooms from: €95 ✉ Via Speranzella 137/A, Toledo ☎ 081/403977 ⊕ www.hotelilconvento.com 14 rooms Free Breakfast Ⓜ Toledo.*

Hotel Toledo

$ | **HOTEL** | A onetime brothel, this centuries-old palazzo has been tastefully transformed into a boutique hotel in a good location only a two-minute walk up from Via Toledo beside the Teatro Nuovo and not too far from the Centro Storico. **Pros:** convenient to Via Toledo shopping; helpful reception staff; two suites have a private roof garden. **Cons:** hotel is a steep walk up Via Montecalvario; can be noisy at night, with popular bar nearby; rooms are small. $ *Rooms from: €96* ✉ *Via Montecalvario 15, Toledo* ☎ *081/406800* 🌐 *www.hoteltoledo.com* 🛏 *14 rooms* 🍽 *Free Breakfast* Ⓜ *Toledo.*

Mercure Napoli Angioino
$$ | **HOTEL** | Right off Piazza Municipio, in the shadows of Castel Nuovo, this popular hotel is a good choice if you're taking a boat from Molo Beverello. **Pros:** good location near the port; early check-in/late check-out available; fine views from the breakfast terrace. **Cons:** breakfast is €15; lacks character compared to many Naples hotels; on a busy road. $ *Rooms from: €180* ✉ *Via Depretis 123, Toledo* ☎ *081/5529500* 🌐 *mercure.accor.com/* 🛏 *99 rooms* 🍽 *No Meals* Ⓜ *Muncipio.*

Palazzo Turchini
$ | **HOTEL** | Just a few minutes' walk from the Castel Nuovo, Palazzo Turchini is one of the city center's more attractive smaller hotels. **Pros:** good location for the port; rooftop terrace; more intimate than neighboring business hotels. **Cons:** rooms on the small and stuffy side; rooms a tad business-like; close to a busy traffic hub. $ *Rooms from: €118* ✉ *Via Medina 21, Toledo* ☎ *081/5510606* 🌐 *www.palazzoturchini.it* 🛏 *27 rooms* 🍽 *Free Breakfast* Ⓜ *Municipio.*

Renaissance Naples Hotel Mediterraneo
$$ | **HOTEL** | A modern, efficient business hotel, the Mediterraneo is within walking distance of both the Teatro San Carlo and the Centro Storico. **Pros:** convenient to the port; good for those who want a modern hotel; attractive rooftop breakfast terrace. **Cons:** not for those who want historic atmosphere; some of the rooms are poorly maintained; in a busy part of town. $ *Rooms from: €180* ✉ *Via Nuova Ponte di Tappia 25, Toledo* ☎ *081/7970001* 🌐 *www.mediterraneonapoli.com, www.marriott.com* 🛏 *189 rooms* 🍽 *Free Breakfast* Ⓜ *Toledo, Municipio.*

Nightlife

Barrio Botanico
COCKTAIL LOUNGES | Situated in the leafy courtyard of 16th-century Palazzo Fondi, this all-day, late-night bar is a favorite with young upcoming Neapolitans. ✉ *Via Medina 24, Port* ☎ *081/4246186* 🌐 *www.facebook.com/barriobotanico* Ⓜ *Municipio.*

Cammarota Spritz
BARS | A favorite of students and alternative revelers who crowd the tiny street outside this hole-in-wall *cantina*, where a Spritz costs just €1. ✉ *Vico Lungo Teatro Nuovo 31, Toledo* ☎ *320/2775687 mobile* 🌐 *www.facebook.com/cammarotaspritz* Ⓜ *Toledo.*

Performing Arts

Galleria Toledo
CONCERTS | The hip set comes here to watch high-quality fringe and avant-garde theater presentations. ✉ *Via Montecalvario 36, Toledo* ☎ *081/425037* 🌐 *www.galleriatoledo.org* Ⓜ *Toledo.*

Teatro Augusteo
CONCERTS | A large, centrally located theater off Via Toledo, the Augusteo usually presents commercial Italian theater and concerts, but Bruce Springsteen did play here once in 1997. ✉ *Piazzetta duca d'Aosta 263, Piazza Augusteo, Toledo* ☎ *081/414243* 🌐 *www.teatroaugusteo.it* Ⓜ *Toledo.*

Teatro Mercadante
CONCERTS | A Belle Époque theater with an ultramodern foyer, Teatro Mercadante hosts high-quality touring productions. ✉ *Piazza Municipio 1, Piazza Municipio* ☎ *081/5513396* 🌐 *www.teatrodinapoli.it* Ⓜ *Municipio.*

Teatro Nuovo
CONCERTS | Another exciting venue for avant-garde performances, Teatro Nuovo occupies a historic theater building. ✉ *Via Montecalvario 16, Toledo* ☎ *081/425958* 🌐 *www.teatronuovonapoli.it* Ⓜ *Toledo.*

CLOTHING AND ACCESSORIES

Barbaro

MEN'S CLOTHING | "Made in Italy" is the trademark of this popular shop that showcases the fashions of top-name designers. ✉ *Galleria Umberto I 1/7, Toledo* ☎ *081/414940* 🌐 *www.barbaro.eu* Ⓜ *Municipio.*

JEWELRY

Ascione

JEWELRY & WATCHES | A family firm established in 1855 and known for its traditionally made coral jewelry and artwork, Ascione has a showroom/gallery on the second floor of a shabby wing of the Galleria Umberto. A hidden secret, aficionados should not miss the guided tour (€5, book ahead) describing the company's rich history, with displays including Egypt's King Farouk's elaborate wedding gift to his bride Farida and what many consider the most beautiful cameo in existence. ✉ *Piazzetta Matilde Serao 19, Piazza Municipio* ☎ *081/4211111* 🌐 *www.ascione.it* Ⓜ *Municipio.*

Brinkmann

JEWELRY & WATCHES | An institution in timepieces since 1900, Brinkmann made the clocks for the city's funicular stations. ✉ *Piazza Municipio 21, Toledo* ☎ *081/5520555* 🌐 *www.brinkmann.it* Ⓜ *Municipio.*

Leonardo Gaito

JEWELRY & WATCHES | For antique wonders or eclectic creations in gold, precious stones, and silver, make yourself at home on one of the velvet chairs inside Leonardo Gaito (operating since 1864) and get ready to be regaled with some fabulous Neapolitan-style jewels. ✉ *Via Toledo 278, Toledo* ☎ *081/421104* Ⓜ *Toledo.*

Chiaia, Santa Lucia, and Nearby

The Lungomare is the city's grandest stretch of city's waterfront. In the 19th century, Naples's waterfront harbored the picturesque quarter that was called Santa Lucia, a district dear to artists and musicians and known for its fishermen's cottages. The fishermen were swept away when an enormous landfill project extended the land out to what is now Via Nazario Sauro and Via Partenope, the address for some of Naples's finest hotels. Huge stretches of the waterfront are blessedly traffic-free, only enhancing their distinctly Neapolitan charm. The area also boasts the chic Chiaia neighborhood surrounding Piazza dei Martiri and the gilded 19th-century Villa Pignatelli.

Chiaia and San Pasquale, two Metro Linea 6 stops due to open in 2022, take you to the eastern part of this area and to the Villa Comunale, close to Villa Pignatelli. Bus 151 passes here from the station, and Piazza Vittoria is the departure points for buses to Mergellina and Posillipo. This area is easily explored on foot.

Sights

★ **Aquarium**

AQUARIUM | FAMILY | Originally named by the Greeks after the Mermaid Parthenope (who slew herself after being rejected by Odysseus, at least in the poet Virgil's version), it's only fitting that Naples should have established one of Europe's first public aquariums in 1874. At the time—when, not so incidentally, the public imagination was being stirred by Jules Verne's Captain Nemo and Hans Christian Andersen's Little Mermaid—technological innovations came into place to funnel seawater directly from the bay into the aquarium tanks, which showcase fish and marine plants from the Bay of Naples, with a tank devoted to tropical fish. Officially named the Stazione Zoologica, founded by the German scientist Anton Dhorn, and housed in a Stile Liberty building designed by Adolf von Hildebrandt, the aquarium quickly became the wonder of Naples for children and art-exhausted adults. Reopened in 2021 after a six-year major overhaul, the foundation added the Museo Darwin-Dohrn (Da-DoM) a few steps away in the leafy Villa Comunale—the 19th-century naturalist and Dohrn were regular correspondents. The highlight is the skeleton of a sperm whale washed up in Ischia in 2018, in a room opening up to the bay. ✉ *Villa Comunale, Naples* ☎ *081/5833442 aquarium, 081/5833642 DaDoM* 🌐 *www.fondazionedohrn.it* 🎫 *Aquarium €7, museum €6, both €10* 🕒 *Closed Mon.* Ⓜ *San Pasquale.*

Castel dell'Ovo (*Castle of the Egg*)
CASTLE/PALACE | The oldest castle in Naples, the 12th-century Castel dell'Ovo dangles over the Porto Santa Lucia on a thin promontory. Built atop the ruins of an ancient Roman villa, the castle these days shares its views with some of the city's top hotels. Its gigantic rooms, rock tunnels, and belvederes over the bay are among the most striking sights that Naples has to offer. Some rooms are given over to temporary art and photography shows.

You enter the castle through its main entrance, below its forbidding trio of cannons. On the right is a large picture of the castle in Renaissance times. Turn left and look through the battlements to the intimate Borgo Marinaro below. An elevator on the right ascends to the castle top, or you can also continue along the walkway overlooking the ramparts. The roof's Sala della Terrazze offers a postcard-come-true view of Capri. This is a peaceful spot for strolling and enjoying the views.

As for the castle's name, the poet Virgil is supposed to have hidden inside the villa an egg that had protective powers as long as it remained intact. The belief was taken so seriously that to quell the people's panic after Naples suffered an earthquake, an invasion, and a plague in quick succession, its monarch felt compelled to produce an intact egg, solemnly declaring it to be the Virgilian original. ✉ *Santa Lucia waterfront, Via Eldorado 3, off Via Partenope, Santa Lucia* ☎ *081/7956180* 🎫 *Free.*

Museo Diego Aragona Pignatelli Cortes
NOTABLE BUILDING | Set behind what would be a very English expanse of lawn (minus the palm trees), this salmon-pink building with its Athenian-style porch was built in 1826 for Ferdinand Acton, the son of English aristocrat Sir John Acton. In 1841 it was bought by the Rothschild banking family, who brought in Gaetano Genovese—he of the Palazzo Reale's sumptuous staircase—to design the Salotto Rosso and the ballroom. The villa then passed to a distant ancestor of Spanish conquistador Hernán Cortés, and eventually to the Italian State in 1955. The villa contains a sumptuous collection of porcelain and a *biblioteca-discoteca*—a collection of classical and operatic records. It exhibits part of Banco di Napoli's collection of paintings, including works by masters of Neapolitan Baroque, and has 18th- and 19th-century landscapes. ✉ *Riviera di Chiaia 200, Naples* ☎ *081/7612356* 🎫 *€5, gardens only €2* 🕒 *Closed Tues.* Ⓜ *San Pasquale.*

Palazzo delle Arti di Napoli (*PAN*)
ART MUSEUM | Occupying the enormous Palazzo Rocella, PAN, as this arts organization calls itself, mounts temporary art exhibitions and operates a center for art research and documentation. Past exhibits have included the photographs of Joel-Peter Witkin, and internationally recognized contemporary artists working in other media have received shows, but the large space showcases works by up-and-coming talents as well. Film and other events also take place here. ✉ *Via dei Mille 60, Chiaia* ☎ *081/7958605* 🌐 *www.facebook.com/Panpalazzoarti* 🎫 *Free (fee for some exhibitions)* Ⓜ *Piazza Amedeo.*

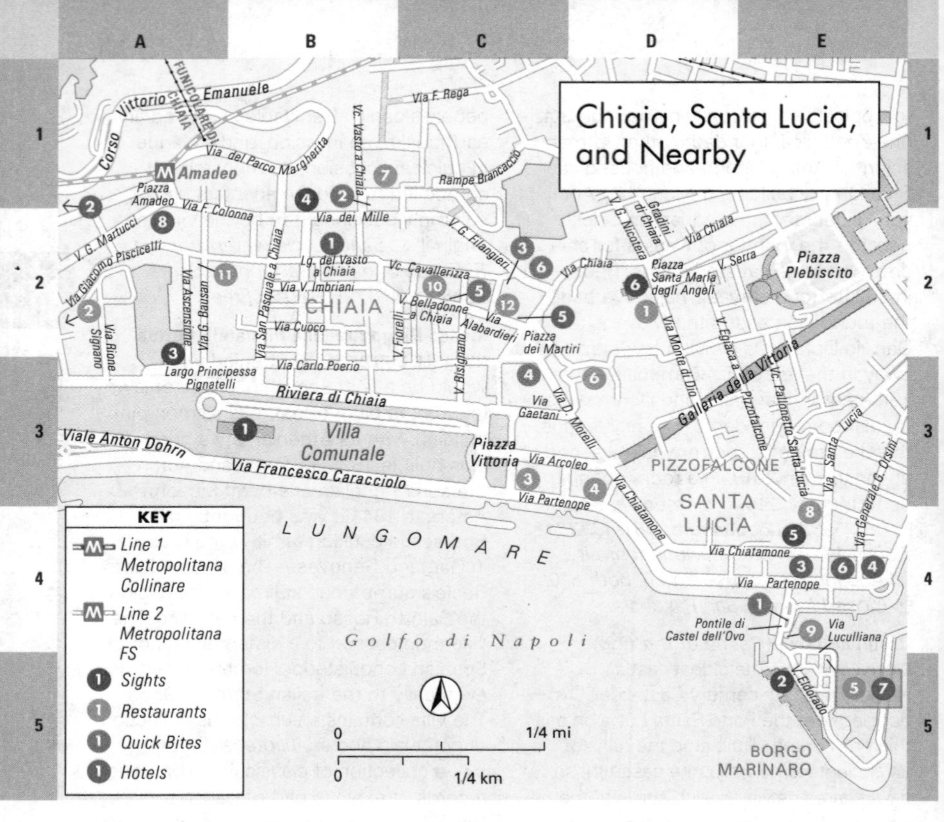

Sights	
1 Aquarium	B3
2 Castel dell'Ovo	E5
3 Museo Diego Aragona Pignatelli Cortes	A2
4 Palazzo delle Arti di Napoli	B1
5 Pizzofalcone	E4
6 Santa Maria degli Angeli a Pizzofalcone	D2

Restaurants	
1 Amici Miei	D2
2 Dora	A2
3 Gino Sorbillo Lievito Madre al Mare	C3
4 I Re di Napoli	D3
5 Il Transatlantico	E5
6 L'Altro Coco Loco	D3
7 L'Ebbrezza di Noè	B1
8 Marino	E4
9 'O Tabaccaro	E4
10 Pescheria Mattiucci	C2
11 Trattoria dell'Oca	A2
12 Umberto	C2

Quick Bites	
1 Al Barcadero	E4
2 Bar Guida	B1
3 Gran Caffè Cimmino	C2
4 Gran Caffè La Caffettieria	C3
5 La Focaccia	C2
6 La Torteria	C2

Hotels	
1 Exe Majestic	B2
2 Grand Hotel Parker's	A1
3 Grand Hotel Vesuvio	E4
4 Hotel Excelsior	E4
5 Hotel Palazzo Alabardieri	C2
6 Hotel Santa Lucia	E4
7 Il Transatlantico Napoli	E5
8 Pinto-Storey Hotel	A2

A Good Walk: The Lungomare

From the Amedeo funicular or metro station take the delightful Passeggiata Colonna on the left down to Via Colonna. Stop at the rambling **Palazzo delle Arti Napoli** if there's an exhibition that catches your eye; otherwise, take the first right turn down off Via Colonna onto the steps at the top of Via Bausan. The steps will take you down toward the Riviera di Chiaia (*chiaia* means "beach" in the Neapolitan dialect), where a final right turn brings you to the **Museo Diego Aragona Pignatelli Cortes.** From here cross the Riviera to the waterfront park of the Villa Comunale and its world-famous **Aquarium.**

Follow the Riviera past the Piazza della Vittoria for a stroll down Via Partenope to reach the spectacular **Castel dell'Ovo.** From here, a walk north on Via Chiatamone takes you to the Piazza dei Martiri, where you can join chic Neapolitans shopping the boutiques, bookstores, and antiques shops lining the streets that radiate off the piazza (particularly the designer-dense stretch between Via Carlo Poerio and Via dei Mille).

The area around Piazza dei Martiri is excellent for both snacking and more substantial meals. From here it's a relatively short walk back to one of the funiculars (the Centrale and Chiaia are roughly equidistant from the piazza), or you can catch any number of buses westward along the area's main artery, the Riviera di Chiaia.

Timing

Allow a few hours to take in the area around the seafront. If you prefer a leisurely wander or wish to visit an exhibition at Castel dell'Ovo, go straight to the Borgo from the Riviera di Chiaia following the seafront, and then swing back to Villa Pignatelli and the Aquarium.

Pizzofalcone (*Falcon's Beak*)
HISTORIC DISTRICT | In the 7th century BC, Pizzofalcone *was* Naples. The ancient Greeks had settled here because, legend says, the body of the siren Parthenope had washed ashore on the beach at the foot of the Pizzofalcone Hill, then known as Monte Echia. In the 18th century, the hill, mere feet from the bay and the Castel dell'Ovo, became a fashionable address as Naples's wealthy sought to escape the congestion and heat of the city center. The rocky promontory soon became studded with Baroque palaces and Rococo churches. The leading sights these days are the palazzi along Via Monte di Dio—including Palazzo Serra di Cassano—and the churches of La Nunziatella and Santa Maria degli Angeli. As with other parts of Naples, Pizzofalcone harbors both palaces and slums; unlike other parts, it's off-the-beaten path, so make sure to be aware of your surroundings at all times. ✉ *Piazza Santa Maria degli Angeli, accessed via elevator at Ponte di Chiaia on Via Chiaia, Pizzofalcone.*

Santa Maria degli Angeli a Pizzofalcone
CHURCH | In 1590 the princess of Sulmona, Costanza Doria del Carretto, donated the land not far from her palace on Pizzofalcone to the Theatine order, who built a small church. It was enlarged in the 17th century with lively vault and dome frescoes by Giovanni Beinaschi of Turin, better known as a painter of genre scenes. There are some good paintings by Luca Giordano and Massimo Stanzione tucked away in the smaller side chapels and

Castel dell'Ovo provides impressive views of the bay, the city, and looming Vesuvius.

oratory. ✉ *Piazza Santa Maria degli Angeli, Pizzofalcone* ☎ *081/7644974* Ⓜ *Chiaia.*

Restaurants

Amici Miei

$$$ | **SOUTHERN ITALIAN** | Favored by meat eaters who can't abide another bite of bream, this dimly lit cozy dining den is known for dishes such as tender carpaccio with fresh artichoke hearts. There are also excellent house-made pasta selections, including orecchiette with chickpeas or *alla barese* (with chewy green turnips), but the highlights are the extravagant grilled meat plates. **Known for:** superb, friendly service befitting the name; Art Nouveau decorative flourishes; a choice of quality meat dishes. $ *Average main: €25* ✉ *Via Monte di Dio 78, Chiaia* ☎ *081/7646063* 🌐 *www.ristoranteamicimiei.com* ⏲ *Closed Mon. and late July–early Sept. No dinner Sun.* Ⓜ *Chiaia.*

Dora

$$$ | **SEAFOOD** | Despite its location up an unpromising-looking *vicolo* (alley) off the Riviera di Chiaia, this small restaurant has achieved cult status for its seafood platters. It's remarkable what owner-chef Renato can produce in his tiny kitchen: start with linguine *alla Dora,* laden with local seafood and fresh tomatoes, and perhaps follow up with grilled *pezzogna* (blue-spotted bream). **Known for:** great service; simple, attractive nautical-theme decor; freshest seafood, both raw and cooked. $ *Average main: €26* ✉ *Via Fernando Palasciano 30, Chiaia* ☎ *081/680519* 🌐 *www.ristorantedora.it* ⏲ *Closed Mon.* Ⓜ *San Pasquale.*

Gino Sorbillo Lievito Madre al Mare

$ | **PIZZA** | For excellent pizza and a spectacular view, head to this hip little pie palace on the seaside promenade, on the corner of a street that includes more than 20 restaurants and bars. Locally grown or made peppers, olives, basil, prosciutto, ricotta, mozzarella, and other

Continued on page 310

AN APPETITE FOR NAPLES

"But there's nothing to it!" cry food snobs when Neapolitan cuisine is mentioned among the higher rungs of the world's culinary ladder. And they might be right—after all, there are no secret spices or special skills needed in its preparation.

The best fresh ingredients are all you need when the local produce is this good

But indeed, simplicity is the key, and the best fresh ingredients are what Napoli has in spades. Long, fleshy, deep-red San Marzano tomatoes grow on the fertile slopes of Vesuvius. The olive groves of the Cilento provide fragrant oil. Buffalo chew the grass on the plains toward Caserta, north of Naples, producing milk that makes the best mozzarella cheese in the world. And Neapolitans have long used the fish-filled waters of the bay to their gastronomic advantage. Tiny fish are marinated, fried, and eaten whole, or used to flavor sauces.

Swordfish are sliced up to make steaks. Clams, mussels, and octopus are ubiquitous, and usually enhanced with oil, lemon juice, garlic, and parsley, rather than masked with sauces.

With it all being so simple, you'd think you could replicate it at home. But it's never quite the same: perhaps it's that the water is different, or that you can never quite get the right variety of tomato. Or maybe it doesn't taste the same simply because you're not in Napoli anymore.

PIZZA NAPLES STYLE: The Classic Margherita

Locally grown San Marzano tomatoes are a must.

The best pizza should come out with cheese bubbling and be ever-so-slightly charred around its edges.

Only buffalo-milk mozzarella or fior di latte cheese should be used.

The dough must be made from the right kind of durum wheat flour and be left to rise for at least six hours.

Be prepared: ranging from the size of a plate to that of a Hummer wheel, Neapolitan pizza is different from anything you might find elsewhere in Italy—not to mention what's served up at American pizza chains. The "purest" form is the marinara, topped with only tomatoes, garlic, oregano, and olive oil.

OTHER FAVORITES ARE . . .

- **CAPRICCIOSA** (the "capricious"), made with whatever the chef has on hand.
- **SICILIANA** with mozzarella and eggplant.
- **DIAVOLA** with spicy salami.
- **QUATTRO STAGIONI** ("four seasons"), made with produce from each one.
- **SALSICCIA E FRIARIELLI** with sausage and a broccoli-like vegetable.

A PIZZA FIT FOR A QUEEN

During the patriotic fervor following Italian unification in the late 19th century, a Neapolitan chef decided to celebrate the arrival in the city of the new Italian queen Margherita by designing a pizza in her—and the country's—honor. He took red tomatoes, white mozzarella cheese, and a few leaves of fresh green basil—reflecting the three colors of the Italian flag—and gave birth to the modern pizza industry.

ONLY THE BEST

An association of Neapolitan pizza chefs has standardized the ingredients and methods that have to be used to make pizza certified DOC *(denominazione d'origine controllata)* or STG *(specialità tradizionale garantita)*. See the illustration on the opposite page for the basic requirements.

FIRED UP!

The Neapolitan pizza must be made in a traditional wood-burning oven. Chunks of beech or maple are stacked up against the sides of the huge, tiled ovens, then shoved onto the slate base of the oven, where they burn quickly at high temperatures. If you visit Pompeii, you will see how similar the old Roman bread-baking ovens are to the modern pizza oven. The *pizzaiolo* (pizza chef) then uses a long wooden paddle to put the pizza into the oven, where it cooks quickly.

PIZZERIE

Hundreds of restaurants specialize in pizza in Naples, and the best of these make pizza and nothing else. As befits the original fast food, *pizzerie* tend to be simple, fairly basic places, with limited menu choices, and quick, occasionally brusque service.

THE REAL THING

Naples takes its contribution to world cuisine seriously. The Associazione Verace Pizza Napoletana (www.pizzanapoletana.org) was founded in 1984 in order to share expertise, maintain quality levels, and provide courses for aspiring pizza chefs and pizza lovers. The group also organizes the annual Pizzafest—three days in September dedicated to the consumption of pizza, when *maestri* from all over the region get together and cook off.

Margherita of Savoy

Buffalo-milk mozzarella

A pizzaiolo at work

Typical pizzeria in Naples

Simple, fresh toppings

MORE NEAPOLITAN DISHES

Studded with clams, spaghetti con vongole is a top menu favorite.

The most famous of Neapolitan foods can be eaten standing up, but there's more to local cuisine than pizza. Don't leave Naples without sitting down to a few of these Napoli classics.

HOW SIMPLE IS NEAPOLITAN CUISINE?

Take a handful of tomatoes and squeeze them into a pan along with a drizzle of olive oil, a pinch of salt, and some fresh basil leaves. Leave them in just long enough to warm through. Boil some pasta for just as long as it needs. Put it all together, and you have pasta al pomodoro fresco, one of the most delicious dishes Italy has to offer. There really is nothing to it!

- **SPAGHETTI CON LE VONGOLE:** spaghetti topped with different kinds of clams, from the tiny lupini to the big red fasullari, still in their shells.
- **IMPEPATA DI COZZE:** mussels, thrown in a pot, heated up, and served with lots of fresh black pepper.
- **BACCALÀ:** dried salt cod, fried and served with some fresh herbs. Once you try it, you'll understand why many Neapolitans regard it as the authentic taste of home.
- **POLPETTINE AL RAGÙ:** meatballs in tomato sauce. Italian food's biggest export has never tasted as good as in Napoli.
- **PESCE ALL'ACQUA PAZZA:** fish in "crazy water," with garlic, a few small tomatoes, then some of the water from the fish added to the hot oil. The bubbles are what make it "crazy."
- **PARMIGIANA DI MELANZANE:** layers of eggplant, mozzarella, and tomato sauce baked in the oven.
- **PASTA ALLA GENOVESE:** not from Genoa, as its name might suggest, but, some claim, invented by a Neapolitan chef named Genovese. Beef and onions are slow-cooked for hours and then folded into the pasta.

"POOR FOOD"

During the winter when the best fresh produce isn't so abundant, Neapolitans head for the store cupboard and soak large quantities of dried cannellini beans, chickpeas, and lentils. These are then made into hearty soups, to which any kind of pasta can be added. They're great as filling and warm dishes, but because *pasta e fagioli, pasta e ceci*, and *pasta e lenticchie* are regarded as "poor food" (the kind of thing you make at home), they aren't often found on restaurant menus.

Baccalà alla vicentina, a traditional Italian codfish stew

LA FRITTURA

Forget all that stuff about the Mediterranean diet being so healthy. Lots of pizzerie and roadside stalls will offer you a selection of *frittura*—deep-fried balls of dough and seaweed, fried sliced eggplant, fried potato croquettes, fried zucchini flowers. Eat them with your fingers, and don't feel guilty.

Fried zucchini flowers

CAKE SEASON

Like everything else, cakes are seasonal. If you're visiting over Christmas, check out the teeth-challenging *rococò*, made of hazelnuts, or the softer *struffoli*, tiny balls of fried pastry doused in honey. Carnival time (mid-February to mid-March) is for *chiacchiere*—large, flat slices of light pastry sprinkled with icing sugar—while Easter sees rivalries for the best *pastiera*, a rich cake filled with ricotta, sifted grain, and orange or rose water. Around All Souls' Day (late October), cake shops fill up with *torrone* (soft or hard nougat). Two Napoli classics are, thankfully, available year-round: the large soft sponge *babà*, soaked in rum, and the *sfogliatella*, sweet and spicy ricotta cheese wrapped in short crust or puff pastry.

Divine pies and pasteria

LIMONCELLO

No serious meal is complete without a final *liquore*, and the local limoncello is the best of the lot. Made from the zest of lemons, lots of sugar, and pure alcohol, limoncello is very sweet, very strong, and must be served very cold.

Many brands of limoncello

O' CAFÈ

Whether to help you digest a big meal, give you a morning pickup, or accompany a cake, *o' cafè* (to give coffee its name in the local dialect) is a Neapolitan rite. You can have it in its pure state, small and black with a teaspoonful of sugar, or order *nocciola* (with hazelnut syrup), *macchiato* (with a dash of frothy milk), or *corretto* (with a shot of liqueur) varieties. If you want to keep to local customs, never ask for a cappuccino after a meal. It's considered bad for digestion.

O' Cafè

ingredients top a masterful wood-fired crust made with the *lievito madre* yeast starter. **Known for:** fresh ingredients; people-watching; glorious views. *Average main: €12* *Via Partenope 1, Santa Lucia* *081/19331280* *www.sorbillo.it.*

I Re di Napoli

$$ | PIZZA | The first restaurant to open on the seafront, this elegant pizzeria has been an essential hangout for Naples's gilded youth since 1994. Offering 36 kinds of pizza—including gluten-free—plus a fine selection of salads and an ample buffet make this a refreshing change from the more minimal *pizzerie.* The various stuffed pizzas named after kings are classics with a modern twist: try the Boccone di Re Ferdinando, filled with *salsiccia* (sausage), *friarielli* (broccoli rabe), and *provola* (smoked mozzarella) cheese, or the half-fried, half-oven cooked *Re di Napoli.* **Known for:** large selection; friendly staff; seafront's oldest pizziera. *Average main: €15* *Via Partenope 9, Santa Lucia* *081/7647775* *www.iredinapoli.it.*

Il Transatlantico

$$ | SEAFOOD | Within the picturesque Borgo Marinaro harbor, in the shadow of Castel dell'Ovo, it's as if you're eating aboard a transatlantic cruise ship. With the Bay of Naples nearby and Vesuvius in the background, you can understand the nautical decor, blue tablecloths, and the menu abrim with fish delicacies. (Foodies should also note that this was the site of the Roman villa of Lucullus, the moneyed aristocrat famous for his passion for luxurious dining.) A best bet is the *schiaffoni* with *astice* and *pescatrice* (large flat tube pasta with lobster and angler fish), or one of the tasty pizzas, but leave room for the dolce of the day (great house-made tiramisu or pear cake with ricotta). **Known for:** good location on the bay; fresh fish dishes; dining fit for a Roman aristocrat. *Average main: €18* *Via Luculliana 15, Borgo Marinaro, Santa Lucia* *081/7648842* *www.transatlanticonapoli.com* *Closed Tues.*

L'Altro Coco Loco

$$ | SOUTHERN ITALIAN | This stylish place took the Naples dining scene by storm a few years back, and it remains popular thanks to the innovative cuisine of master chef Diego Nuzzo. A bar runs the length of the restaurant, where salami and other glorious tidbits are served. **Known for:** vast wine list; convival atmosphere; high-quality cuisine. *Average main: €18* *Vicoletto Cappella Vecchia 4/5, east of Piazza dei Martiri, Chiaia* *081/7641722* *www.cocoloco.rest/napoli* *Closed 3 wks in Aug. No lunch Mon.–Sat.; no dinner Sun.*

L'Ebbrezza di Noè

$ | ITALIAN | A simple enoteca by day, L'Ebbrezza has a dining area in the back that fills up in the evening. Owner Luca's enthusiasm for what he does is quite moving—as you sample a recommended wine you can sense that he hopes you like it as much as he does. **Known for:** good wine list; quality cuisine; cheese selection. *Average main: €12* *Vico Vetriera a Chiaia 8b/9, Chiaia* *081/400104* *www.lebbrezzadinoe.com* *Closed Mon., and Aug. No lunch* *Piazza Amedeo.*

Marino

$ | SOUTHERN ITALIAN | Just around the corner from the Borgo Marinaro and the Hotel Vesuvio, this famous restaurant and pizzeria offers up its delights in a cool white-and-blue room. Try the house specialty, the Pizza Anastasia, with cherry tomatoes and lots of premium mozzarella. **Known for:** moderate prices; display of football memorabilia; fresh ingredients. *Average main: €7* *Via Santa Lucia 118/120, Santa Lucia* *081/7640280* *www.facebook.com/ristorantepizzeriamarino* *Closed Mon., and Aug.*

'O Tabaccaro

$ | SEAFOOD | If you're trying to keep to a budget but want to enjoy a seafood feast alongside the yachts of the Borgo Marinaro harbor, head to this former tobacco store. While your eyes feast on all the pretty boats, the Lungomare hotels, the Castel dell'Ovo, and Vesuvius, you can savor classic Neapolitan seafood spaghetti or an *impepata di cozze* (mussels with pepper and garlic). **Known for:** family service; portside dining; relatively inexpensive fare. *Average main: €13 Via Luculliana 28, Santa Lucia 081/7646352.*

★ Pescheria Mattiucci

$$ | **SOUTHERN ITALIAN** | In the evening, this fourth-generation fish shop becomes a trendy spot to enjoy an aperitif and a light meal. If you want to experience superb Neapolitan sushi and cold wine while sitting on a buoy stool, get here early: service is 7:30–10:30. **Known for:** fish lunches; intimate and small place, so get here early or call ahead for dinner; pescheria counter displaying today's catch. *Average main: €15 Vico Belledonne a Chiaia 27, Chiaia 081/2512215 www.pescheriamattiucci.com Closed Sun. and Mon. San Pasquale.*

Trattoria dell'Oca

$$ | **SOUTHERN ITALIAN** | The bright, clean, and simple decor reflects this place's lighter take on traditionally heavy Neapolitan food. The soupy pasta *e piselli* (with peas) is a wonderful surprise for anyone who has bad memories of pea soup, and the penne *alla scarpariello* (pasta with fresh tomato, basil, and pecorino cheese) is a specialty to set taste buds quivering. **Known for:** improved take on well-known dishes; pastel decor; cosy atmosphere. *Average main: €16 Via S. Teresa a Chiaia 11, Chiaia 081/414865 www.trattoriadelloca.it Closed 3 wks in Aug. and Tues. No lunch weekdays Piazza Amedeo.*

★ Umberto

$$ | **SOUTHERN ITALIAN** | Run by the Di Porzio family since 1916, Umberto is one of the city's classic restaurants, combining the classiness of its neighborhood, Chiaia, and the friendliness one finds in other parts of Naples. Try the *paccheri 'do tre dita* ("three-finger" pasta with octopus, tomato, olives, and capers); it bears the nickname of the original Umberto, who happened to be short a few digits. **Known for:** classic Neapolitan meat sauce alla Genovese; charming hosts; authentic Pizza DOC (smaller, with chunky cornicione rim). *Average main: €17 Via Alabardieri 30–31, Chiaia 081/418555 www.umberto.it No lunch Mon. Chiaia.*

Coffee and Quick Bites

Al Barcadero

$ | **SOUTHERN ITALIAN** | Located below the walkway to Castel dell'Ovo, Al Barcadero is a romantic outdoor setting for a snack and a coffee or aperitif. Take a break at one of the tables and gaze at Mt. Vesuvius beyond the masts of the nearby luxury yachts. **Known for:** light snack beside the castle; the city's most romantic setting; portside outdoor seating. *Average main: €5 Banchina Santa Lucia 2, Santa Lucia 333/2227023 mobile www.albarcaderonapoli.blogspot.com.*

Bar Guida

$ | **ITALIAN** | A fave with Via dei Mille shoppers is Bar Guida, which offers you not only the luxury of being able to sit down, but also has a decent range of savory light meals. **Known for:** fresh pastries; efficient service; crostoni (tiny bruschette). *Average main: €4 Via dei Mille 46, Chiaia 081/18893451 www.facebook.com/barguidaviadeimille Piazza Amedeo.*

Gran Caffè Cimmino

$ | **CAFÉ** | Connoisseurs often say the most refined pastries in town can be found at Gran Caffè Cimmino. Many of the city's lawyers congregate here, to celebrate or commiserate with crisp, light cannoli; airy lemon eclairs; *choux* paste in the form of a mushroom laced with chocolate whipped cream; and delightful wild-strawberry tartlets. **Known for:** terrace for watching Chiaia's finest; babà to die for; Neapolitan breakfast favorite. *Average main: €3 Via G. Filangieri 12/13, Chiaia 081/418303 Chiaia.*

Gran Caffè La Caffettieria

$ | **ITALIAN** | A classic address in the chic Chiaia district, in the summer months this bar sells their famous coffee-flavored chocolates in the shape of tiny coffee-pots. **Known for:** outdoor seating; delicious coffee; Art Deco design. *Average main: €3 Piazza dei Martiri 30, Chiaia 081/7644243 www.grancaffelacaffettiera.com No credit cards Chiaia.*

La Focaccia

$ | **ITALIAN** | While flat, pan-cooked focaccia can make some pizza fundamentalists wince, this place makes mouthwatering slices of the crunchy-bottomed snacks with a variety of toppings. Skip the predictable tomato variations and go for the delicious potato-and-rosemary focaccia with melted provola. **Known for:** ideal late-night snack spot; location among the Chiaia bars; fresh crispy focaccia. *Average main: €3 Vico Belledonne a Chaia 31, Chiaia 081/412277.*

La Torteria (*Pasticceria Varriale*)

$ | **ITALIAN** | This café is beloved not only for its excellent coffee but also for its beautiful cakes—concoctions of cream, chocolate, and fruit whose swirls of color make them look like Abstract Expressionist paintings. They also have a lunch menu. **Known for:** more than 50 years of service; perfect for a quick snack; fantastic cakes. *Average main: €3 Via Filangieri 75, Chiaia 081/405221 www.pasticceriavarriale.com Chiaia.*

Hotels

Exe Majestic

$$ | **HOTEL** | In a rather unspectacular blue-tiled building, the Exe Majestic is perfectly located near the swish Via dei Mille shopping street, the buzzing Chiaia nightlife, and the PAN contemporary art gallery. **Pros:** located in chic Chiaia; great for shopping; helpful staff. **Cons:** no bar; small breakfast; uninteresting 1950s building. *Rooms from: €180 Largo Vasto a Chiaia 68, Chiaia 081/416500 www.exemajestic.com 114 rooms Free Breakfast Piazza Amedeo.*

Grand Hotel Parker's

$$$ | **HOTEL** | A little up the hill from Chiaia, with fine views of the bay and distant Capri, this landmark hotel, first opened in 1870, continues to serve up a supremely elegant dose of old-style atmosphere to visiting VIPs. **Pros:** excellent restaurant; historic hotel; fabulous views. **Cons:** terrace sometimes closed when hosting weddings; not quite as grand as it once was; a very long walk or taxi ride from city center and seafront. *Rooms from: €250 Corso Vittorio Emanuele 135, Chiaia 081/7612474 www.grandhotelparkers.it 79 rooms Free Breakfast.*

★ **Grand Hotel Vesuvio**

$$$$ | **HOTEL** | You'd never guess from the modern exterior that this is the oldest of the city's great seafront hotels—the place where Enrico Caruso died, where Oscar Wilde dallied with lover Lord Alfred Douglas, and where Bill Clinton charmed the waitresses—fortunately, the spacious, soothing interior compensates for what's lacking on the outside. **Pros:** luxurious atmosphere; directly opposite Borgo Marinaro; historic setting and traditionally furnished rooms. **Cons:** not all rooms have great views; reception staff can be snooty; spa and pool cost extra. *Rooms from: €400 Via Partenope 45, Santa Lucia 081/7640044 www.vesuvio.it 160 rooms Free Breakfast.*

Hotel Excelsior

$$$ | **HOTEL** | Maharajahs, emperors, and Hollywood legends have stayed at this grand-tradition outpost that opened in 1908. **Pros:** delicious breakfasts; great views from breakfast room and rooftop

terrace; spacious rooms. **Cons:** some rooms are noisy; not all rooms have sea views; decor seems dated. *Rooms from: €205 Via Partenope 48, Santa Lucia 081/7640111 www.eurostarsexcelsior.com 122 rooms Free Breakfast.*

★ Hotel Palazzo Alabardieri

$$ | **HOTEL** | Just off the chic Piazza dei Martiri, this is a solid choice among the city's smaller smart hotels—with comfortable guest rooms and a fab location for sights, shopping, and eating. **Pros:** impressive public salons; polite, pleasant staff; central yet quiet location. **Cons:** small rooms; cell reception and a/c are patchy; no sea view. *Rooms from: €178 Via Alabardieri 38, Chiaia 081/415278 www.palazzoalabardieri.it 44 rooms Free Breakfast M Chiaia.*

Hotel Santa Lucia

$$ | **HOTEL** | Neapolitan *lungomare* enchantment can be yours if you stay at this luxurious, quietly understated hotel that overlooks the port immortalized in the song "Santa Lucia." Hundreds of boats bob in the water, seafood restaurants line the harbor, and the medieval Castel dell'Ovo presides over it all. **Pros:** great views from most rooms; fab pastries and baked goods; proximity to the port is convenient for trips to the islands. **Cons:** not near a metro stop; extra charges at breakfast; rooms can be small. *Rooms from: €200 Via Partenope 46, Santa Lucia 081/7640666 www.santalucia.it 85 rooms Free Breakfast.*

★ Il Transatlantico Napoli

$$ | **B&B/INN** | Enjoying perhaps the most enchanting setting in all of Naples, this modestly priced hotel tops many travelers' dream list of places to stay. **Pros:** fabulous location and views; boat hire available; reasonable prices for maritime-style rooms. **Cons:** sometimes loud music in the Borgo; no elevator; dated furniture and fabrics. *Rooms from: €140 Via Lucullliana 15, Santa Lucia 081/7648842 www.transatlanticonapoli.com 8 rooms No Meals.*

Pinto-Storey Hotel

$ | **HOTEL** | The name combines a 19th-century Englishman who fell in love with Naples with a certain Signora Pinto; together they went on to establish this hotel that overflows with warmth, charm, and late 19th-century (but fully renovated) decor. **Pros:** safe neighborhood; traditional Anglophile atmosphere; near public transit. **Cons:** two-night minimum in high season; no views; not close to major sights. *Rooms from: €100 Via G. Martucci 72, Chiaia 081/681260 www.pintostorey.it 6 rooms No Meals M Piazza Amedeo.*

Nightlife

BARS

Ba-Bar

BARS | Connoisseurs of fine wines sit at wooden-top tables or at the bar in this convivial, dimly-lit bar. As the evening progresses it's standing room only, with guests mingling to the sounds of chill-out tunes. *Via Bisignano 20, Chiaia 081/7643525 www.ba-bar.it M San Pasquale.*

★ Enoteca Belledonne

WINE BARS | Between 8 and 9 in the evening, it seems as though the whole upscale Chiaia neighborhood has descended into this tiny space for an aperitivo. The small tables and low stools are notably uncomfortable, but the cozy atmosphere and the pleasure of being surrounded by glass-front cabinets full of wine bottles with beautiful labels more than makes up for it. Excellent local wines are available by the glass at great prices. *Vico Belledonne a Chiaia 18, Chiaia 081/403162 www.enotecabelledonne.it M San Pasquale.*

66
BARS | The bar entitled simply 66 describes itself as a "fusion bar." Some prefer it as a chic place to have an aperitivo (help yourself to the snacks beautifully laid out on the bar). Other patrons, who look like they've just popped out of one of the area's designer-clothing shops, come here to dine or gather in one of the upstairs rooms. ✉ *Via Bisignano 58, Chiaia* ☎ *081/415024* 🌐 *www.facebook.com/66Baretti* Ⓜ *San Pasquale.*

Performing Arts

Associazione Alessandro Scarlatti
MUSIC | The association organizes chamber-music concerts at Teatro Sannazaro with occasional performances at the Music Conservatory in the Centro Storico. ✉ *Piazza dei Martiri 58, Chiaia* ☎ *081/406011* 🌐 *www.associazionescarlatti.it.*

Centro di Musica Antica Pietà de' Turchini
MUSIC | Based in the early Baroque church of Santa Caterina da Siena, the center presents an excellent season of early music that runs from October to early May. Even if madrigals aren't your thing, it's worth visiting just for the location. Some performances are also held in other locations in the city. ✉ *Via Santa Caterina da Siena 38, Toledo* ☎ *081/402395* 🌐 *www.turchini.it.*

TAM Tunnel
CONCERTS | For those with knowledge of the Italian language, the TAM Tunnel has a solid program of cabaret and stand-up. ✉ *Gradini Nobile 1, Chiaia* ☎ *081/682814* 🌐 *www.madeinsud.it* Ⓜ *Piazza Amedeo.*

Teatro Politeama
CONCERTS | This venue presents a challenging bill of fare that includes a healthy dose of contemporary dance. The Teatro San Carlo company uses the space to present contemporary works that are a little too modern for their hallowed headquarters. ✉ *Via Monte di Dio 80, Chiaia* ☎ *081/7645001* 🌐 *www.teatropoliteama.it* Ⓜ *Chiaia.*

Teatro Sannazzaro
CONCERTS | For a satisfying Neapolitan "soul" experience, catch a local singer like Lina Sastri or Lara Sansone here at Teatro Sannazzaro. Traditional Neapolitan plays by Edoardo di Filippo are also often presented here, and the venue also books shows by younger Italian bands and singers. Associazione Scarlatti hosts its classical music season here. ✉ *Via Chiaia 157, Chiaia* ☎ *081/411723* 🌐 *www.teatrosannazaro.it* Ⓜ *Chiaia.*

Villa Pignatelli
CONCERTS | The 19th-century residence of the Rothschild banking family makes a fitting venue for the concerts that are often held in the summer here. ✉ *Riviera di Chiaia 200, Chiaia* ☎ *081/7612356* Ⓜ *San Pasquale.*

Shopping

ANTIQUES

Domenico Russo e Figli
ANTIQUES & COLLECTIBLES | This shop continues the centuries-old Neapolitan tradition of marble-inlay work, creating precious tables and console tops. ✉ *Via Bisignano 51, Chiaia* ☎ *081/7648387* 🌐 *www.marmirussonapoli.it* Ⓜ *San Pasquale.*

ART GALLERIES

Galleria Lia Rumma
ART GALLERIES | Marina Abramović, Anselm Kiefer, and Vanessa Beecroft are among international artists represented by this gallery. ✉ *Via Vannella Gaetani 12, Chiaia* ☎ *081/19812354* 🌐 *www.liarumma.it* Ⓜ *Chiaia.*

Galleria Trisorio
ART GALLERIES | The gallery exhibits the works of international artists of the caliber of Rebecca Horn and William Eggleston. ✉ *Riviera di Chiaia 215, Chiaia* ☎ *081/414306* 🌐 *www.studiotrisorio.com* Ⓜ *San Pasquale.*

Umberto Di Marino
ART GALLERIES | Young and promising Italian and international artists are shown here, along with their established counterparts. ✉ *Via Alabardieri 1, Chiaia* ☎ *081/2159001* 🌐 *www.galleriaumberto-dimarino.com* Ⓜ *Chiaia.*

BOOKS AND PRINTS

Bowinkel
ANTIQUES & COLLECTIBLES | For antique prints, postcards, watercolors, photographs, and engravings, the most famous shop in town is Bowinkel (here since 1879), where the lucky collector can often pick up pricey treasures, including delectable views of 19th-century Naples. ✉ *Piazza dei Martiri 24, Chiaia* ☎ *081/7644344* 🌐 *www.bowinkel.it* Ⓜ *Chiaia.*

La Feltrinelli
BOOKS | The largest bookstore in town carries books, CDs, and DVDs, and has an inviting coffee bar on the lower ground floor. The branch in Stazione Centrale also has a large selection of English books. ✉ *Via Santa Caterina a Chiaia 23, Chiaia* ☎ *081/2405411* 🌐 *www.lafeltrinelli.it* Ⓜ *Chiaia.*

CLOTHING AND ACCESSORIES

Argenio
MEN'S CLOTHING | An exclusive address for men's accessories, Argenio is the former supplier of scarves, cuff links, buttons, tiepins, and so forth to the royal Bourbons of the House of the Two Sicilies. ✉ *Via Filangieri 15/E, Chiaia* ☎ *081/418035* 🌐 *www.argenionapoli.it* Ⓜ *Piazza Amedeo, Chiaia.*

Eddy Monetti
MEN'S CLOTHING | The original Eduardo Monetti opened his doors in 1887 as a hat designer, soon bringing in customers such as the tenor Enrico Caruso. The shop remains a landmark Neapolitan name in sartorial splendor for men. Women can now find Monetti fashions on nearby Via Santa Caterina. ✉ *Via dei Mille 45, Chiaia* ☎ *081/407064* 🌐 *www.eddymonetti.com* Ⓜ *Piazza Amedeo.*

Emporio Armani
MIXED CLOTHING | Designer Giorgio Armani's mass-market brand does business in chic Piazza dei Martiri. ✉ *Piazza dei Martiri 61, Chiaia* ☎ *081/425816* 🌐 *www.armani.com/it* Ⓜ *Chiaia.*

Furla
HANDBAGS | The shop carries bags at surprisingly accessible prices. ✉ *Via Filangieri 26, Chiaia* ☎ *081/414218* 🌐 *www.furla.com* Ⓜ *Piazza Amedeo, Chiaia.*

Hermès
HANDBAGS | The French brand Hermès has a shop on the increasingly chic Via Filangieri. ✉ *Via Filangieri 53/57, Chiaia* ☎ *081/4207054* 🌐 *www.hermes.com* Ⓜ *Piazza Amedeo, Chiaia.*

Jossa
MEN'S CLOTHING | Menswear by Italian and international designers can be found here. ✉ *Via Carlo Poerio 43, Chiaia* ☎ *081/7649835* 🌐 *www.facebook.com/jossastores* Ⓜ *San Pasquale.*

Livio de Simone
WOMEN'S CLOTHING | The Neapolitan designer Livio de Simone was famous for his bright, printed-textile designs worn by 1950s and '60s celebrity femmes, and now his daughter Benedetta runs the still sexy line. ✉ *Via Domenico Morelli 15, Chiaia* ☎ *081/7643827* 🌐 *www.liviodesimone.com* Ⓜ *Chiaia.*

Mariano Rubinacci
MEN'S CLOTHING | If you feel like indulging in a custom-made suit or shirt, try this world-famous haberdashery that's been in business since the 19th century. In the 16th-century Palazzo Cellamare, you can watch the tailors at work. ✉ *Palazzo Cellammare, Via Chiaia 149e, Chiaia* ☎ *081/415793* 🌐 *www.marianorubinacci.com* Ⓜ *Chiaia.*

Marinella
MEN'S CLOTHING | Count the British royal family among the customers of this shop that has been selling old-fashioned made-to-measure ties for more than 100 years. ✉ *Via Riviera di Chiaia 287, Chiaia* ☎ *081/7642365* 🌐 *www.emarinella.eu* Ⓜ *Chiaia, San Pasquale.*

Salvatore Ferragamo
MIXED CLOTHING | Although based in Florence, Ferragamo is also beloved by Neapolitans who appreciate fine Italian taste and craftsmanship. ✉ *Piazza dei Martiri 56, Chiaia* ☎ *081/415454* 🌐 *www.ferragamo.com* Ⓜ *Chiaia.*

LEATHER GOODS

IDEM
LEATHER GOODS | Run by the next generation of renowned artisan Aldo Tramontano, IDEM sells handcrafted leather bags in a location with original 19th-century furnishings. ✉ *Via Belledonne a Chiaia 12, Chiaia* ☎ *081/406852* 🌐 *www.idemlab.com* Ⓜ *San Pasquale.*

Louis Vuitton
LUGGAGE | Lose yourself in this emporium of luxury travel accessories spread across two floors. ✉ *Via dei Mille 2, Chiaia* ☎ *081/7646606* 🌐 *www.louisvuitton.com* Ⓜ *Piazza Amedeo, Chiaia.*

Tramontano
LEATHER GOODS | Since 1865, this place has been crafting fine leather luggage, bags, belts, and wallets. ✉ *Via Chiaia 143, Chiaia* ☎ *081/414837* 🌐 *www.tramontano.it* Ⓜ *Chiaia.*

JEWELRY

Bulgari
JEWELRY & WATCHES | The posh brand showcases its internationally famous jewelry on posh Via Filangieri. ✉ *Via Filangieri 40, Chiaia* ☎ *081/409551* 🌐 *www.bulgari.com* Ⓜ *Piazza Amedeo, Chiaia.*

Damiani
JEWELRY & WATCHES | Since 1924, award-winning Damiani has sold high-end watches and jewelry to the likes of Sophia Loren, Brad Pitt, and Gwyneth Paltrow. ✉ *Via Filangieri 15, Chiaia* ☎ *081/405043* 🌐 *www.damiani.com/it* Ⓜ *Piazza Amedeo, Chiaia.*

DoDo
JEWELRY & WATCHES | The unusual jewelry at DoDo comes in the form of gold, silver, and other charms. ✉ *Via Filangieri 58, Chiaia* ☎ *081/418245* 🌐 *www.dodo.it* Ⓜ *Chiaia.*

Ventrella
JEWELRY & WATCHES | One of Naples's oldest traders, operating since 1850, the chic salon of this most exclusive contemporary jewelry workshop sells the original designs of its gifted artisans. ✉ *Via Carlo Poerio 11, Chiaia* ☎ *081/7643173* 🌐 *www.ventrella.it* Ⓜ *San Pasquale.*

MARKETS

Bancarelle di San Pasquale
MARKET | High-quality shoes, bags, and clothing can be found every morning at this market in Chiaia that also has a large section of foods, spices, fruits, and vegetables. ✉ *Via Vittorio Imbriani, Chiaia* Ⓜ *Piazza Amedeo, San Pasquale.*

Vomero

The hill that towers over Naples is the largely residential Vomero. From the balcony belvedere of the Museo di San Martino, a rich spread of southern Italian amplitude fills the eye: hillsides dripping with luxuriant greenery interspersed with villainously ugly apartment houses, streets short and narrow (leading to an unspeakable as well as unsolvable traffic problem), countless church spires and domes, and far below, the reason it all works, the intensely blue Bay of Naples.

Four *funicolari*—the funicular system that runs up and down the hill on four separate routes—tie the lower parts of the city with Vomero. Metro stop Vanvitelli, on Line 1, takes you to the heart of the area.

Sights

Castel Sant'Elmo

CASTLE/PALACE | Perched on the Vomero, this massive castle is almost the size of a small town. Built by the Angevins in the 14th century to dominate the port and the old city, it was remodeled by the Spanish in 1537. The parapets, configured in the form of a six-pointed star, provide fabulous views. The whole bay lies on one side; on another, the city spreads out like a map, its every dome and turret clearly visible; to the east is slumbering Vesuvius. Once a major military outpost, the castle these days hosts occasional cultural events. Its prison, the Carcere alto di Castel Sant'Elmo, is the site of the Museo del Novecento Napoli, which traces Naples's 20th-century artistic output, from the Futurist period through the 1980s. *Largo San Martino, Vomero* *848/800288, 081/5587708* *www.beniculturali.it/luogo/castel-sant-elmo-e-museo-del-novecento-a-napoli* *€5* *Museo del Novecento closed Tues.*

★ **Certosa e Museo di San Martino**

RELIGIOUS BUILDING | Atop a rocky promontory with a fabulous view of the entire city and majestic salons that would please any monarch, the Certosa di San Martino is a monastery that seems more like a palace. The *certosa,* or charter house, had been started in 1325, but by the 18th century, it had grown so sumptuous that Ferdinand IV was threatening to halt the religious order's government subsidy. Although the Angevin heritage can be seen in the pointed arches and cross-vaulted ceiling of the Certosa Church, over the years dour Gothic was traded in for varicolor Neapolitan Baroque. The sacristy leads into the Cappella del Tesoro, with Luca Giordano's ceiling fresco of Judith holding aloft Holofernes's head and paintings by Jusepe de Ribera (the *Pietà* over the altar is one of his masterpieces). The polychrome marble work of the architect and sculptor Cosimo Fanzago (1591–1678) is at its finest here, and he displays a gamut of sculptural skills in the Chiostro Grande (Great Cloister). Fanzago's ceremonial portals at each corner of the cloister are among the most spectacular of all Baroque creations, aswirl with Michelangelo-esque ornament. The nearby Museo dell'Opera, not always open, contains sociology-theme rooms that add up to a chronological tour of the city. One room has 13 gouaches of Vesuvius, and another has paintings depicting the Plague. The Quarto del Priore (Prior's Quarters), the residence of the only monk allowed contact with the outside world, is an extravaganza of salons filled with frescoes, majolica-tile floors, and paintings, plus extensive gardens where scenic *pergolati* (roofed balconies) overlook the bay.

Entering from the Quarto del Priore side, you come upon two splendid gilded coaches and then the "Vessels of the King" naval museum, with a 20-meter (65-foot) boat occupying a whole room. Beyond this lie two rooms with Early Renaissance masterpieces; subsequent rooms hold works by later artists, including the tireless Luca Giordano. Past the library, with its heavenly majolica-tile floor, comes the Sezione Presepiale, the world's greatest collection of Christmas cribs. Pride of place goes to the *Presepe* (Nativity scene) of Michele Cuciniello. Equally amazing in its own way is a crib inside an eggshell. *Piazzale San Martino 8, Vomero* *081/2294503* *www.beniculturali.it/luogo/certosa-e-museo-di-san-martino* *€6* *Closed Wed.* M *Vanvitelli.*

A Good Walk: Vomero

Begin in the Toledo area at the main station of the Funicolare Centrale, on the tiny Piazza Duca d'Aosta, on Via Toledo. After two hillside stops, get off at the end of the line, Stazione Fuga, near the top of the Vomero Hill. To get to the Castel Sant'Elmo/Certosa di San Martino complex, head out from the station, turning right across the pedestrianized Piazza Aldo Masullo toward the escalator, then left on Via Morghen. At the next junction, Via Scarlatti—the main thoroughfare of the neighborhood—turn right uphill and take the escalator (or steps), cutting twice across the snakelike Via Morghen, then follow the path around the left side of the Montesanto funicular until you run into the Via Tito Angelini. This street, lined with some of Naples's best Belle Époque mansions, leads to the **Certosa di San Martino** past the adjoining **Castel Sant'Elmo,** which commands magnificent 360-degree vistas over city and sea to Vesuvius.

After viewing this enormous complex, the more energetic will want to hike down the 414 Pedamentina di San Martino steps to Spaccanapoli, but you can also backtrack to Via Scarlatti until you make a left on Via Bernini at Piazza Vanvitelli. This piazza, with its smart bars and trattorias, remains the center for the Vomero district.

Walk right onto Via Cimarosa for two long blocks until you reach the entrance to the **Villa Floridiana,** today a museum filled with aristocratic knickknacks and surrounded by a once-regal park. After viewing the villa, make a right from the park entrance on Via Cimarosa for two blocks until you reach the Stazione Cimarosa of the Chiaia funicular, which will take you back down to the Lungomare area.

Timing

As always in Naples, it's best to start out early in the morning to fit most of your sightseeing in before the lunch break—and summer's midday heat. Aim to get to the San Martino complex atop the Vomero hill at opening time and allow at least three hours to take it in along with the Castel Sant'Elmo and an additional half hour for the Villa Floridiana.

Villa Floridiana

OTHER MUSEUM | Now a chiefly residential neighborhood, the Vomero Hill was once the patrician address of many of Naples's most extravagant estates. La Floridiana is the sole surviving 19th-century example, built in 1817 on order of Ferdinand IV for Lucia Migliaccio, duchess of Floridia—their portraits hang in a room to the left of the villa's main entrance. Only nine shocking months after his first wife, the Habsburg Maria Carolina, died, Ferdinand secretly married Lucia, his longtime mistress, when the court was still in mourning. Scandal ensued, but the king and his new wife were too happy to worry, escaping high above the city to this elegant little estate. Immersed in a delightful park done in the English style by Degenhardt (also responsible for the park in Capodimonte), the villa was designed by architect Antonio Niccolini in the Neoclassical style. It now houses the Museo Nazionale della Ceramica Duca di Martina, a museum devoted to the decorative arts of the 18th and 19th centuries. Countless cases on three floors display what Edith Wharton described as "all those fragile and elaborate trifles the irony of fate preserves when brick and marble crumble": Sèvres, Limoges, and Meissen porcelains, gold watches, ivory fans, glassware, enamels, majolica vases, as well as one of the most significant collections of Oriental antiquities in Italy. Sadly, there are no period rooms left to see. ✉ *Via Cimarosa 77, Vomero* ☎ *081/5788418* 🌐 *www.musei.campania.beniculturali.it/le-collezioni-del-museo-duca-di-martina* 🎫 *Free* ⏲ *Closed Tues.* Ⓜ *Vanvitelli.*

Restaurants

Acunzo

$ | **PIZZA** | If you see a line of hungry-looking patrons between the Funicular stations of Toledo and Chiaia, you'll know you are close to Pizzeria Acunzo. To avoid anxious waits, many like to get here as soon as it opens at 7, just as the busier evening session starts. **Known for:** best pizza in Vomero; new covered seating area outside; signature pasta pizza pie. Ⓢ *Average main: €8* ✉ *Via Cimarosa 60, Vomero* ☎ *081/5785362* 🌐 *www.acunzo1964.it* ⏲ *Closed 1 wk Aug.* Ⓜ *Vanvitelli.*

Trattoria Vanvitelli

$ | **ITALIAN** | A small low-key entrance on Piazza Vanvitelli opens into a labyrinth of underground cellars and a large covered courtyard surrounded by palazzos. This bustling eatery suits a range of palates and budgets: pizzas and several variants of *filletto* (steak) come highly recommended. **Known for:** outdoor garden dining area; convivial atmosphere; lavish fixed-price lunch menu. Ⓢ *Average main: €12* ✉ *Piazza Vanvitelli 9c, Vomero* ☎ *081/5563015* 🌐 *www.facebook.com/trattoria.vanvitelli1* Ⓜ *Vanvitelli.*

Coffee and Quick Bites

Ambrosino

$ | **SOUTHERN ITALIAN** | At Ambrosino, ideal for a quick snack, you can take your pick of the pizzas and pasta dishes, or ask the owners to whip up a panino made from the excellent cheeses, vegetables, and meats on display. The uniformly high-quality ingredients make up for this place's spartan surroundings. **Known for:** its bustling atmosphere; a quick bite; local fare. Ⓢ *Average main: €7* ✉ *Via Scarlatti 49, Vomero* ☎ *081/3721170* 🌐 *www.ambrosinonapoli.it* ⏲ *Closed 2 wks in Aug.* Ⓜ *Vanvitelli.*

Friggitoria Vomero

$ | **SOUTHERN ITALIAN** | Since 1938, this place has been popular with kids (and decidedly not with health-conscious adults) thanks to its greasy brown-paper bags filled with deep-fried eggplant, zucchini, zucchini flowers, *zeppole* dough balls, and potato croquettes—the Neapolitan versions of French madeleines. Forget all that stuff about the Mediterranean diet being so healthy and indulge in some oil-drenched bliss. **Known for:** traditional street food; a quick bite; deep-fried delights. Ⓢ *Average main: €3* ✉ *Via Cimarosa 44, Vomero* ☎ *081/5783130* 🌐 *www.facebook.com/friggitoria.vomero* ⏲ *Closed Sun., and Aug.* Ⓜ *Vanvitelli.*

Hotels

Hotel San Francesco al Monte

$$$ | **HOTEL** | This high-end hotel retains hints of its former life as a Franciscan monastery; the small lobby leads to narrow corridors lined with doors that look dauntingly cell-like, until you enter and find surprisingly spacious, simply decorated rooms, many with their own hot tubs and furnishings no monk would dream of. **Pros:** rooftop pool; several nice dining options; a monk's wildest dream. **Cons:** taxi needed to go out at night; on a main traffic route; a little far from the action. Ⓢ *Rooms from: €210* ✉ *Corso Vittorio Emanuele 328, Vomero* ☎ *081/4239111* 🌐 *www.sanfrancescoalmonte.it* 🛏 *45 rooms* 🍽 *Free Breakfast.*

Nightlife

BARS

Fonoteca

BARS | By day the city's best independent record store, by night this is *the* place to hear eclectic tunes and mingle in Vomero. They serve decent bar snacks, pasta dishes, cakes, and drinks. ✉ *Via Morghen 31, Vomero* ☎ *081/5560338* 🌐 *www.fonoteca.net* Ⓜ *Vanvitelli.*

Riot Laundry Bar

CAFÉS | By day a clothing store and bar, this favorite with trend-setters becomes a late-night haunt after dark. ✉ *Via Michele Kerbaker 19, Vomero* ☎ *081/19578491* 🌐 *www.facebook.com/riotconceptstore* Ⓜ *Vanvitelli.*

Swig

BARS | This tiny bar is where trendy *Vomeresi* grab a predinner cocktail or postdinner *cicchetto* (shot). ✉ *Via Alessandro Scarlatti 50/a, Vomero* ☎ *081/5568861* 🌐 *www.swigbar.net* Ⓜ *Vanvitelli.*

Shopping

MARKETS

Mercatino di Antignano

MARKET | For low-price and surprisingly high-quality clothing and linen, head to the Mercatino di Antignano. ✉ *Piazza degli Artisti, Vomero* Ⓜ *Medaglie D'Oro.*

Mergellina and Posillipo

A small fishing port until the 17th century, Mergellina in western Naples is now a major traffic hub and very much a part of the city. Fishermen still gather here, but can be difficult to spot among the private yachts and pleasure craft lining the long pier.

Climbing the hill to Capo Posillipo, this is *the* address to have. Sumptuous villas and gardens with private beaches line the coast; the imposing white mansion Villa Rosebery, the Italian president's Neapolitan residence, is the most noteworthy (and is visible only from the sea). Naples's most famous panorama is also here, immortalized in countless postcards and pizzeria paintings: a lone umbrella pine on a bluff overlooking the bay and the city, with Vesuvius in the background. The iconic pine tree no longer exists, but the view remains magnificent.

The Metro station Mergellina (Line 2, with Line 6 in construction) is just five minutes walk from the sea, and bus 140 climbs the Posillipo hill from here and Piazza Vittoria in Chiaia. The funicular from Via Manzoni also arrives here, although this has been closed in recent years.

Sights

Parco Vergiliano a Piedigrotta

CEMETERY | An often overlooked sight in western Naples, the park is named for the poet Virgil and is reputedly his burial site. Not to be confused with the Parco Virgiliano, at the western end of the Naples suburb of Posillipo, the sign at the park's entrance indicates that not only (by legend) is Virgil's tomb here, but also the tomb-memorial of Giacomo Leopardi, the author of the evocative poem "L'infinito," who died during the 1837 cholera epidemic. As a safety precaution, victims of the disease were usually buried in mass graves, but the writer (and later politician) Antonio Ranieri, a close friend, arranged for this monument, which until 1939 was located elsewhere. From the Mergellina metro station, walk south to Salita della Grotta and turn right just before the church of Santa Maria di Piedigrotta; the park's entrance is just before the road tunnel. ✉ *Salita della Grotta 20, off Piazza Piedigrotta, Mergellina* ☎ *081/669390* 🎟 *Free* 🕒 *Closed Tues.* Ⓜ *Mergellina.*

Parco Virgiliano

VIEWPOINT | Perched 500 feet above the Bay of Naples, this large urban park is worth the trip for its stunning vistas that face the islet Nisida with the formerly industrial area of Bagnoli stretching out below. A raised central area has a sports field where the Naples American Football team often trains. ✉ *Viale Virgilio, Posillipo* 🎫 *Free.*

★ Pausilypon Archaeological Park

RUINS | Located at the top of Posillipo's hill, this small yet magical complex has a 1st-century villa and two amphitheaters; access is though the Grotta di Seiano, a 2,500-foot tunnel cut though the *tufa* rock over two millenia ago. Free guided tours (in Italian, book ahead) are given at 9:30 and 10:30, weekdays, with more detailed tours given at weekends. Evening concerts are often held here in the summer. ✉ *Discesa Coroglio 36, Posillipo* ☎ *081/2301030 to book tours weekdays, 081/2403235 to book tours weekends* 🌐 *www.gaiola.org* 🎫 *Free weekdays, €6 weekends.*

Restaurants

'A Fenestella

$$ | **SEAFOOD** | This restaurant is perched overlooking a beach in Posillipo near the end of a long winding side road, and has long capitalized on its location. The landmark also comes with its own piece of Neapolitan folklore: in the 19th century the owner's great-grandmother Carolina was one day standing at the window (*fenestella* in the local dialect) and was spotted by musician Salvatore Di Giacomo below, thus inspiring the Neapolitan folk song "Marechiaro." Today, the restaurant is straightforwardly traditional, with comfortable decor and the usual suspects on the menu. **Known for:** glorious views; close to the beach; part of the city's folklore. 💲 *Average main: €22* ✉ *Calata del Ponticello a Marechiaro 23, Posillipo* ☎ *081/7690020* 🌐 *www.ristoranteafenestella.it* 🕓 *Closed Tues. Sept.–May.*

50 kalò

$ | **PIZZA** | In the Neapolitan *smorfia*, a list of numbers used to analyse dreams (and play the lottery), 50 means bread, and kalò is the Greek for good. And good dough is on the menu here, with this airy pizzeria gaining accolades since opening in traffic-busy Piazza Sannazaro in 2014—the *New York Times* hailed the pizza among the best in Italy. **Known for:** vegetable pizza; international accolades; a local favorite. 💲 *Average main: €7* ✉ *Piazza Sannazzaro 201/b, Mergellina* ☎ *081/19204667* 🌐 *www.50kalò.it* Ⓜ *Mergellina.*

★ Palazzo Petrucci

$$$$ | **SOUTHERN ITALIAN** | Overlooking the beach at the 15th-century Palazzo Donn'Anna, the Michelin-starred Palazzo Petrucci doesn't lack for dramatic dining options. On three levels, one of which is their lounge bar, diners are practically on the beach, with a glass partition revealing the kitchens. **Known for:** magical location; three tasting menus; fine beach dining. 💲 *Average main: €38* ✉ *Via Posillipo 16b/c, Mergellina* ☎ *081/5757538* 🌐 *www.palazzopetrucci.it* 🕓 *Closed 2 wks in Aug. No dinner Mon.* Ⓜ *Mergellina.*

★ Trattoria da Cicciotto

$$ | **SEAFOOD** | Chic and charming Da Cicciotto corrals more than a few members of the city's fashionable set—if you dine here, there's a fair chance you'll find a Neapolitan count or off-duty film star enjoying this jewel with a tiny stone terrace (with seats and a canopy) that overlooks a pleasant anchorage. You can also opt for the large covered patio across the way and appreciate the outdoor setting at either lunch or dinner. **Known for:** freshest seafood; venue for a special occasion; fabulous views over the harbor and bay. 💲 *Average main: €24* ✉ *Calata del Ponticello a Marechiaro 32, Posillipo* ☎ *081/5751165* 🌐 *www.trattoriadacicciotto.it.*

Hotels

BW Signature Collection Hotel Paradiso
$$ | HOTEL | This impressive hotel on the hillside of Posillipo is famous for its Bay of Naples view, its roof-garden Paradiso Blanco restaurant, and its garden terrace. **Pros:** sweeping bay views; posh Posillipo neighborhood is quieter and safer than city center; lovely rooftop restaurant. **Cons:** removed from Naples, so guests miss out on city life; the cheaper rooms have no views; funicular service is patchy. *Rooms from: €160* ✉ *Via Catullo 11, Posillipo* ☎ *081/2475111* 🌐 *www.hotelparadisonapoli.it* *72 rooms* *Free Breakfast.*

Nightlife

Palazzo Petrucci
CAFÉS | With its views of the bay at the start of the Posillipo hill, Palazzo Petrucci's rooftop lounge bar is one of the most romantic locations in the city to enjoy an evening cocktail. ✉ *Via Posillipo 16b/c, Posillipo* ☎ *081/5757538* 🌐 *www.palazzopetrucci.it* Ⓜ *Mergellina.*

Teatro Posillipo
DANCE CLUBS | Perched on the hill of Posillipo, this one-time cinema now hosts cabaret dinner shows, followed by local and international DJs. ✉ *Via Posillipo 66, Posillipo* ☎ *081/7691742* 🌐 *www.teatroposillipo.it.*

Shopping

MARKETS

Mercatino di Posillipo
MARKET | The market takes place on Thursday morning. Get here early for the best bargains. ✉ *Viale Virgilio, Posillipo* ☎ *339/4200584 mobile* 🌐 *www.facebook.com/cirotitti.*

Index

M

N

O

P

Photo Credits

Front Cover: Freeartist / Alamy Stock Photo [Picturesque Atrani village in amalfi coast of Italy]. **Back cover, from left to right:** Cezary Wojtkowski /istockphot, ElenaPhotos/istockphoto, J-wildman/istockphoto. **Spine:** RomanBabakin/istockphoto. **Interior, from left to right:** Oleg Voronische/shutterstock (1). Inu/shutterstock (2-3). Eric Valenne geostory/Shutterstock (5). **Chapter 1: Experience the Amalfi Coast, Capri, and Naples:** Minnystock/Dreamstime (6-7). Rudi1976/Dreamstime (8-9). Lesia Popovych/Shutterstock (9). Laszlo Konya/Dreamstime (9). Ig0rzh/Dreamstime (10). Leklek73/Dreamstime (10). Leklek73/Dreamstime (10). Villa Cimbrone (10). Courtesy of Le Sirenuse (11). Photogolfer/Dreamstime (11). Courtesy of Il San Pietro di Positano (12). Lucamato/Dreamstime (12). Inu/Shutterstock (12). Neirfy/Dreamstime (12). Peeradontax/Shutterstock (13). Thecriss/Dreamstime (14). Nataliia Gr/Shutterstock (14). Luca Rei/Shutterstock (14). Roman Plesky/Dreamstime (14). Alkan2011/Dreamstime (15). RKCharlton/Shutterstock (15). Ghischeforever/Shutterstock (20). Associazione Verace Pizza Napoletana (21). S-F/Shutterstock (22). Alexey Pevnev/Dreamstime (22). CherylRamalho/ Shutterstock (22). MihaelGrmek, [CC BY-SA 2.0]/Wikimedia Commons (23). Ravello Festival | ph Pino Izzo (23). Mariyasiyanko/Dreamstime (24). Javarman/Dreamstime (25). Boris-B/ Shutterstock (26). Crazy nook/Shutterstock (27). Massimo Santi/Shutterstock (28). Enrico Della Pietra/Dreamstime (28). Jeremy Brown/Dreamstime (28). Danilo Mongiello/Dreamstime (29). Lucamato/Dreamstime (29). Mazerath/Shutterstock (30). Giannis Papanikos/ Shutterstock (31). Neirfy/Dreamstime (32). Angelo Pesce/Shutterstock (32). Simona Flamigni/Dreamstime (32). Simona Pavan/Dreamstime (33). Elenaphotos/Dreamstime (33). **Chapter 3: The Amalfi Coast:** Canadastock/shutterstock (55). Mikadun/Shutterstock (64). Lina Harb/ Shutterstock (71). Khirman Vladimir/Shutterstock (72). George green/Shutterstock (72). Robert Fisher (73). Ollirg/Shutterstock (73). Nicolette Van der Vlerk/Shutterstock (73). Alfio Ferlito/Shutterstock (74). Khirman Vladimir/Shutterstock (74). Robert Fisher (75). Allerina & Glen, [CC BY 2.0]/Flickr (75). Ollirg/Shutterstock (75). Robert I.C Fisher (76). Robert I.C Fisher (80). Elephotos/ Shutterstock (84). Tanialerro.art/Shutterstock (87). Mitzo/Shutterstock (92). Nikolpetr/ Shutterstock (94). IgorZh/Shutterstock (100). Maciej Matlak/Shutterstock (105). Maciej Matlak/ Shutterstock (110). Gimas/Shutterstock (112). **Chapter 4: Capri, Ischia, and Procida:** IgorZh/shutterstock (115). Neirfy/Shutterstock (118). AlexMorozov1204/Shutterstock (119). Vacclav/Shutterstock (119). Satoshi Nakagawa, [CC BY-SA 2.0]/Flickr (130). IgorZh/Shutterstock (132). Inu/Shutterstock (135). Ken Gillham/AgefotoStock (139). Danilo donadoni/AgefotoStock (140). Kiedrowski, R / AgefotoStock (140). Deepblue-photographer/Shutterstock (141). Fototeca ENIT (141). Caprirelaxboats.com/salsa/it (141). Colin Sinclair / AgefotoStock (142). Capri Tourism (142). Capripalace.com (142). SCPhotos / Alamy (143). Caprirelaxboats.com/salsa/it (143). Roman Babakin/Shutterstock (146). Capri Tourism (152). Guido Amrein Switzerland/ Shutterstock (154). Paola Ghirotti/Fototeca ENIT (160). Francesco Bonino/Shutterstock (167). **Chapter 5: Sorrento and the Sorrentine Peninsula:** Bahdanovich Alena/Shutterstock (173). Barmalini/Shutterstock (176). Campania Tourism (177). Gianluca Foto/Shutterstock (177). Angelafoto (187). Robert Fisher (188). **Chapter 6: The Bay of Naples:** Mariia Golovianko/ Shutterstock (199). Ferdinando Marfella, [CC BY-SA 2.0]/Flickr (202). Angela Sorrentino/ iStockphoto (203). Angela Sorrentino/iStockphoto (203). JethroT/Shutterstock (211). Versta/Shutterstock (215). Wjarek/Shutterstock (219). TheFaunInPompeii/SuperStock (219). Kated/Shutterstock (220). Antonina Tadeush/Shutterstock (221). Balounm/Shutterstock (221). Ivan bastien/Shutterstock (222). Freevideophotoagency/ Shutterstock (222). Boris Stroujko/ Shutterstock (222). Leonid Andronov/Shutterstock (223). Katie Hamlin (224). Alfiya Safuanova/Shutterstock (225). Alexander Gold/Shutterstock (230). Imma Gambardella/ Shutterstock (234). **Chapter 7: Naples:** Xtoforens/shutterstock.com (237). Hotel Luna Convento (240). Gallimaufry/Shutterstock (241). Shebeko/Shutterstock (241). Massimo Santi/Shutterstock (251). Vololibero/ Shutterstock (251). DinoPh/Shutterstock (251). Lalupa, [CC BY-SA 2.5]/wikipedia.org (252). Eric Valenne geostory/Shutterstock (252). Boris Stroujko/Shutterstock (252). Enrico Della Pietra/Shutterstock (253). Maurizio De Mattei/Shutterstock (253). Juraj Kamenicky/Shutterstock (253). Nadezhda Kharitonova/Shutterstock (253). Cristian Puscasu/Shutterstock (257). The York Project, [CC BY-SA 2.0]/Wikimedia Commons (259). CuboImages srl / Alamy (263). Guarino/Dreamstime (280). Boris Stroujko/Shutterstock (283). Lucamato/Dreamstime (287). Photogolfer/ Dreamstime (290). Khirman Vladimir/Shutterstock (292). EvrenKalinbacak/Shutterstock (294). Certosa di San Martino (295). Wikipedia Commons (295). CuboImages srl / Alamy (296). Angelo Chiariello/Shutterstock (296). CpaKmoi/Flickr (296). Marcobrivio6/Dreamstime (297). MuseoNazionaleDiSanMartino (297). Public Domain (297). De Agostini Picture Library/Fototeca ENIT (304). ChiccoDodiFC/Shutterstock (305). Campania Tourism (306). Marzolino/Shutterstock (307). Elena Elisseeva/Shutterstock (307). Mazur Travel/Shutterstock (307). Pixiemoments photography/Shutterstock (307). Romanadr/Shutterstock (307). Paolo Gallo/Shutterstock (308). Euripides/Shutterstock (309). Campania Tourism (309). Giuseppe Parisi/Shutterstock (309). MissyH, [CC BY-ND 2.0]/Flickr (309). Gimsy/Shutterstock (309). **About Our Writers:** All photos are courtesy of the writers.

**Every effort has been made to trace the copyright holders, and we apologize in advance for any accidental errors. We would be happy to apply the corrections in the following edition of this publication.*

Notes

Notes

Notes

Notes

Notes

Fodor's THE AMALFI COAST, CAPRI, AND NAPLES

Publisher: Stephen Horowitz, *General Manager*

Editorial: Douglas Stallings, *Editorial Director*, Jill Fergus, Amanda Sadlowski, *Senior Editors;* Kayla Becker, Brian Eschrich, Alexis Kelly, *Editors;* Angelique Kennedy-Chavannes, *Assistant Editor*

Design: Tina Malaney, *Director of Design and Production;* Jessica Gonzalez, *Graphic Designer;* Erin Caceres, *Graphic Design Associate*

Production: Jennifer DePrima, *Editorial Production Manager*, Elyse Rozelle, *Senior Production Editor;* Monica White, *Production Editor*

Maps: Rebecca Baer, *Senior Map Editor*, David Lindroth, Mark Stroud (Moon Street Cartography), *Cartographers*

Photography: Viviane Teles, *Senior Photo Editor;* Namrata Aggarwal, Neha Gupta, Payal Gupta, Ashok Kumar, *Photo Editors;* Eddie Aldrete, *Photo Production Intern;* Kadeem McPherson, *Photo Production Associate Intern*

Business and Operations: Chuck Hoover, *Chief Marketing Officer*, Robert Ames, *Group General Manager*, Devin Duckworth, *Director of Print Publishing*

Public Relations and Marketing: Joe Ewaskiw, *Senior Director of Communications and Public Relations*

Fodors.com: Jeremy Tarr, *Editorial Director;* Rachael Levitt, *Managing Editor*

Technology: Jon Atkinson, *Director of Technology;* Rudresh Teotia, *Lead Developer*

Writers: Nick Bruno, Fergal Kavanagh

Editor: Jill Fergus

Production Editor: Elyse Rozelle

10th Edition

ISBN 978-1-64097-535-4

ISSN 1542-0728

All details in this book are based on information supplied to us at press time. Always confirm information when it matters, especially if you're making a detour to visit a specific place. Fodor's expressly disclaims any liability, loss, or risk, personal or otherwise, that is incurred as a consequence of the use of any of the contents of this book.

SPECIAL SALES
This book is available at special discounts for bulk purchases for sales promotions or premiums. For more information, e-mail SpecialMarkets@fodors.com.

PRINTED IN CANADA

10 9 8 7 6 5 4 3 2

About Our Writers

Nick Bruno is an Italy specialist and frequent Fodor's contributor. As well as authoring and updating books and features, he makes radio packages for the BBC. A lifelong interest in history and Italian language has led to a project researching his paternal Italian family during the Il Ventennio Fascista period. Nick updated Experience, the Amalfi Coast, Sorrento and the Sorrentine Peninsula, and the Bay of Naples chapters. Follow him on Instagram and Twitter @ nickjgbruno and 🌐 *barbruno.com*.

Fergal Kavanagh travels extensively throughout Italy with his Tune Into English Roadshow, where he teaches English through pop music (🌐 *www.tuneintoenglish.com*). In his twenty-five years in the country there is hardly a town square he has not passed through. He updated Travel Smart; Capri, Ischia, and Procida; and Naples.